Digging Miami

UNIVERSITY PRESS OF FLORIDA

Florida A&M University, Tallahassee
Florida Atlantic University, Boca Raton
Florida Gulf Coast University, Ft. Myers
Florida International University, Miami
Florida State University, Tallahassee
New College of Florida, Sarasota
University of Central Florida, Orlando
University of Florida, Gainesville
University of North Florida, Jacksonville
University of South Florida, Tampa
University of West Florida, Pensacola

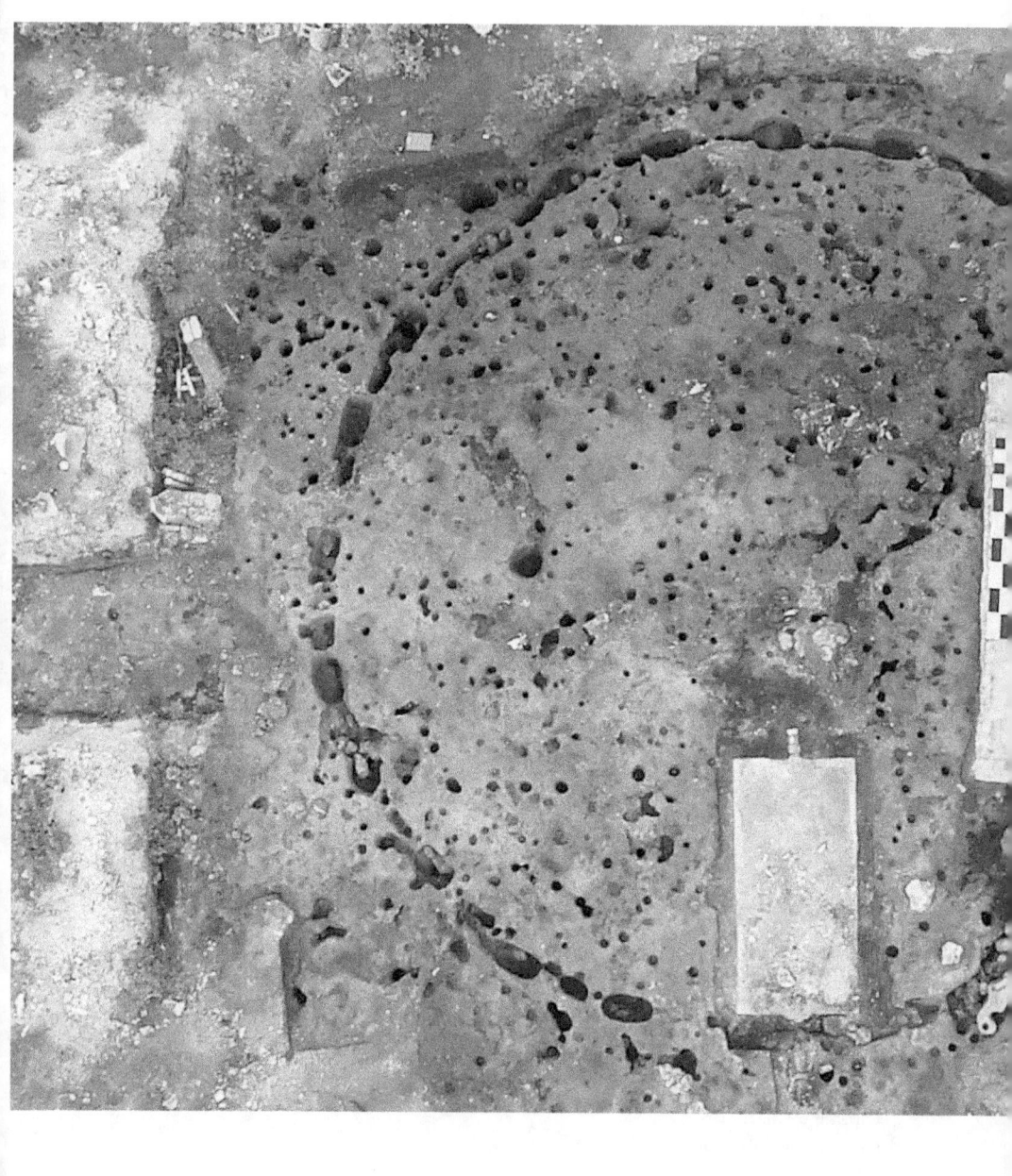

Digging Miami

Robert S. Carr

University Press of Florida
Gainesville
Tallahassee
Tampa
Boca Raton
Pensacola
Orlando
Miami
Jacksonville
Ft. Myers
Sarasota

Frontispiece: Miami Circle with scale.

Copyright 2012 by Robert S. Carr
All rights reserved
Published in the United States of America

First cloth printing, 2012
First paperback printing, 2023

28 27 26 25 24 23   6 5 4 3 2 1

Library of Congress Cataloging-in-Publication Data
Carr, Robert S.
Digging Miami / Robert S. Carr.
p. cm.
Includes bibliographical references and index.
Summary: An exploration of the archaeological findings of one of Miami's best archaeologists.
ISBN 978-0-8130-4206-0 (cloth)
ISBN 978-0-8130-8005-5 (pbk.)
1. Indians of North America—Florida—Miami—Antiquities. 2. Seminole Indians—Antiquities. 3. Excavations (Archaeology)—Florida—Miami. 4. Miami (Fla.)—Antiquities. I. Title.
E78.F6C37 2012
975.9'381—dc23   2012018863

The University Press of Florida is the scholarly publishing agency for the State University System of Florida, comprising Florida A&M University, Florida Atlantic University, Florida Gulf Coast University, Florida International University, Florida State University, New College of Florida, University of Central Florida, University of Florida, University of North Florida, University of South Florida, and University of West Florida.

University Press of Florida
2046 NE Waldo Road
Suite 2100
Gainesville, FL 32609
http://upress.ufl.edu

Contents

List of Illustrations   vii
Preface: More than Just Seashells   xi

1. Diggers, Scientists, and Antiquarians: History of Archaeological Research   1

Part I. Prehistoric Miami

2. The First People: The Cutler Fossil Site   27
3. The South Florida Archaic   46
4. The Perfect Balance: Adapting to the Land and Sea   62
5. Sacred Geography: The Prehistoric Settlement System   92

Part II. Failed Settlements: The European Legacy

6. European Contact: The Transition to Extinction   121
7. The English and Bahamian Legacy   143

Part III. Seminole Legacy

8. Seminole Archaeology   157
9. Stockades and Musket Balls   180

Part IV. Pioneer Miami

10. The Archaeology of Arrowroot: Miami's First Industry   201
11. Tropical Homesteads: Artifacts of Miami's Pioneers   215

Part V. Urban Archaeology: A Past with a Future

12. The Miami Circle and Beyond   233

Epilogue   249

Acknowledgments   251
Notes   255
References Cited   265
Index   287

Illustrations

Chapter 1. Diggers, Scientists, and Antiquarians: History of Archaeological Research

1.1 Portrait of Jeffries Wyman 5
1.2 Destruction of Miami Burial Mound 8DA14, 1897 9
1.3 John Goggin in the Everglades, 1949 12
1.4 WPA archaeologists excavating at Opa-Locka 1, 1934 15
1.5 Dan Laxson at the Trail site 17
1.6 Excavating the Cheetum site, 1971 19
1.7 Discovery of the 1855 Key Biscayne survey marker 20
1.8 View of the Granada site excavations, 1976 22

Part I. Prehistoric Miami

Hermann Trappman, *A Tequesta Family on the Miami River*, 1983 25
Prehistoric sites of Miami-Dade County 26

Chapter 2. The First People: The Cutler Fossil Site

2.1 Archaeologists at the Cutler site, 1986 28
2.2 Map of the Cutler site and excavation units 30
2.3 Uncovering a jaguar mandible at the Cutler site 33
2.4 Bifaces and points from the Cutler site 37
2.5 Limestone turtleback scraper from the Cutler site 38
2.6 Limestone scraper from the Cutler site 38
2.7 Human ulna with carnivore tooth perforation from the Cutler site 40
Table 2.1 Fire-altered bones from the Cutler Fossil site 35

Chapter 3. The South Florida Archaic

3.1 Aerial photo of Weston Pond and solution holes, c. 1968 47
3.2 Limestone biface from the Cheetum site, 8DA1058 51

3.3 Chert projectile point from 8DA411 51
3.4 Incised bone handle from 8DA1058 52
3.5 Fiber-tempered pottery from Miami-Dade County 53
3.6 Map of units and human remains at Santa Maria West, 8DA11246 60

Chapter 4. The Perfect Balance: Adapting to the Land and Sea

4.1 Pottery sherds 64
4.2 Pottery sherds 71
4.3 *Strombus* celt 75
4.4 *Busycon* ladle 76
4.5 Drilled shark teeth 78
4.6 Bone awls and point 80
4.7 Stone anchor with pecked design 81
4.8 Carved pumice float 83
4.9 Carved shell pendants 83
4.10 Wooden pestle found in the Everglades 85
4.11 Map of the Royal Palm Circle, 8DA11 87
4.12 Map depicting a plan of the MDM parcel solution holes and cemetery, 8DA11 89

Chapter 5. Sacred Geography: The Prehistoric Settlement System

5.1 Aerial photo of Dade Circle, 1926 99
5.2 Indian canoe trail in the Everglades, c. 1910 100
5.3 Flagami Island after 16 inches of rain, 1981 106
5.4 Robert Carr at the Flagami site, 8DA1073, 1981 107
5.5 Dan Laxson at Madden's Hammock, 8DA45, 1959 110

Part II. Failed Settlements: The European Legacy

Hermann Trappman, *Approaching the Polly Lewis Homestead on the Silver Bluff, Biscayne Bay,* 1983 119

Spanish and English-Bahamian colonial sites of Miami-Dade County 120

Chapter 6. European Contact: The Transition to Extinction

6.1 Portrait of Pedro Menéndez de Avilés 125
6.2 Bronze Bible hinge from 8DA11 133
6.3 Eighteenth-century rosary bead from 8DA11 133

6.4 Three brass bells, from 8DA11 and 8DA34   134
6.5 Wooden statuette of a corsair from Elliott Key   135
6.6 Wooden statuette of the Virgin Mary from Elliott Key   135
6.7 Majolica sherds   138
6.8 Olive jar found in the eastern Everglades   139
6.9 Carnelian bead and Punta Rassa pendant   142

Chapter 7. The English and Bahamian Legacy

7.1 Terracotta tobacco pipe bowl from 8DA2132   146
7.2 Menu cover for Black Caesar's Forge   150

Part III. Seminole Legacy

Hermann Trappman, *Construction of Fort Henry*, 1983   155
Seminole and Seminole War sites of Miami-Dade County   156

Chapter 8. Seminole Archaeology

8.1 Perforated William and Mary half-penny, 1689–94   161
8.2 Persian snuff box lid from 8DA411   173
8.3 Trade beads from the Brickell Trading Post   173
8.4 Lightkeeper's cap insignia from 8DA45   174
8.5 Copper ornaments from 8DA411   175
8.6 Copper ladle from 8DA411   176
8.7 Lead musket-ball mold   177
8.8 Kaskaskia projectile point from 8DA411   177
8.9 Glass knife from the Bamboo site, 8DA94   178

Chapter 9. Stockades and Musket Balls

9.1 Flask sherd depicting Zachary Taylor from 8DA411   183
9.2 Military buttons from 8DA411   184
9.3 Musket ball and minie ball from 8DA411   184
9.4 Gerdes map of Fort Dallas, 1849   188
9.5 Pipe bowls from Fort Dallas   190
9.6 View of Fort Russell by Capt. John Rodgers Vinton   191
9.7 Whiteware with fort motif from "Fort Desolation"   195

x Illustrations

Part IV. Pioneer Miami

Hermann Trappman, *Operations at the Arch Creek Coontie Mill,* 1983   199
Pioneer sites of Miami-Dade County   200

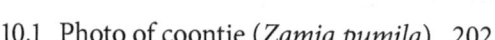

Chapter 10. The Archaeology of Arrowroot: Miami's First Industry

10.1 Photo of coontie (*Zamia pumila*)   202
10.2 Aerial photo depicting Woods's mill race, 1926   204
10.3 Curry comb from Arch Creek Mill, 8DA1655   206
10.4 Gerdes map of Ferguson Mill, 1849   208

Chapter 11. Tropical Homesteads: Artifacts of Miami's Pioneers

11.1 Maude and Belle Brickell, c. 1900   220
11.2 Kaolin pipe with effigy of eagle's claw   223
11.3 Brickell porcelain doll leg   223
11.4 William Jennings Bryan at Villa Serena   225
11.5 African Bahamian settlement in Coconut Grove   228

Part V. Urban Archaeology: A Past with a Future

Guy LaBree, *Tequesta Skyline,* 1984   231
Map of the Miami Circle depicting test units and features selected for faunal analysis   232

Chapter 12. The Miami Circle and Beyond

12.1 Aerial photo of the Miami Circle   234
12.2 Miami Circle foundation basins   236
12.3 Deptford Stamped pottery sherd from the Miami Circle   238
12.4 "Eye" basin cut into the bedrock at the Miami Circle   239
12.5 Shark skeleton at the Miami Circle   242
12.6 Shell buzzard ornament from 8DA1058   248

Preface
More than Just Seashells

If urban archaeology in Miami has accomplished anything during the past thirty years, it is that it has forged a sense of community from the flotsam of artifacts and sites representing ten thousand years of human endeavor. To reach back and touch the source of who we are and to know that Miami is more than the dream of entrepreneurs to create a tourist mecca and a city built on top of dredged rock and sand is to move closer to the truth.

Archaeology matters because we are curious and vain about ourselves. We are often temporal-centric in believing that we are living in the best of times and astonished that humans could have been fulfilled in that ancient dark age of B.C. (before computers). Though living in the high rise of civilization may have its rewards, with endless choices of products, restaurants, and leisure time, it is the look backward that can illuminate our understanding of who we are. Below our high-rise view of modern life is the basement of civilization, where concrete blocks are underlain by nineteenth-century red bricks, and below the bricks are the wooden post molds of Indian houses constructed a thousand years before.

Who is to say with authority that today's Miami is somehow superior to the ancient Miami of endless forests and sweet water rushing seaward in the Miami River from the Everglades. We have reshaped the land, cut its forest, and bulldozed most every square foot in the county at least once. Some downtown properties are on their fourth generation of new buildings, each construction preceded by the demolition of an older building that had become obsolete. Only the hammock forests that survive at Simpson Park, Alice Wainwright Park, and the Deering Estate at Cutler have missed the ache of heavy equipment gouging deep into the muck and limestone, stripping the skin of rich organic soils to create the economy of modern life.

It is this enterprise of progress that continues to erase the monuments and traces of the indigenous people and historic pioneers. Ironically, it is this same progress that has uncovered much of the archaeological record described in this book. The yin-yang of archaeological discovery is that it is often the very act of new development that creates the opportunity to discover what has lain dormant for centuries. It is a favorable testimony to county and city governments that the permit that allows new development often requires another permit to document the vestiges of the archaeological record that may be disturbed or destroyed. Surprisingly, this oversight has accounted for over 90 percent of Miami-Dade County's archaeological discoveries. By 2012, forty-two archaeological sites and zones had been designated within the county. Interestingly, state and federal preservation laws had no effect on the discovery or preservation of the Miami Circle. Likewise, all of the sites uncovered on Brickell Avenue and at Crandon Park on Key Biscayne after Hurricane Andrew would have been destroyed during the post-hurricane cleanup if not for local ordinances. The rich archaeological deposits at Villa Serena would have been lost to landscape redevelopment if not for the implementation of the City of Miami preservation ordinance. And there are dozens of other examples throughout the county of local efforts creating a public good by documenting and preserving sites that are exempt from any state or federal regulations.

Who benefits from local historic and archaeological preservation? We do. By becoming custodians and not just consumers of the land, we assure our community that the important monuments of the human experience will not disappear or be marginalized by appearing only in photographs, interpretive signs, or displays of artifacts in a museum. Not that these interpretative measures lack great educational value, but preservation of an archaeological site can assure the public a sense of place and provide a bank of scientific data that can be carefully assessed by future scholars.

Protecting the past need not involve the taking of property. In some cases, pending developments have required green space areas and archaeological sites can be used to meet those green space requirements. It's worth noting that since 1980, all of Miami-Dade County's archaeological designations have proceeded without lawsuits because existing regulatory land-use guidelines have been balanced with a respect for private property rights.

Common sense and bureaucratic flexibility allow sites to be documented by archaeological investigations and innovative preservation, such as the last sliver of the Tequesta village site buried at the Hyatt Convention Center in downtown Miami. When it was announced that a swimming pool would be excavated on the parcel's "preservation area," the solution was to create an alternative design and construct an elevated swimming pool on piers that destroyed less than 10 percent of what would have been lost. When architect Raul Rodriquez designed a structure to sit above the Miami River Rapids site rather than use deep footer trenches, his innovative approach helped preserve much of that important site.

Planners, government regulators, and archaeologists should not see this juggling act between preservation and development as forces in opposition, but as a way for the public good and private property owners to find common ground, a process that involves adequate surveys and education to identify areas of known and potential sites and a comprehensive due diligence by developers and property owners to minimize surprises with regard to what may be hidden beneath the earth.

1

Diggers, Scientists, and Antiquarians

History of Archaeological Research

South Florida is a region generally unfamiliar to American archaeologists. Until the 1980s, relatively few archaeologists conducted research in the area, in part because of several geographic and educational forces. First, the remoteness of the area contributed greatly to the lack of investigations. Before Henry Flagler's Florida East Coast Railroad arrived in the newly formed city of Miami in 1896, getting there was difficult and usually involved traveling by water. While the railroad brought tourists and settlers, few archaeologists traveled to South Florida. Second, most of Miami-Dade County's coastal prehistoric sites were quickly destroyed or built over during Miami's first building boom, which lasted from 1896 until the bust of 1925. (Ironically, many of the sites that had been covered and preserved by fill in the 1920s were uncovered in the 1980s and 1990s during a building boom that spread southward from downtown Miami to Brickell Avenue, uncovering a scientific bonanza of artifacts and information.) Third, although the University of Miami had been established in 1926, courses specializing in Florida archaeology were not offered until recently. South Florida was not the home of a four-year state university until the 1960s. The absence of a state academic institution meant that professional archaeologists, traditionally employed by state colleges, rarely had the opportunity to be employed south of Gainesville (home of the University of Florida). It is no accident that until the 1980s the largest number of prehistoric sites of any of Florida's counties was recorded in Alachua and Leon Counties, where long-established state universities are located. Until the 1960s archaeological projects often were situated within driving distance of universities.

The documentation and preservation of Miami-Dade County's archaeological resources did not begin in earnest until protective legislation was enacted. The federal Historic Preservation Act of 1966 established guidelines to help preserve and conserve archaeological sites located on federal property, such as Everglades National Park and Biscayne National Park. These standards eventually filtered down to state, county, and municipal levels. The Florida Division of Historical Resources (FDHR) began in 1967 under the authority of Florida Statute 267. However, because of the agency's small budget, and with an office only in Tallahassee, an additional seven years elapsed before state archaeologists were able to conduct investigations in southeastern Florida. It was not until 1981 that Dade County (so named prior to 1997's name change to Miami-Dade) passed its own historic preservation ordinance, followed by the city of Miami's ordinance in 1986. It was only after these local ordinances were in place that archaeological sites received protection and requirements for their documentation if threatened by development.

Despite circumstances that discouraged scientific archaeological research in southern Florida prior to protective ordinances, artifacts and information from the area's prehistoric culture were collected and cataloged by a large number of people, from winter visitors and explorers to scientists and avocational archaeologists. What follows is a summary of those contributions, but undoubtedly, the full story could be a book in itself.

Explorers and Surveyors

Even though Spanish colonization proceeded vigorously throughout much of the Caribbean and South America during the sixteenth century, the Spanish domination of Florida moved at a slow pace, encountering greater resistance from the Indians and fewer material rewards for the colonizers' efforts. However, many of the Spanish visitors in early Florida left valuable records that document not only Spanish intentions but also Native American customs.

One of the most important witnesses to southern Florida's Native American cultures was Hernando d'Escalante Fontaneda, who was shipwrecked in the 1540s and rescued by the Pedro Menéndez de Avilés expedition seventeen years later. Fontaneda lived with the Indians during those years and learned their languages and customs. The description of his captivity is one of the most important eyewitness accounts of sixteenth-century Native Americans in southern Florida.[1]

Gonzalo Solis Meras, the official chronicler of the Menéndez expedition, recorded their encounters with the Tequesta and Calusa Indians. Descriptions of Indian religion were also contained in letters written by a Spanish priest, Brother Francisco Villareal, who had attempted, unsuccessfully, to maintain a Jesuit mission at the mouth of the Miami River. Extensive records have been translated into English and are now accessible in books and articles about the Calusa.[2]

Among the most valuable sources of information on Florida Indians are the illustrations of Timucuan culture by Jacques Le Moyne, who accompanied the French colonists on the St. Johns River in northern Florida in 1564. Although the Timucua lived several hundred miles north of the Tequesta and Le Moyne used artistic license in his renderings, the Timucua shared many details of dress, ornament, and customs with the Tequesta. A late-seventeenth-century account by the shipwrecked Pennsylvania Quaker Jonathan Dickinson near Hobe Sound also contains observations about the customs of the Indians and their attitudes toward the English, which by that time had become distinctly pro-Spanish.[3]

The transition from observing Tequesta Indians and their culture firsthand to reporting only their abandoned villages occurred in the eighteenth century, after the last of the Indians from southern Florida had been relocated to Cuba in 1763. It is appropriate that the first description of a South Florida archaeological site is the abandoned Spanish fort and village of Tequesta, which was described by the English surveyor Bernard Romans in 1775 during his visit to the Miami River: "At its mouth are the remains of a savage settlement."[4] After Romans's visit, there are no descriptions of South Florida antiquities until the beginning of intensive government surveys of Florida's interior. In 1847, this alluring description of a mysterious site in the eastern Everglades was provided by surveyor George McKay:

> On the subject of the settlement of the islands of the Everglades, I saw nothing that indicated civilization, excepting upon a small island . . . where are to be seen fallen walls of a stone building, broken earthenware, and bottles of a shape I have never before seen, and of an age I will not venture to determine.[5]

Two years earlier, McKay had discovered a circular earthwork while conducting a survey along the Miami River at present-day NW Twelfth Avenue. In his field notes he described an old "redoubt" surrounded by a ditch that formed a circle 200 feet in diameter. Within the center of the redoubt were earthworks in the form of a cross. The antiquity of the site was indicated by a large pine tree that had grown on top of the earthworks after its construction.[6]

McKay's discoveries were probably never shared with the scholars of his day, many of whom were involved in a raging debate about the origins of the people who had built the mounds and earthworks of eastern North America. Even if scholars had been aware of the Miami River earthwork, they almost certainly would have classified it as a European fortification, or in the very least, a monument built by any group of people but Native Americans. During the nineteenth century, mounds all over America were being probed, potted, and excavated to produce evidence that could affirm one theory or another about the origin of the mound builders. Some scholars gave credit to colonists from Atlantis, others to the Phoenicians, Irish monks, the Lost Tribe of Israel, and even the De Soto expedition. Most of these scholars believed that the American Indians were not capable of building mounds and that all monuments and artifacts that reflected any degree of "civilized" art, engineering, or thinking must have an Old World origin. This type of "scholarship" represented the prevailing intellectual atmosphere and reflected a national policy of forced Indian emigration and of a reservation system that attempted to terminate Native American culture.

Archaeologists, Antiquarians, and Diggers

Jeffries Wyman, often regarded as the father of forensic anthropology, was the first scientist to excavate in what is now Miami-Dade County (fig. 1.1). In 1869, Wyman, the first curator of Harvard University's Peabody Museum, arrived in Biscayne Bay on the yacht *Azalea* and described some of the mounds at the mouth of the Miami River. Through the efforts of Christopher Eck a complete transcription of his South Florida diary entries is available.[7] Among some of the most interesting entries are the following:

> Concluded to spend another day [March 9, 1869] here instead of moving on—Went on shore after breakfast & dug in the shell-heap in front of Mr Hunts house—Large quantities of bones pottery & shells—the accumulation of long series of years 3 to 4 ft thick. Bones of fish, turtle, coon, birds, deer, shark verteb. Very common—"two pieces of worked bone" & two or three chisels of conch shell.[8]

Hunt's house was on the north bank of the Miami River at the Fort Dallas officers' quarters. This location would later be known as the Granada site component of the Miami One site, 8DA11.

Figure 1.1. Jeffries Wyman, first director of the Peabody Museum, was the first archaeologist to investigate the prehistoric mounds of Miami.

On March 10, Wyman began an exploration of a mound on the north side of the Miami River west of the Granada site. His work there represents the earliest scientific investigation of a rock mound in southern Florida:

> Spent whole day in excavating mound on the Miami. This is a few rods from right bank & ¼ mile from mouth—60 ft long 40 broad & 11 high of an oval shape & covered with a young growth of trees.... Long diameter very nearly N. & S., deviating (—help of Andrew & Mr Hunt) into side yesterday & found loose stones—too late to make complete exam.
>
> Light rain, followed by great numbers of mosquitoes. Conical trench nearly to center—throwing out many tons of stone—for we worked steadily.
>
> Thursday, March 11th, 1869
> Started soon after breakfast for mound. Capt. of A[zalea], Capt. Crowell, Henry & Andrew worked till noon; built & in shield & finished excavations but found nothing buried. No trees of great age on top. Having opened the mound beyond the center & [searched] to right and left. Mound consists of large stones in middle on which smaller ones had been piled.
>
> Failed to find any contents returned at noon, just in time to escape a thunder shower. Hunt & Crowill came on boat & lunched. Heat disagreeable air sultry—Thermom. 76°—Barom. 29'90".[9]

Although his documentation of the Miami sites was minimal, Wyman's investigation of mounds on the St. Johns River in northern Florida was important, proving that the mounds were manmade and predated the time of the historic Indians.

In 1876, Henry E. Perrine (son of the famous botanist murdered at Indian Key) amused himself by excavating a burial mound near Biscayne Bay in present-day Charles Deering Estate Park while he visited the Addison family. He provided the following account:

> Using the pick and spade we soon came to skulls and bones of both adults and children, the skulls in nearly every instance showed that they had been buried with the face downwards, and with the toes toward the center of the mound.[10]

Perrine collected two of the best preserved skulls with the intention of delivering them to the Academy of Natural Sciences in Buffalo, New York. He forgot to pack them on his return trip north, however, and their present location is unknown.

Perhaps the most ambitious of the nineteenth-century investigators was archaeologist Andrew Douglass, who in 1884 arrived at the mouth of the Miami River on his yacht *Seminole*. He visited three mounds near the river, first meeting and receiving permission from William Brickell to visit a mound located south of the Brickell House. Douglass also noted that Brickell believed that the Brickell House had been built on top of a mound:

> On Wednesday morning I started to find Brickell's mound by going in boats along the bayshore and striking into the dense scrub to a live oak that was quite conspicuous. It was not more that 200 yards from the shore but among brambles and Spanish bayonets and wild lime trees loaded with fruit which the men found refreshing. The mound was covered with the same dense vegetation. It proved to be about 10 ft high with a base diameter of about 120 feet. I dug out a space about 16 ft square on the summit; it was intensely hot and we were compelled to send the boat for a tent fly to shade us, as it was impossible to work in the sun. By 3 P.M. we had completed the excavation and had found numerous burials about 4 feet below the surface and of great antiquity. The only object I secured was a little earthenware cup or pot of great beauty for such material I think very remarkable. It was quite whole, not even having the bottom knocked out as is the invariable custom in such deposits. It was found in the centre of the mound and within 6 inches of the surface. It was this fact that probably preserved

it from our shovels, for when the banks caved in it dropped out like a lump of earth. It is 4 ½ in high, 5 in long and 4 in broad.[11]

Additional information on this mound's location was secured by avocational historian William Straight, who obtained another description of the mound's location from the catalog entry of the earthenware cup at the American Museum of Natural History. The entry indicated that the pottery vessel was found 8 inches beneath the surface of a mound referred to as the Brickell Mound, located 500 yards south of the Miami River and 300 yards west of Biscayne Bay. Based on that description, the mound's location is approximately between present-day SW Eighth and SW Ninth Streets, east of Miami Avenue. This location is likely in error because Gilpin in his 1890 diary indicates that this elusive mound is actually located south of the Brickell House, later recorded as 8DA15, and thus the "300 yards west" should read "300 feet." According to the photo provided by the Smithsonian to William Straight, the earthenware bowl is decorated with an intricate pattern of herring-bone incising and punctuates that is not typical of southern Florida ceramic decorations.[12] It was likely imported from some other region outside of Florida. It also is possible that the reconstructed exotic bowl was incorrectly assigned at the Smithsonian, the result of a cataloging error.

Douglass subsequently met with J. W. Ewan, who ran a store on the river's north bank. Ewan led Douglass a quarter-mile through a great tangle of briars and wild lime trees to the largest of Miami's mounds (8DA14):

> It was built of stones and about 15 feet high, 150 feet long and 75 broad at the base. It was quite impossible for me to dig such a mound with my force had I been so disposed. . . . This had several burials upon it fenced in and with headstones. The interments were of soldiers and officers of Fort Dallas which in 1856 & 7 was the name of the post here, so that alone would have prevented my excavation.[13]

Douglass would have been shocked if he had known that 21 years after his visit this magnificent mound and the soldiers' graves would be destroyed to build the Royal Palm Hotel. Douglass explored the south bank of the Miami River and described the third mound he encountered:

> We found it about 150 yards back from the river, but much to our disappointment it was not a sand mound but built of rocks like the one described [previously]. . . . Neither of these rock mounds is circular

but as it were ridges. This one was 75 ft long on top and 6 ft broad, while at the base it was 150 feet long 45 broad. The sides were quite steep and the surface was covered with large trees.[14]

Other nonscientific excavations occurred in Dade County in the 1890s. These investigations included a picnic outing to excavate a burial mound at Arch Creek (destroying most of the mound) and the collection of surface artifacts by Commodore Ralph Munroe on his property, 8DA10, at the Barnacle in Coconut Grove along Biscayne Bay. In 1892, another Grove resident, Kirk Munroe (unrelated to Ralph), led an expedition into the Everglades to gather Indian artifacts for the Florida exhibit at the Chicago World's Fair, although it is not known what was collected and whether the items were ever exhibited. In 1896, surveyor A. L. Knowlton reported finding a large stone artifact while surveying the streets of the newly subdivided town of Miami. The artifact's present whereabouts are unknown.

While the new city seemed to be teeming with people curious about their newly found tropical paradise, the area's rapid development began to take its toll on significant archaeological sites. The most staggering loss was the leveling of Miami's largest mound (8DA14) during the construction of the Royal Palm Hotel in 1897 (fig. 1.2). Ironically, this 15-foot-high mound was not even on the site of the hotel proper but near the proposed hotel's northeastern veranda close to present-day Biscayne Boulevard, where the mound blocked part of the view of Biscayne Bay. In a more politically correct time the mound would have been preserved. Instead, the mound was leveled and its contents spread and used as topsoil for the gardens of the Royal Palm Hotel. John Sewell, the foreman of the clearing crew, reported that he found only some beads and "Indian trinkets." Gone and lost forever were thousands of artifacts that were unrecognizable to the untrained eye. Sewell's men collected 50 to 60 skulls. Sewell gave many of them away to anyone for the asking. Ironically, as Douglass had previously observed, some of these bones may have belonged to the numerous soldiers from Fort Dallas who were buried there during the Seminole Wars. Many skulls made their way to the Girtman Brothers general store, where they were reportedly sold as curios to visiting tourists. Sewell stored the other bones in a tool shed near the hotel, and when the hotel construction was completed, he noted,

> I took about four of my most trusted negroes and hauled all of these skeletons out near by where was a big hole in the ground, about twelve

Figure 1.2. The destruction of Miami Burial Mound 8DA14 at the mouth of the Miami River in 1897 by the workers building the Royal Palm Hotel. Courtesy of the Archaeological and Historical Conservancy.

feet deep, and dumped the bones in it, then filled the hole up with sand and instructed the negroes to forget this burial . . . and I suppose they did. . . . There is a fine residence now standing over the bones—and the things that the owners don't know will never hurt them. And the Indian's bones are now resting in peace.[15]

Their eternal rest was brief, however, since that house was eventually demolished. Another account by the daughter of Capt. W. H. Weatherly, who was a supervisor of construction at the Royal Palm Hotel, sheds more light on the mound's destruction and the exact location of reburial in a manuscript describing the mound's contents:

Papa was in charge of a crew of laborers who began at the eastern base and gradually brought it down. They found a great many skeletons, lots of items which may have belonged to soldiers stationed at the Ft.

Dallas such as handmade metal canteens, odds and ends of pottery jars—glass beads and other objects. We had several of these but over the years have lost all except some blue and white glass beads and a hand made flattened gold earring found in a grave occupied by a small skeleton.

. . . Other skeletons found higher up in the layers near (the) top of the mound were removed and bones deposited in barrels, the skulls ranged up on boards placed on top of barrels. After all the bones were removed and placed in barrels, they were buried in a deep sink-hole not far away. This was a natural deep pit, with a large wild fig tree growing tall with its top many feet above the rim. The pit was gradually filled and ground leveled. As near as I can recall, this pit was located at about what is now S.E. Second Street and Second Avenue. The Watson home in later years was built on this spot.[16] Christopher Eck, former director of Miami-Dade County's Historic Preservation Division, reports that this location is now occupied by a 12-story commercial building, and it is presumed that the bones were destroyed during the building's construction in 1967.[17] The artifacts described now repose at the Loxahatchee Historical Museum in Jupiter, Florida.

In 1904, workers, while clearing the hammock for construction of the Roome House (a.k.a. Coral Cliff) overlooking Biscayne Bay at 1725 Brickell Avenue, uncovered an Indian skeleton buried in a sitting position.[18] Most of the bones disintegrated after being uncovered, but Mr. Roome saved the teeth and larger bones. Their current whereabouts are unknown.

By 1926, five of the six burial mounds reported in the vicinity of the mouth of the Miami River had been destroyed. Except for several beads and ornaments that are now at the Loxahatchee Historical Museum, the whereabouts of other artifacts and bones from the Miami River mounds are unknown.

Although development destroyed many sites, it also led to the uncovering of many artifacts. Dredging operations uncovered several important artifacts. About 1909, when the Miami Canal was being excavated to drain the Everglades water into the Miami River, workers had to dynamite their way through the limestone ridge at the river's north fork. Capt. C. J. Rose, a Miami resident, happened to be at the excavation when workers uncovered a copper kettle weighing 35–40 pounds.[19] The kettle was cemented over with "rock" or concretion. Its antiquity and origin were greatly debated, and the "archaeologist" of the James Deering Estate in 1922 opined that it was made of metal obtained from a "Spanish conquerors or pirates." The artifact has since disappeared. Two wooden artifacts were discovered on Julia Tuttle's property when a boat slip was being dredged. In 1913, a beautiful wooden club made of black mangrove was found during the dredging of the Collins Canal on Miami Beach. It is now in the collection of the Historical Museum of Southern Florida in Miami.

Although chance discoveries of artifacts continued to occur throughout the period of the earliest development of the Biscayne Bay area, no scientific studies were conducted on any archaeological sites. Only one man, John Kunkel Small of the New York Botanical Garden, dutifully recorded the many sites he encountered during his botanical studies in southern Florida. He first visited the area in 1903 and returned almost every year until his death in 1938. Small was the first to observe and record the variety of plant species that grew exclusively on aboriginal sites. He also recorded many of the Indian uses for native plants. In 1924, he wrote in dismay of the needless bulldozing of the Surfside burial mound on Miami Beach.

In 1931 and 1932, John M. Goggin, then only 16 years old (fig. 1.3), visited the leveled remnants of the Surfside Mound and the cratered Flagami Mound. It marked the beginning of 30 years of investigations by a man who contributed more to our knowledge of Florida archaeology and anthropology than any other person up to that time.[20] Goggin's contributions were enormous. Biographer Brent Weismann notes that in Goggin's 15-year professional career, he published three dozen reports, monographs, and articles, including his unpublished tome "The Archaeology of the Glades Area, Southern Florida" and unpublished articles on glass beads and Spanish majolica. "No one before or after Goggin has approached Florida archaeology with such intellectual zeal and range or with his depth of knowledge or capacity for intense focus," Weismann writes. "John Goggin taught us how to think about Florida archaeology."[21]

Goggin was born in Chicago in 1916, and his family moved to Miami during the boom. As a boy, he was attracted to the Everglades wilderness and traveled it extensively, studying its plants, animals, and, particularly, Indian sites. Goggin was the first to classify and describe the entire range of Native American material culture of southern Florida.[22] He successfully constructed the first chronological ordering of prehistoric pottery types—a seriation that has withstood the test of modern radiocarbon dating. Goggin contributed major papers on Seminole ethnography and material culture,

Figure 1.3. John Goggin (*right*) stuck in the muck in the Everglades in a swamp buggy, February 1949. Courtesy of the Archaeological and Historical Conservancy.

and on Spanish artifacts such as olive jars and majolica. He was a founder of the Florida Anthropological Society and editor of the *Florida Anthropologist*.

One of Goggin's major contributions was the creation of a Florida site file which was an inventory of archaeological sites from across Florida. He recorded 49 sites in Miami-Dade County, learning about many of them through local informants such as Charles Brookfield and Donald Poppenhager. Although he did not visit all of the sites he recorded, he did conduct excavations at several of them that helped interpret the area's prehistory. His most important excavations in Miami-Dade County were at Snapper Creek, Surfside, and various sites in Everglades National Park.

Goggin was instrumental in influencing Matthew Stirling of the Smithsonian Institution to conduct excavations at the Surfside site on Miami Beach in 1934–35. This was conducted as part of the Works Progress Administration (WPA) program during the Depression and was the first scientific work to be done in southern Florida since Douglass's investigations of the 1880s. Gene Stirling, Matthew's brother, was the field director and was assisted by Vernon Lamme. Although not a trained archaeologist, Lamme was appointed Florida's first state archaeologist by Governor Scholtz in 1935. The position was soon terminated under a cloud of accusations about Lamme's fiscal management. Lamme spent some of his time investigating sites in Miami-Dade County, but his plans to expand investigations into the proposed Everglades National Park met with fierce opposition from Ernest F. Coe, chairman of the Everglades National Park Association, who sent a telegram to Governor Sholtz stating that the Everglades should be omitted from the WPA project.[23] Aleš Hrdlička of the Smithsonian joined the fray and wrote to the governor and Coe opposing the proposed work:

> It would be easy to destroy, but no one could rebuild. The mounds and shell heaps will constitute one of the most attractive and characteristic features of the Park, and only careful, thoroughly scientific work should be permitted.[24]

Coe's concern won out and Governor Scholtz ordered that the WPA excavations were not to include the Everglades. Lamme focused on other sites and made several important discoveries. He and Karl Squires, a professional surveyor and civil engineer, were the first investigators to break through the concretion on an Everglades tree island and discover evidence of Archaic period occupation in the Everglades. Lamme described the discovery:

> [We] found that what we had at first thought was base rock was in reality a sort of hard pan that could be broken with a hand axe. This hard pan is a depth of around 16 inches and today we penetrated this strata with difficulty and in one shovel full of debris taken from [sic] below the hard pan we found a beautifully turned needle of deer bone, a shark's tooth with a hole in it which appeared to be cut in rather than drilled as were all the others found in Dade County.[25]

Karl Squires also supervised the Surfside project in 1935, as did Julian Steward later the same year. Squires, an avid student of southern Florida prehistory and natural history, was eventually made director of the federal relief archaeological projects for the South Florida district. He and Lamme created the South Florida Archaeological Research Society, which apparently had no other members than themselves. Squires maintained a small museum at the Halcyon Arcade on Flagler Street. Unfortunately, Squires's extensive personal collection and field notes have since disappeared. Likewise, the scores of human skeletons removed from the Surfside Mound have met a similar fate, since they were reportedly stolen from the Opa-Locka train station while being shipped to the Smithsonian Institution.[26] Lamme reports that other craniums were stolen or broken by vandals coincidentally, including approximately 50 skulls and long bones. Excavations at the Surfside site continued the following year. An additional 22 graves were uncovered from the midden under the field direction of D. L. Reichard and Alfred Coe.

The WPA was also responsible for excavations of tree island sites in the Opa-Locka area, and unconfirmed informant reports exist of work done at the El Portal Burial Mound. A total of five eastern Everglades tree island sites and the Honey Hill site, 8DA411, located on the western edge of the Atlantic Coastal Ridge, were targeted for excavation. The WPA efforts used an army of workers—up to 125 at the Surfside site—and dozens of largely untrained workers crowded onto Everglades tree islands (fig. 1.4). Nonetheless, the close supervision by archaeologist W. E. Reicherd resulted in well-documented excavations.

Although it took the Depression to stimulate archaeological research in southern Florida, the results of this important work were not published until 1949. They probably would not have been published at all if it had not been for the Caribbean Program initiated by the Department of Anthropology of Yale University in 1944. Southern Florida fit well into this program because it was the logical location to search for clues that might indicate cultural contact between the Southeast and the Caribbean. Goggin was a major contributor to this program, first, by continuing to compile a survey of archaeological sites in southern Florida, and second, by codirecting a stratigraphic excavation with Frank Sommer at Upper Matecumbe Key.[27]

Southern Florida was first recognized as a distinctive prehistoric cultural area by M. W. Stirling in 1936. However, John Goggin defined three distinctive prehistoric subareas within southern Florida. These are the Calusa subarea in southwest Florida, the Tekesta subarea for southeast Florida and

Figure 1.4. WPA archaeologists and laborers excavating at Opa-Locka 1, 8DA48, in 1934. Collection of Robert S. Carr.

the Florida Keys, and the Okeechobee subarea surrounding Lake Okeechobee. Goggin classified these subareas on the basis of his recognition of their distinctive natural environments, differences in the archaeological record, and the predominant tribes—the Calusa and the Tequesta—who lived there during the first Spanish period. Since Goggin's work, there have been considerable amendments and revisions to his culture area definitions.

Goggin continued to work in the area between 1948 and 1952 while teaching for the Department of Sociology and Anthropology of the University of Florida. When the department was later restructured as the Department of Anthropology, he became its first chairman. He remained with the university until his death in 1964.

One of the most interesting salvage efforts of this period was the removal of a 400-pound carved limestone sea turtle from near a burial mound at 609 Brickell Avenue. The mound, 8DA15, was destroyed in 1949 during construction of the First Presbyterian Church on Brickell Avenue. The turtle's prehistoric antiquity is debatable since there is a possibility that it was made by Bahamians or Europeans rather than Indians as has usually been asserted. The turtle sculpture was reportedly vandalized in 1898 by a Spanish-American War soldier who broke off the head and took it as a souvenir. However, an 1890 account reports the head was already missing.[28] Prior to the church's construction, the turtle was moved and donated by Hervey Allen to the Historical Museum of Southern Florida in 1953.

The Era of the Avocational Archaeologist

John Goggin discontinued much of his South Florida field work when he moved to Gainesville. This left a scientific vacuum in the area for almost 25 years. Not a single Dade County university or college hired a professional archaeologist with a Florida orientation, nor did any college establish a local archaeological program. Dade County's population tripled between 1950 and 1970, and archaeological sites were destroyed at a rapid pace. Fortunately, a number of avocational archaeologists and archaeological societies emerged to fill the gap.

An excavation project was undertaken in 1952 by Mark Brooks at Grossman's Hammock, now located in Everglades National Park, but the most important of all the avocational archaeologists of the 1950s and 1960s was Dan D. Laxson (fig. 1.5), an Eastern Airlines radio operator.[29] Born in 1910, Laxson began excavating sites in 1951 in Hialeah, where he lived. In total, Laxson's research spanned twenty years and resulted in nineteen published articles. He was greatly influenced by Goggin's Glades ceramic types and seriation.[30] In 1955 he wrote that "it is important that representative material be removed from these sites and their presence noted before the bulldozers and draglines destroy them forever."[31] Among his most notable works were his excavations at Madden's Hammock,[32] an article on shell tools,[33] and his discovery of a nineteenth-century Seminole "warrior's" grave in Hialeah only months before the site's destruction by the construction of a church.[34]

Laxson's site investigations were always small and manageable and never significantly impacted any site. Laxson was the first avocational archaeologist in South Florida to collect zooarchaeological specimens and submit them for analysis.[35] He also placed all of his collections in museums. Laxson's investigations set the standard at the time for other avocational archaeologists, whom he greatly influenced by establishing a local archaeological society and teaching students at the Museum of Science in Miami. Laxson, in many respects, was Dade County's first urban archaeologist by staying one step ahead of the bulldozer.

In 1962, anthropologist Henry Fields, who was a research Fellow at the

Figure 1.5. Dan D. Laxson with a cannonball discovered at the Trail site, 8DA34, in the eastern Everglades, c. 1960s. Courtesy of the Archaeological and Historical Conservancy.

Peabody Museum of Archaeology and Ethnology between 1950 and 1969, resided in Coconut Grove at the former homestead of Kirk Munroe. Fields began an archaeological club for local children dubbed the Fields Junior Archaeologists. He brought students to numerous sites throughout South Florida, including Madden's Hammock, and excavated at an unrecorded prehistoric midden site at the Harris School on Biscayne Bay.[36]

Charles Brookfield, an Audubon warden in the Everglades and a long-time informant for John Goggin, continued his visits to area sites collecting historic artifacts at the Brickell Trading Post and Madden's Hammock. His small collection of artifacts are at the Historical Museum of Southern Florida.

The emergence of archaeological societies during this time period had both positive and negative effects. On the positive side, these societies acted as a focus for individuals interested in learning about local archaeology and provided valuable public awareness of archaeological sites and prehistory.

They also conducted excavations on sites that have since been destroyed by development. On the negative side, many of the members of these societies had little training in excavation techniques and destroyed more information than they uncovered. Also, many societies indiscriminately dug on significant sites that were not endangered by development, including sites preserved within public parks. Unfortunately, some of the most important excavation work by local societies has never been published and the recovered artifacts have been lost.

Dade County's first archaeological society, founded in 1952 by Dan Laxson, was the Tequesta Archaeological Society, which would later become the Dade County chapter of the Florida Anthropological Society (FAS). The chapter dissolved sometime in the 1960s. In the 1970s, FAS chapter status was presented to the Miami–West India Archaeological Society (MWIAS). This later society was founded in 1969 and had the commendable policy of placing all artifacts collected by its members into a small museum they operated in Opa-Locka. Although the society's name suggests some rather diverse geographical interests, most of the members' work was done in southern Florida. Under the leadership of Wesley Coleman and Ted Huna, the society was among the first to promote site preservation, actively lobbying government officials to preserve certain endangered sites. They worked closely with local environmental advocates to save the Arch Creek site. Also to their credit was their help toward preserving a burial mound, 8DA25, on the Oleta River and the numerous excavations of endangered sites they conducted throughout Dade County. Most of their artifacts were eventually donated to the Historical Museum of Southern Florida, and more recently, former member Bill Carson donated his collection to the Archaeological and Historical Conservancy.

When MWIAS disbanded in 1978, the role of societal archaeological leadership had already been inherited by the Archaeological Society of Southern Florida. This society had its roots in an older group called the Peninsula Archaeological Society. However, the Peninsula Archaeological Society left few records and no documented collections representing their 10-year span of operations in Dade County.

The Archaeological Society of Southern Florida was the first archaeological organization in Florida to adopt a policy of excavating only endangered sites. Currently, that society makes important contributions to archaeological education and conducts salvage excavations in cooperation with Miami-Dade's Historic Preservation Division and other professional archaeologists (fig. 1.6). Many of their most significant artifact finds are

Figure 1.6. Members of the Archaeological Society of Southern Florida excavating at the Cheetum site, 8DA1058, in 1971. Courtesy of the Archaeological and Historical Conservancy.

donated to the Historical Museum of Southern Florida, while others are at the Everglades Trading Post near Florida City.

Other avocational archaeologists emerged during the 1950s–1970s. Among the most noteworthy were Ron Card, Wesley Coleman, Stan Cooper, C. M. Duggar, Bill Carson, Mark Greene, Jim Lord, Bill Lyons, Ted Riggs, and Jim Shafer. All kept good records of the sites associated with the artifacts they had collected and, in the case of Shafer and Card, maintained an excellent photographic record. Duggar's work was highlighted by the several unpublished excavation reports he wrote and the educational artifact exhibits he took to many of Dade County's schools. More recently, John Reiger, former professor of history at the University of Miami, wrote several important articles describing various types of prehistoric shell tools of southern Florida, and ongoing research by Jim Clupper and by the late William Straight has added to our knowledge of the area's history and pre-

Figure 1.7. The discovery of the 1855 Key Biscayne survey marker during the construction of the county golf course in 1970. County surveyor J. S. Frazier on left and unidentified person on right. Courtesy of the Historical Museum of Southern Florida.

history. Several of these individuals maintained large personal collections, which sometimes created conflicts with professional archaeologists who were anxious to place important specimens and information into local museums. Important collections have been donated by Coleman, Cooper, and Reiger to the Historical Museum of Southern Florida.

Perhaps the most unusual discovery of a historical feature made during this period was a heavy granite survey marker found in 1970 during the clearing of the county golf course on Key Biscayne (fig. 1.7). Dating from 1855, the base marker was preserved in place and its history subsequently documented by former county surveyor J. C. Frazier. Additional survey markers were discovered near the Key Biscayne lighthouse by surveyor Ted Riggs with the help of former county archaeologist John Ricisak.

The Reemergence of Scientific Study

While avocational archaeologists were doing the majority of work in Dade County during this time period, scientific work was restricted to inventories of sites in Everglades National Park and Biscayne National Park. Informal surveys were conducted by park rangers Richard Stokes, Barney Parker, and Fred Dayoff. Archaeologists John Griffin and William Kennedy compiled information on all the known sites in Everglades National Park. Griffin did important excavations of the Bear Lake site in 1964, producing a series of radiocarbon dates that were important contributions toward interpreting the chronological placement of ceramic types associated with the site.

A more comprehensive inventory of Everglades National Park was compiled by the Southeast Archaeological Research Center under the direction of John Ehrenhard, with some of the major field work being conducted by Robert Taylor. From 1977 to 1981, Ehrenhard directed a similar assessment of archaeological sites in the Big Cypress National Preserve. In 2002, John Griffin's comprehensive Everglades studies were published by the University Press of Florida. In the same year, I completed an analysis of tree island sites in the Everglades,[37] and additional tree island studies were conducted by the National Park Service archaeologist Margot Schwadron.[38]

Other excavation projects in Dade County were sponsored by the Florida Division of Historical Resources. This state agency sponsored a three-week dig at the Arch Creek site in 1974,[39] investigations at 8DA33,[40] and 1979 salvage excavations at the prehistoric midden at Chekika Park before part of the site was covered with fill for the construction of a campground.[41]

The most important project in Dade County sponsored by the FDHR was the two-phase salvage excavation of the Granada site (8DA11), located on the north bank of the Miami River, where the Hyatt and Knight Convention Center is now located. These investigations encompassed an estimated 10 percent of the original area of the prehistoric village of Tequesta. The first phase of investigations was conducted in 1974 under the direction of Ross Morrell, and a second larger phase was completed in 1976–77 (fig. 1.8). The second phase of the Granada site excavation was directed by Carlos Martinez. After he left the project, Shaun Bonath continued the work. However, it was John Griffin who completed the analysis and report in 1983,[42] generating information from tens of thousands of artifacts and animal bones of one of the largest excavations attempted in southern Florida since the WPA

Figure 1.8. View east of the Granada site, 8DA11, in 1976. The Hyatt Center currently occupies the site. Courtesy of the Historical Museum of Southern Florida.

work of the 1930s. The Granada report includes a comprehensive reconstruction of prehistoric subsistence and diet completed under the direction of Elizabeth Wing of the Florida State Museum in Gainesville.[43]

The Historic Preservation Division of Miami-Dade County

In 1978, the Dade County Community Development Block Grant Program and the Florida Division of Archives, History, and Records Management awarded grants to Dade County to assess and create an inventory of the historical, architectural, and archaeological sites in the county. This funding provided the basis for establishing the Dade County Historic Survey, directed by Ivan Rodriguez. In July 1978, as staff archaeologist, I was hired to conduct the archaeological portion of the survey. The survey was initially administered by the Parks and Recreation Department, but in 1981, the program was transferred to the Office of Community and Economic Development. The Historic Preservation Division became its own department in 2000, renamed the Office of Historic and Archaeological Resources. In 2007, with looming budget cuts, the agency was transferred to the county's Planning Department.

The focus of the archaeological survey was metropolitan Dade County since that area was most subject to development. Western boundaries of the study area included State Road 27 in northern Dade County (north of U.S. 41) and the 836 Levee in central Dade. Some tracts west of these boundaries also were surveyed, but most sites in the Everglades conservation areas were not assessed other than by using aerial photographs, nor were any sites within the Everglades or Biscayne National Parks. The field survey was completed in November 1981, with a total of 350 archaeological sites being documented.

In addition to an assessment of archaeological sites, the Dade County Historic Preservation Division began monitoring and conducting salvage excavations in 1978 at numerous sites that were threatened by development. Some of the most important projects include salvage work at the Granada site during excavations for a swimming pool (8DA11), monitoring, and excavations at the Brickell site (8DA12) during the construction of the Hyatt Hotel; the Santa Maria cemetery (8DA2132); the Atlantis site (8DA1082); the Flagami sites (8DA1053 and 8DA1073); the Cutler Fossil site (8DA2001); and the Miami Circle in 1998. During that time, the agency discovered several significant historic sites, such as the Ferguson Mill (8DA1655), the

Lewis Homestead (8DA2132) on Biscayne Bay, and the Arch Creek coontie mill (8DA1657).

One of the first county ordinances in Florida to address the preservation of archaeological sites was drafted by local preservationists. In 1981, Dade County Ordinance 81-13 was passed by the Miami-Dade Board of County Commissioners. It established the authority for the Miami-Dade Historic Preservation Board and provided guidelines for the designation of historical, architectural, and archaeological sites. Since 1980, there have been four county archaeologists: Robert Carr (1980–95), John Ricisak (1996–99), Gary Beiter (1999–2004), and Jeff Ransom (2005–present).

A total of 42 archaeological sites and zones have been designated across the county as of 2012. Since 1978 the Historic Preservation Division has accessioned over 3,000 groups of artifactual and data samples into the Historical Museum of Southern Florida. These materials provide one of the largest research collections of archaeological materials from southern Florida.

Part I
Prehistoric Miami

Hermann Trappman, *A Tequesta Family on the Miami River*, 1983. Pencil on paper, 8 × 10. Collection of the Archaeological and Historical Conservancy. By permission of the artist.

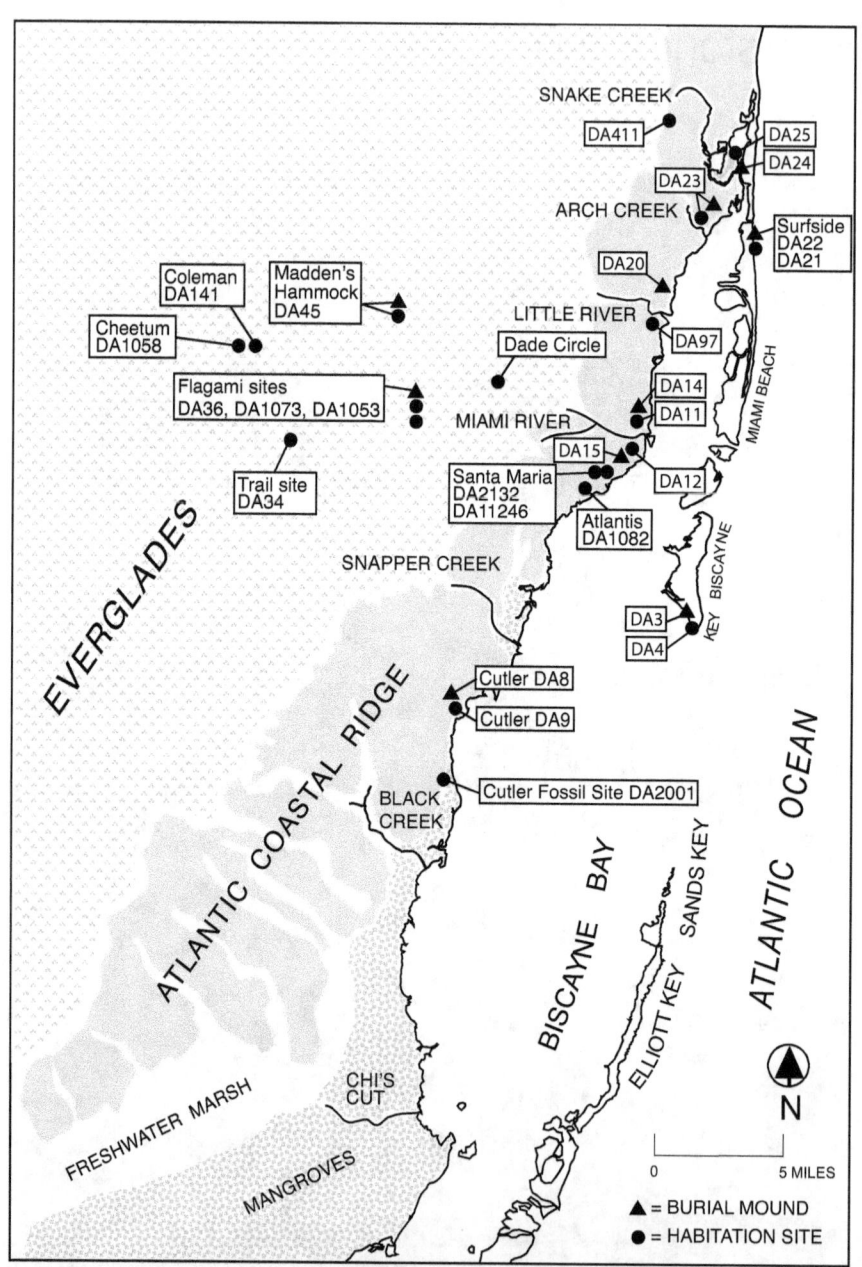

Prehistoric sites of Miami-Dade County. Map created by John G. Beriault. Courtesy of the Archaeological and Historical Conservancy.

2

The First People

The Cutler Fossil Site

If there is such a thing as a hole within the thin carpet of civilization that plunges to the darkest recesses of Florida's prehistory, then the solution hole at Charles Deering Estate Park at Cutler is such a place (fig. 2.1). Across southern Miami-Dade County, the ancient Miami oolitic limestone rises to 19 feet above sea level. Over the millennia, rainwater transporting carbonic acid combined with humic acids from rotting vegetation has dissolved deep fissures that finger into the rock, creating caves and solution holes. This process is called karsification. The holes grew larger through time as the eroded rock opened into shafts that now vary from 6 inches in diameter to some 30 feet wide. These solution holes slowly fill with vegetative debris, rocks, and soil. Many of these holes contain the bones of animals that have fallen into them. With no easy way out, these animals were fatally injured, died from starvation, or became easy prey for carnivores. Some larger solution holes became dens for carnivores.

The solution hole at Charles Deering Estate Park is no larger than a small bedroom—only about 10 meters in diameter. It became known as the Cutler Fossil site and has yielded evidence of South Florida's most ancient people, the so-called Paleo-Indians ("paleo" meaning old since there was no name passed down by Native Americans identifying these earliest prehistoric people).

South Florida is a long way from the Bering Strait: 4,500 miles as the bird flies. It is North America's cul-de-sac, where animals and people can travel no farther south without bumping into the Florida Straits, obstructed by the swift currents of the gulf stream. It perhaps is not surprising that most of the earliest discoveries and investigations of Paleo-Indian sites occurred at locations in western North America closer to the proposed entry point of the Bering Strait and only a quick march southward to Mexico

Figure 2.1. Archaeologists working at the Cutler site, 8DA2001, in 1986. Courtesy of the Archaeological and Historical Conservancy.

and South America. Early discoveries of Paleo-Indian artifacts at Clovis and Folsom in New Mexico dominated scholarly research during the first half of the twentieth century. It was not until recently that scholars began to seriously consider that prehistoric sites in eastern North America might provide important understanding on the earliest peopling of the Americas. Florida emerged into the scholarly debate on the antiquity of man in the New World with the discovery of the "Vero Man" during the excavation of a canal at Vero in 1911. Controversy raged when human bones were found in association with extinct fossil animal bones, including the mammoth and Pleistocene horse. The antiquity of the human remains were unknown because the fossils and artifacts had been mixed by the dredge and radiocarbon dating hadn't yet been discovered. It would not be until the 1960s that the age of Florida's Paleo-Indian sites would be firmly established with the discoveries of human remains deep within Warm Mineral Springs and Little Salt Spring in southwest Florida. Investigations by archaeologists Carl Clausen at Little Salt Spring[1] and Wilburn "Sonny" Cockrell[2] at Warm Mineral Springs resulted in the radiocarbon dating of organic samples associated with human activity dating to 12,000 to 13,000 years. More recent investigations of Paleo-Indian sites in Florida, including Aucilla River,[3] Little Salt Spring,[4] and Wakulla Springs,[5] have added valuable information and new radiocarbon dates, some as early as 14,500 years ago.

No Paleo-Indian sites were discovered in southern Florida until 1979, when one of Florida's most important fossil sites was discovered near present-day Cutler Ridge in Miami-Dade County. The discovery was made by Wonda and Jim Simons, who manufactured hand-crafted knives and were searching in the Deering Hammock for wood to use as knife handles. When they climbed into a large solution hole they found pieces of wood that were unusually hard and polished. Fortunately, they brought the curious pieces to me (I was then the county archaeologist). I identified them as fossil horse teeth and asked them to take me to the site. When I climbed into the solution hole, I quickly realized its tremendous potential for yielding additional fossils, but the discovery was kept secret until it was certain that the site could be properly excavated and protected.

Beginning in the early 1980s, attempts were made to acquire the Charles Deering Estate as a county park. In 1985, the 30-acre parcel that encompassed the site, to the surprise of many, was deleted from the 300 acres acquired to create the park. While negotiations assured the purchase of most of the Deering Estate, the smaller parcel containing the fossil site was omitted to allow for the development of residential housing and a shopping center. In response, the county's Historic Preservation Board designated the Cutler Fossil site as a historic site. This designation and pending development resulted in the property owners, the Danielson family, donating funds to have the site excavated and documented. Those investigations began on October 15, 1985, under the direction of the Historic Preservation Division with an archaeological team provided by the Archaeological and Historical Conservancy.[6]

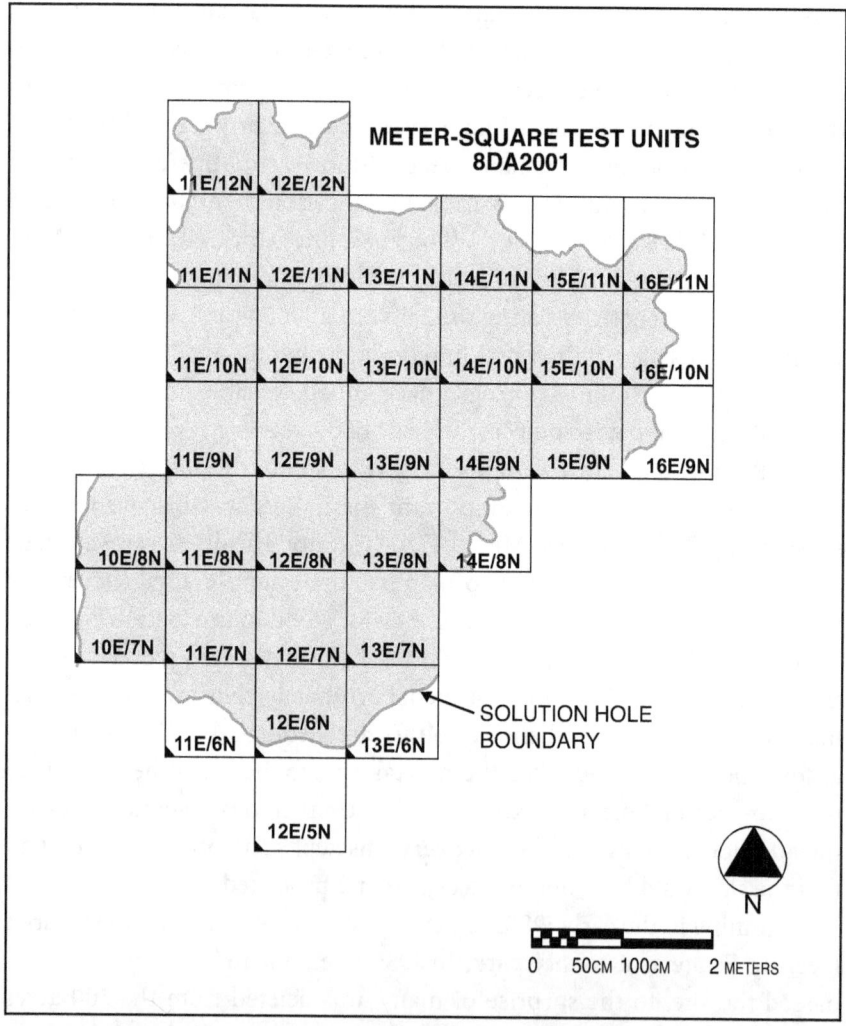

Figure 2.2. Map of the Cutler site and excavation units. Map created by John G. Beriault. Courtesy of the Archaeological and Historical Conservancy.

Excavations continued over a 14-month period resulting in 32 1-meter squares being dug within the 8-×-10-meter solution hole (fig. 2.2). A cardinal grid was extended across the hole. The excavations encompassed all of the accessible and exposed sediments within the feature. To access the site, the archaeological team had to cut steps into the limestone to descend into the steep solution hole, which was about 7 feet below the surface of the hammock forest.

Unfortunately, in the six years since the site's original discovery, 11 pits had been dug by a local collector, causing disturbances deep into the sediments and leaving redeposited soils as well as holes and gaps in the archaeological record. The archaeologists dug away the disturbed soils to uncover intact sediments below, which varied from unit to unit, but disturbances were as deep as 2 feet. Fossil bones and teeth were uncovered throughout the disturbed sediments. When the undisturbed sediments were encountered, the archaeologists began digging at 10-centimeter arbitrary levels, sifting the soils through a one-quarter-inch mesh screen.

On the second day of excavation a bone artifact was encountered., the first evidence of human activity found at the site. It would not be the last. The biggest surprise occurred at the depth of 120 centimeters, where a human tooth was discovered in direct association with fossil animal bones. Soon afterward, bone and chert tools were discovered in unit after unit, providing conclusive evidence of human activity at this ancient site. Despite the excitement of uncovering what appeared to be ancient artifacts in association with a fossil deposit, the significance of the overwhelming number of fossil bones and teeth required an expert opinion.

The Fossil Record

I invited paleontologists from the Florida Museum of Natural History to help in the investigations. Gary Morgan and Steven Emslie, as well as several of their students, provided valuable field assistance and important insights into the identification and population of the fossil assemblage. Morgan and Elmslie's analysis resulted in identifying the Cutler site as containing one of the most southern continental fossil deposits. Morgan identified the site as dating from the Late Pleistocene (Late Rancholabrean) period, representing an age of 130,000 to 10,000 B.P. He interpreted the species assemblage as having affinities with Neotropical influences.[7]

A total of 119 vertebrate species were identified, including 47 mammalian fauna, of which 16 were extinct Pleistocene fauna that represented grazing herbivores such as horse (*Equus* sp.), Columbian mammoth (*Mammuthus columbi*), American mastodon (*Mammut americanun*), camels (*Palaeolama marifica* and *Hemiauchenia macrocenhala*), and bison (*Bison antiques*). At the top of the food chain were the carnivores, of which 14 species were identified,[8] including the dire wolf (*Canis dirus*) with a total of 42 individuals represented, mostly juveniles. Morgan notes that the remains of pecaries, which abound at the site, are often represented by only teeth and the ends of limb bones, some gnawed, suggesting that they may have been the principal meal of the wolves.

The second most abundant ungulate was the horse (*Equus* sp.), also likely victims of carnivores as attested by the preponderance of teeth and juveniles. The second most common carnivore was the bear (*Tremaretos floridanus*), with at least nine individuals being identified, and a single species of the South American spectacled bear (*Tremarctos orratus*). Other carnivores included coyotes (*Canis lantrans*), with at least five individuals represented, and jaguar (*Panthera onca*), with four individuals represented (fig. 2.3). In smaller numbers were bobcat (*Lynx rufux*), a single black bear (*Ursus americanus*), and Florida panther (*Puma concolor*), Florida lion (*Panthera atnox*), and saber-toothed cat (*Smilodon fatalis*).

Other fauna included birds, bats, amphibians, reptiles, and smaller mammals, whose presence provide important clues to the micro-environment of the Cutler Fossil site as well as to the general environment of the area 11,000 years ago. A total of nine reptiles, seven amphibians, five fish, and 51 bird species were identified, including at least seven extinct species of avifauna, reflecting a diversity of environments that included hardwood hammocks, pinelands, marshes, coastal habitats, and open grasslands.[9] Elmslie identified two species of caracara, including the extinct *Milvago readri*, indicating the proximity of a savannah or forest-fringed habitats. Also present were the hawk-eagle (*Spizartus grinnelli*) and the California condor (*Gymnogyps californianus*). The presence of the Peregrine falcon (*F. peregrinus*) was interpreted to indicate open grasslands and savannahs near the site. Mammals included 16 extinct and 31 extant fauna, including the pine vole (*Pitymys pinetorum*), coyote (*Canis latrans*), and pocket gopher (*Geomys pinetis*), which no longer occur in South Florida except for the recent return of the coyote to the area.

Amphibians and reptiles represent the most abundant bone elements found. These and other smaller fauna provide important clues to the Paleo

Figure 2.3. Uncovering a jaguar mandible at the Cutler site. Courtesy of the Archaeological and Historical Conservancy.

environment of the Cutler Fossil site. Amphibians indicate that the solution hole had standing water in it at least part of the year. Whether water was there as a result of collected rain and/or a spring is unclear, but the presence of water may have created an oasis effect attracting animals, particularly during drier periods. The absence of any large bodies of freshwater is suggested by the complete absence of freshwater turtles, water snakes, and alligators. Gary Morgan identified one bat species (*Myotis austropraparius*), suggesting that perhaps the site may have once been part of a dry cave.

John Gifford of the University of Miami excavated five cores across the site which demonstrated that a deep fossil deposit occurred at least 4 meters below the site surface and below the water table.[10] The depth of the deposit suggested that the earliest fossils are likely to be tens of thousands of years old.

Thousands of fossil bones were recovered from the site, including large concretions of fossil wolf and horse. One large mass of concretion is currently on exhibit at HistoryMiami (the Historical Museum of Southern Florida), although most of the fossil bones are at the Florida Museum of Natural History in Gainesville.

The Archaeological Record

Although the density and diversity of the fossil bone was in itself an important scientific discovery, the rocket of excitement generated by the discovery of human artifacts and bones mixed with fossil animal bones was understandable. The media coverage had trumpeted this association, and I certainly believed in what I was observing. Enough excitement was generated to bring Pleistocene expert Paul Martin from the University of Arizona to the site for a personal visit. His comments were illuminating. He too saw the obvious association of human tools lying adjacent to extinct horse and wolf bones, but seeing is not always believing. In a soft voice he explained that there was another way to view this evidence: It was possible that the human occupants were not there at the same time as the megafauna but that humans had moved into an empty cave—vacant because the animals were long dead and their bones were simply littering the floor. These people had moved into an empty apartment to become the latest tenants in a long history of solution hole occupation. But how could I identify and separate those bones which were related to those animals using or dying in the solution hole versus those bones left behind by human occupants? Aside from the obvious artifacts shaped by human hands and the human bones, what was the best way to isolate those animal bones deposited by human activity as opposed to natural deaths and carnivore meals? I hypothesized that the bones that were burnt or charred likely represented direct evidence of human meal preparation. These burnt bones could be identified and sorted from the other bones to determine whether humans and extinct megafauna were cohabitating this area at the same time. I reasoned that the burnt bones were cultural and not natural because of the unlikeliness that natural forest fires would have occurred within a small, moist solution hole amid a hardwood hammock, a habitat rarely affected by natural fires. That some of the fire-altered bones had turned white or greenish blue from the intensity of the heat reinforced a cultural explanation for the fires. Paleontologist Steve Esmlie, then at the University of Florida, conducted the analysis. Looking at 802 burnt or charred bones and teeth, he determined that the fire-altered bones represent at least 19 different species and a minimum number of 22 different individuals (the identified species are presented in table 2.1).

After these bones were identified, it was clear that most of the animals that were cooked and eaten by Paleo-Indians were not the extinct megafauna but extant animals such as deer, rabbit, and possibly dog. Morgan notes that the burnt bones of a *Canis latrans* may actually represent *Canis familaris,* the domestic dog.[11] This would be a more likely candidate for the culinary hearth than the coyote. If it is proven to be a domestic dog, it is among the earliest documented in Florida.

Table 2.1 Fire-altered bones from the Cutler Fossil site

Taxon	Number of bones	MNI
Sylilagus sp. (cottontail rabbit)	24	7
Sigmodon hispidus? (cotton rat)	3	1
Neotoma floridiana? (eastern wood rat)	2	1
Dasypus bellus* (giant armadillo)	1	1
Didelphis virginiana (opossum)	5	1
Procyon lotor (raccoon)	2	1
Lynx rufus (bobcat)	3	1
Canis latrans?** (coyote)	6	1
Mephitis mephitis (striped skunk)	2	1
Mammuthus sp.,* (mammoth)	1	1
Odocoileus virginianus (white-tailed deer)	29	3
Artiodactyla (even-toed ungulate)	1	—
Buteo sp. (hawk)	1	1
Aves	2	—
Chelonia (unidentified turtle)	3	—
Pseudomys? (pond slider)	1	1
Serpentes (unidentified snake)	6	—
Anura (unidentified frog)	4	—
Unidentifiable fragments	652	—
Total	802	22

Source: Steven Emslie, unpublished report prepared for the Archaeological and Historical Conservancy, 1986.
Note: MNI = minimum number of individuals represented by the bones for each taxon.
*Extinct taxon.
**Morgan notes that these bones may represent domestic dog, *Canis familaris.*

Only two extinct species were identified from the burnt bones: mammoth (*Mammuthus* sp.) and the giant armadillo (*Dasypus bellus*). After Emslie's analysis other burnt bones were recovered, including a large vertebrae from a paleolama (*Paleolama mirifica*) in Unit N and burnt horse (*Equus* sp.) teeth from Level 14 in Unit H. The heat alteration observed on some of the extinct bones and teeth indicates direct contact with fire.

In addition to the charred and burnt bone, sixteen marine-shell specimens were recovered. The shells were another important clue to human activity because it is unlikely that most of the shells entered the solution hole naturally. Included are whelk (*Busycon*), conch (*Strombus gigas*), tulip (*Fasciolara sp.*), clam (*lunciae*), and a single bleeding tooth (*Nerita peloronta*) recovered from Level 10. Among several shell tools were a *Busycon* scraper and a columella hammer. These marine shells may represent some of the earliest shell artifacts identified from a North American archaeological site.

Although most of the marine shell has a cultural association, it is possible that shells like the tulip (*Fasciolara sp.*) may have entered the site on the back of a hermit crab, since marine shells are often recycled by crabs. Once they fall into a solution hole there is no easy way out. Other recovered invertebrates such as the apple snail (*Pomecea paludosa*) may have found their way into the site as the result of birds. The snail kite (*Rostrhamus sociabilis*) is well known to eat the apple snail as the principal part of its diet. Even certain vertebrates such as fish, represented by gar (*Lepisosteus platyrhincus*), and small reptiles and mammals could have entered the site from birds perching or nesting over the solution hole. Other invertebrates include a single specimen of a bleached tree snail (*Liguus fasciatus*) uncovered in Level 5 of Unit 15E/11N.

A total of 192 lithic artifacts were recovered, including artifacts made from local limestone as well as tools made from nonlocal chert. These included seven projectile points represented by Bolen Beveled, Dalton, and Greenbriar (fig. 2.4). These point types have been dated from about 8000 to 10,000 B.C. from other sites in central and northern Florida, but until their discovery at the Cutler Fossil site, no points of similar antiquity had been found in southern Florida. Also uncovered were one chert core, three micro blades, and 21 chert flakes. Three of the flakes are reddish, suggesting thermal alteration. Archaeologist and lithic expert Robert Austin analyzed the chert flakes and identified them as having been quarried from sources hundreds of miles away from the Cutler site in the northern and central Gulf Coast.[12] The most common material is Suwannee limestone chert from the

Figure 2.4. Chert bifaces and projectile points from the Cutler site. Collection of the Historical Museum of Southern Florida.

Upper Withlacoochee Quarry, with at least one specimen originating in the Rock Ridge region of Polk County. He also identified two flakes of Tampa limestone chert likely from the Hillsborough River Quarry and one of Ocala limestone chert that likely had its origin at the Lake Panasoffkee Quarry Cluster.[13] Austin also identified a uniface retouch flake and other flakes that represent tool maintenance—exactly the kind of curation and reshaping that would be expected to maintain tools made more valuable by a distant source of lithic raw materials.[14]

Other lithic artifacts include a stone bead and several tools made from local oolitic limestone, including a turtleback scraper (fig. 2.5), a flaked axe, and a possible knife or scraper (fig. 2.6). An analysis of the limestone artifacts was conducted by Marilyn Masson (1987). She assessed 61 limestone objects, including axes (or celts), biface knives, scrapers, blades, and spoke shaves. This assemblage of expedient artifacts is important because it reveals that the people at the Cutler Fossil site were able to adapt to an environment lacking chert or other hard stones. Masson observed tooling marks and use marks on some of the artifacts suggesting manufacturing techniques consistent with chert tools, an observation indicating that old techniques were being adapted to new materials. Many of the limestone artifacts appear to have been burnt or heat treated.[15]

Other recovered cultural materials include burnt pumice (FS 1073) re-

Figure 2.5. Limestone turtleback scraper from the Cutler site. Collection of the Historical Museum of Southern Florida.

Figure 2.6. Limestone scraper from the Cutler site. Collection of the Historical Museum of Southern Florida.

covered from Unit 14E/10N, Level 10. This volcanic rock floats and was probably recovered from the ocean shore. This specimen is undoubtedly one of the earliest examples of culturally associated pumice found in eastern North America. Another unusual discovery was orange-red ochre. Two small lumps were found, one in 15E/10N at Level 11 and another from Unit 13E/6N. Ochre is significant in the archaeological record because it is often used as a pigment for body painting and often occurs in association with human graves.

Human Remains

Human bones and teeth were uncovered throughout the site. Most were isolated and fragmentary. An analysis of the human remains was conducted by George Armelagos, although other human remains were identified in the collection after his analysis. He identified a minimum of five individuals: three adults and two subadults.[16] Most of the remains were recovered from Units 12E/N and 12E/7N. Six other units—11E/7N, 11E/8N, 12E/8N, 13E/7N, 13E/8N, and 13E/9N—had human remains.

The three adults are represented by three distinct frontals, including the midline and part of the sagital sulcus.[17] The most complete cranium is associated with a mandible that represents an older male. Sex was determined by visual assessment of the cranial fragments and the mandible. Age was estimated based on the complete fusion and near obliteration of the coronal and sagital sutures and antemortem loss of the posterior teeth with attendant marked alveolar resorption. Many of the postcranial elements are also representative of an adult male, presumably the same individual, including at least the right and left femora, innominates, and a portion of the distal humerus. Based on the large size and robosity of the bones, Armelagos identified the individual as a male.

Of the other two adults, at least one is likely female. The postcranial elements are much smaller and gracile in comparison to the adult male. The cranial vault fragments of the two remaining adults are gracile and thinner and lack the bony characteristics indicative of males.

Excavation of Unit 12E/7N resulted in the largest quantity of human remains recovered from the site. Bones from an adult were found in Levels 5 through 7 (50 to 70 centimeters below surface). They were disarticulated, extending along a general northeast-southwest axis, and were located beneath a group of large limestone rocks. Cranial fragments and long bones occurred at the southwest end and other cranial fragments occurred in the adjacent Unit 12E/8N. No obvious grave goods were apparent, but a possible limestone scraper was documented near the bones in Level 6, and other artifacts found in that unit include a Bolen Beveled projectile point (fig. 2.4) in Level 4 and a shark tooth in Level 5, although there is no evidence that they were deliberately interred with the grave. It is possible that the artifacts represent concurrent or subsequent habitation at the site.

One of the two subadults (Individual 4) was found beneath the ledge in Units 12E/5N and 12E/6N and is represented by cranial and dental elements. This subadult is the site's most intact individual and is aligned roughly east-west with the cranium at the east end. This individual is three to four years of age, an estimate based on development of the permanent molars using the standards presented by Moorees, Fanning, and Hunt.[18] The grave provides a clue to the changing climate of South Florida. Adjacent to the child were three hazelnuts (*Corlylus* sp.). Today hazelnuts grow no farther south than northern Florida. Hazelnuts growing in Miami 10,000 years ago suggest a shifting climate change that has become increasingly subtropical since that time.

Although most of the human remains were undoubtedly associated with graves, some fragments raise questions about other activities associated with the human remains. One distal radius fragment found in Unit 11E/8N at Level 5 is burnt. Other burnt bones include phlanges from Unit 14E/11N and fragments of rib, ulna, and radius from 11E/9N. It is unlikely that the extent of burning exhibited on these bones could have occurred as an in-

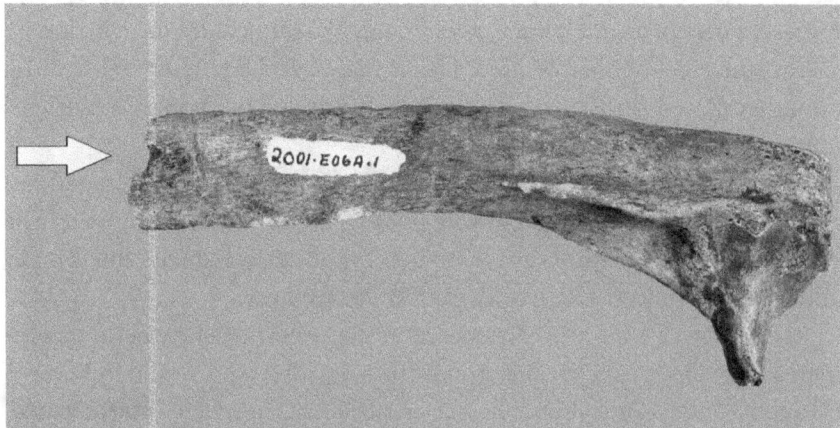

Figure 2.7. Human ulna with carnivore tooth perforation from the Cutler site. Collection of the Historical Museum of Southern Florida.

direct result of being on the ground exposed to a cooking fire. The burnt surfaces of the bones appear to have been fully encompassed by the heat or fire source. These burnt surfaces are similar to the burnt animal bones recovered from across the site. The presence of burnt human bones raises the possibility of cremation burials or burial preparation rites, and even ritual cannibalism cannot be ruled out. One unusual altered human bone is an ulna, perforated by a carnivore tooth at its center (fig. 2.7). Whether it represents a victim of a carnivore attack or a scavenged grave is difficult to say.

Botanical Analysis

A total of 43 botanical remains were analyzed by ethnobotanist Lee Newsom.[19] She identified a wide range of plants using seeds, charcoal, and other plant remains uncovered at the site. Not surprisingly, most of the specimens were found in Unit 12E/6N, within the inundated soils beneath the southern ledge. Species represented there include pine (*Pinus*), cypress (cf. *Taxodium*), oak (*Quercus virginiana*), and tropical hardwoods such as *Ficus*, cherry (cf. *Prunus myrtifolia*), mahogany (cf. *Swietenia*), buttonwood (*Conocarpus erectus*), stopper (*Eugenia*), and plants of the marlberry family (*Myrsinaceae*). The most common specimens in the collection are pine, oak, and wild fig. Of particular interest are hazelnuts, which are not native to south Florida, and cypress, which does not currently occur in the immediate area of the site.

Radiocarbon Dates

A total of 15 samples were subject to radiocarbon dating. Five of the samples were dated by Beta Analytic and 10 samples of faunal bone were dated at the University of Arizona under the coordination of Steven Emslie. Most of the samples failed to produce reliable dates. Carbon extracted from soil samples (0.3%) indicated an age of 3000 B.P. for the carbon and was not useful in interpreting the archaeological and fossil context of the site. Likewise, bone samples submitted by Emslie had little or no collagen and could not be dated. Surprisingly, one of the hazelnuts tested with a modern date despite its context beneath the ledge and its association with a human burial, suggesting some type of contamination. The two charcoal samples (FS 115, 717), both likely to have been associated with hearths and uncovered from the horizon of Paleo artifacts, are statistically the same date. Calibrated, the corrected age is 11,270 to 10,680 B.P. or a mean date of 10,875 B.P. (9320 B.C.)

The Great Extinction

Perhaps one of the most important insights provided by the fossil record at the Cutler site is the extraordinary view it offers of environmental changes in South Florida 10,000 to 12,000 years ago. The site preserved thousands of animal bones representing at least 119 vertebrate species of fauna—many of them extinct. Uncovered species included herbivores such as the mammoth (*Mammuthus columbi*), horse (*Equus* sp.), tapir (*Tapiris* sp.), and camel (*Paleolama marifica*), as well an assemblage of carnivores such as the dire wolf (*Canis dirus*), saber-toothed tiger (*Smilodon fatalis*), Florida lion (*Panthera atnox*), and jaguar (*Panthera onca*). The importance of this array of fauna is not only its testimony to species diversity during the late Pleistocene but also its usefulness as a snapshot of South Florida's environment, offering a dramatic contrast to modern South Florida characterized by the Everglades and an adjacent coastal ridge of pinewoods and hammocks. Twelve thousand years ago, when many of these extinct species were at their zenith, there was no Everglades or Biscayne Bay. Both are relatively recent features that are no more than 5,000 to 7,000 years old. Prior to that time, South Florida was drier and freshwater wetlands more intermittent. The sea level was dramatically lower, with seawater impounded in massive glaciers during the Late Wisconsin glacial maximum in present-day Canada, Greenland, and Alaska; enough ice impacted in these glaciers that sea levels were approximately 60 to 80 meters lower during peak glaciation 18,000 years ago than today.[20] Lower sea levels meant that Florida was a much wider peninsula that extended several hundred miles west of today's shores of the Gulf of Mexico. The submerged continental shelf opposite Miami presented a narrow shelf, and thus the coastline was only several kilometers east of its present alignment. Ten thousand years ago Biscayne Bay may have been an area of fresh and brackish water marshes. The current configurations of the barrier islands of Key Biscayne and Miami Beach did not exist. Scientific data from cores from other parts of eastern North America suggest an accelerated sea-level rise between 10,500 and 10,000 B.P.[21] Studies indicate a gradually decreasing rate of sea-level rise at about 6,000 years ago.[22]

The South Florida of 12,000 years ago contained vast savannahs of grasslands with mixed forests, providing an ample food supply for grazing animals, which in turn provided a healthy diet for a wide range of carnivores that included dire wolf, jaguar, Florida lion, and at least two species of bear. Forests of pinewoods probably did not occur at the same scale and density as the Dade County pine forests of only a century ago, and the range of tropical hardwood hammocks may not have extended north of the Florida Keys. Forest growth was tempered by lower rates of precipitation as well as foraging by large populations of herbivores that may have constrained new sapling growth. Warmer temperatures may have been the rule, as suggested by Morgan, who believes much of Florida was subject to Neotropical influences and was largely frost free.[23]

The Cutler site 12,000 years ago was a deep solution hole beneath an outcrop of elevated limestone rising only a few feet higher than the surrounding forest and savannahs. The limestone was undercut with fissures, creating a shallow overhang cave. The solution hole may have been vegetated by a ring of oaks and intermittent pine, a forest oasis surrounded by grasslands. The solution hole and its spring of fresh water provided a secure den for carnivores, such as jaguars and dire wolves, although different species probably never shared the feature at the same time.

Studies of the extinction of various species of megafauna within North America based on a review of radiocarbon dates suggest that these extinctions across the continent may have been completed by 10,800 B.P., with some species surviving as recently as 10,000 years B.P. The peccary may have survived to 9500 years B.P., and the horse and camel into the early Holocene. Evidence from both eastern and western North America indicates that the mammoth had disappeared between 10,500 and 10,600 B.P.[24] It is worth noting that this date coincides with evidence of an accelerated sea-level rise and the appearance of humans at the Cutler site.

The question as to exactly when these extinctions began and ended, and whether they were gradual or catastrophic, remains to be fully resolved. However, the larger debate as to what caused this great extinction has fallen into two general schools of thought: those scholars who believe that human intervention, specifically the overkill theory, led to the demise of the megafauna and those who believe that climate was the principal impetus for the extinction. More recently the idea of a catastrophic event—the impact of a comet—has been proposed and debated widely, with proof of such a collision being offered by the discovery of nano-diamonds formed by the explosive heat associated with a sediment horizon dating from megafauna extinction.[25]

The Cutler site, with its South Florida context, presents some tantalizing evidence that could contribute to an understanding of the great megafauna extinction. It was observed during the excavations there that dense fossil deposits at the lower depths of the site occurred within a reddish brown sediment, a soil that is typical of many of the deeper solution hole deposits throughout central and southeastern Miami-Dade County. The soils were deposited into the solution cavities and holes that pocket the bedrock. At the Cutler site, shifting water tables transported organic carbonates from the bones through the sand, causing some of these sediments to cement into lumps and lenses of concretion and ultimately cementing thousands of bone fragments and soil together.

At the Cutler site there is a dramatic contrast between the deeper fossil-bearing strata and the strata above. From the surface to about 125 centimeters in depth, thousands of limestone rocks occur from small pebbles to 100-pound chunks. Below 100–125 centimeters there is a dramatic decrease in the number of rocks. In some deeper levels no rocks were encountered, particularly in the fossil horizon.

These rocks in the 100–125 centimeter horizon represent pieces that have fallen from the adjacent walls and the overhang of the solution hole, although some of the rock debris may be explained by human intervention, specifically from Paleo-Indians excavating cooking pits, placing rocks over graves, and possibly constructing a mortuary wall enclosure beneath the southern overhang. Most of these rocks undoubtedly entered the hole by the forces of erosion when large volumes of rainwater broke off the rock, causing overhangs and ceilings to collapse and sloughing off thousands of pounds of limestone. This erosional process continues today, but evidence at the site suggests that it began as a dramatic singular event, perhaps as a result of unrelenting torrential rains that marked the beginning of a wetter cycle. That event occurred between 11,000 and 12,000 years B.P. The Cutler rock debris horizon at a depth of 100–125 centimeters is the record of this dramatic climate change.

Another piece of evidence of torrential rains are the erosional flow channels uncovered at depths of 125–150 centimeters, all running across the top level of the concreted sediments. The channels average 20 centimeters in width and cut across the fossil bone bed. Characterized by soft gray organic sands, the channels were filled with redeposited sand. No bones occur in the channels, suggesting that they were washed away since harder fossil bearing sediments occur on both sides of the channels.

This great deluge—what appears to be an event or episode of accelerated precipitation—was of unknown duration. Whether it lasted a year or less, or 10 years or longer, the flooding was sufficient to disrupt the food chain. Savannah grasslands were drowned and grazing animals began to starve. A possible temporary spike of carnivore population as easy prey became abundant, but eventually large carnivores found their food supply severely disrupted and they too became extinct. This scenario played out not only in Florida but also around the world.

The Cutler site, once a thriving den for dire wolves, was abandoned after the great extinction. The driving torrents of rain eroded deep gullies across the den floor, washing out bones as the water and sediments poured into the hole and eventually flooded it. It is unknown whether a hundred years or a thousand years passed before the first humans climbed into the hole. The dangerous carnivores were gone; only scattered bones and teeth remained. The site may have served its first human hosts as both a shelter and a source of fresh water. The evidence of fires and burnt bones attest to meal preparation, and the artifacts reveal their technology and subsistence. Human remains representing at least five individuals were found at the site, and it is obvious that most of these were associated with intentional graves. Although largely fragmentary, the human bone clusters suggest that some may have been primary interments.

Today the Cutler Fossil site is preserved within the Charles Deering Estate Park. Because of its rugged, rocky terrain it is not yet accessible to the public, but eventually a trail and boardwalk may allow visitors to see Miami's earliest site of human habitation.

3

The South Florida Archaic

Although the 11,000-year-old Cutler site set the stage for the earliest known human occupation of South Florida, sites from the early Archaic period (c. 6500–5000 B.C.) are conspicuously absent. There is an inexplicable 4,000-year gap in the archaeological record, and it is not known whether this hiatus represents a low human population and/or the destruction of these scarce sites by modern development.

South Florida's Early and Middle Archaic people were likely small bands who lived at strategic locations along the coast and within the interior. They maximized the use of shellfish, fish, and other local animals and plants. Habitation on the coast may have been at sites currently inundated by Biscayne Bay and the Atlantic Ocean. Habitation in the interior of southern Florida occurred in a pre-Everglades environment, which was drier than today's Everglades. Prior to 5000 B.P., the interior of South Florida was a "neverglades"—a mosaic of ponds and marshes interspersed with pine flatwoods and oaks. There was less marsh and more upland knolls and islands of pine and hammock, intermixed with ponds, perhaps not unlike the current Big Cypress National Preserve. Scientific data accumulated from soil borings and radiocarbon dates indicates that the Everglades is a relatively recent creation, beginning about 5,000 to 6,000 years ago. It was at this time that the cypress swamps and hardwood forests typical of the subtropics began to emerge in southern Florida.[1] The wetlands developed in concert with rising sea levels and increasing precipitation. The Everglades basin began to fill, becoming the principal drainage for waters overflowing out of Lake Okeechobee.

Evidence of South Florida's oldest known wetlands was discovered in 1988 by archaeologists at a previously undocumented rocky ridge in what is now the city of Weston in Broward County.[2] The ridge extends seven miles southward from Weston to Hollywood. Mucky and peaty sediments shield a karst limestone substrate characterized by hundreds of solution holes (fig. 3.1). Although other rocky knolls and ridges occur across the eastern Ev-

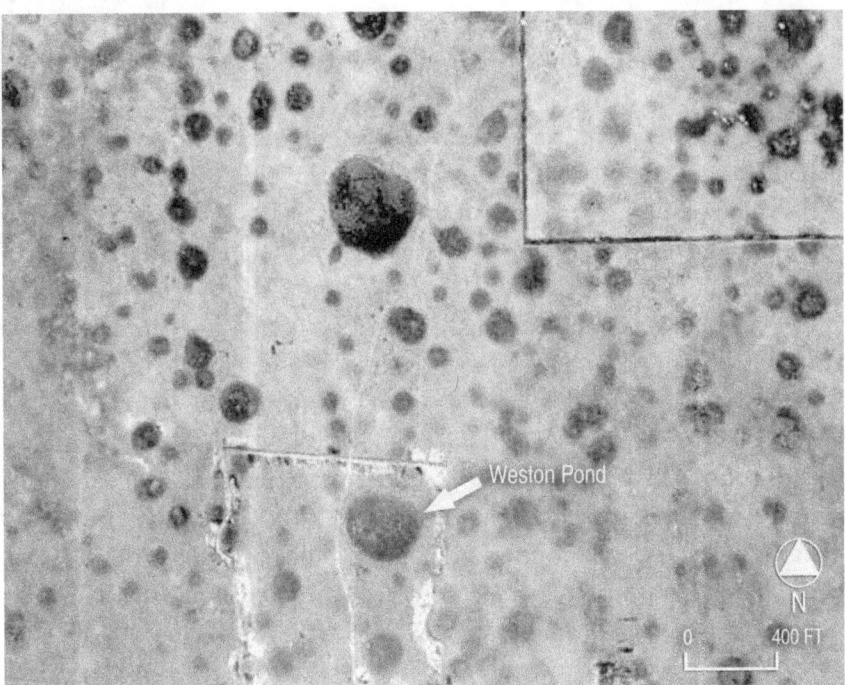

Figure 3.1. Aerial photo of Weston Pond and solution holes, c. 1968. Courtesy of the Archaeological and Historical Conservancy.

erglades, the Weston limestone ridge was undoubtedly more pronounced and exposed 5,000 years ago.

Located on the northern part of the ridge is a large solution hole, dubbed Weston Pond by archaeologists, measuring 125 meters in diameter.[3] Two prehistoric sites were discovered on the rim of the pond dating from 3500 B.P. Although these sites are ancient, the real surprise occurred when the pond was excavated with a trencher. Eleven holes were dug to a depth of 2 meters below the surface. Three of these trenches resulted in the discovery of small animal bones preserved within freshwater peaty sediments. In the peat 1.5 meters below the surface, perfectly preserved leaves—still green— were uncovered. The sediment's radiocarbon dates revealed an age of 5315 ± 70 B.P. for this organic stratum of leaves and bones and 7030 ± 70 B.P. for the pond's basal organic deposits, indicating that it is one of the oldest freshwater features documented in South Florida.

One of the few known sites dating from the Middle Archaic period (c. 5000–3000 B.C.) is 8BD1119, located on Pine Island in Broward County. This site yielded a large number of Middle Archaic–style chert bifaces and chert flakes.[4] The site is located on top of a sandy knoll once surrounded by freshwater wetlands in the eastern Everglades. Artifacts occur across an area 20 meters in diameter. The site has a conspicuous absence of bone, shell, or any other organic materials. The well-drained sandy soils are probably the reason for the absence of any organic materials suitable for radiocarbon dates. The site was likely a small camp that probably supported no more than 20 people, possibly representing an extended family or a small band.

Between 1500 B.C. and 500 B.C. Native Americans utilized elevated tree islands across the Everglades; however, options for settlements continued to decrease as tree islands with lower elevations became inundated. The lowest islands and knolls were abandoned by about 1500 B.C., but higher islands continued to be used. Some of the larger tree islands with elevations up to 4 feet above the sawgrass have yielded evidence of occupation as early as about 3000 B.C. with continuous habitation through historic times. Evidence of pre-ceramic Archaic deposits on larger tree island sites has been documented at the Cheetum site, 8DA1058,[5] and Taylor's Head, 8BD74.[6] More recently, Archaic horizons have been documented in Everglades National Park.[7]

The author's investigations at the western edge of the Everglades revealed a large number of small sites located on top of rocky knolls and ridges, many of which had been historically inundated and were beneath peat until recent drainage and farming activities.[8] Griffin (1988) identifies a date of 2700 B.P. (c. 300 B.C.) as being significant for settlement shifts in the Everglades, but recent evidence indicates that this change may have begun at least a thousand years earlier. Many of these sites have no evidence of prehistoric occupation after circa 1500 B.C., suggesting that they were abandoned, likely because of rising water tables. Site 8HN56 provided marine-shell dating from 3620 ± 60 B.P.[9] Similar abandoned Late Archaic period sites have been discovered on low tree islands and knolls throughout the eastern rim of the Everglades in Broward and Palm Beach Counties.[10]

Investigations at the Silver Lakes site (8BD1873), located on a tree island in the eastern Everglades in present-day Hollywood, uncovered evidence of occupation dating from the Glades II period, circa A.D. 700–1200, however, demucking excavations by a developer in the adjacent sawgrass wetlands revealed an Archaic component 1 to 1.5 meters below the peat.[11] This wetland component extended 50 meters north and eastward from the existing tree island. Mixed within the Archaic period artifact and faunal bone assemblage were splinters and cut pieces of pine wood, representing refuse from woodworking activities and possibly indicating that pine trees were growing on the island or in close proximity. Currently, the site is about 4 miles west of the closest pinewood communities. A radiocarbon date for a marine-shell artifact from the lower levels of 8BD1873 indicates an age of 4770 ± 70 B.P. These investigations provide evidence of a contracting tree island drowning by rising water tables and suggest the disappearance of adjacent pinelands by about 3500 years B.P (c. 1500 B.C.).

Archaeological data from Everglades tree islands indicate that human activities have had a significant impact on the geomorphic character and development of those islands. Undoubtedly, the accretion of midden soil created by human activities has contributed to overall tree island development. Prehistoric occupation and subsistence activities have, in some instances (i.e., 8DA33, 8DA1058), significantly added to the elevation of the islands, contributing from 1 to 1.5 meters of organic midden soil to the island's northern end. These elevations in turn have affected microhydrology by inhibiting sheet flow, providing an elevated soil mantle and soil chemistry that promotes certain types of vegetation, such as gumbo-limbo and hackberry, and indirectly creating habitat for certain fauna. For example, increasing tree island elevations possibly promoted the survival and expansion of *Liguus* tree snail populations during prehistoric times.

My observations of tree island sites indicate that the majority are underlain by limestone bedrock. However, in several instances no underlying bedrock was encountered during testing. Sites such as Beal Smith (8DA1043), Sheridan (8BD127), and Black Island (8DA4737) revealed an underlying strata of either peat or other wet sediments, suggesting that the initial prehistoric occupation occurred on a low, wet location.[12] An alternate hypothesis is that these initial occupations occurred during drier periods, but observations of underlying peat formations revealed no compression or degradation of the peat as might be expected to occur from exposure to dry conditions or human activity. The natural peat horizon underlying the midden at 8DA1043 indicates a date of 3945 ± 90 B.P. Likewise, a similar age for underlying peat at the Black Island site is 4490 ± 60 B.P.[13] It is possible that these sites initially may have been occupied by the construction of wooden scaffold houses or platforms above a wetlands pond that had been selected because of an abundance of fish and other fauna such as turtles and eels. These structures may have collapsed, creating a barrier to sheet-water flow and thus an opportunity for soil buildup and colonizing vegetation. This type of human occupation using constructed wooden platforms may have played a key role in the development of certain tree islands. It is interesting to note that a possible fishing station or platform in the wetlands may have been discovered in Everglades National Park when dredging near the Anhinga Trail at Royal Palm Hammock uncovered a large quantity of bone points in the marsh sediments.

Evidence of changing water tables and "recent" tree island development was discovered at the Hog site, 8DA1045, a small tree island in the eastern Everglades.[14] The site measures 16 by 20 meters and rises about 75 centimeters above the surrounding wetlands. A single test unit resulted in uncovering a horizon of *Helisoma* snail shells at a depth of 85 centimeters below the cultural horizon. The stratum of snails indicates that the island was once inundated. A radiocarbon date indicates this flooded condition occurred at 2210 ± 75 B.P. Whether this occurrence was a single storm-related episode or a longer period of time is uncertain, but it was of sufficient duration to provide a habitat for the *Helisoma*.

Archaic Period Material Culture

The adaptation of Native Americans to an emerging Everglades and a shrinking coastline was neither dramatic nor catastrophic, but an imperceptible shifting of floral communities and hydrology. Any change in the range and population of certain terrestrial fauna, such as deer, were probably not meaningful in the daily rhythm of life. The adaptive responses to a largely wetlands environment were based on well-developed cultural kits using handed-down fishing, hunting, and harvesting strategies anchored in ancestral experiences from other parts of Florida and the Southeast.

What was different in South Florida was its lack of hard stones with which to manufacture tools. North America's lithic tradition of flaking chert and grinding hard stone into tools, which had developed over millennia, was useless in South Florida, where only friable limestone characterized the landscape. Experiments with local limestone did occur. Several crude attempts at chipping limestone into projectile points have been found, including one example from the Cheetum site, 8DA1058, in the eastern Everglades (fig. 3.2).

In southern Florida's Archaic period, chert was a rare commodity. It may have been initially brought by migrations of people from central and northern Florida, but eventually chert was obtained by trade. Several examples of archaic chert bifaces, particularly from 8DA411, have been found in Miami-Dade County (fig. 3.3).

Figure 3.2. Limestone biface from the Cheetum site, 8DA1058. Collection of the Historical Museum of Southern Florida.

Figure 3.3. Chert projectile point from 8DA411. Collection of the Historical Museum of Southern Florida.

The most important response to this paucity of hard, workable stone was the shift to using other local materials. Axes made from conch shells (*Strombus gigas*) became the norm. The lip of a conch was broken from the shell and then chipped and hammered into a preform. The shell was polished (possibly using coral or volcanic pumice, which often washed ashore) and sharpened into a nearly identical version of its stone prototype. The shell celt was then mounted into a wooden handle by cutting an opening in the wood where the pommel end of the axe could slide, eventually being wedged at the celt's midsection, where the tool became larger than the hole. A soaking of the axe and handle in water would swell the wood, gripping the axe even tighter. Leather thongs could be added to further secure the axe. The final product is an effective and surprisingly hard tool that can cut trees and shape wooden poles and canoes. The Late Archaic celt is often thicker and more robust than more recent examples suggesting increasing exploitation of the conch through time, which resulted in a scarcity of larger specimens. And while *Strombus* axes were manufactured in southeastern Florida, a distinctive version of a shell axe and adze was created from the outer wall of the *Busycon* in southwestern Florida and along the Palm Beach County coast, where whelks commonly occurred. This *Busycon* version of a cutting tool was created by grinding a beveled edge onto a section of the outer shell wall after it was removed from the shell.

During the Late Archaic period, bone points and pins, not unlike those found at sites in central and northern Florida, continued to be manufactured in southern Florida. Simple geometric designs were incised onto bone hair pins. One example was discovered at the Atlantis site, 8DA1082. Most other pins and awls were simple forms, generally undecorated and polished.

One unusual incised bone composite tool is a beautifully incised handle with what appears to be a barracuda tooth placed into a small aperture at one end (fig. 3.4). It was discovered in the Archaic horizon below the concretion at the Cheetum site by Wesley Coleman. Perforated shark teeth that were part of a composite knife were common during the Late Archaic period. The base of the tooth was perforated with either a single hole or two

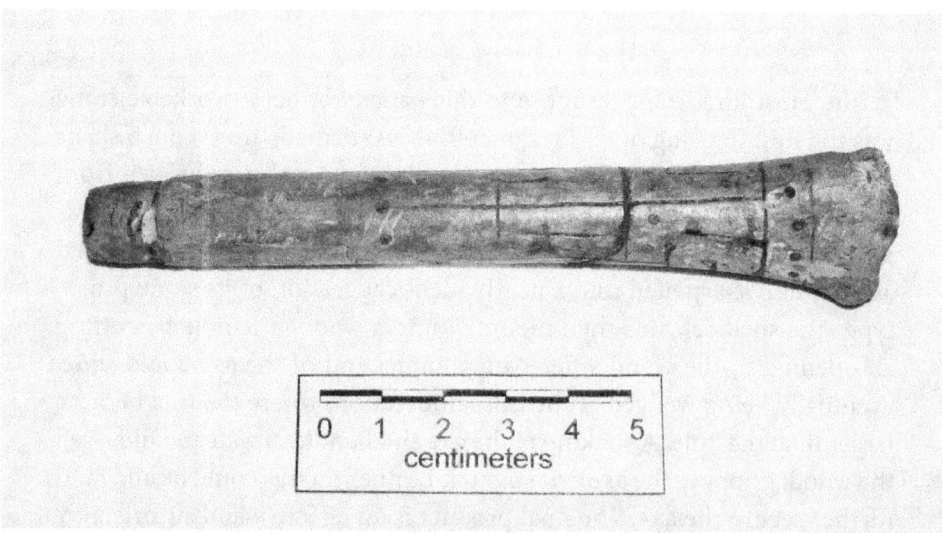

Figure 3.4. Incised bone handle from 8DA1058. Collection of the Archaeological and Historical Conservancy.

Figure 3.5. Fiber-tempered pottery from Miami-Dade County. Collection of the Archaeological and Historical Conservancy.

holes to allow it to be bound to a wooden handle. Interestingly, double-hole shark teeth rarely occur after the Archaic period.

Pottery vessels appear by about 1000–1500 B.C., but examples are scarce. The earliest known type is a fiber-tempered ware characterized by pin-sized holes in the clay where the tracks of fibers that had been burnt away are visible as a result of the firing of the bowl (fig. 3.5). The pottery is distinctive because of its light and chalky texture. Fiber-tempered pottery appears in peninsular Florida as both plain and decorated vessels. The most noteworthy type is the Orange series occurring in northeastern Florida at sites located along the St. Johns River and first documented in large quantities in southern Florida at Marco Island.[15] Plain examples also have been found at several sites in coastal Miami-Dade County, but never in large quantities. The pottery is distinctive because of its light weight and chalky texture. Pottery development evolved to an intermediate type of tempering that included sand mixed into the clay, which resulted in a harder type of ware. By 500 B.C.–A.D. 1, pottery with both fiber and sand tempering, St. Johns Plain and sand-tempered plain, occur together. This mixed ceramic assemblage was found at the Atlantis site, 8DA1081.[16]

Archaic Subsistence Patterns

The Archaic period was characterized by an increased reliance by native populations on the shellfish and marine resources of the coast and an expanded hunting, fishing, and plant gathering within the emerging Everglades. Archaeologist Randolph Widmer observed that faunal remains recovered from Marco Island in southwest Florida revealed an increasing trend toward marine adaptation, up from the 44.4 percent at about 3000 B.C. to 78.2 percent at 1500 B.C.[17] By the Glades period, about A.D. 280, marine materials rose to 86.3 percent.

The foundation of prehistoric subsistence patterns in southern Florida are clearly part of a long tradition that began in the Archaic period. The wetland environment provided numerous subsistence options and was a mainstay of resources that remained largely unchanged for at least three thousand years. Evidence of prehistoric subsistence is well documented in South Florida's archaeological record. The organic soils associated with black earth middens combined with the carbonates of shallow limestone and bone calcium create a base environment favorable for bone preservation. Also preserved are charred seeds and wood, which provide valuable clues to botanical exploitation.

Late Archaic period deposits are well represented at coastal sites, particularly at the Atlantis (8DA1082) and Santa Maria sites (8DA1655). Important fauna represented at coastal sites include sea turtle, fish (particularly shark), and conch. The calories consumed from these marine taxon dominate food consumption, with lesser quantities of meat provided by deer and smaller mammals, reptiles, amphibians, and birds.

Faunal remains from a Late Archaic/Glades I period site, recovered from a black-earth and shell midden, 8BD259, located on the north bank of New River in Fort Lauderdale several miles inland from the Atlantic, were analyzed by zooarchaeologists Quitmeyer and Blessing.[18] Their analysis indicates the following percentages: invertebrates (bivalves) 65 percent and vertebrates 35 percent. Of the invertebrates, the American oyster (*Crassotrea virginica*), 45 percent, are the most common, followed by lucine (*Lucina pecinata*) at 17 percent. These two latter species reflect the brackish and freshwater conditions of the New River. Of the vertebrates fish, the most common include (in order of decreasing MNI) sunfish (*Amia clava*) and freshwater catfish (*Ameiurus* spp.). Marine fish were less frequent and included Jack (*Carangidae*), snapper (*Lutjanidae*), grunt (*Haemulon*), surgeonfish (*Acanthururus spp.*), barracuda (*Sphyraena barracuda*), and shark (*Centrarchidae*).

Reptiles account for 10.5 percent of the recovered vertebrate fauna, including freshwater turtles and at least two terrestrial species: box turtle (*Terrapene carolina*) and gopher tortoise (*Gopherus polyhemus*). Mammals are scarce, representing only about 7.5 percent of the MNI, including white-tailed deer (*Odocoileus*), opossum (*Didelphis virginiana*), marsh rabbit (*Sylvilagus palustris*), and otter (*Lutra canadensis*), with deer being the largest meat contributor.

Of particular interest to Quitmeyer and Blessing's analysis is their identification of nine habitats exploited for food at 8BD259, which they compared to the Miami Circle/Brickell site, 8DA12. They determined that 47 of the species MNI (42%) at 8BD259 derive from freshwater habitats compared to only five species (3.11%) at the 8DA12 on the Miami River. Likewise, a much smaller percentage of coastal and offshore resources are represented at the 8BD259 (15.3%) versus 8DA12 (72.64%). This contrast reflects the proximity of freshwater and marine habitats to the respective sites.

Food deposits recovered from Late Archaic and Formative period sites in the Everglades have been analyzed from three sites: MacArthur 2, 8BD2591, and Sheridan Hammock 8BD191[19] and 8BD2572. The MacArthur site was not occupied after circa A.D. 1, probably because of rising water tables that eventually inundated the island. In contrast, 8BD191 was inhabited through the Glades III period, Fradkin's analysis identified 49 taxa from MacArthur 2 and 52 taxa from Sheridan Hammock. She identified the most important contributor to the diet in regard to meat as being alligators, snakes, and lizards (Sheridan Hammock at 46.34% and MacArthur 2 at 45.76%). The importance of alligators to prehistoric diet may seem obvious despite the dangers of hunting mature alligators. With hard scutes providing a coat of armor, an alligator hunt may have been dependent on striking at the most vulnerable spot, and a log in the alligator's open mouth and a subsequent clubbing, as depicted in Le Moyne's engraving, may have been the preferable method. It is also possible that alligators are underrepresented in the archaeological record because it may have been more convenient to dress a gator and remove the meat at or near the kill site rather than drag the entire carcass to the village. Fradkin notes the importance of snakes—including venomous rattlesnakes and moccasins—to the prehistoric South Florida diet, being well represented at both coastal and Everglades sites.[20]

Mammals, large and small, are represented by abundant remains in middens. Deer (*Odelcoileus virginianus*) is the biggest meat provider, but rabbits (*Sylvilagus* spp.) are the most common species represented in the Everglades middens. Medium-sized mammals include opossums, raccoons, river otter, and mink. Small mammals represented include muskrat (*Neofiber alleni*) and the cotton rat (*Sigmodon hispidus*). Probably underrepresented are manatees. Only a few sites have yielded any manatee bones. Weighing hundreds of pounds, it is unlikely that their carcasses were taken to the camp or village. Instead, manatees were likely butchered on the nearest shore to where they were killed and only the butchered meat was transported to the camp.

Carnivores are generally scarce in the archaeological record, although smaller carnivores, such as fox, bobcat, and dog, occur. Man's best friend may have been at times man's best meal, although there is substantial evidence of a cozy relationship between man and canine. Dog burials of small- to medium-sized dogs have been found at sites in the Everglades and at the mouth of the Miami River.

The Florida panther and black bear are rarely represented in the archaeological assemblage. This is not surprising considering that these are largest carnivores in the food chain. They are powerful and dangerous, and evidence of their high status is reflected by the several drilled canine teeth used as ornaments or amulets that have been found (8DA12). It is unlikely that these animals were ever considered an important source of food but rather were symbols of power.

Of particular interest are marine mammals such as dolphins, whales, and seals. These animals likely were of some importance to the prehistoric people of South Florida, with whale and porpoise teeth discovered at 8DA11 and 8DA12[21] and a whale vertebrae from 8DA12 at the mouth of the Miami River. Seal teeth have been found on both sides of the Miami River.

Also scarce in the archaeological record are birds. Fradkin reports that the pied-billed grebe (*Podilymbus podiceps*) was the most common bird at the Late Archaic Everglades tree island site. Other birds present include the great blue heron (*Arden herodias*) and marsh duck (*Anas* sp.). Birds have a limited potential as a food source because of their small size, and with little meat to offer, some species may have had greater value for their feathers.

An analysis of faunal remains at a Late Archaic site, 8BD2572, looking mainly at refuse pits[22] revealed that the highest quantity of faunal bones by weight was reptile (nearly 23%), with turtle being the most prominent (14.31%). Snake represented 8.3 percent and alligator less than 1 percent.

The occurrence of numerous burnt snake bones reinforces their importance to the local diet.

Fish was next as the highest contributor to the faunal assemblage, representing 14.3 percent by weight. Prominent were bowfin (*Amia calva*), Florida gar (*Lepisosteus platyrhincus*), red ear sunfish (*Lepomis microlophus*), and large-mouth bass (*Micropterus saloides*).

Mammals represent 11.85 percent of the faunal remains, with deer (*Odocoileus virginianus*) having the highest element count and weight as well as providing the greatest calorie contribution. Other mammals identified in the assemblage are rabbit (*Sylvilagus* sp.), Florida water rat (*Neofiber alleni*), raccoon (*Procyon lotor*), river otter (*Latra canadensis*), and dog (*Canis familiaris*).

Like Fradkin's findings, birds were rare, with the pied-billed grebe (*Podilymbus podiceps*) being the only identified species. Amphibians were equally scarce, with *Siren lacertina* and various frogs represented.

Mortuary Practices

Numerous Archaic period cemeteries have been reported throughout southeastern Florida.[23] At least four Late Archaic cemeteries have been discovered in Miami-Dade County since 1980, all found as a result of archaeological investigations prompted by development. Human burials for the Archaic period are of two principal types: primary and secondary. Primary burials are interred in the ground in either an extended or flexed position. Secondary burials represent individuals that have either been defleshed or stored in a charnel house prior to interment, resulting in burials that are comingled and disarticulated.

Archaic period graves have been uncovered at the eastern and western Santa Maria sites (8DA2132 and 8DA11246) near Biscayne Bay and at the Cheetum and Flagami sites (8DA1053 and 8DA36) in the eastern Everglades. The first documented primary graves found on the coast by archaeologists were discovered at the Santa Maria site, 8DA1658, along Brickell Avenue in 1981 on property owned by former Miami mayor Maurice Ferrer, during the parcel's redevelopment into a high-rise condominium. This is the same location where human graves were uncovered in 1904 during the construction of the Roome House (see chapter 1). I had previously discovered an early-nineteenth-century homestead on the parcel near the bluff overlooking Biscayne Bay (see chapter 7). Mixed with the historic artifacts were prehistoric pottery, shells, and animal bones, all dating from the Glades II and III periods. Soon after the archaeological documentation of the site, heavy equipment began to excavate a construction pit for the new building's foundation. The pit was dug to a depth of about 20 feet into the limestone bedrock. While inspecting the pit walls, I observed what appeared to be two roots extending from the pit wall. University of Miami student Mark Duda was sent up a ladder to investigate. The "roots" turned out to be human femora—the leg bones from a single grave. Most of the body had been destroyed by the backhoe and only the feet and legs had survived. Subsequent archaeological investigations uncovered an additional four individuals. Three were aligned in an east-west direction while the fourth was north-south. The graves had limestone rocks placed on top the bodies. All of the graves had been placed in a solution hole where deposits of sediments were deep enough to allow for digging a grave shaft. Generally, sediments on the Atlantic Coastal Ridge are very shallow—less than 2 feet thick on top of the limestone bedrock—however, within solution holes the soil can be 10 feet deep and deeper.

Bioarchaeologist Yasar Iscan examined the Santa Maria skeletons at 8DA2132 and determined that five individuals had been interred in the solution hole. Individual 3 was the best preserved, although only the upper half of the skeleton had survived the backhoe.[24] This individual was lying face down and was identified as being a female 30 to 35 years old. Interestingly, although no obvious grave goods accompanied this individual or any other individuals, a second cranium (Individual 4) was found on top the back of Individual 3. Only the cranial vault of this overlying individual was found suggesting a single cranial burial. The partial skull of Individual 4 was identified as being a male.[25] This skull may have been a trophy from a slain individual or an heirloom. Individual 2 was the least disturbed by construction activity. The body was extended east-west with the face turned eastward. This individual was identified as a female approximately 25–30 years of age.

All of the bones had lesions. It was hypothesized by Iscan that some of the lesions may have been the result of osteomyelitis caused by an infection that entered from the blood into the bones. Other holes and cavities in the bone may have been postmortem, including the Individual 4 cranium, as I have observed similar holes on sea turtle bones buried in black-earth middens. Some of these postmortem holes may have been created by beetles or other insects.

Radiocarbon dates were determined for two soil samples recovered from the burial pit. Sample UM-2406 was recovered from within the cranial vault of Individual 2 and sample UM-2407 was taken from soil outside and adjacent to the same skull. It is assumed that the organic component being dated was likely associated with the decomposition of soft tissues associated with the individual. The dates were statistically the same; the cranial sediments dating to 3000 ± 110 B.P. (corrected age of 3100 ± 110 B.P.) and the external soils dating to 2870 ± 60 B.P. (corrected age of 2950 ± 60 B.P.) indicated that the burials date from roughly 1000–1200 B.C.[26]

A second Archaic cemetery was discovered during the construction of the Atlantis condominium, also known as the Brickell Bluff site, 8DA1082.[27] The site dates from about 2000–500 B.C. and was associated with a mix of fiber-tempered pottery, St. Johns Plain, and gritty sand-tempered plain. Analysis by bioarchaeologists indicated that only four individuals were represented by the badly fragmented and poorly preserved bones.[28] Despite Iscan's assertion that they were secondary bundle burials, the extensive bioturbation caused by a nearby ficus tree and two millennia of disturbances prevents the original mortuary context from being easily discerned and thus the burials may have been primary interments.

The third discovery of an Archaic cemetery occurred within a stone's throw of the Santa Maria site. Dubbed Santa Maria West, 8DA11246, the site is located on the west side of Brickell Avenue within a lot that had once been home for several families, with the first house built in the 1920s. In the home's front yard facing Brickell Avenue was a low solution hole. Archaeological investigations that were required prior to the parcel's development in 2006 revealed that the hole had been gradually filled from trash dumped into the hole beginning about A.D. 1900, including artifacts from an army encampment from the Spanish American War. Archaeologist Richard Haiduven conducted the initial assessment and discovered human remains, and subsequent excavations by Archaeological and Historical Conservancy archaeologists Joe Mankowski and Ryan Franklin uncovered a total of 19 individuals.[29] Of those, 12 were extended along general northeast–southwest alignments with the heads facing west (fig. 3.6).

Late Archaic period cemeteries also have been documented in the eastern Everglades, particularly in Broward County. At least four discrete cemeteries have been discovered there. These cemeteries, unlike the Miami-Dade assemblage, are all associated with sand islands or ridges located in the eastern Everglades. Site 8BD1113 is a midden and cemetery located at

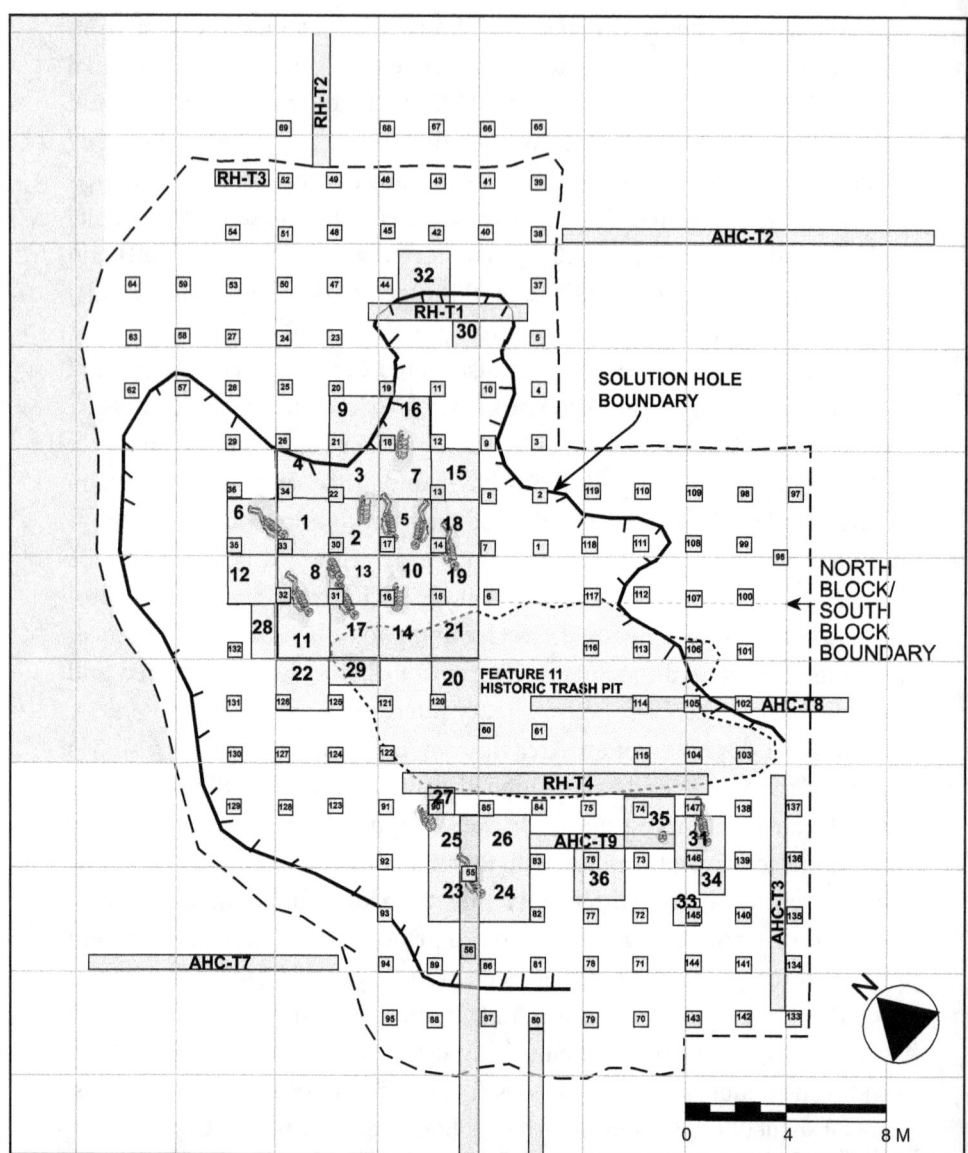

Figure 3.6. Map of units and human remains at Santa Maria West, 8DA11246. Map created by John G. Beriault. Courtesy of the Archaeological and Historical Conservancy.

the eastern end of Pine Island. Three individuals were identified as a result of salvage excavations prior to the widening of Pine Island Road in Davie.[30] Felmley estimated a stature of five feet eight inches for the male and a little less for the female.[31]

In 2001–2, excavations prior to residential development at nearby Long Lake, 8BD3283, uncovered grave pits in a sandy knoll.[32] This circular knoll measured 60 meters in diameter and was only about 1 meter above the surrounding marsh. Two of three radiocarbon dates indicate a Late Archaic age of 3050 ± 40 B.P. (Beta 165676) to 2540 ± 40 B.P. Interestingly, evidence of habitation activities possibly postdating the use of these sites as a cemetery also were found. Bioarchaeologist Alison Elgart identified a minimum number of 30 individuals associated with the site, including 22 adults, two adolescents, and nine children. Five discrete burial features were identified at the site that include two males, two females, and one of undetermined sex. These individuals included three adults, two adolescents and four children. The oldest individual was a small female, probably 50-plus years, who had suffered two broken and healed humeri. She was exceptionally small—only four feet four inches to four feet six inches tall. The overall cross-section of age and an apparent lack of grave goods with the Long Lake and Pine Island Archaic period graves suggest an egalitarian society.

In 2001, archaeological investigations were conducted on a similar sandy knoll in Miramar where a new housing development had been approved in western urban Broward County.[33] The site, 8BD2572, measures 48 by 39 meters, although only a portion of the area was used as a cemetery. A total of six burial features were uncovered, of which four appear to have been primary interments and two secondary. Three were adults and one a child. The adult burials appeared semiflexed with the heads to the northwest and the feet to the southeast, the lower limbs lying flexed on the left side and the long axis of the vertebral column running northeast to southeast. One of the two secondary burials was located 5 meters from the primary burial area. It included a burial characterized by a cranium on top of the forearm bones. A minimum number of six individuals were uncovered, five adults and one child. No grave goods were found, and ample evidence of the site's reuse for habitation was documented. It is likely that when the knoll was reused for habitation, the new occupants had no knowledge of the graves below.

4

The Perfect Balance

Adapting to the Land and Sea

Three thousand years before the birth of Christ, South Florida's Native Americans inhabited a land dotted with thousands of ponds, sloughs, and coastal isles. It was a watery land not unlike the marshy tributaries of northeastern Florida, an area that archaeological evidence suggests may have been the point of origin for southeastern Florida's Tequesta. Although Paleo-Indians reached Florida by 9000 B.C., the ancestors of the Tequesta may not have arrived at Florida's southern tip until about 3000 B.C. The recent documentation of numerous Archaic period sites throughout the Everglades and along Biscayne Bay indicate that by that date, the first continuous habitation of South Florida had begun (see chapter 3).

The ancestors of the Tequesta may have brought with them artifacts typical of northern Florida, such as chert projectile points. They also brought a tradition of manufacturing bone artifacts such as bipoints, socketed points, awls, and carved-bone hair pins. Perhaps their most important cultural baggage was their previous experience in the wetlands of northern and central Florida—knowledge that guaranteed good fishing and successful food procurement in South Florida.

That the South Florida environment challenged the new arrivals seems certain. Chert, once easily accessible for tools and projectile points from quarries and outcrops in central and northern Florida, was no longer available except by trade or by nearly a week's journey northward. Certain plants more common to northern Florida, such as persimmon and hickory, were scarce or absent in the south, and instead, a variety of new plant species offered themselves. Divine guidance or trial and error must have been in order, because some of these plants that may have been used for food, such as coontie (*Zamia integrifolia*), are poisonous if not prepared properly. The Indians of southeastern Florida manufactured tools from the plentiful marine shells since they could not use the soft oolitic limerock that characterizes most of the area. Axes made from the lip of the conch shell were as effective as stone axes, and finding the material to replace a broken tool was no more difficult than picking up a conch shell. These shell axes, or celts, as they are called by archaeologists, are one of the distinctive traits of southeastern Florida's prehistoric material culture and are similar to shell axes manufactured in north-central and northeastern Florida prior to 500 B.C.

The Native American adaptation to the subtropical environment of South Florida is best characterized by John M. Goggin as the Glades Tradition, which he describes as being "based on the exploitation of the food resources of the tropical coastal waters, with secondary dependence on game and some use of wild plant foods. Agriculture was apparently never practiced but pottery was extensively used."[1]

The Glades period subsistence strategies were well established by the Late Archaic period (see chapter 3) and continued without significant variations through European contact. Two major studies of zooarchaeological remains dating to the Glades period have been completed: the Bear Lake site (8MO30) in the southern Everglades and the Granada site, 8DA11, at the mouth of the Miami River (fig. 4.1). The Bear Lake site dates from the Glades I Late period through Glades IIIA. The site was tested in 1968 by John Griffin, who dug a transect of units[2] within an elongate black-earth midden mound (Mound 1). Faunal remains from Test Unit C were identified with 31 taxa. By weight, oyster (*Crassostrea virginica*) is the most common, representing almost 50 percent. *Merceraria campechiensis*, a robust hardy shell, is the second most common, with *Busycon contratium* and *Macrocallista nimbosa* being major contributors. *Strombus gigas*, a mainstay of coastal sites along Biscayne Bay and the Atlantic, is relatively scarce (about 1% of the total mollusca weight), reflecting the fact that the site's principal marine exploitation is focused on Florida Bay, where *Strombus gigas* is not as common as in the Atlantic. Griffin notes that the highest incidence of oyster, a brackish water species, in Level 13 suggests a possible shift in salinity of the coastal estuaries during that period.[3]

Vertebrate remains likewise emphasize the importance of the marine environment, with fish accounting for up to 91.1 percent of the phyla represented. Using otoliths as an index element, sea catfish (*Galeichthys felis*) and the crevalle jack (*Caranax hippos*) are likely overrepresented. Underrepresented, but likely a principal food source, are sharks. Reptiles in general are a poor second in the Bear Lake assemblage, representing a range of 6.7 to 48.6 percent by period. Birds and mammals are even scarcer, but the pres-

Figure 4.1. Pottery sherds: (A) Fort Drum Punctate, (B) Cane Patch Jab and Drag, (C and D) Opa-Locka Incised, (E) Miami Incised. Collection of the Historical Museum of Southern Florida.

ence of deer represents an important food contributor and a single black bear was represented.

Contrasting the near-coastal assemblage of Bear Lake is the assemblage of Panther Key, farther north in the Everglades, where more emphasis on freshwater turtles and mammals was documented.[4] A general trend of decreasing marine resources was observed in other sites in the Big Cypress National Preserve as their distance increases from Florida Bay.[5]

In contrast to sites in the southern Everglades and Big Cypress, where canoe access favored Florida Bay, the Granada site at the mouth of the Miami River and next to Biscayne Bay is strategically located adjacent to freshwater habitats of the Miami River and is only 4 miles from the Everglades. Fresh water flowed through the Miami River and vacillated in salinity at its mouth with ebbs and flows of brackish and salt water according to the season.

The Granada site was investigated in 1978.[6] A total of 37,719 bones and teeth were examined by Elizabeth Wing and Jill Loucks (1983). Ninety-nine species were identified from contexts representing the Glades I through Glades IIIB periods. Of these, 76 are aquatic and 23 are terrestrial. Their analysis of the vertebrates indicates a constant exploitation pattern through time.[7]

Sharks and rays are well represented and provided a significant percentage (61.2%) of the biomass of fish. Fourteen different shark species were identified.[8] Other fish include both fresh-water and saltwater species. Sea turtle represents the largest bone contributor by weight to the faunal assemblage. Mammals (5–7%) are of particular interest because of the presence of marine species. Teeth of the West Indian seal (*Monachus tropicalis*) were found in midden at both the north and south banks of the river,[9] and the bones of bottle-nosed dolphin (*Tursiops truncates*) occurred at both the Granada site and the Miami Circle. A whale vertebra was found at Brickell Point in 1980 during the construction of the Holiday Inn.

Plants are a small but important part of the archaeological record in southeastern Florida. Six fruits are prominent in the botanical materials recovered from the Honey Hill site, 8DA411,[10] located in the eastern Everglades and at the Granada site (8DA11) at the mouth of the Miami River.[11] Seeds of mastic (*Mastichodendron foetidissium*), cocoplum (*Chrysobalanus icaco*), cabbage palm (*Sabal palmetto*), saw palmetto (*Serena repens*), sea grape (*Coccoloba* sp.), and hog plum (*Ximenia americana*) were recovered. The presence of mastic at Honey Hill suggests to the archaeobotanists that the site was inhabited in the spring and/or summer.

The most intensive ethnobotanical study done to date has been at the Granada site.[12] Using charcoal and seeds, Scarry identified plant species and reconstructed the site's catchment area, identifying likely habitats.[13] Although the map depicts mangrove forest along parts of the Biscayne Bay shore where they did not exist, the map accurately indicates the proximity of the important habitats in the region. Scarry summarizes all of the edible and contributing plants associated with the area's diverse plant communities.[14] By analyzing the wood charcoal, she indentifies two principal habitats that were exploited for firewood—pinelands and the low hammock/mangrove—which indicates that the coastal maritime hammocks typical of the barrier islands were being utilized as well as mangrove forest, with the largest and closest communities being in Biscayne Bay on the lee side of the barrier islands.

Although the archaeological evidence suggests that plants played a small role in daily subsistence, ethnographic documents indicate otherwise. In the sixteenth-century account of Spanish captive Juan Escalante de Fontaneda, who spent 13 years with the Calusa, he provides the following description of the role of plants in the indigenous diet:

> They have bread of roots which is the common food the greater part of the time and because of the lake, which rises in some seasons so high that the roots cannot be reached in consequence of the water, they are for some time without eating this bread.... There is another root, like the truffle over here [Spain], which is sweet and there are other different roots of many kinds; but when there is hunting, either deer or birds, they prefer to eat meat or fowl.[15]

Fontaneda may be referring to coontie, but scholars are still uncertain as to whether this is the plant to which he refers. Other historic commentary specifically refers to sea grape (*Coccoloba uvifera*), cocoplum (*Chrysobalanus icaco*), sabal palmetto, and saw palmetto (*Serenoa repens*).[16]

The Material Culture

Archaeologists classify the artifacts of a society into discrete types of tools, ornaments, and pottery types. Often these type names reflect functions such as cutting, hammering, and adornment. The following summary based on raw materials provides an outline of the most important artifact types of southeastern Florida.

Pottery

Pottery is among the most important types of artifacts for the archaeologist to analyze. The importance of pottery for archaeologists probably exaggerates its importance to Native Americans—not that the invention of pottery did not have significant consequences for cooking, storage, and the transportation of food and water, and in certain cases, as a medium for religious and artistic expression. For archaeologists, pottery can indicate different chronological periods because pottery styles changed through time. Certain pottery styles occurred more or less frequently at certain time periods and were often specific to a particular geographic region. Clay sources and chemical analysis of pottery can also provide clues for trade and the movement of people.

Most of the South Florida ceramic types were first described by John Goggin during his pioneer work on southern Florida archaeology.[17] The temporal framework he developed for his ceramic serration has held up well with the advent of radiocarbon dating. The only important revision to Goggin's ceramic sequence for South Florida is the addition of fiber-tempered and several other minor types and the determination that the St. Johns series has both an early and late manifestation in South Florida

Although decorated pottery types have been classified with specific geographic place names, it does not mean that these styles are exclusively found in or had their origin from those areas. These type names are merely labels given by archaeologists for the purpose of classifying pottery styles—usually with an attempt to reflect the geographic location where the type was first discovered. This can sometimes be misleading. For example, Sanibel Incised occurs rarely on Sanibel Island and actually is common only in the Ten Thousand Islands, a hundred miles farther south. Likewise, Key Largo Incised occurs with regularity throughout the Keys and southern mainland as far north as Broward County and as far west as the Ten Thousand Islands.

If the Tequesta were alive today and discovered that time periods of their cultural history were being classified on the basis of stylistic changes of their cooking pots, they might find the Western mind very strange. It would be similar to dividing the twentieth century on the basis of style changes in coke bottles (in fact, coke bottles have changed so appreciably through time that they provide a useful chronological index for the various decades of the twentieth century). For example, if archaeologists excavating twentieth-century trash heaps in Hialeah were to discover that the words on soda bottles made a dramatic change from English to Spanish, this change would accurately reflect a fairly significant cultural event: the increase of Hispanic populations after 1960. Likewise, changes in Indian pottery may be able to tell us about significant political and social changes.

If there are differences in something as simple as pottery between one group and another, then it is possible pot sherds may shed light on less discernable traits, such as religious ideas, social customs, and language, which also separated these groups. For example, between about A.D. 1200 and A.D. 1500, the pottery types of southeast and southwest Florida became increasingly homogeneous. If one assumes that women were the principal pottery makers in South Florida (as was the case in most Native American groups), then it might be expected that if men of one tribe married women from another tribe, pottery designs could become increasingly similar between the two tribes or areas. Tribes raiding other areas and capturing women would produce the same result. Archaeologist John Griffin believes that the sudden disappearance of decorated pottery in southeastern Florida during the Glades IIC period might reflect the rise of Calusa dominance over the Tequesta since the sixteenth-century Tequesta were paying tribute to the Calusa, who had a tradition of plain pottery. Of course, alternative explanations for ceramic variations might be trade, the infusion of new ideas by religious or social diffusion, or even the migration of new people into a region.

Sand-Tempered Plain (c. 500 B.C–A.D. 1700)

Sand-tempered plainware is a ubiquitous type formerly called Glades Plain by Goggin. This pottery is moderately to heavily tempered with quartz sand. The heaviest tempered pottery feels gritty to the touch. There seems to be a tendency for the pottery to become less gritty and have a smoother surface finish through time, until much of the pottery of the Glades III period looks well smoothed and sometimes has a slip-like surface, possibly because the vessel surface has been floated while still in a plastic state. Bowls were constructed by the coiling method, using long coils of clay that were built up from the vessel base. The pottery after firing varies in color from black or gray to tan or even bright red or orange. Much of this color variation reflects different firing environments. Since Goggin's classification, archaeologists agree that if one were to mix sand-tempered plain pottery from the Gulf Coast or from central Florida into a bag containing sand-tempered pottery from southeast Florida, no archaeologist using their powers of observation could accurately separate the southeast Florida sherds from those of the other areas. The day has now arrived when chemical testing (e.g., PIXIE testing) will permit a trace element analysis of pottery to allow for its classification according to the source of clay and thus, presumably, allow it to be classified by geographic region.

Another interpretive difficulty with sand-tempered plain pottery is that an archaeologist counting pottery sherds will often have over 90 percent of the sherd count represented by sand-tempered plain pottery because designs were generally confined to the area on or near the vessel rim. Thus if a decorated bowl such as Opa-Locka Incised were broken into one hundred pieces and hopelessly scattered and mixed with other sherds in the site, the vast majority of the Opa-Locka bowl would be without decorations and be classified as sand-tempered plain. A simplistic completion of this sampling bias would be demonstrated by the following example: If only ten of the one hundred pieces of the Opa-Locka bowl had evidence of the design, and all of the sherds were mixed with four hundred undecorated sherds representing four plain bowls, then a count of the sherds might indicate that 2 percent of the pottery was from decorated bowls rather than the actual 20 percent. This type of sampling problem indicates that reconstructing percentages of decorated versus plain pottery is best considered by focusing only on rim sherd counts.

Glades Red (c. A.D. 100–1600, Glades I–III)

Glades Red, a sand-tempered plainware, is distinctive because red paint was applied to the vessel walls. This paint pigment appears to be a red ocher and is often visible only as a faint reddish brown residue on the pottery walls. One must be cautious not to confuse the red or orange color caused by oxidation firing with paint pigment.

Fort Drum Punctate (A.D. 700–1000)

Fort Drum Punctate is characterized by one to four rows of punctuates below the rim (fig. 4.1A). Sometimes the punctuates are directly on top the rim lip. Often the rows of punctuates are zoned into clusters or form downward curves from the rim. Fort Drum, dating from the beginning of the Glade II period, is among the earliest decorated styles.

Fort Drum Incised (A.D. 700–1000)

Patterns of vertical ticking on the rim or just below the lip characterize Fort Drum Incised (fig. 4.1). Sometimes these incisions are lightly done and inconspicuous. The bowl form is usually open mouthed and hemispheric. This type is among the earliest decorated types of the Glades II period.

Cane Patch Jab and Drag (c. A.D. 500–800)

Cane Patch Jab and Drag is a ware decorated with a drag-and-jab technique (fig. 4.1B). Often the design is executed as a curve or straight line extending diagonally from the lip. This type occurs infrequently but is reported from a number of sites in southeastern Florida, particularly in the Everglades.

Opa-Locka Incised (c. A.D. 750–900)

Small, open arcs or fingernail impressions define Opa-Locka Incised (fig. 4.1C, D). Generally these impressions/incisions occur in either a single horizontal row or as vertical columns below the rim. This type occurs in southeastern Florida from Broward County to the upper Florida Keys.

Miami Incised (c. A.D. 750–900)

Miami Incised pottery is distinguished by groups of two to six diagonal parallel lines extending downward from the lip (fig. 4.1E). Usually the design elements are clustered in groups and are separated by an undecorated space of equal width. Most of the sherds are from open, shallow bowls. This type occurs throughout southeastern Florida.

Dade Incised (c. A.D. 750–1000)

Dade Incised, a Glades II type, is characterized by one to three concentric arcs or straight lines beneath the rim. All of the arcs curve upward to the rim. The lines are usually diagonal and incised at an angle of less than 30 degrees to the rim.

Plantation Pinched (c. A.D. 1000–1150)

Characterized by a heavy pinching, Plantation Pinched has two punctuates with an elevated ridge between them that occur below the vessel rim. It often appears coarsely or crudely made. Griffin believes that it is a distinctive type marker for the Glades IIC period. It occurs infrequently and is a minor type in the Glades decorated series but important because of its narrow chronological placement.

Glades Noded (A.D. 1000 (?)–1200)

Glades Noded is a newly recognized type characterized by one or two rows of circular embossments beneath the exterior lip caused by partial punctuates to the interior of the vessel wall creating a noded or embossed pattern on the exterior wall. This type is occasionally found on coastal and interior sites. Its exact chronological range is not certain, but it appears to date from the Glades II period.

Key Largo Incised (A.D. 1000–1400)

Key Largo Incised is one of the common decorated types of the Glades II period in southern Florida. It is characterized by incised arches below the rim, usually as a single row, although sometimes as a row of two concentric loops (fig. 4.2A). The vessel lip profile is generally rounded, with vessel shapes being open mouthed and globular. Key Largo Incised resembles Opa-Locka Incised and probably evolved from it. However, Key Largo Incised is more common and widespread.

Figure 4.2. Pottery sherds: (A) Key Largo Incised, (B) Matecumbe Incised, (C) Surfside Incised, (D) Glades Tooled Rim, (E) St. Johns Check Stamped. Collection of the Historical Museum of Southern Florida.

Matecumbe Incised (A.D. 1200–1400)

Matecumbe Incised pottery is decorated by incised cross-hatching forming diamond-shaped areas below the lip (fig. 4.2B). The vessel shape often has a constricted neck. While Goggin reported that this type is commonly found on sites along the edge of the Everglades, subsequent investigators have found that it is apparently more common in the Florida Keys.

Surfside Incised (c. A.D. 1200–1600)

Surfside Incised pottery is well made and has a smoothly finished exterior. The design varies from a single incised line to up to four parallel lines that circle the bowl below the lip (fig. 4.2C). The rim is usually thickened near the top and shallow; two long grooves often occur longitudinally on the lip. The bowls are usually open and hemispheric, but an important Surfside variant has rim lugs, or appendages, extending above the rim. The lugs are generally triangular and truncated at the top with small notches near the truncation. Incised lines occur on the lug, sometimes on both the obverse and reverse sides. It is interesting to note that Surfside Incised appears to be more common at coastal sites than interior sites. It is a marker for the Glades IIIA period.

Glades Tooled (A.D. 1400–1750)

Decorated by notching, grooving, or incising upon the vessel lip, Glades Tooled is a well-made, distinctive pottery. The design ranges from a fine to a bold execution (fig. 4.2D). Latter expressions of this type usually have a flattened and expanded lip, giving the rim a T-shaped profile. The bowls are either hemispheric, with a slightly incurved rim, or shallow and plate-like. The late expanded type is rarely found outside of southeast Florida, although the earlier notched and incised rims that occur throughout the Ten Thousand Islands of southwest Florida are more likely Fort Drum Incised. Glades Tooled Rim is the major ceramic marker for the Glades III period. Rare variants combine Key Largo incising or Surfside incising with the tooled lip.

Nonlocal Pottery Types

A wide variety of prehistoric, nonlocal pottery types have been reported in southeastern Florida. Nonlocal types have their origins from northeastern and northwestern Florida, the Lake Okeechobee area, and northern Florida. Below is a description of the most common of the nonlocal wares.

St. Johns Chalkyware (c. 500 B.C–A.D. 200, c. A.D. 900–1750)

The relatively large quantity of St. Johns ceramics found in southeast Florida originally prompted Goggin to believe that it was a local type, which he labeled as Biscayne Plain, but he and other scholars subsequently revised this type's nomenclature to St. Johns Plain. This chalkyware may have been made in northern Florida, although the exact source of the clay used has not been identified. This pottery is made from saltwater marl-clays as indicated by the fossil sponge spicules that can be observed in the fired clay. Some of the pottery has been tempered with plant material, leaving white, ashy fibers that are sometimes observed in the clay.

St. Johns chalkyware is particularly interesting because it has two separate chronological appearances in South Florida: during the Late Archaic period from about 500 B.C. to A.D. 200 and during the Late Glades II throughout the Glades III period, about A.D. 900–1750. St. Johns vessels are lightweight and characterized as large deep bowls with either cylindrical or straight walls, although smaller flat-bottomed bowls also occur. On the exterior, the color of the paste can be white, buff, gray, or pink. The interior core is often black or gray.

In addition to plainware, its earliest occurrence includes several decorated types, including St. Johns Incised. Although rare in southeast Florida, some specimens were found at the Atlantis site, 8DA1082. A variety of simple-stamped and complicated-stamped designs on chalkyware have been discovered at the Miami Circle, 8DA12,[18] and at 8BD252 on the New River.[19] This scarce type appears during the Glades I period and is similar to the various Deptford stamped types that occur in North Florida and along the Gulf Coast.

The most common of the decorated St. Johns wares is St. Johns Check Stamped. The vessel shape, paste, and temper are the same as St. Johns Plain pottery with the addition of a pressed rectangular checker pattern that usually covers the entire exterior vessel wall (fig. 4.2E). The check size varies from 3 to 10 millimeters, with the smaller size generally associated with the Glades IIIB and IIIC periods. This stamping is applied to the vessel while the clay is still wet with a carved wooden paddle. St. Johns Check Stamped pottery first appears in the Glades I period, circa A.D. 100–300, then disappears and then reappears after circa A.D. 900 and continues to the period of European contact.

Belle Glade Plain

Belle Glade Plain has its origins in the Lake Okeechobee area. Heavily tempered with sand, this plainware often has a chalky feel. The most distinctive attribute of this type are its surface striations or abrasions caused by the use of a smoothing tool dragging the quartz particles across the vessel walls, probably while the clay was dry. The vessel is usually a large, open-mouth bowl with a rectangular or chamfered rim profile. This ware occurs sporadically in southeastern Florida with increasing frequency during the late Glades II and Glades III periods, suggesting increasing contact between the Tequesta and the Belle Glade cultures of Lake Okeechobee.

Miscellaneous Ceramic Artifacts

Although rare, several fragmentary and complete pottery pipes have been reported in southeastern Florida. Specimens of a tubular and platform pipe are known from Brickell Point (8DA12), including five complete and fragmented specimens uncovered at the Miami Circle and from nearby Brickell Park.[20] Several complete platform pipes have been reported from sites in both Broward and Dade Counties. Many of these pipes are made with a paste and exterior finish similar to the Belle Glade pottery of the Lake Okeechobee area. The large number of similar pipes excavated by William Sears at the Fort Center site[21] suggests that the Lake Okeechobee area may be the principal source for South Florida's pipes. Those pipes uncovered from 8DA12 likely date from the Glades I period.

Problematic types of ceramic artifacts include discs and pendants cut from sherds. Two types of pottery discs are known: one is perforated at the center and the other is unperforated. Known specimens range in diameter from 1 to 6 centimeters. Their function is unknown, but perforated specimens are suggestive of spindle whorls, although there is no evidence to demonstrate that they were used that way. All of the known specimens appear to have been carved from pottery sherds salvaged from broken bowls. Other sherd artifacts are cut into forms suggesting pendants or gorgets.

Shell Tools

When an archaeologist classifies the tools of an extinct culture, the function of these artifacts is not always apparent. An artifact's function has been often assumed or guessed at by many scholars, and only recent scientific studies of wear patterns, tool replication, and ethnographic analogy have made determining function more certain. However, there is still considerable research needed on South Florida's prehistoric tool assemblage, particularly shell tools, and the classifications that follow are offered with those limitations in mind.

Strombus Celt

The *Strombus* celt is one of the most important and common tools of the Glades Culture Area. Manufactured from the lip of the *Strombus gigas*, this tool can be classified into a number of subtypes according to shape, size, and blade shape. Celt shapes vary from the relatively rare leaf shape to triangular- and parallel-sided types (fig. 4.3). The tool's likely function is for cutting wood. It is probable that the celts with edged blades would have been used for cutting trees and that the single beveled blade was an adze used for shaving or chipping wood and was particularly important for canoe manufacture.

Although the celt may appear, on cursory examination, to be a hand-

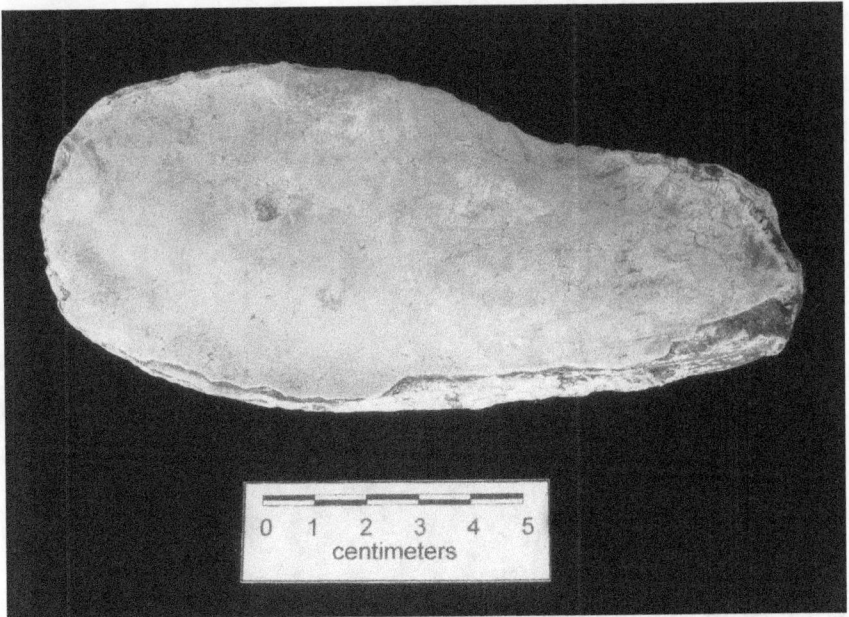

Figure 4.3. *Strombus* celt. Collection of the Archaeological and Historical Conservancy.

held tool, it was likely hafted to a wooden handle. Specimens found at Key Marco were fastened to a wooden handle with a bone socket holding the celt's pommel.[22] Other specimens, particularly the grooved celts, suggest hafting by cordage or rawhide.

Celts range from 3 to 25 centimeters in length, and these different sizes suggest more specialized functions. For example, the smaller celts may have been used for fine or delicate carving while the larger tools may have been important for canoe manufacture and cutting trees.

Shell Ladles, Dippers, and Cups

The most common ladle, dipper, or cup is the *Busycon* dipper (fig. 4.4). The columella and inner whorls of the *Busycon contrarium* were removed, leaving an open container with the shell's beak providing a handle. John Goggin notes that the specimens he examined held a volume ranging from 5.5 to 18 fluid ounces.[23] These dippers were likely associated with the ceremonial use of the "Black Drink" made from the plant *Ilex vomitoria*. I observed a cache of *Busycon* dippers at a burial mound in St. Lucie County, and another cache was uncovered at the Orchid Jungle in Miami-Dade County after Hurricane Andrew. However, it is possible that *Busycon* dippers also served a utilitarian purpose. This artifact type was apparently highly re-

Figure 4.4. *Busycon* ladle. Collection of the Archaeological and Historical Conservancy.

garded by Indians outside of southern Florida. Exported specimens found in northern Florida are usually better finished than those found in southern Florida.

Other less common vessels, manufactured from *Melongena fasciolaria* and Triton shells, also have been reported. Cups or ladles made from the *Cypraea exanthema*, a highly polished mahogany-and-cream-colored shell, was used as a spoon or a ladle and is reported from several sites in the Keys and Miami-Dade County.

Perforated Busycon Adze

A common shell tool often found in southwest Florida and the Florida Keys but somewhat less common in the rest of southern Florida, the perforated *Busycon* adze occurs with some regularity at both coastal and interior sites. Goggin and some other investigators have referred to this tool as a pick, but this is misleading since it suggests a digging tool, and most of the best preserved specimens indicate a chisel-like blade on the end of the columella rather than a pointed one. This chisel blade is compatible with a woodworking tool. Furthermore, the angle of the tool during use, as suggested by the location of the handle in relation to the perforation, also supports an adze-like use.

The tool is characterized by a number of alterations to the natural shell. First, the thin edge of the lip is chipped or pounded back to a uniform thickness. Part of the lower beak or columella is removed and the resulting edge is shaped into a chisel-like blade. A semicircular notch is cut into the lip a short distance below the shoulder. Apparently this is where a wooden handle extended through the shell to a circular perforation on the opposite side of the shell. Other perforations on the top of the shell allowed for lashing the handle to the shell. A good example of how these tools were lashed is provided by a specimen recovered by John Reiger at 8MO17 in Upper Matecumbe Key. This is stained from the original rawhide thong, showing the hafting pattern.

John Goggin described other variations of this tool, including a type without holes. It is possible that this unperforated type is a precursor to the perforated types. Goggin also notes that after continued use this *Busycon* tool is often reworked, with the bit reshaped increasingly closer to the crown.

Miscellaneous Shell Tools

Important shell tool types include the robust columella of the horse conch, *Plueroplaca giqantea,* modified with a beveled blade. Some gastropods were used as pounders or hammers. Entire shells with tips that are rounded and abraded from pounding have been found throughout the area. Sometimes pieces of *Strombus* lip or columella with similar wear have been found suggesting pounding.

One of the simplest but most important shell tool types is the *Pleuroploca gigantea,* ingeniously adapted for use as a canoe anchor. Cushing recovered specimens from Key Marco that had been pierced and lashed together so that the beaks radiated outward. The shells had been filled with sand, making them heavy enough to do the job. Specimens of these perforated shells have been found throughout southern Florida, including sites within the Everglades. Other specimens have been dredged from the Miami River and more recently found at 8DA11[24] (see also rock anchors).

There are other types of shell tools documented only by a few examples. A tool that appears to be a *Busycon* scraper was found at DA1053. Examples of shell pins, awls, and a possible stylus or needle are known. Some perforated shells were likely used as net weights. There are even some possible candidates for shell projectile points, but these examples are not conclusive. The archaeologist must be particularly careful about assigning tool categories to every smooth and pointed piece of shell that is collected at a site. Most shells suffer greatly from being buried and by being subject to humic acids and water actions that can modify a broken shell fragment into a smooth and sharpened "tool."

Bone Tools

Readily available from the many animals that were obtained for food, bone became the favorite choice for creating projectile points, hair pins, awls, and many other items. Although animal bones were the usual choice, there are some rare examples of tools made from human bones. A well-polished disc made from the parietal of a human cranium was uncovered at an Everglades site, as was a human tooth pendant found at the Granada site.

Shark Teeth

Among the most important artifacts are modified shark teeth, which were used as composite knives, and saws (fig. 4.5). The razor sharp teeth of hammerheads, tigers, and other sharks were perforated to allow them to be attached to a handle. Shark teeth still attached to wooden handles have been found at Key Marco. Perforated shark teeth usually have a single hole drilled through the base of the tooth near the center. In Archaic period

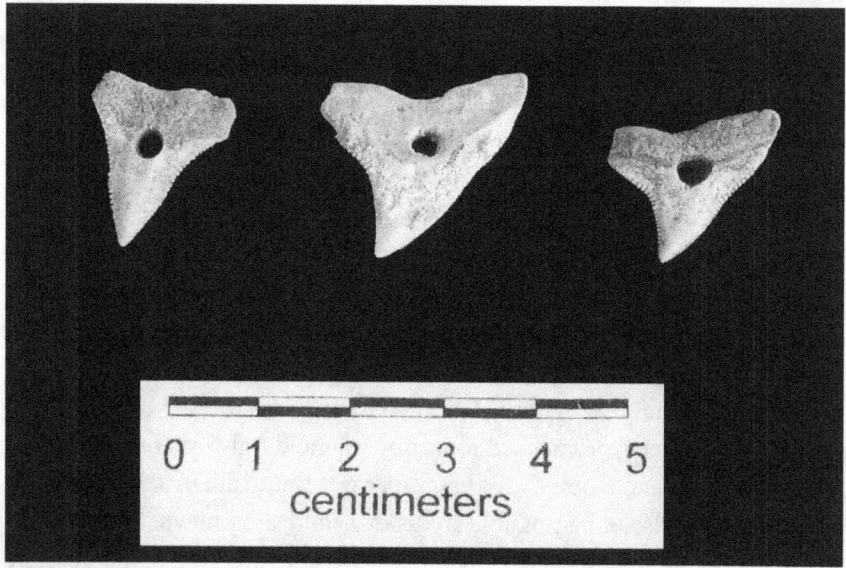

Figure 4.5. Drilled shark teeth. Collection of the Archaeological and Historical Conservancy.

examples, two drill holes are present. Sharks teeth are also found undrilled with notches on the tooth's enamel edge to allow for lashing to the wooden handle. Modified shark teeth occur in both coastal and interior sites. An excellent example of a shark-tooth knife with a preserved handle was found at the Granada site (8DA11) during excavations for a swimming pool.

Bone Socket Handle

The bone socket handle is part of a composite tool handle. Some may have functioned as sockets for the atlatl or "throwing stick," an ingenious spear thrower that allows for an individual to increase the power of the throw by incorporating an extension to the shaft. Examples of composite tools were recovered from Key Marco by Frank H. Cushing. Other bone "sockets" were attached to *Busycon* adze or celt handles. Two examples are known, with one found at the Trail site, DA34.

Sharpened Bone Points

Pieces of flattened bone, polished and bipointed, are common in South Florida sites and have been often characterized as projectile points. These specimens range in length from 3 to 5 centimeters, but larger examples are known, and in the latter cases, it is possible that the artifact could have been a needle or awl. Some archaeologists have argued that the smaller points might have actually been fish gorges or part of a composite fish hook. Socketed bone points were manufactured from the hollow long bones of small mammals or birds. One end is evenly cut across the width, and the other end of the shaft is cut diagonally to form the point (fig. 4.6, center). This bone point tradition was in existence during the Glades II and III periods but may have had its roots in the Archaic period, when similar point types are found in other parts of the Southeast.

Bone Awls

Bone awls were used for perforating or piercing (fig. 4.6, bottom, top). They are often polished and sharpened at one end. An unusually long awl or needle made from a bird bone was found at 8DA1058.

Lithic Artifacts

The use of stone, usually an important resource of the prehistoric material culture in North America, is less significant in southern Florida because of the absence of any hard lithic resources that easily lent themselves to chipping, grinding, or polishing. The local limestone was relatively soft and

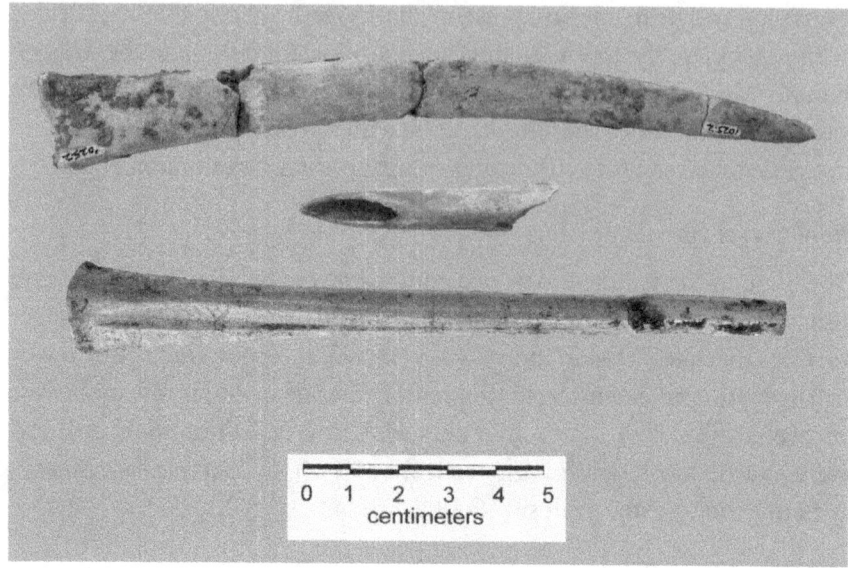

Figure 4.6. Bone awls and point. Collection of the Archaeological and Historical Conservancy.

friable. Nonetheless, limestone artifacts are part of the southeastern Florida tool assemblage, and some of the most common types are described below.

Anchor Stones

Often overlooked by investigators, anchor stones are simply large rocks that were used as anchor weights for canoes. This artifact required little modification. A large boulder would be used or selected because it had a natural hole through it which was sometimes enlarged. A cord was then tied to the rock through the hole. One specimen found along Biscayne Bay at 8DA10 has a groove around the center that allowed a cord to be wrapped around it. Another found on the south bank of the Miami River had a natural hole on one end with a geometric-pecked design around the hole (fig. 4.7). These specimens weigh between five and ten pounds each.

Stone and Coral Plummets/Pendants

There is some debate among prehistorians as to whether "plummets" were ornamental or utilitarian. Their overall similarity in form and shape to the shell pendants has prompted some researchers, such as John Reiger, to conclude that the limestone and coral versions were ornaments too.[25] Reiger describes the same flattened "back" for the stone specimens that also characterize the shell pendants. Other scholars disagree, citing their basic unattractiveness as being their reason for interpreting a utilitarian use. They

Figure 4.7. Stone anchor with pecked design found on the south bank of the Miami River. Collection of the Historical Museum of Southern Florida.

suggest that these artifacts were used as fishing-line weights. However, one should be careful not to confuse our standards of beauty with those of Indian cultures. It should be noted that in addition to the shell pendants, specimens are reported made from pumice, fossilized bone, and pottery sherds.

Limestone Balls

In 1963, two limestone balls were recovered from Brickell Point (8DA12). One ball is somewhat rough, with a facet worn or ground into it suggesting that it served as a grinder or a sharpener. It is 6 centimeters in diameter. They may also have been used as weapons or heating stones.

Exotic Lithic Artifacts

While one might conclude that flint/chert projectile points were not manufactured in South Florida because of the lack of local quarries, there is evidence in the form of chert debitage representing tool or biface manufacture, as well as fist-sized chert nodules, indicating that some lithic tools were manufactured locally. At the Brickell site (DA12), hundreds of chert flakes were found at the Miami Circle excavations in 1998.[26]

Although rare, polished stone celts have been reported with some regularity in Miami-Dade County. Most of these are typical of types that occur in Georgia, Alabama, and the Carolinas, where natural deposits of hard metamorphic rock occur. About a dozen specimens are known from Miami-Dade County, including three from the Miami Circle. All except one were found at coastal sites.

Pumice

Pumice, a volcanic glass, is found at most sites along Florida's east coast. Pumice is not native to Florida. Its light weight, which allows it to float, explains its occurrence along the coast, where it has been washed ashore from sea currents. Pumice found in middens often has been smoothed or has grooved surfaces suggesting its use as grinders, "smoothers," and spoke shaves. A few examples are known to have been carved into pendants or floats (fig. 4.8), including at least two specimens from the Florida Keys carved in the form of birds. Goggin has suggested the Lower Antilles, the Azores, and even Peru (by way of the Amazon River) as good candidates for the origin of South Florida's pumice. An analysis of pumice from Brickell Point identifies several possible sources, including the eastern portion of the Trans-Mexico Volcanic Belt.[27] The large quantity of pumice found at the Miami Circle indicates a Glades I period for that assemblage. Testing by thermoluminescence may determine the exact date of the eruptions that were responsible for South Florida's sudden wealth of workable stone.

Ornaments

Ornaments were made from shell, stone, and bone. Types range from simple beads to intricately carved gorgets with zoomorphic or geometric designs. Some shells were simply perforated and used as ornaments because of their beautiful natural colors and shapes. Most perforated shells, however, such as *Codakia orbicularis* and *Lucina tigrina*, were probably net weights, as indicated by similar specimens of *Nuetia* shells recovered with preserved cordage at the Key Marco site[28] (Gilliland 1975). Some *Busycon* shells were cut and carved into circular discs and used as gorgets.

The most intriguing ornaments are the many pendants (fig. 4.9) that have been uncovered throughout South Florida. Shell pendants are often made from the columella of the *Pleuroploca gigantea* or the *Busycon contrarium*, however, some pendants were manufactured from the shell lip or the shell wall. Specimens vary from approximately 3 to 22 centimeters in length, although most are 5 to 8 centimeters long. Similar pendant forms

Figure 4.8. Carved pumice float. Collection of the Archaeological and Historical Conservancy.

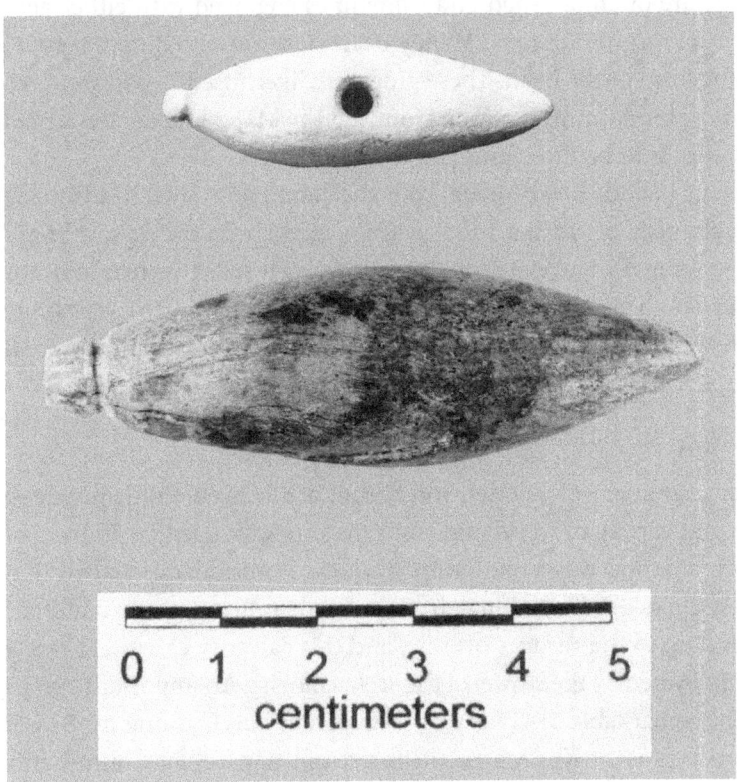

Figure 4.9. Carved shell pendants. Collection of the Archaeological and Historical Conservancy.

occur in bone and stone. A groove occurs at one end and, in rare cases, on both ends to allow suspension. Many specimens have the peculiar trait of having one side flattened. This trait was first observed by John Reiger, who believes that this may have been done to keep the pendant from turning and twisting the cord while being suspended.[29] The function of these objects as pendants is substantiated by Sparke's report that the Timucua Indians of northern Florida were wearing pieces of "unicorn horn" around their necks and illustrations by Le Moyne in the sixteenth century that depict columella-like pendants suspended from the hip and legs.

The phallic appearance of these artifacts has drawn speculation by some scholars that this resemblance is not accidental and that these artifacts represent a sexual amulet. D. L. Reichard was among the earliest to note this similarity after observing pendants excavated from the Surfside site, 8DA20.[30] Reiger is also a major proponent of this interpretation.[31]

The most common ornamental bone objects are hair pins. These cylindrical bone artifacts were modified with prepared heads and sharpened points. They are often polished and sometimes engraved with either geometric or zoomorphic designs. Willey describes fourteen different types based on the form of the head. These pins were likely used as hair pins. An anthropomorphic painting on a shell found at the Marco site depicts a man with what appear to be three pins placed in his hair.[32]

Ornaments include beads made from shell and bone. Shell beads made from the columella of whelks, tubular beads made from the hollow bones of birds, perforated bone elements, and perforated shark vertebrae occur throughout South Florida. It should be noted that perforated vertebrate should not be confused with unmodified vertebrae that has a natural neural hole through the centrum.

Wood Artifacts

This cursory summary of wooden and fibrous artifacts does little justice to the extent and variety of wood and plant materials used by the Indians of South Florida. Wood was a medium that offered considerable artistic and utilitarian expression. Unfortunately, wood and similar organic materials do not stand up to the ravages of time, and this category of artifact rarely has been uncovered by the trowel of the archaeologist. An important exception was the remarkable discovery by Frank Hamilton Cushing in 1896 of wooden artifacts at the Key Marco site in present-day Collier County. This assemblage, in terms of beauty and variation, is yet to be duplicated from any other site. It was regarded as such a unique treasure at the time of its discovery that many scholars doubted its authenticity. Today, this discovery ranks as the major source of our knowledge of prehistoric wood craftsmanship of South Florida. An inventory and description of the Key Marco artifacts is provided in Gilliland's *Material Culture of Key Marco, Florida*, a well-illustrated book of considerable value to the prehistorian and student because of its unparalleled glimpse into prehistoric material culture.[33]

It is likely that a similar variety of wooden artifacts existed in southeastern Florida. Tequesta and pre-Tequesta material culture included wooden mortars, pestles, and bowls (some of the Key Marco bowls have incised parallel lines similar to the Surfside Incised design of ceramic bowls). Isolated discoveries of wooden artifacts within the silt of Miami River and a wooden club uncovered during dredging at Miami Beach provide a glimpse of the prehistoric wooden artifact assemblage. Fishing nets, tool handles, and even wooden stools may have been commonplace. In the 1980s several wooden pestles (fig. 4.10) were discovered in the wetlands adjacent to an Everglades tree island, and in 1981 a wooden handle of a shark-tooth knife was discovered at the Granada site.

However, nothing could have been more important to the prehistoric people of the Glades than the wooden dugout canoe, a mainstay of South Florida prehistoric life. In an area dominated by wetlands, extensive coastal estuaries and islands, the canoe connected all of these environments, making a trip from the eastern Everglades to Biscayne Bay by way of the Miami River easily accomplished within several hours. Historic accounts provide

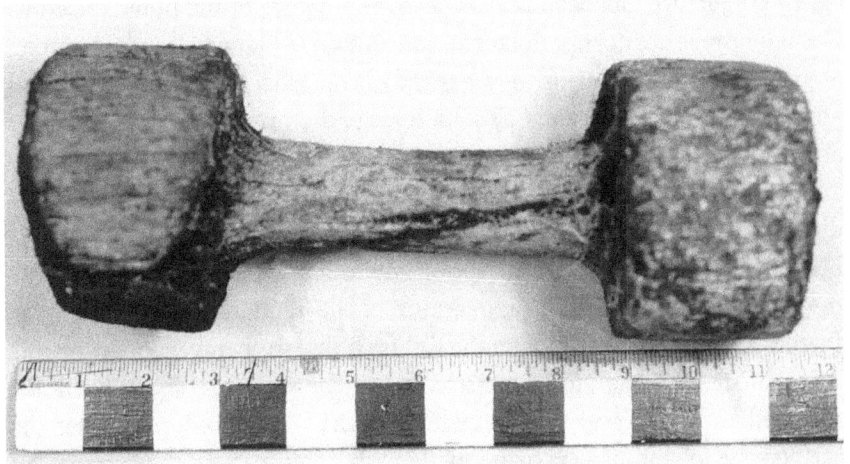

Figure 4.10. Wooden pestle found in the Everglades. Collection of the Historical Museum of Southern Florida.

some insight about the Tequesta and Calusa canoes. In one account, the chief's canoe required sixteen paddlers. In another account, the Calusa are described as occasionally lashing two canoes together, straddling the space between the canoes with a deck, and then constructing a cabin with poles and thatching on top the deck similar to a catamaran.[34] The importance of the canoe is indicated by a possible "toy" canoe made from bone that was uncovered at the Granada site, 8DA11, during excavations by the Florida Division of Archives, History, and Records Management.[35]

Although scores of prehistoric canoes from central and northern Florida have been found, few have been reported from South Florida that can be attributed to prehistoric cultures. The one likely prehistoric example is the specimen reported by Cushing at Key Marco. A wooden canoe found by Britt in 1903 in the vicinity of present-day Coco Plum in Coral Gables is of an unknown origin and its present whereabouts is unknown. Other canoes reportedly found along the mangrove coast have always proven to be of historic manufacture—generally Seminole or Miccosukee—or the flotsam of Indian tribes from Central or South America. It is unfortunate that no specimens of southeast Florida prehistoric canoes are available for measurements to provide data for a scientific comparison of types and sizes of canoes. In all probability, however, they were similar to the dugout canoes found in other parts of the peninsula.

The Indian Dwelling

Much conjecture has been offered as to the nature of the houses used by the Tequesta. The most popular misconception is that when the Seminoles arrived in southern Florida they learned to construct their open-sided rectangular chickees by copying the structures of their predecessors, the Calusa and Tequesta. There is no historical documentation to prove this. Recent archaeological discoveries of post holes at the mouth of the Miami River indicate that prehistoric structures were oval. These discoveries are important because despite extensive descriptions of Indian customs by the Spanish, none of them addressed the appearance of the Tequesta houses. However, there is a Spanish description of the Calusa houses as being wooden, round, and thatched.[36] Jonathan Dickinson, a shipwrecked English captive of the Jobe Indians in the seventeenth century in the vicinity of Jupiter Inlet, described the Jobe houses as being made with poles stuck in the ground and bent over toward the middle and then covered with thatch. This may be similar to the construction techniques for the Tequesta.

The Perfect Balance: Adapting to the Land and Sea   87

In 2004 a circular structure defined by post holes was discovered by archaeologists from the Archaeological and Historical Conservancy at the MDM parcel encompassing a portion of 8DA11 on the north bank of the Miami River. Incredibly, the feature had survived the construction of the Royal Palm Hotel. This prehistoric structure, dubbed the Royal Palm Circle, is characterized by two concentric circles of post holes (fig. 4.11).

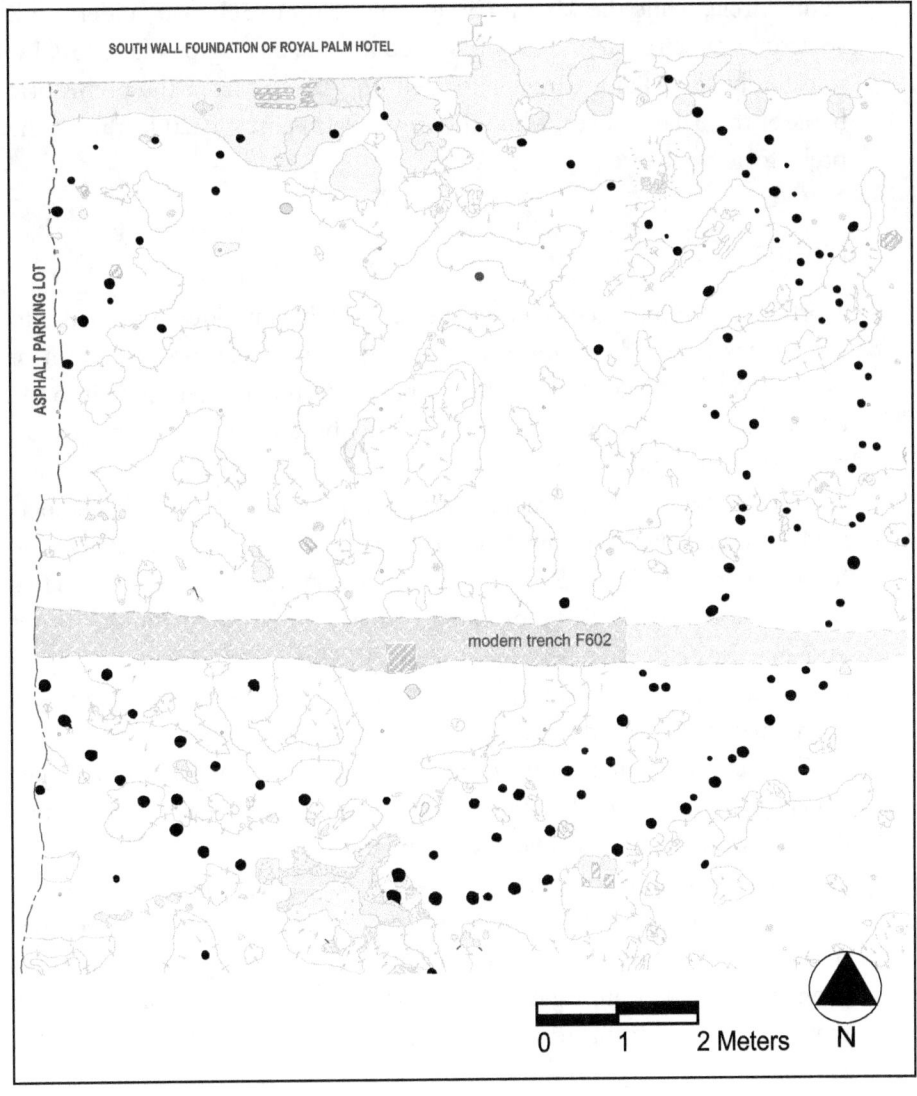

Figure 4.11. Map of the Royal Palm Circle. Map by John G. Beriault based on field map created by Briana Delano. Courtesy of the Archaeological and Historical Conservancy.

While the structure has no obvious door, there is a gap between the inner and outer wall on the northeast quadrant that suggests an entryway.

The Royal Palm Circle has an outer wall diameter of about 36 feet and inner wall diameter of about 29 feet. In contrast, the Miami Circle measures 38 feet in diameter. Also, the Miami Circle has a robust construction plan that used large foundation basins, while the Royal Palm Circle is characterized by walls supported by posts averaging about 20 centimeters in diameter. Radiocarbon dates suggest an A.D. 600–700 age for the Royal Palm Circle, while the Miami Circle may be up to 500 years older. Both structures are circular and may have had an elite or religious function. Interestingly, the Miami Circle is located only 25 feet from the prehistoric bank of the Miami River, while the Royal Palm Circle is 20 feet from the prehistoric bay shore.

Mortuary Patterns

Mortuary customs established in the Late Archaic period continued into the Glades I period. Solution hole burials, a principle mortuary trait of the Late Archaic characterized by primary interments, continued into the Glades period, although secondary burials became more common than primary interments.

At DA11 thousands of fragmentary comingled human remains associated with secondary interments were discovered below and adjacent to the foundations of the Royal Palm Hotel. All the bones were located within five solution holes (fig. 4.12).[37] Only a few primary burials were found. It is not known if the distinction between primary and secondary interments represents changing religious/mortuary customs through time and/or whether individual status played a role.

The second mortuary pattern that continues from the Late Archaic period is the midden burial. Interments commonly occur in black-earth middens across southern Florida. These human remains occur in the same locations as habitation activities, which at first blush suggests that individuals were being buried within active camps or villages. This may not have been the case. It is possible that midden burials were occurring after a camp had been abandoned or during intervals between occupation. It is also possible that some burials occurred prior to that part of the site being used for habitation.

The complexity of interpreting midden burials was revealed when hu-

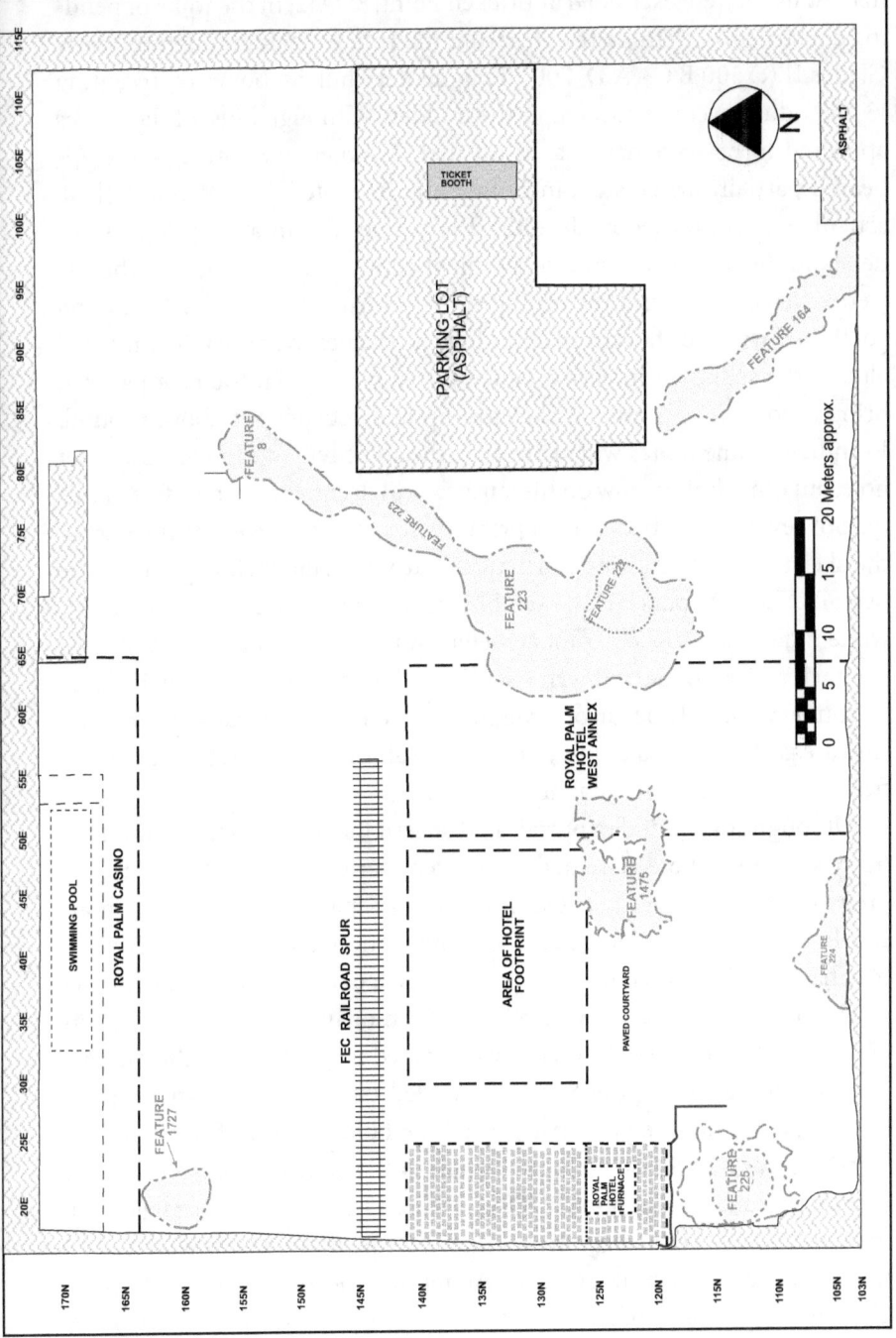

Figure 4.12. Map depicting a plan of the MDM parcel solution holes and cemetery, 8DA11. Map created by John G. Beriault. Courtesy of the Archaeological and Historical Conservancy.

man remains were excavated at Brickell Point, 8DA12, in the wake of pending construction.[38] This site dates from the Late Archaic through the early Glades II (c. 500 B.C.–A.D. 700). Fragmentary human bones representing 13 individuals were uncovered in the midden. Although most of the graves appeared to be secondary based on their fragmentary nature, some appeared partially articulated, including an articulated arm. Was a fleshed, articulated arm buried at the site? The answer lies in attempting to understand the overall site and its sediment context. Disturbances of the site were extensive. Ground-disturbing activities from centuries of habitation combined with tree falls from countless hurricanes over the millennia had altered the sediment integrity. When a tree blows over, the root ball can bring a portion of a human skeleton up and redeposit it above ground. Eventually some bones will settle with the soil back into the original root hole, but other bones, now on the surface, will decompose. The effect of this type of severe bioturbation on a primary interment may leave only part of the skeleton, such as a single articulated arm or hand, below ground. The overall effect, of course, is the semblance of a largely secondary cemetery, while in fact the Brickell Point cemetery was likely a combination of both primary and secondary interments. Like the coastal sites, disarticulated "secondary" burials occur on Everglades tree islands. Because Everglades sites are generally small, most graves were subject to intensive disturbances from tree falls and continual human activity.

Although some midden burials had shared loci for habitation and mortuary activities, there is evidence that cemeteries and possible mortuary preparation areas were selected in locations separate from habitation areas. In some cases, as indicated above, habitation and mortuary activities may have occurred at different times at a particular location. In other cases small, isolated tree islands were selected for mortuary activities. One Everglades tree island, 8DA34, intensely excavated in the 1970s by the Miami–West India Archaeological Society, revealed two discrete mortuary areas located away from the principal area of habitation.[39] One of the mortuary locations was a small island located about 100 meters east of the main tree island. This small area, dubbed TR-4, yielded hundreds of comingled human bones and teeth, suggesting a major cemetery or a possible preparation area used prior to interments. At another location south of the principal midden, an area of human remains was discovered in the wetlands at the edge of the island. These remains appeared to be deliberate interments placed within small solution holes on the water's edge. A *Strombus* celt cache and part of an alligator skeleton were discovered in close proximity to the remains. It is not clear what the relation of these features had to the human remains.

The third and most conspicuous mortuary site type of the Glades period is the constructed mound. At least 15 mounds are known in Miami-Dade County, of which only four have survived. Some mounds were constructed of sand and others of limestone rocks. This distinction may simply reflect the availability of suitable materials in that sand is scarcer south of the Miami River, where all of the rock mounds are reported to occur. Burials with constructed mounds have not been well documented, but both secondary and primary burials as well as single instances and groupings of human crania are reported. Burial mounds may have been reserved for the elite or higher status individuals. (See chapter 5 for further discussion of burial mounds.)

5

Sacred Geography

The Prehistoric Settlement System

In the world of Tequesta geography, the land, sea, and Everglades were inextricably linked. Each location used for settlement favored water access for transportation and fishing and had sufficiently high ground to stay dry. Mangrove estuaries became prime locations for fishing, and no doubt families and clans claimed and regulated fishing rights on the most productive locales. Perhaps there were spirits attached to principal rivers and estuaries and each special place, special tree, and offshore reef had its own sacred significance. We do not know the Tequesta perception of sacred space, but in the Native American world, there is less a distinction between the sacred and secular as there is an integrated whole—an operating cosmology in which all actions have consequences in both the natural and supernatural worlds.

The Tequesta settlement system includes the locations used for resource procurement, habitation, and disposal of the dead. This encompasses all of southeastern Florida, reflecting an effective adaptation to the region's major natural features: the Everglades, the rivers and creeks that drain from the Everglades across the Atlantic Coastal Ridge, the shores of Biscayne Bay, and the barrier islands that parallel the coast, such as Key Biscayne and Miami Beach. All of these areas were easily accessible by canoe. The rivers, creeks, and sloughs that drained from the Everglades into Biscayne Bay allowed canoes to travel between the interior and the bay within hours, making all of the coast and Everglades, including the upper Florida Keys, easily accessible within hours.

Questions about whether the Tequesta were "nomadic" or sedentary are frequently asked of prehistorians. More specifically, the discussion focuses on whether sites were used year around or only periodically. Studies in other parts of eastern North America often reveal evidence of shifts of settlements in response to seasonal changes and/or the availability of various food resources, and similar shifts of settlement and resource procurement in South Florida undoubtedly occurred. Archaeologists have been able to identify specific animal and plant remains within the archaeological record that can often be correlated with their availability at specific times of the year, however, this record of seasonal availability does not necessarily indicate that the site was not in use during other times of the year when such seasonal evidence might be absent, nor is it diagnostic.

Descriptions of prehistoric settlement in South Florida should avoid terms like "nomadic" or "seminomadic." The word "nomadic" conjures images of a homeless people drifting aimlessly through a hostile environment, whereas in reality, the Tequesta were very much at home in the South Florida wetlands. They probably lived in bands of extended families, perhaps varying in size from a dozen to 40 people, in camps and villages on both the coast and interior. They made frequent trips throughout the region to procure food and other resources, using smaller camp sites as temporary bases to gather specific resources, such as sea turtles on Key Biscayne.

One of the ongoing debates among scholars is whether the Tequesta were predominantly coastal dwellers who traveled into the Everglades exclusively for the purposes of hunting and fishing, thus using the Everglades tree islands only briefly during hunting and fishing trips, or whether they used the Everglades for long-term camps or even permanent villages. Archaeological investigations demonstrate that some Everglades sites were intensively used and may have been more than temporary camps. Many of these black-earth middens are large and deep with up to 4 feet of cultural deposits. Most of these tree island sites include cemeteries. Evidence gleaned from Everglades excavations has revealed marine shells and sea turtle bones obtained from fishing and foraging on the coast. Although coastal sites were the primary location for prehistoric habitation, the evidence suggests that some Everglades sites may have been used for primary habitation, with foraging and food gathering being directed to the coast rather than the reverse.

Site Types

The Dade County Historic Survey was conducted between 1978 and 1981. It resulted in the documentation of 350 prehistoric archaeological sites across the county. This is by no means all of the sites that once existed there, but it is a large enough sample to provide the basis for classifying these sites into types and develop a predictive site model and thus create a regional settlement model. These site types are described below.

Habitation Sites

A habitation site is among the most important site types because it contains cultural remains that can provide information about how people lived. A wide spectrum of activities are associated with habitation, such as food preparation, tool manufacture, and tool usage, and these daily activities can be interpreted from the artifacts and food refuse that occurs there.

Archaeologists refer to the larger prehistoric habitation sites as black-earth or shell middens. A midden is an accumulation of cultural debris that may actually cause an increase in the ground elevation. Some middens in southeast Florida are up to 4 feet deep. The midden is characterized by organically enriched soil mixed with cultural debris—the refuse of centuries of subsistence and habitation activities. A single shovelful of midden soil may contain parts of broken and discarded tools, pottery sherds, hundreds of animal bones, charcoal from cooking fires, and charred plant remains. A midden is generally associated with house locations where meal refuse and other garbage were often tossed in close proximity. In some instances evidence of post holes has been uncovered in middens.

South Florida has prehistoric habitation sites that range from as small as 15 feet in diameter, where a few individuals ate and lived for a short period of time, to areas of 50 hectares where hundreds of people lived nearly year around over a period of hundreds and even thousands of years. Smaller habitation sites or camps are characterized by an isolated scatter of artifacts or cultural materials. I have observed one small island in the Big Cypress National Preserve 15 feet across that had been used as a camp. A good example of a large habitation site is the village of Tequesta, 8DA11 and 8DA12, at the mouth of the Miami River, representing at least 2,500 years of continuous occupation. This village was the largest and one of the most populated settlements in southeastern Florida encompassing middens and constructed mounds along both banks of the River. At least five mounds are recorded as being in proximity of the Miami River's mouth.

Most habitation sites occur near waterways that allowed for efficient canoe travel. Not surprisingly, most of South Florida's prehistoric sites are located along creeks, rivers, islands in the Everglades, and Biscayne Bay. Sites also occur on the barrier islands along the Atlantic Ocean but are rarely encountered because of the dual effects of development and erosion from storms.

The rivers of southern Florida were the roadways of prehistoric times. Although Miami-Dade County's rivers and creeks are hardly imposing, they provided canoe access between the Everglades and Biscayne Bay on to the Atlantic Ocean. From the Oleta River and Arch Creek southward to Snapper Creek, the Indians inhabited the elevated river banks, fishing and hunting across the pristine countryside.

Tree islands were the principal focus of prehistoric habitation in the Everglades. Tree islands have a wet and dry component. The dry component occurs on the uplands at the northern end of the tree island, often referred to as "hammocks." These upland hammocks range in size from 30 to 200 feet in diameter. The higher elevations are often characterized as rocky knolls that provide sufficient elevation to support a hardwood community of gumbo limbo, ficus, paradise trees, and other tropical plants. The elevated hammock provided a high and dry location for prehistoric settlement. The effects of millennia of occupation and sheet-water flow was to accumulate additional sediments onto the island, thus making it even more attractive and convenient for human use.

Constructed Mounds

The term "Indian mound" often has been used by the public to refer to any Native American site. In South Florida, the term "mound" often referred to tree island sites in the Everglades. Actually, there are few constructed mounds in southern Florida. Constructed mounds are often confused with black-earth middens. Although both types of sites are elevated, the mound is purposely constructed while the midden's elevation is usually an unintentional byproduct of long-term occupancy and natural forces that resulted in accumulations of sediment that through time added to the elevation of the site. The constructed mounds of southern Florida are similar to others throughout eastern North America, most of which were part of a Native America religious-social tradition for burying the dead and/or for creating earthen platforms for religious structures. These mounds were constructed from either sand or limestone rocks.

While southeastern Florida is one of the few regions of North America that has rock mounds, that distinction is the result of the simple fact that the Tequesta used the building material that was most easily available in the vicinity of the site. It is noteworthy that most rock mounds occur from the Miami River southward to the Florida Keys, where loose rocks abound in the hardwood hammocks. Deep deposits of sand occur less frequently south of the Miami River, and not surprisingly, sand mounds tend to occur more frequently from the Miami River northward, where sand deposits are deeper and more accessible.

Historical records and accounts by archaeologists who visited Miami prior to intensive development indicate that there were at least 15 mounds in present-day Miami-Dade County, of which three were rock mounds and the others were sand, although one is reported as a muck burial mound (8DA36) that was located on Flagami Island. Eleven of the 15 mounds have been destroyed by development, and those that survive have been the targets of skull collectors and treasure hunters, making the task of preserving the few remaining mounds difficult at best.

Among the most accessible of the surviving burial mounds in Miami-Dade County is the El Portal Mound (8DA20) along the Little River. This mound has the distinction of being Dade County's first intentionally preserved archaeological site, dedicated as an archaeological park in 1925 as part of the Sherwood Forest Subdivision. Although the mound's integrity greatly suffered in the 1930s–1940s from the neighborhood children and avocational archaeologists, in general, the mound's form and its many beautiful oak trees make it one of the most attractive and charming vistas in all of the county.

Similar destructive curiosity had targeted the burial mound at Cutler (8DA8), located in a county park. What is heralded as the county's largest oak tree grows stoically upon the mound's crest, its roots undoubtedly rearranging whatever graves might have been missed by looters. The Cutler Mound measures about 38 by 20 feet at the base and rises about 5 feet above the surrounding terrain. In the 1860s Henry Perrine Jr. removed and then lost several human skulls from the site (see chapter 1). In the 1890s Ralph Munroe of Coconut Grove led a digging expedition to the mound. In 1940 John Goggin and Charlie Brookfield visited the site without conducting any excavations.[1] Disturbances continued through the 1980s, when neighborhood children jumped the property wall and dug into the mound. Fortunately, several of these people, now adults, returned the skeletal material. All of the bones were reinterred after the property became a park. Today the mound is preserved within the Charles Deering Estate at Cutler county park and is accessible to visitors by guided tour.

Cemeteries

Prehistoric human interments were not confined to constructed mounds. They also occur in solution holes—one of the few places that had sufficiently deep soils for the placement of a human remains because much of Miami-Dade County is underlain with shallow limestone bedrock. Not to be confused with sink holes, solution holes are natural openings in the limestone bedrock formed by water and organic acids slowly dissolving the rock. Sometimes these actions resulted in creating cave-like formations or deep depressions, as at the Cutler site, that are from 5 to 10 feet below the surface and up to 100 feet in diameter. Others are depressions filled with sand and clay-like the soils at 8DA11246 on Brickell Avenue. In some cases, even small solution cavities only several feet in diameter have been used for isolated human interments. To date, five solution hole cemeteries have been discovered within a 3-mile area of downtown Miami and Brickell Avenue. These include the Atlantis site, Santa Maria, Santa Maria West, the Bristol site, and the largest and most significant of them all, the MDM parcel in downtown Miami.

The first solution hole burial documented by archaeologists was in 1981 at 8DA1082 during construction of the Atlantis condominiums east of Brickell Avenue.[2] This shallow solution hole occurs about 30 feet from the bay. Fragmented human remains with fiber-tempered pottery and St. Johns Plain sherds were uncovered from beneath a large ficus tree. Likewise, a solution hole cemetery was uncovered in 1981 at the Santa Maria parcel, home of former Miami mayor Maurice Ferrer. The Santa Maria cemetery was of particular interest because unlike the human remains at Atlantis, grave pits were discernable, with three individuals present, each primary, and with limestone capstones placed above the bodies.[3]

In 2005, a previously undocumented portion of the Santa Maria cemetery, DA11246, was discovered during development of a parcel on the west side of Brickell Avenue by archaeologist Richard Haiduven. Additional investigating were completed there by archaeologists from the Archaeological and Historical Conservancy.[4] Like Santa Maria East, the human remains were primary and extended, and many were covered with limestone rocks. A total of 19 individuals were documented and later reinterred.

Since 1990, several other solution hole cemeteries have been documented, but no one could have anticipated that the largest Tequesta cemetery had somehow survived until its discovery in downtown Miami in 2005. The cemetery is located within a group of five large solution holes, some interconnected, and several smaller ones discovered beneath a commercial parking lot between SE Second and SE Third Street. The lot once contained the northwest quadrant of the Royal Palm Hotel, opened in 1897 and demolished in 1930. The solution holes were directly beneath the northwest annex of the hotel, and in some instances the brick foundations had been placed within inches of human skulls without disturbing them, although many others were destroyed by the hotel construction.

Several hundred individuals were identified based on largely fragmentary remains. The human remains were mostly secondary and comingled with a few primary graves. One group of bodies was interred within a limestone crypt, where unfinished limestone slabs and rocks were loosely placed around and above several bodies within a solution hole (Feature 164).

An analysis of human remains from two of the five solution holes reveals that Feature 225, a solution hole about 4 meters in diameter, contained 38 individuals, including 28 adults and 14 juveniles. Most of these bones were comingled but at least two were primary.[5] Feature 164 represents the largest ossuary on the site. The minimum number of individuals there was determined to be 63, based on using the most common element (MCE), the petrus, as an indicator, resulting in 49 adults and 14 juveniles being identified.[6] Echazabal determined that 26 were males and 20 were females; the others were indeterminate.

Overall, the MDM cemetery suggests an egalitarian population that includes males and females and both adults and children. Grave goods are rare, which suggests that personal possessions may have been redistributed and/or that certain possessions were owned by the clan or family. Evidence indicates that the cemetery was used from Glades I through Glades II periods, A.D. 400–1200. A similar practice of secondary interments occurred at other coastal as well as interior sites. There are numerous reports of fragmentary human skeletal remains within Everglades black-earth middens on tree islands.

Earthworks

Earthworks are among Florida's most mysterious sites. For reasons still unknown, numerous circular and linear earthen ridges were constructed across southern Florida, particularly around Lake Okeechobee. Many of these sites are visible only from the air. William Sears believed that the earthworks of Fort Center located adjacent to Fisheating Creek were constructed to facilitate drainage for the cultivation of maize.[7] However, his theories are unproven and likely incorrect. I believe that these circular earthworks were used as fish weirs based on my study of earthworks in the Lake Okeechobee area.[8]

At least two prehistoric earthworks are documented in Miami-Dade County. They are circular ditches. One is 180 meters in diameter and the other is 60 meters in diameter. The smaller one is near the Miami River and was first described by surveyor George McKay in 1845 near present-day Twelfth Avenue (described in chapter 1). I discovered the second circle studying 1926 aerial photographs (fig. 5.1). It was located in the vicinity of present-day NW Forty-second Avenue and NW Seventh Street at what would have been the headwaters of the south fork of the Miami River.

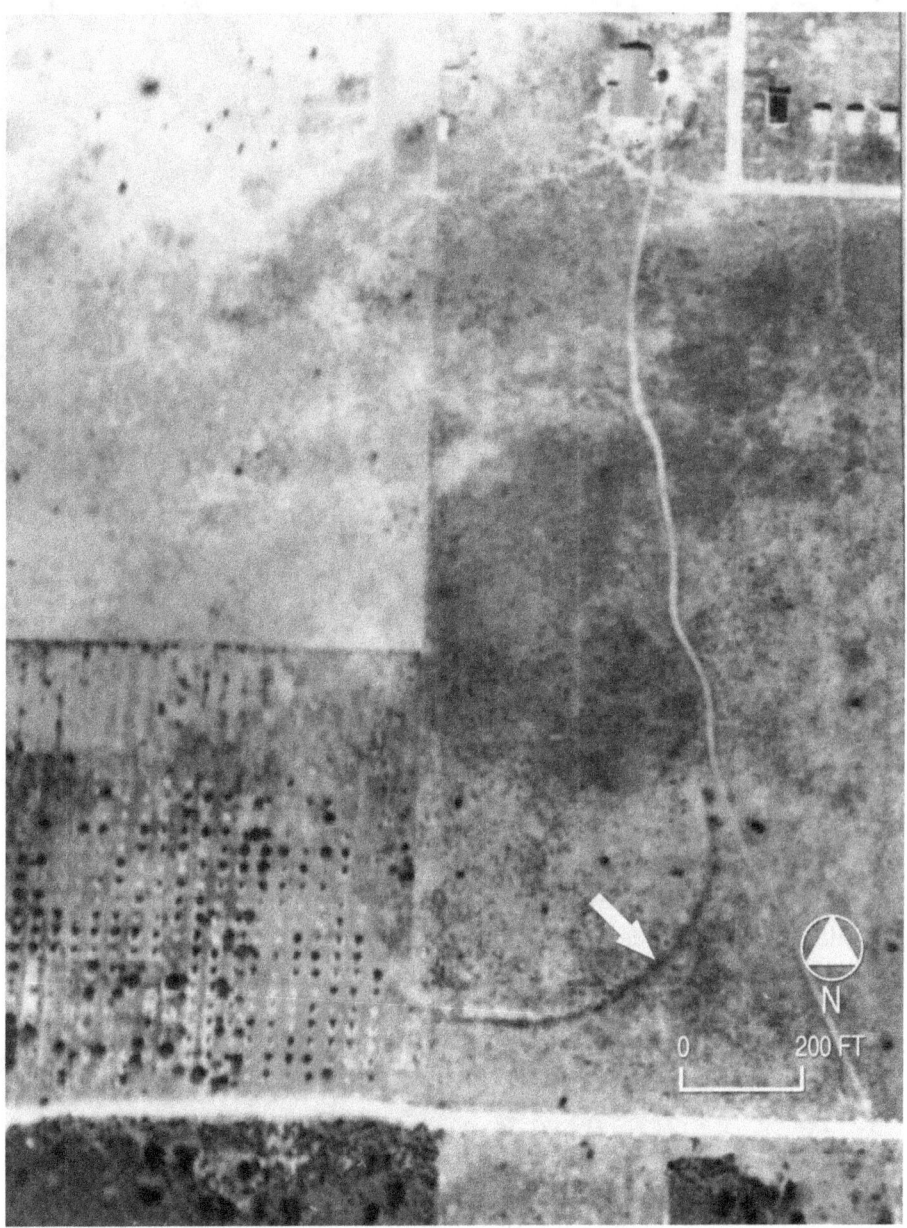

Figure 5.1. Aerial photo of Dade Circle earthworks, 1926. Collection of Robert S. Carr.

Figure 5.2. Indian canoe trail in the Everglades, c. 1910. Collection of Robert S. Carr.

Indian Trails

There are two types of Indian trails: land and water. Land trails were simply foot paths, the best documented being the Indian trail that connected Coconut Grove to the mouth of the Miami River. The trail is still visible where it traverses Barnacle State Park in Coconut Grove, crossing the property from north to south as a narrow clear path largely void of vegetation. This segment of the trail is the only part that has survived of what was once a 5-mile trail that extended northward to the Miami River.

Canoe trails at one time criss-crossed the Everglades (fig. 5.2). After the demise of the Tequesta, these trails were used by the Seminoles and, subsequently, by the military during the Seminole Wars to pursue the Indians. It is likely that many of the earliest airboat trails followed canoe trails that are hundreds of years old.

Tequesta Sites

Tequesta daily life was intertwined with the land and sea. Their principal town was at the mouth of the Miami River, and from that strategic vantage overlooking Biscayne Bay, the Atlantic was an hour away by canoe and the Everglades even closer. The Miami River sites are on both the north and south banks of the Miami River (8DA11, 8DA12) and have yielded some of the most important evidence of Tequesta culture uncovered by archaeologists.

Miami Midden 1 (8DA11)

Archaeologists refer to the principal site at the mouth of the River as the Miami Midden site. John Goggin designated the site as Miami Midden 1 (8DA11). He never excavated there as undoubtedly it would have been a difficult task when he lived in the area, in the 1930s and 1940s, since the site was under commercial parking lots and beneath the lawn of the Granada Apartments.

The site encompasses approximately 25 acres, extending over 1,000 feet along the north bank of the river and about 1,000 feet northward along Biscayne Bay to the vicinity of present-day Flagler Street. The deepest and most significant deposits of archaeological material were concentrated near the river's mouth and on the bay shore. Scattered refuse and artifacts have been found as far inland as the Dade County Cultural Center on Flagler Street and NW Second Avenue. The site's broad extent reflects the magnitude of prehistoric activities that once occurred there. A slightly elevated ridge is visible in several pre-1910 photographs of Flagler Street's eastern termination at Biscayne Bay. This elevation was probably part of the midden. Several years ago, crane operator Bob Holt told me that when he worked on the construction of the Brickell Tower Building between SE First Street and Second Street, he uncovered several deep, shell-lined pits. Unfortunately, because the discovery occurred prior to local preservation laws, archaeologists were not able to document these features before they were destroyed. Recently, the name "Granada site" has been used to refer to Miami Midden 1 because of the state's archaeological excavations at the Granada Hotel (now the Knight Convention Center). The Granada component, however, represents only about 10 percent of the original Miami Midden 1. The state's Granada project was at that time the most ambitious archaeological project in the county since the WPA work of the 1930s, with Florida's Division of Historical Resources employing dozens of laborers under supervising archaeologists. The analysis of the Granada site data provides one of the best reconstructions of plant and animal subsistence completed for southeastern coastal Florida (see chapter 4). The final Granada report edited by archaeologist John Griffin includes detailed zooarchaeological analysis.[9]

As originally proposed, the convention center development would have destroyed the entire site, however, efforts were made to set aside a greenspace preservation area on a small, triangular sliver of land between the new structure and the Brickell Bridge. When the preservation agreement was ignored two years later to construct a swimming pool within the "archaeological preservation area," the county archaeologist insisted that the pool be constructed on an elevated deck above the site, thus restricting subsurface disturbances only to the pits dug for concrete support pilings. The county archaeologist monitored the pit excavations and had the dirt transported in a dozen truckloads to the yard of avocational archaeologist Wesley Coleman, where members of the Archaeological Society of Southern Florida and anthropology students from the University of Miami spent the next year sifting the dirt piles. Each pile was designated according to the construction pit from which it was excavated. Although the artifacts were hopelessly mixed from their original context, the recovery project provided new information about the site as well as allowing students to become familiar with artifact classification and cataloging techniques. All of the materials are now at the Historical Museum of Southern Florida.

In recent years, monitoring has been conducted at other construction projects that have impacted Miami Midden 1. Monitoring of the construction of the People Mover and the Southeast Bank Building between SE Second Street and SE Third Street uncovered intact prehistoric deposits. The Southeast Bank project (formerly occupied by the northeast lawn of the Royal Palm Hotel) revealed an area of prehistoric occupation dating from A.D. 200–400 directly on top the limestone bedrock.

As the development boom reached a crescendo in the late 1990s, archaeologists knew it was only a matter of time before the three parking lots located on the grounds of the former Royal Palm Hotel would be developed. These lots were regarded as potentially significant locations that could unravel the mysteries of the prehistoric and historic contact period town of Tequesta, with the promise of providing information that could reveal shifting locations of the settlement through time. I hypothesized that the overall Miami Midden site was never fully occupied at any one time, but that settlement may have been shifted to new locations as one area became unsanitary from rotting food refuse and human activity.

Before the developer could begin construction on the three parking lots, an archaeological investigation had to be completed. The Archaeological and Historical Conservancy conducted investigations there from 2001 to 2006, determining that despite a century of disturbances, there were intact cultural deposits beneath the asphalt parking lots. Lot C, the most southwestern of the three parking lots, was the most disappointing. Despite its location in the southern gardens of the Royal Palm Hotel, the property had been intensely disturbed down to the bedrock because Miami's first sewer system had been built there to service the Royal Palm Hotel. Although many interesting artifacts were found, few intact prehistoric features were observed.

In contrast, Lot B, located directly east of Lot C, revealed hundreds of post holes cut into the bedrock; one group of post holes represented the footprint of a circular structure (see chapter 4 for description). Lot D held the biggest surprise. Although evidence of prehistoric occupation occurred throughout the lot, the most important discovery was a Tequesta cemetery located within five deep solution holes buried beneath the Royal Palm Hotel and its northern gardens. Thousands of disarticulated human bones representing several hundred individuals were uncovered. Despite the construction of the Royal Palm Hotel in 1897 directly on top of much of the cemetery, many of the human remains had survived just below and near the hotel foundations.

The three lots revealed habitation and mortuary activities dating back at least 2,000 years; however, little evidence of habitation from the Glades III period was found. The mystery of the missing Glades III component was solved when a thin horizon of redeposited Glades III midden and cultural material was found near the hotel's foundations and around its massive swimming pool. It is likely that when the construction crews cleared the land they stockpiled the rich organic midden soil. After the hotel was completed they spread the soil throughout the hotel gardens.

Miami Midden 2 (DA12)

The Miami River's south bank became known as the Brickell Point site (8DA12) after the Brickell family, early settlers to the area who owned the property. Although not as deep as the north bank midden, the Brickell site was the location of substantial habitation activity. Curiously, the south bank may not have been occupied for as long a time period as the north bank. The archaeological materials excavated from the Brickell site indicate an occupation from as early as 750 B.C.–A.D. 1200. In contrast, the north bank settlement was occupied from the same early period, then more or less continuously until the time of European contact.

The Brickell site has been severely diminished over the last century. Settlers had cleared and cultivated the land as early as the mid-nineteenth century, and with the arrival of the Brickell family in 1871, several structures were built on the property, including homes and a store. The Brickell house may have been placed directly on top the remnants of a sand burial mound as indicated by the discovery of a layer of white sand, human teeth, and several possible grave goods by Carr and Mark Greene in 1961 beneath the Brickell House.[10] In 1932, the Brickell Bridge was constructed, destroying archaeological deposits on both sides of the river. The Brickells sold a portion of their property adjacent to the bridge where the developers then built the Brickell Apartments in 1949. Construction there included the leveling of the parcel, which had the effect of removing site sediments to below bedrock on the parcel's south end but preserving a portion of the site beneath fill on the north end near the river bank (where the Miami Circle would eventually be discovered).

John Goggin never had a chance to dig at the Brickell site, undoubtedly rebuffed by the reclusive Maude Brickell. The first investigation there was by avocational archaeologist Dan Laxson, who dug in 1958 after part of the property was sold to the Elks Club.[11] Laxson collected two shell tools and 272 pottery sherds from a modest excavation during construction of the club's building. During the same period avocational archaeologist Stan Cooper collected numerous artifacts from the site, many of which are now at the Historical Museum of Southern Florida.

The construction of the Brickell Holiday Inn in 1981 resulted in the monitoring and testing at the site before part of it was destroyed. This was the first monitoring project coordinated by Dade County's Historic Preservation Division, beginning Miami's legacy of urban archaeology. A feature of post holes associated with a small prehistoric house was discovered after a bulldozer had scraped the topsoil from the bedrock on top of the bluff. The prehistoric structure was defined by an elongated oval pattern of post holes cut into the bedrock and was the first evidence of a prehistoric structure uncovered in southeast Florida.[12]

Monitoring of construction of the hotel on the natural ridge along the 10-foot contour revealed fragments of human bones. Similar human remains were found in 2002 in Brickell Park when the city of Miami weighed the option of selling or trading the park to developers.[13] The discovery of the cemetery stopped the deal.

In 1996, the Brickell Apartments were demolished to make way for a new high rise. The city of Miami's historic preservation ordinance required that an archaeological assessment be conducted prior to new construction, and archaeologists soon discovered that intact midden had survived beneath the fill of the Brickell Apartments. While monitoring demolition of the apartments, several units dug by Carr and Ricisak revealed basins cut into the limestone bedrock.[14] Surveyor Ted Riggs observed the basins and hypothesized that they were part of a circle, and using geometry he predicted the exact location and size of the circle. This feature became known as the Miami Circle (discussed in detail in chapter 12). The developer, increasingly concerned about the archaeological discoveries on his property, confined the archaeologists to working in a small area around the circle. It was not until public acquisition that state archaeologists were able to test the entire parcel and determine the full extent of the midden.[15]

Another opportunity to investigate what was left of the Brickell midden occurred when the Sheraton Hotel (formerly the Holiday Inn) was scheduled for demolition in 2004. Although much of the site had been destroyed during the 1981 construction of the hotel, at the insistence of the county archaeologist, a preservation area had been set aside within the driveway island where the Brickell House cellar had been and around the hotel swimming pool and gardens. Unexpectedly, a 20-foot swath representing a road easement within the adjacent Brickell Park was included in the proposed development. Archaeological excavations lasted from 2005 to June 2006 and resulted in uncovering fragmentary human remains and hundreds of post holes cut into the bedrock.[16]

These and other recent investigations west of Brickell Avenue revealed the extent of prehistoric occupation on the south side of the Miami River with midden extending hundreds of feet inland from the river and the bay. In the 1990s, when a sidewalk was being replaced in front of 500 Brickell Avenue, I collected a perfect shell celt that lay beneath the old sidewalk.

Although the county's vigorous archaeological program monitored much of Miami's new downtown construction, it provided only a glimpse of Tequesta culture. Thousands of artifacts had been found by archaeologists, but lost forever was the fabric of an entire Native American group that had reigned over a water world of estuaries and creeks for thousands of years. Understanding the robustness of Tequesta culture meant seeing the broader patterns of settlement across area. The mouth of the Miami River and the town of Tequesta was a beginning point. It was a destination but also a point of departure that linked the river to the bay and to the Everglades.

Flagami Island (DA36, DA1053, DA1073)

The Tequesta's canoe trail started and ended at the river's mouth. It was a vigorous paddle for 40 minutes until you reached the mouth of the south fork of the Miami River, then made a southwest turn into the south river fork. With a southeastern breeze pushing from your left, you were now heading toward the Everglades.

As you paddled westward into the Everglades, leaving the headwaters of the south fork of the Miami River, the dark silhouette of a large tree-covered island loomed on the sawgrass horizon (fig. 5.3). What name the Tequesta had for this place we do not know, but it may be the "Micco Island" depicted on nineteenth-century maps from the Seminole Wars.[17] The island was half a mile in length—one of the largest in the eastern Everglades.

During prehistoric times, a canoe trail touched directly against the island's northern tip. Ironically, the canoe trail is covered now by the 836 Expressway, moving cars from downtown to suburbia on part of the same route that canoes once traveled from the Miami River to the Everglades. In the 1960s concrete warehouses and an auto body shop were constructed on what once was a large prehistoric village. Eventually, the site would become the location of a new intermodal facility for the county's rapid transit system.

Flagami Island first came to the attention of archaeologists in 1931 when 16-year-old John Goggin learned about the site from artifact collector Roy Montgomery, who had been digging on the burial mound. Goggin observed the gaping collectors' pits. His observations of the Flagami burial mound (DA36) and their demise were the first recorded of the site.[18] State archaeologist Vernon Lamme and Karl Squires visited the site in July 1934.

Figure 5.3. Flagami Island, looking west, after 16 inches of rain in 1981. Courtesy of the Archaeological and Historical Conservancy.

Lamme described the burial mound as 100 feet in diameter, composed of black muck and nearly completely dug.[19] Unknown to Goggin or Lamme was that buried beneath the thick hammock underbrush around the mound, there was a habitation site with numerous scattered human burials.

In the summer of 1980, Flagami Island was rediscovered during the Dade County Historic Survey, its location having been "lost" after Goggin's and Lamme's visits there. As fate would have it, the rediscovery of Flagami Island occurred on the eve of its destruction. The island, then only a rise of higher ground west of NW Seventy-second Avenue, was covered with small wood-frame houses and several businesses. In 1981, the homes were razed to make way for a new group of warehouses. Over a period of two years, the county archaeologist with student volunteers from the University of Miami monitored preconstruction clearing and excavated exposed fragmentary prehistoric burials. The results of this field work demonstrated that the island had been in use from as early as 1500 B.C., as indicated by radiocarbon dates of a shell celt (fig. 5.4). Although the major area of habi-

Figure 5.4. Robert Carr uncovering shell celts during bulldozing of Flagami site, 8DA1073, in 1981. Courtesy of the Archaeological and Historical Conservancy.

tation was on the northern portion of the island, scattered activity areas, including numerous graves, dotted the island. The Flagami graves were all secondary burials and badly fragmented. Analysis of the human remains by bioarchaeologist Yasar Iscan indicated an MNI of 16 individuals.[20] The burials included a few possible grave goods, including perforated turkey-wing shells that may have been the remnants of a necklace or cloak.

The Trail Site (DA34)

Continuing west southwest from Flagami, the ancient canoe trail traversed the open Everglades. Sawgrass lay ahead, while to your back the pine trees on the Atlantic Coastal Ridge stretched across the horizon to the southeast. Within an hour, the tall ficus trees of a tree island were visible. This tree island is known as the Trail site, 8DA34.

John Goggin recorded the site and identified it as one of the largest of the Everglades sites. With the help of several students, Goggin excavated test pits there in 1952; however, the results of these tests were never published. Other investigators, such as avocational archaeologists Dan D. Laxson and Wesley Coleman of the Miami–West India Archaeological Society have left us the only written reports about the site, a fortunate circumstance considering the site's destruction in 1972 to make way for townhouses.

The excavations by MWIAS uncovered evidence of specialized mortuary activity areas.[21] Although earlier investigators, such as the Broward County Archaeological Society, had uncovered human burials at midden sites before, no specialized or isolated mortuary areas had previously been identified.

Coleman identified a small island 100 meters east of the main site that he believed was a burial preparation area. The island measured 17.5 by 22 meters and was designated by the society as TR-4-B. Although no maps showing the specific location of the test pits or any features are included, a general contour map depicting the site is in his report.[22] Coleman reports that human bones were recovered from all 150 excavation units. Human remains included small bones such as phalanges, teeth, and skull fragments, as well as fragments of long bones. Although Coleman attributes much of this to burial preparation activities, a more likely interpretation is that the bones represent a cemetery of secondary burials and/or disturbed primary graves.

A second mortuary component associated with 8DA34 was an area of secondary burials located in what was once a wetlands south of the upland tree island midden. Fragmentary skull and limb burials associated with *Strombus* celt caches were discovered. This was the first evidence of a wetland mortuary found in southeastern Florida. It was also one of the few instances where celt caches were found in close proximity to human burials.

One of the most extraordinary discoveries reported at DA34 was the recovery of a single burial represented by only the right side of the individual. Even the skull had been cut laterally. The burial was placed in a semiflexed position, and adding to the curiosity of this macabre burial was the discovery of an alligator skull situated on top of the individual's pelvis.[23]

Madden's Hammock (DA45)

Ten miles north of the Trail site, about a two-hour canoe trip, is the highest natural elevation in Miami-Dade County, a 19-foot-high sand mound located at Madden's Hammock that towered above the Everglades. From its summit, the vast horizon of the Everglades stretched westward. The pines of the Atlantic Coastal Ridge filled the eastern view. Camp fires from villages five miles distant or more could easily be seen.

The site measures 600 feet north to south and 500 feet east to west, encompassing 7 acres. A dense, black-earth midden is located on the northern end of the island, and a cemetery is situated on the island's south end, although human remains have been found throughout the island.[24]

The site has a crescent shape, not unlike a parabolic dune, with its open side to the east. A large mound occupies the center of the crescent. The large mound is composed entirely of fine-grained quartz sand. Archaeologists debated for years as to whether the mound was manmade or natural. Goggin believed that the mound was constructed of sand transported by the Tequesta inland from Miami Beach, while others disagreed and believed that the sand is a remnant Pleistocene beach on the site. The truth is that the sand is typical of the local area and was not transported from the coast. The format and geology of the island indicates that it is not a typical Everglades tree island but a relic parabolic dune composed of windblown sand, an isolated remnant of the Atlantic Coastal Ridge where sand commonly occurs.

This conspicuous site has long attracted the interest of the curious. Unfortunately, during the 1950s and 1960s the mound was the continual target of diggers, both the informed and uninformed, from treasure hunters to Boy Scouts and the occasional avocational archaeologist. The results of decades of collecting were gaping holes in the mound, its native vegetation stripped and human bones scattered across the sand. To date, only a single fragmented cranium of the dozens of human burials removed from the sand mound has been preserved. Local hunter Tom Shirley reports that he visited the site in 1955, when he and several friends excavated a group of human graves on the south end of the site. He described the burials as having the heads in one central area with the bodies radiating outward.[25] In 2009 Shirley returned the human bones that he had collected and they were reinterred at the site later that year.

In 1955 the site also caught the attention of avocational archaeologist Dan Laxson, who lived in nearby Hialeah. Laxson earnestly pursued information about the Seminole use of the site and its historic significance in an open letter of inquiry to the Pioneer Club of Miami. He dug several test units there and published the first scientific report on the site.[26] Laxson also was there during the initial bulldozing of the site (fig. 5.5).

Many important collections were made at the site by the late James Sha-

Figure 5.5. Dan Laxson at Madden's Hammock, 8DA45, in 1959. Courtesy of Barbara Tansey.

fer and the late Patrick Maddalino. Part of the Shafer collection is at the Historical Museum of Southern Florida. Numerous pits were excavated by Maddalino, but his collection has not been made available for research, nor have the bones been returned for reinterment. Maddalino told me that he had uncovered and removed a female burial with an associated child. Undoubtedly, other important collections from the site exist and will eventually be made available to the public. Fortunately, the owners of Madden's Hammock stopped the vandalizing of the site in 1965 after several unfortunate incidents, which included the beating of a security guard by treasure hunters and the subsequent shooting and wounding of one of the diggers.

A Phase I archaeological survey of the site was conducted by John Gifford.[27] Additional testing to determine the exact boundaries of the site was done in 2005 by the Archaeological and Historical Conservancy.[28] Their investigations reveal that the island was occupied from the Late Archaic period through the time of Spanish contact by the Tequesta and that a large prehistoric cemetery occupies a portion of the island. Archival research reveals that when the Tequesta left the site, it was occupied by the Seminoles and became an important cultural center where the green corn dance was performed (see chapter 8).

Arch Creek Site (DA23)

During prehistoric times, an Indian canoe trip from the town of Tequesta at the mouth of the Miami River 7 miles northward to Arch Creek probably took about one hour. The view and landscape would have been beautiful: clean bay bottom, a continual green fringe of mangroves, and a distant curtain of pine trees that announced the upland coastal ridge just behind the mangroves. On entering Arch Creek the view would soon change from beautiful to spectacular.

Mangrove branches overhung the mouth of Arch Creek, and dead, still air greeted canoe travelers as the fresh bay winds were blocked by the thick mangrove forest. The 1-mile canoe trip westward was uneventful, the low swampy banks giving no hint of what lay upstream. As the creek made its first major bend northward, solid cliffs of white limestone suddenly thrust out of the black mangrove muck. Hardwood trees lushly draped in Spanish moss, orchids, and bromeliads grew above the creek. It was near the foot of the rock cliff that the canoes landed, and upon the rocky ridge that the Indians had built one of their largest coastal villages.

Just 300 feet beyond the landing was a spectacular feature that must have impressed the Indians as much as it marveled the white settlers who followed: a natural bridge of limestone that straddled the creek, an arch of unyielding rock that had been shaped by millennia of rushing water.

The Arch Creek village encompassed much of the ridge north of the creek, probably in excess of 5 acres. It encompassed a deep black dirt midden that was the result of continual occupation since at least circa 750 B.C. in a village probably populated by fewer than 100 people.

In the 1920s botanist John Kunkel Small visited the site and offered the following description: "There are evidences of much activity, in the way of kitchen middens, village sites, and burial mounds." Avocational archaeologist Karl Squires dug there in the 1940s, and John Goggin recorded the site for the Florida Master Site File in the early 1950s. By that time the site had already been diminished by development and Goggin could locate none of the burial mounds referred to by Small.

The only description of a burial mound at the site is the following account from 1899 by Florence Miller, who had dug there with friends during a picnic outing at the natural bridge:

> A short distance west of the bridge was an elevation, into which we dug. We found skeletons buried on a level in a circle, head in feet out. An apparently perfect skull would crumble when exposed to air. There were shells on the skeletons, flat shells arranged as a necklace would be, a large one on the breast and smaller ones toward the neck. Each shell had two holes, as for a cord or string, but whatever held them was gone.[29]

Miller's picnic dig may have been an ominous sign of the future, because the twentieth century has not been kind to Arch Creek, nor to its natural or archaeological treasures. The site is among the most disturbed of all sites in Dade County. No less than five different excavation projects have been conducted there since Dan Laxson's dig in 1957, when he dug eight excavation squares.[30] The data provided by these excavation projects, particularly those done jointly by the Miami–West India Archaeological Society and the Broward County Archaeological Society, lobbying by activist Harvey Rubin, and finally the 1975 excavation project conducted by Florida's Division of Archives, History, and Records Management,[31] greatly contributed to the state's decision to acquire a large part of the Arch Creek site and preserve it as a park on the eve of its near destruction by development.

Among the major impacts to the site was the construction of NE 135th Street across the midden, permanently dividing the site into two sections. While most of the archaeological integrity of the southern component was permanently damaged by bulldozing in 1956 and again in the 1960s, the limestone bluffs and canoe landing have survived, along with part of the mangroves behind a shopping center.

The most ominous threat to the site was the proposed 1972 development of the area north of NE 135th Street as a car lot. Community activists rallied to preserve the property to prevent it from being just another paved development, and eventually their efforts succeeded when the land was acquired in 1974 as a public park. However, on the very eve of public acquisition, the natural bridge mysteriously collapsed into a pile of limestone rubble into the creek. Some suspected the developer who had lost his bid for the property. Others blamed a nearby passing train that jolted the ancient arch with its weight and vibrations.

Today, the land is a county park and is comanaged by the Arch Creek Trust, a group of citizens dedicated to maintaining and restoring the property's original hardwood hammock. A small museum and nature center was constructed there in 1983, and in 1986 the Arch Creek site was listed in the National Register of Historic Places. A replica of the stone bridge was reconstructed in 1986 by the county and Arch Creek Trust. The southern segment of the site, still on private lands, was eventually built over with a shopping center, although the river landing has survived.

Surfside Site (DA24)

A Tequesta canoeing from Arch Creek eastward across Biscayne Bay would arrive at Indian Creek, an estuary that twists through the mangroves on the lee side of the barrier island at present-day Surfside near Miami Beach. It is here that a large Tequesta village thrived in close proximity to a sand burial mound. A foot trail probably crossed the island, connecting the village to the Atlantic Ocean and allowing canoes to be hauled from the bay to the ocean. Today the site has disappeared beneath a modest neighborhood of homes and asphalt roads.

The Surfside midden and burial mound afforded easy access to the ocean and was not visible to enemies approaching from the sea. The ovoid midden had north-south dimensions measuring 372 feet and about 200 feet east-west. Vernon Lamme theorized that the midden may have been in the shape of a crescent, with the concave portion facing the waters of the bay, forming a possible harbor for canoes.[32] The midden ridge was reported to be as high as 6.31 feet from the bay bottom by surveyor Karl Squires. The crescent-shaped midden ridge is a type reported at other sites in Florida, and its shape is suggestive of the Archaic shell rings reported in other parts the southeastern United States, including Jupiter and the Ten Thousand Islands.[33] The possibility of an Archaic shell ring lying below the formative Glades period midden is tantalizing, suggesting that other parts of the site may lie underwater in the bay bottom. Reinforcing this possibility is that excavations on the midden encountered cultural material below the water table, suggesting that rising water tables may have encroached on the site.

The sand burial mound was situated about 100 feet north of the midden. The mound measured 70 feet east-west by 21 feet north-south. Its height was nearly identical to that of the midden mound. Botanist John Kunkel Small first reported that the burial mound was bulldozed in 1923 in preparation for development.[34] After the site's discovery was publicized, locals descended on the site with a vengeance and at least 100 burials were looted or destroyed.[35]

State archaeologist Vernon Lamme and Karl Squires were instrumental in initiating the WPA work at the Surfside site. The public works project began in May 1934 and continued through September 1934. Squires completed maps of the site while Lamme directed the excavations and dug. Lamme reports on his excavations:

> I dug up most of the street which ran through the burial mound [sic] but found that the steam roller which was used broke all the skeletal material into small bits; all except one skull down in the bottom of the creek bottom marl which had hardened into stone.[36]

Lamme describes most of the burials as secondary with at least two primary burials. He also recovered 19 skulls from near the center of the mound, but it is unclear as to whether other bones accompanied them. From the east side of the mound he uncovered human remains embedded in concretion, and under one skull he found a drilled fossil shark's tooth. Lamme reports that a total of 50 skulls were collected and that he then hid them in the mangroves, where they were later discovered by vandals who destroyed them by pitching the skulls against the coconut trees:

> The work however was stopped May 28th. And when the mound was visited the first of June it was discovered that all of the skeletal material which had been hidden in the mangroves had been visited by vandals and the material destroyed. The skulls had been ruthlessly cast against the surround [sic] coconut palm trees, evidently by small boys and the long bones broken and lying in the street.[37]

In September 1934, Lamme had uncovered enough artifacts and skeletal material to ship to Washington, D.C. He advised Matt Stirling that he had two barrels of artifacts and bones. "I have some good stuff," he quipped.[38] In the same year the habitation mound was a focal point of investigations by the WPA, with 125 workmen descending on the mound under the coordination of D. L. Reichard of the Smithsonian Institution. A total of 19 trenches were excavated across the midden. A lens of concretion characterized by hardened soil mixed with animal bone was uncovered below the loamy midden soil.

Artifact types were consistent with the Glades II and III periods, including Key Largo Incised and St. Johns Check Stamped pottery. D. L. Reichard shipped hundreds of artifacts to the Smithsonian Institution, including the following items:

5 shell celts
1 pottery knob
7 pkts. charcoal
32 pcs. deer horn
2 bdls shark teeth not drilled
10 shark teeth not drilled
2 post holes in coquina composition
6 shoe boxes burial bones
4 sacks burial bones[39]

Upon completion of the excavations, the midden mound was reconstructed by the WPA team on January 15, 1936, to its original form only to be destroyed again when it succumbed to residential development in the 1940s. Today only a few residential lots in a Surfside neighborhood preserve the remnants of what was once one of Florida's most significant sites.

Key Biscayne Site (DA3, DA4)

In prehistoric times, water travel on the leeward side of the barrier island provided the most ease of travel. Tequesta canoes would have encountered few breaks in the green wall of mangroves. Leaving the Surfside site southward you would soon pass present-day South Beach and Fisher Island, which prior to dredging Government Cut, was part of one island. It was here that the waters were treacherous as one crossed the cut with the open Atlantic Ocean to your left. If the tides are strong it requires vigorous paddling to reach Virginia Key, half a mile distant, where at least one prehistoric camp is reported in the dunes of the island's Atlantic side. Onward, past Bear Cut to Key Biscayne, food is plentiful, sea turtles nest in the summer, sea grapes abound, and the most extraordinary numbers of fish occur in the channel at the island's southern tip. Along the way are numerous camps and way stations for collecting the island's resources. One camp, 8DA5, at the island's midsection, is located at the head of an estuary through the mangroves. Today homes cover the site.

A large site on the bayside half a mile south of 8DA5, near the present-day canal that bounds the north side of Bill Baggs State Park, yielded evidence of habitation and prehistoric graves during monitoring of wetlands restoration in the 1990s. The largest site, 8DA3, is located at the southern tip of the island. John Goggin documented the disappearance of part of the site to the erosion of waves and storms. Much of the site is now several feet beneath the Atlantic, but after Hurricane Andrew, when park crews were clearing tree debris, hundreds of pieces of shell, animal bones, and artifacts were found, including Glades Tooled and St. Johns Check Stamped pottery sherds, indicating a Glades III occupation of the site. A large sand mound, 8DA4, was once located north of the lighthouse. Today only waves wash the beach sand where the palmetto-covered mound once existed.

Sands Key Site (DA2, DA4582)

From Key Biscayne southward a Tequesta canoe had to cross the swift currents of the channel known today as the Safety Valve, continuing across the tepid flats to the northern islets of the Florida Keys. Gliding on the lee side of Boca Chita, Tequesta canoes would have reached Sands Key. A narrow estuary led through the mangroves to a rocky upland hammock. It is here, hidden from view and obscured by forest, that one of the county's greatest archaeological sites was discovered.

In 1985, local residents Virginia Tannehill and Joe Knowles had braved the difficult terrain searching for bottles and driftwood when they stumbled onto large piles of conch shells over 3 feet high. There were at least 20 of these shell features with what appeared to be cleared paths between them. Tannehill and Knowles alerted Park Ranger Bill Hudson to their discovery.

In 1990 I conducted an assessment of the site in coordination with National Park Service staff.[40] A plane table map was completed at this site by John Beriault, Walter Buschelman, and Joe Long. My team and I excavated shovel tests and units revealing that this site is among the best preserved prehistoric sites in southeastern Florida. Testing revealed that the site was occupied primarily through the Glades III period, A.D. 1200–1700, as indicated by diagnostic pottery types such as Glades Tooled, St. Johns Check Stamped, and Surfside Incised.

The site was recorded as 8DA4582 but is probably the same location as 8DA2, recorded by John Goggin though never visited by him. Its location in Biscayne National Park will help assure that this site will be protected and preserved for future research and interpretation.

Cutler Site (DA8, DA9)

A one-hour canoe trip westward from the barrier islands brought the Tequesta to the county's most southerly uplands, which skirts Biscayne Bay. Pinewoods growing on the bay shore were a visual guide easily spotted from across the bay. As Tequesta canoes approached the pines, they made a hard right, aiming for the narrow channel that snaked into the black mangrove forest eventually giving way to a freshwater marsh. The marsh abutted a rocky shore festooned with lush hammock only a stone's throw from a bubbling freshwater spring that was the focal point of habitation.

Centuries of habitation have covered the rocky limestone with a midden mantle of rich organic soil. Only a short distance away are dangerous crevices and solution holes. A sand and rock burial mound lies a thousand feet from the village. Although the mound had been ravaged by Henry Perrine Jr. in the nineteenth century, the first documented visit by an archaeologist was by John Goggin in the 1940s. He persuaded the caretaker of the property to allow him and Charles Brookfield to visit the site, where they made a small surface collection.[41] The private estate owned by the Deering Danielson family of International Harvester fame was off limits for archaeological excavations and it wasn't until the 400-plus-acre estate was offered for development in 1984 that archaeologists were once again allowed onto the parcel. The assessment was conducted as part of the county's bid to acquire the parcel as a public park.

The county assessment documented a Glades II–III period occupation for the site and verified the significance of both the midden and the burial mound. This information contributed to the public acquisition of the parcel, and numerous evaluations of the park by archaeologists followed as the park plan was developed. One of the most interesting facts learned about the site was that some of the midden had been "mined" for use as gardening soil, likely by the Deering estate groundskeeper, who had moved wheelbarrows of midden soil mixed with artifacts to fill rocky solution holes in front of and around Deering's stone house. Such borrowing also may have been done earlier by pioneer homesteaders who built the town of Cutler within the hammock and pinewoods. Large areas of midden may have been redeposited around the Addison Homestead.

From Cutler, a voyage southward across Biscayne Bay and along the 120-mile length of the Florida Keys brought the Tequesta past Matecumbe to Cayo Hueso (Key West), the most southerly extent of their domain. From here it was an easy canoe trip across Florida Bay to Cape Sable, where the Tequesta bumped into the people of the Ten Thousand Islands—likely vassals of the Calusa during the Glades III period—and it was here that Tequesta territory reached its western border.

Part II

Failed Settlements
The European Legacy

Hermann Trappman, *Approaching the Polly Lewis Homestead on the Silver Bluff, Biscayne Bay,* 1983. Pencil on paper, 8 × 10. Collection of the Archaeological and Historical Conservancy. By permission of the artist.

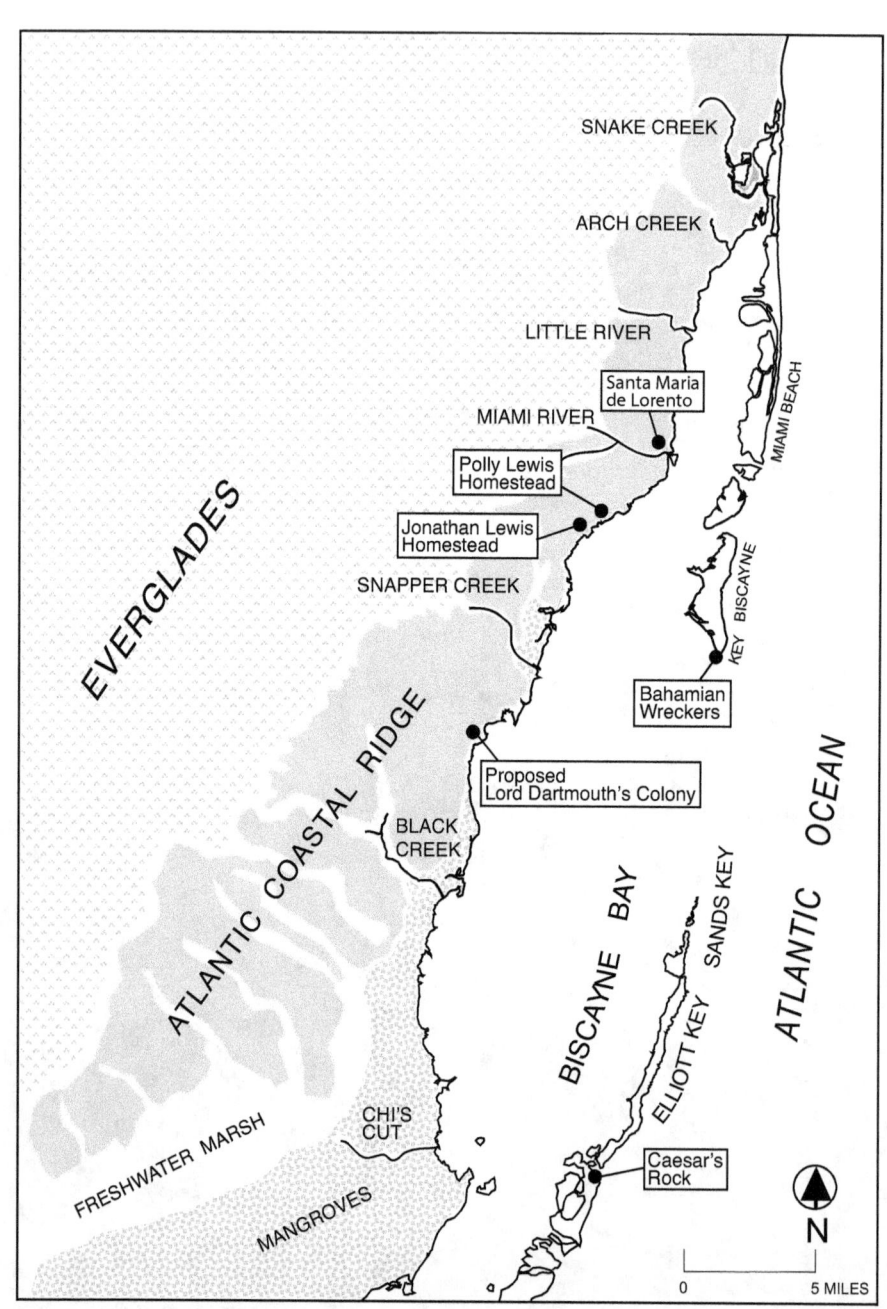

Spanish and English-Bahamian colonial sites of Miami-Dade County. Map created by John G. Beriault. Courtesy of the Archaeological and Historical Conservancy.

6

European Contact

The Transition to Extinction

The arrival of Columbus in the New World was perceived by the peaceful Lucayan Indians of the Bahamas as a celestial event. The Lucayans believed that Columbus and his crew were gods and that they and their three ships had sailed from the heavens. The Indians of Mexico gave similar reverence to Cortes and his mounted army when the Spanish arrived at Veracruz in 1519, but those beliefs were quickly dispelled when it was observed that the Spanish and their horses were subject to bleeding and even death when wounded—obviously less than adequate behavior for gods.

We know nothing of what perceptions Florida's natives had when they viewed their first Europeans. Although Juan Ponce de León is given credit for discovering Florida in 1513, there is a possibility that other Europeans had been shipwrecked on Florida's coast previous to his visit. The vulnerability of shipwrecked Europeans did not invite perceptions of immortality, and it is possible that Indians fleeing the Spanish slave raids in the Bahamas and Cuba may have provided helpful clues to Florida natives as to the true character of Spanish intentions and thus set a somber reception for the earliest European visitors.

It is known that when Ponce de León made his two Florida voyages he was attacked by Indians several times and eventually received a mortal wound from an Indian arrow while somewhere on the southwest Florida coast. The Florida native perception of the Europeans in the early sixteenth century is best summarized in a chilling account of Alvar Núñez Cabeza de Vaca's 1522 Florida expedition when he discovered on a beach near Tampa Bay three packing boxes typically used for shipping goods to Spain—each containing a butchered Spaniard, all apparent victims of the local reception committee.[1] Native Floridians, however, had no monopoly on cruelty. The Spanish equaled them in murders and atrocities, and this climate of hostility continued until Pedro Menéndez de Avilés scored a major diplomatic coup by establishing a shaky alliance with the chiefs of the Calusa and the Tequesta in 1567–68.

The Spanish Landings

It is believed that Ponce de León anchored near Key Biscayne, which is undoubtedly the island he refers to as Santa Marta. There he would have found fresh water, deer, and no shortage of other food. The earliest historic reference to the Indian village of Tequesta at the mouth of the Miami River is Antonio de Herrera y Tordesillas's reference to *Chequesta*.[2] It is possible that his knowledge of this village is based on a visit there by Ponce de León. Historians are uncertain of the exact facts of his Florida exploration because his log books have disappeared and our knowledge is largely attributed to Herrera, who had access to the log books. The Pineda map of Florida (1519) is believed by some historians to have its origins from Ponce's Florida voyages.

Much to the frustration of scholars, the vagueness and omissions in the written record are matched by a shortage of physical evidence buried in the ground to demonstrate the exact location of any landings. This sparseness in the archaeological record is because the early and brief visits by Europeans left little evidence that has been preserved, having been subjected to storms, beach erosion, and development over the centuries.

If Ponce de León filled his water casks at Key Biscayne, short of him carving his name on a limestone slab or leaving a stone cross, there is little that an archaeologist can find that would conclusively identify such a landing. And don't think people haven't looked for his artifacts. The Fountain of Youth Park in St. Augustine rested its claim of authenticity based on the owner's "discovery" of two impressive Ponce de León relics. In 1913, the owner revealed the discovery of an embossed metal goblet. No less impressive was the uncovering by his workmen of a stone cross carefully constructed from rocks. The owner noted that there were thirteen stones forming the horizontal arm and fifteen stones forming the vertical. With obvious satisfaction, he interpreted these numbers as representing the year 1513, the date of Ponce de León's landing. In reality, both the cross and the goblet were forgeries manufactured solely to increase tourism at the park. In fact, some historians suggest that Ponce's most northerly Florida landing was not in St. Augustine but in the vicinity of Cape Canaveral, and that the River of Crosses, where he placed a stone cross, was at Jupiter Inlet or St. Lucie Inlet.

The archaeologist's trowel is more likely to encounter the mundane than the dramatic. A good example of how the mundane can be linked to a significant event is provided by the discovery of some rather ordinary conch shells, apparently the refuse of a long forgotten meal on a beach in Ft. Lauderdale. The discovery was the result of an archaeological survey of the Bartlett Estate, the last undeveloped upland beach parcel in Broward County.[3] In 1984 an archaeological survey of the estate resulted in the discovery of a Tequesta site, 8BD1102. This discovery caused no particular excitement until an unusual pile of conch shells was spotted near the shore of a brackish water lagoon. The pile consisted of 27 *Strombus gigas* shells and numerous oysters. These conch shells may have provided an evening meal for a dozen or so people. But these shell eaters were not Indians. The clue to interpreting the origin and significance of the shells is provided by a single 3-inch hole appearing on the side of each. It is obvious to even the most casual observer that these holes were the result of people breaking the shell to remove the meat inside, but the hole was smashed into the wrong part of shell. The Tequesta were intimately familiar with the anatomy of the conch and easily removed the gastropod by a single small hole placed at the crown of shell, exactly placed to sever the muscle that connects the gastropod to its shell. No Tequesta would smash the shell wall with the inefficient hammer-like blows observed on the New River specimens. The only plausible explanation is that these conchs were opened by non-Indians who were new to Florida and the Caribbean. When the Spanish settled in the Caribbean basin in the early sixteenth century, they quickly learned Indian customs regarding food supplies and how to open conch. The people who ate this meal were newcomers and had not learned the regionally known methods for removing conch meat. The clinching piece of evidence suggesting Europeans was a hole caused by a metal sword or knife blade that had cut into one of the conch shell walls.

All the evidence indicates that Europeans ate these conchs and visited this once desolate beach. Two calibrated radiocarbon dates of the shells indicate a median date of A.D. 1547.5.[4] This culinary feature is physical evidence of the earliest European contact yet found in southern Florida. Who were these visitors? Were they shipwrecked castaways? Or was the site a camp from a landing of northern Europeans, such as English, Dutch, or French? Despite extensive diggings and several metal-detector surveys, only one artifact was found—a piece of lead slag near the shells suggesting that they had been melting lead, possibly to create musket balls. The identity of these visitors remains a mystery.

Spanish Settlement

The Spanish settlement of Florida began with the arrival of Pedro Menéndez de Avilés (fig. 6.1). His first objective was to secure Florida from the French, who had successfully established a fort and colony on the St. Johns River. Menéndez ruthlessly destroyed the French fort, slaughtering hundreds of the fleeing French colonists. In September 1565 he established St. Augustine, the first Spanish colony in Florida. Menéndez then shifted his attention to securing the Florida peninsula and finding a route across Florida that would provide a short cut from the Gulf of Mexico to the Atlantic. Perhaps his real agenda was finding his son, Juan Menéndez, who had been shipwrecked on the Florida coast during a storm several years earlier. He hoped Juan had been captured and was being held by a Florida tribe, like Juan Escalante de Fontaneda, who had been shipwrecked in the Florida Keys in about 1549. Held captive by the Calusa for seventeen years, Fontaneda, now deeply tanned and fully native in his appearance, was rescued by Menéndez. Fontaneda became an important liaison to Menéndez, able to translate the Indian languages of South Florida and provide information on Indian towns and geography. Fontaneda furnished the first written description of Tequesta:

> Toward the north of the Martyrs and near a place of the Indians called Tegesta, situated on the bank of a river which extends into the country the distance of fifteen leagues, and issues from another lake of fresh water, which is said by some Indians to be an arm of the Lake of Mayami [Lake Okeechobee].[5]

He also described the Tequesta people and their lands, likely based on his own firsthand visits:

> These Indians occupy a very rocky and very marshy country. They have no product of mines or things we have in this part of the world. The men go naked, and the women in a shawl made of a kind of palm leaf, split and woven. They are subjects of Carlos [the cacique] and pay him tribute of all the things I have before mentioned, food and roots, the skins of deer, and other articles.[6]

Menéndez successfully created his first alliance in South Florida with the powerful Calusa. Landing on Florida's southwest coast with over five hundred men, he used Fontaneda to arrange a meeting with Carlos. After an exchange of gifts, Menéndez lured Carlos onto his ship with the intent

Figure 6.1. Portrait of Pedro Menéndez de Avilés. Courtesy of the Historical Museum of Southern Florida.

of holding him captive. There he bartered for the release of shipwrecked Christian captives—five women and three men who were subsequently brought to the ship and freed. Carlos provided a feast for the arrival of the powerful Spanish adelanto. Menéndez arrived for the meal at the principal Calusa village—which was likely Mound Key in present-day Estero Bay—with 200 arquebusiers, two fifers and drummers, three trumpeters, one harpist, one violinist, one psalter, a singer, a dancer, and a dwarf.

After Menéndez's forced "marriage" by Carlos to his sister, Menéndez achieved status, power, and an alliance with the southern Florida tribes that could never have occurred using warfare or brute force. His marriage and alliance provided him with an inadvertent opportunity to ally with the Tequesta. In 1567, Menéndez learned that soldiers from St. Augustine had mutinied and fled southward along the Florida coast. Twenty of the mutineers arrived at the village of Tequesta at the mouth of the Miami River. To their surprise they were greeted warmly and welcomed by the Tequesta cacique, who already was aware that Menéndez and Carlos were "relatives." Menéndez's nephew, Pedro Menéndez Marquez, rescued 12 of the mutineers from the Tequesta and reported to his uncle that they had been treated well and had not been taken captive or killed, as formerly had been the case for Spaniards landing or shipwrecked off southern Florida. This shift in Tequesta behavior was because they knew of the Menéndez marriage to Carlos's sister. When the Calusa learned that the Spanish mutineers were in the Tequesta town, they sent a party to "collect" them and transferred them to Carlos, but the Tequesta refused and a fight broke out. Two of the Calusa emissaries were killed. This conflict indicates that the Calusa-Tequesta relationship was dynamic and not a simple "vassal" relationship of the Tequesta to the Calusa.

Although the Tequesta paid tribute to Carlos, they considered the Calusa their enemy, and the Spanish-Calusa alliance that the Tequesta responded to so favorably was more of an awareness that a similar alliance between their tribe and the Spanish was in their interest, not only because of the potential protection it offered but also because of the dazzling array of gifts they hoped to receive. If they could create a similar alliance with the Spanish, a whole new portal for receiving European objects could be opened.

Pedro reported to his uncle that the Tequesta had presented him with gifts and offered to become Christians. He reported that many of the Indians were wearing a red cross painted on their throats and asked for a cross to be erected in their village. The Tequesta cacique surprisingly sent four Indian men and women, including his brother, with Pedro to Havana. Delighted with this turn of events, Menéndez sent a present to the Tequesta cacique and a letter to the seven mutineers still remaining in the village, telling them that if they were willing to stay in the village and help Christianize the Tequesta, learn their language, and help foster an alliance with the natives, he would intercede on their behalf with the king and seek pardons for their act of mutiny and theft of government property.

Menéndez returned to Spain feeling like the victor. On July 20, 1567, he was received in the court of Seville trumpeting his success in taming Florida's indigenous people.[7] In less than two years he had pushed the French out of Florida and established forts and pueblos across the Florida peninsula, including at Tequesta. He had developed alliances with the South Florida Indians that would guarantee a buffer from English and French expansion and hopefully assure that shipwrecked Spaniards would be well treated and not killed or held captive as had been the custom. In his court appearance he was joined by the brother of the Tequesta cacique as proof this new alliance. It appeared that the Menéndez initiative had completely changed the course of Spanish influence in Florida.

Unknown to Menéndez was that the Spanish alliance was quickly unraveling. Brother Francisco Villarreal, a Jesuit priest who had been making progress in converting some of the Tequesta to Christianity, was encountering trouble. When he began treating the sick with prayer, it raised the wrath of the Tequesta shaman, who accused Villarreal of having doomed one ill Indian girl by having touched her. However, Villarreal was having doubts of his own about the effect of his work. In a long letter to Father Juan Rogel, he wrote,

> I need Your Reverence to advise me . . . and also if it is well to go to speak to them when they are ill to persuade them to become Christians, because at such a time they open up readily, and I am in doubt whether they do it out of fear, or with a lack of comprehension, or out of some love or desire for some food of corn, which they desire greatly.[8]

The letter was delivered by a brig under command of Captain Francisco with as many as 30 soldiers on board.[9] Also on the ship were Fontaneda and the Carlos heir, using his new Christian name of Don Pedro. The ship left Tequesta and continued to Carlos, where a new alliance could be nurtured.

In February 1567, Menéndez and his nephew Pedro left Cuba with seven ships bound for Carlos. On board was his new Calusa wife, renamed Doña Antonia, and the Tequesta Indians who had departed with the mutineers.

Also on board were two Jesuit priests, Father Rogel and Brother Villarreal. At Carlos, the Spanish build a chapel, houses for the Christians, and a house for Doña Antonia, and with a final stroke of diplomacy, Menéndez arranged for a peace between the Calusa and Tequesta.

In March, Menéndez departed Carlos and sailed for Tequesta, leaving Father Rogel and the soldiers. He sent Brother Villarreal and his nephew on without him while he pursued another ship of mutineers he encountered, but eventually he joined the entourage at the Tequesta town on the Miami River. Solís de Merás described Menéndez's arrival there:

> He was very well received by the cacique and those Indians: he made great peace with them: they took him for their elder brother: he left there thirty soldiers, and . . . as their captain; and left them a saw, and some carpenters to build a blockhouse. He erected a cross with great devoutness. The Indians worshipped it: he left there Father Francisco [Villarreal] of the Society of Jesus: he remained there four days in that pueblo: great was his satisfaction at seeing that every morning and evening all the Indian men and women, big and little, hastened to the cross to worship it and kiss it with great devotion.[10]

Within months after the Spanish arrival open warfare had broken out between the new settlers and their Indian hosts, ending their brief peaceful coexistence. Father Rogel, in a letter of March 5, 1570, wrote an account of the demise of the Tequesta mission:

> If the Devil had not put an obstacle in the way, using the Christians themselves in order to prevent it. For it is thus that wherever we Spanish are, [we are] so proud and unrestrained that we try to trample everything underfoot, and thus the soldiers of the fort began to treat the natives in the same way [they would have] if they had conquered them by war, subjecting them to grievous insults and mistreatments; because of which, when the Indian could endure it no longer, they first warned them that they should leave, [saying] that this was not a good land for settling; and when they were not able to settle it by warnings, they decided to kill those that they could, among the Spaniards and set fire to their own village and so they did.[11]

Brother Villarreal reports that the conflict began when an old Tequesta chief insulted a Spanish soldier. In response the soldiers killed him, which then led to retaliation by the Tequesta.[12] When Pedro Menéndez Marquez returned to the village with supplies, he discovered 23 Spaniards and Christians, including Villarreal, all hiding in a house without food or water. Four Spaniards had been killed. One of them had been split open and his entrails placed on a pole for everyone to see.[13]

It is likely that after the hasty departure of the Spanish all of the mission structures were burnt. However, after these hostilities forced the Spanish evacuation, the most unexpected event occurred. The cacique's brother, Don Diego, returned from Spain and was able to convince his brother to make peace with the Spanish. Dazzled by what he had seen, Don Diego convinced his tribe to welcome the Spanish and reopen the mission and to build a house for the new Jesuit father, who would arrive soon. Each day an Indian was sent out to look for the returning ship. Finally, on December 4, 1568, the newly appointed priest, Father Antonio Sedeno, arrived at Tequesta after a stormy voyage and reported his dramatic arrival:

> For us the storm lasted three days; and the Lord wished that we should be forced to return to Tequesta, and, when we fired a shot the Indians came on board, and with the chief and Don Diego and we arranged the peace, and he, through a visit of the notary, gave obedience to King Philip, promising to become a Christian with all his people, and as pledge of this they brought two beautiful pines for a cross, which was made and planted where the first one had been, while singing the litanies with great devotion. And all went to adore it with great reverence, and the chief himself with his Indians, showing great joy.[14]

The settlement, manned by 20 to 30 soldiers, was abandoned a second time in 1570, but the reason for this final failure is unknown, since no records have been found to indicate the specifics of this event. Menéndez's diplomatic front was a failure. By 1573, he was providing depositions to the council of the Indies to support his request to wage total war against the Indians. Christians were again no longer safe in South Florida. In 1572, nine shipwrecked sailors were lured ashore and then killed by darts and clubs. Only one, Captain Calderon, was successfully rescued by paying a ransom.[15]

Documentation on the Tequesta during the seventeenth century is scant, but the on-again, off-again relations undoubtedly vacillated based on opportunities for trade and the occasional ransom extracted for shipwrecked captives. In 1622, a salvage expedition was sent from St. Augustine to "Bocas de Miguel Mora," the inlet south of Key Biscayne, to trade for valuables salvaged by the Indians, much of which had traveled by Indian trade northward from the Keys.[16] The real value of the South Florida Indians became apparent to the Spanish during their zealous salvage of shipwrecks along the Florida coast. Indians were highly sought as divers during this period and paid with alcohol, tobacco, iron implements, and beads. Indian divers were used throughout South Florida and even taken as far as the Bahamas to salvage the *Nuestra Señora de las Maravillas*.[17]

It was obvious that a strategic presence in southeast Florida could be instrumental in protecting Spanish interests and safeguarding shipwrecked Spaniards and treasure. The courting of South Florida Indians was successful in 1607 when they were invited by the Florida governor to attend a festival in St. Augustine. Governor Ibarra reported that over 500 Indians attended the event.[18] The governor suggested that a fort be built at the "Head of the Martyrs" with Indian assistance.[19] This site could only be at Key Biscayne or the Miami River, where high ground or a strategic advantage is offered. In 1600 Governor Alonso de los Almas had made an identical request, noting that with 100 men they could control the whole south coast. In 1628, Governor Borjas again invited the South Florida Indians to St. Augustine, hoping they would keep an eye on the expanding Dutch and English presence, but by 1700 the Tequesta cultural disintegration was well under way, including a population decline likely fostered by diseases spread through contact with the Spanish. Even the name Tequesta begins to fade from usage.

In 1675, Bishop Caldron referred to the 13 tribes of southern Florida, including the "Vizcayanos," which was likely the Tequesta Indians of Biscayne Bay. In 1765, cosmographer Fernán de Martínez described the Tequesta and their area as

> head of the Martyrs including the Keys or Cape Florida, which Juan Ponce de Leon discovered [and] on which he landed in the year 1512 ... its coasts by Indians of the Tequesta nation, who today are called Costas Indians.[20]

The disintegration of the Tequesta and other South Florida tribes accelerated in the early eighteenth century. In 1704 Indians from the Keys sought refuge in Havana from the alarming increase in raids by the Lower Creeks.[21] In 1711, a Spanish vessel arrived in Cuba with Indian refugees fleeing Yamassee war parties that were capturing local Indians for sale as slaves to the English for indigo and rice plantations. Bishop Gerónimo Valdéz sent two ships to the Keys to pick up the other besieged Indians—all remnants of Tequesta, Calusa, and other South Florida tribes. There was room for only 270 refugees, but over 2,000 Indians arrived to board the ship. The 270 on board were the tribal elite, including chiefs of the Calusa, Jobe, Maiyami, Concha, Musepa, and Rio Seco. Their elite status provided far less an advantage than they may have wished. Within a short period, four of the chiefs were dead as well as over 200 of the refugees. Approximately 16 to 18 returned to Florida to join an estimated 6,000 Indians who still remained.[22]

In 1732, an attempt was made to round up Indians desiring to emigrate to Cuba, but except for attending a four-day feast on board the ship, all of the Indians departed the ship and returned to their villages. The ships returned to Cuba empty. The governor understandably became dubious about future Indian emigrations and ended them.

On July 13, 1743, the Cuban officials established a mission, Santa Maria de Loreto, on the north bank of the Miami. Father Joseph Maria Monaco and Joseph Xavier Alaña were sent to establish the mission. They found the remnants of three Indian nations—the Keys, Carlos (also a name for the Calusa tribe), and Boca Raton—represented by 180 men, women, and children. At a distance of up to four days travel were three other nations—the Mayami, Santa Luzes, and Maracas—representing another 100 souls.[23]

The Alaña letter was the first vivid description of the Tequesta—or what was left of them—since the sixteenth century. Alaña described their reception as cold. The Indians demanded that if the Spanish intended to build a church in their village, they would have to pay a tax, and if Spaniards were to settle there, they had to pay a tribute to the chief since the lands belonged to him, not the king of Spain. Despite Indian resistance, Alaña had a great vision for the settlement of the Miami River. The land, he wrote, is "capable of so great a settlement that with ten or twelve years of cultivation it will attract the families that have remained in San Augustin, Florida, through so many frights and losses, leaving there only with its fort and garrison." He recommended that convicts be brought to clear the land because the Indian men are only capable of the light work of fishing and the others are the elite or warriors, who are exempt from work.[24]

Alaña believed that the South Florida tribes were on the verge of extinction and would need aid if they were to be preserved:

> If these tiny little tribes fight constantly and they are shrinking, as is testified by the remembrance of the greater number there was twenty years ago, so if they are left to their barbarous ways, they will have disappeared in a few years, whether on account of the skirmishes, or on account of the rum they will drink until they burst, or on account

of the children that they account, or on account of those whom the small pox carries off for lack of a remedy, and, finally whether on account of those who perish at the hand of the Uchises.[25]

Alaña and the priests tolerated the continual insults and abuses by the Tequesta, who claimed that the Spanish had not been invited to their town. To prove to the Tequesta that their fear of their god was unreasonable, the priests broke and burned the wooden idol of a bird—the guardian of the Tequesta cemetery and the temple, which was likely a charnel house of the Indian dead. Not surprisingly this action was not well received by the Tequesta. The Alaña report, with its detailed account on the fundamental listlessness and hostilities of the Indians, was responded to by the governor of Cuba with decisiveness. He promptly ordered the Miami mission closed. By 1744 the last Spanish mission in Tequesta was no more.

The final breath of the town of Tequesta was extinguished in 1761, when the Uchises, Indian allies of the English, forced them to abandon their Miami River settlements and all other villages on the coast except for Cayo Hueso (Key West), their final stand, from where they fled to Havana. On February 28, 1762, 48 Uchises overpowered the canoes of the "coastal" Indians, killing or enslaving them.

In 1763 Spain ceded Florida to England at the end of the Seven Years' War. In 1770 English surveyor Bernard Romans landed on the north bank of the Miami River and saw the ruins of the 1743 mission, which he described as "Pueblo Ratton town," and wrote that Key West and Key Vaca were the last refuge of the Calusa nation, where the "last remnants of these tribes, consisting of about eighty families, left this last possession of their native lands and went to Havannah."[26]

In less than 200 years after the Menéndez expedition, the Tequesta and all of southern Florida's indigenous people had become extinct as a culture. Those who survived were scattered along the coast, fishing and trading with Cuba. Their few descendents became part of the quilt of Cuban mestizos and mulattos, and those who survived in Florida, many also of mixed blood, who became known as the "Spanish Indians," would eventually become absorbed by the Seminoles and Miccosukees. In 1744 the Miami River and its ancient villages were for the first time void of Tequesta voices. Only the wind and birds broke the silence. The Tequesta legacy was reduced to buried artifacts, graves, and mounds. The abandoned villages and camps, once clear and open of vegetation, were quickly overtaken by hardwood hammock forests.

The Spanish mission legacy, marked by violence, disease, and enslavement, has left few clues in the archaeological record. Some of the most interesting artifacts discovered during archaeological excavations include a possible brass hinge from a Bible recovered during the demolition of the Dupont Plaza component of 8DA11 in 2006 (fig. 6.2). Other mission-related artifacts found at the Granada site, 8DA11, include rosary beads, some made from polished stone such as jet and cut crystal, and one fancy glass bead decorated with appliqué glass to create stemmed roses (fig. 6.3).

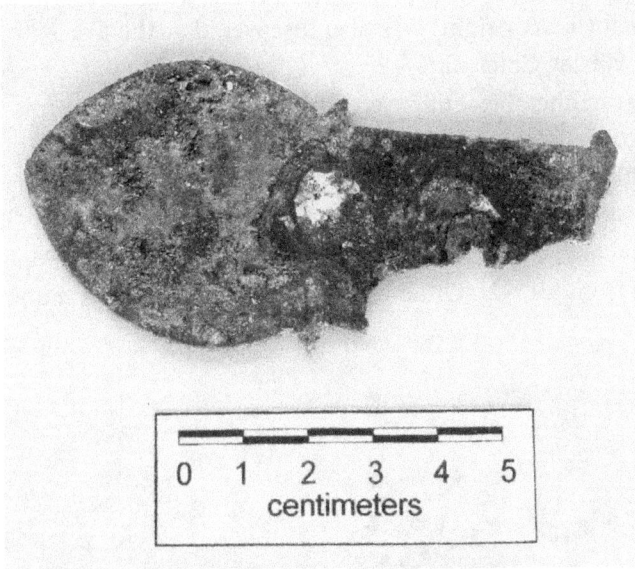

Figure 6.2. Bronze Bible hinge from 8DA11. Collection of the Archaeological and Historical Conservancy.

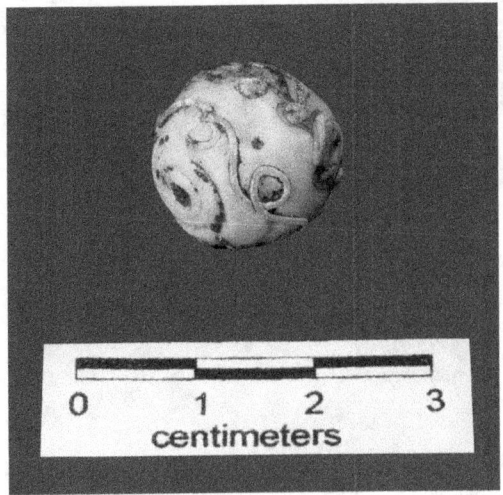

Figure 6.3. Fancy eighteenth-century rosary bead from 8DA11. Collection of the Historical Museum of Southern Florida.

Other trade amulets or artifacts possibly linked to the Santa Maria de Loreto mission in 1743 are two brass bells found by the Archaeological Society of Southern Florida in 2006 while sifting soils salvaged from new construction at the Dupont component of 8DA11 on the east side of the Brickell Bridge. One bell is a "flushloop," a subtype of flush-edged rumbler bell, measuring 35 millimeters in diameter (fig. 6.4 left). From the same spoil pile an open cast-brass bell measuring 57 millimeters in length and 50 millimeters wide at its widest point was found (fig. 6.4 center). It has a remnant silver finish and an attached suspension clip. These bells may have been part of a priest's garb. The flushloop bell dates from about 1600–1670.[27] A brass rumbler bell (fig. 6.4 right) was also discovered at the Trail site, 8DA34, by the late Wesley Coleman.

Perhaps the most telling object uncovered from the South Florida mission effort is the bronze host press allegedly found at Mound Key—site of Carlos—in the 1980s. The host press was manufactured in Potosí Bolivia and used for making communal wafers. The artifact is imprinted with "I am the living bread who descends from heaven Holy Christ of Potosi." Pope Leo X's reign dates from 1513–21. Other important Spanish artifacts found

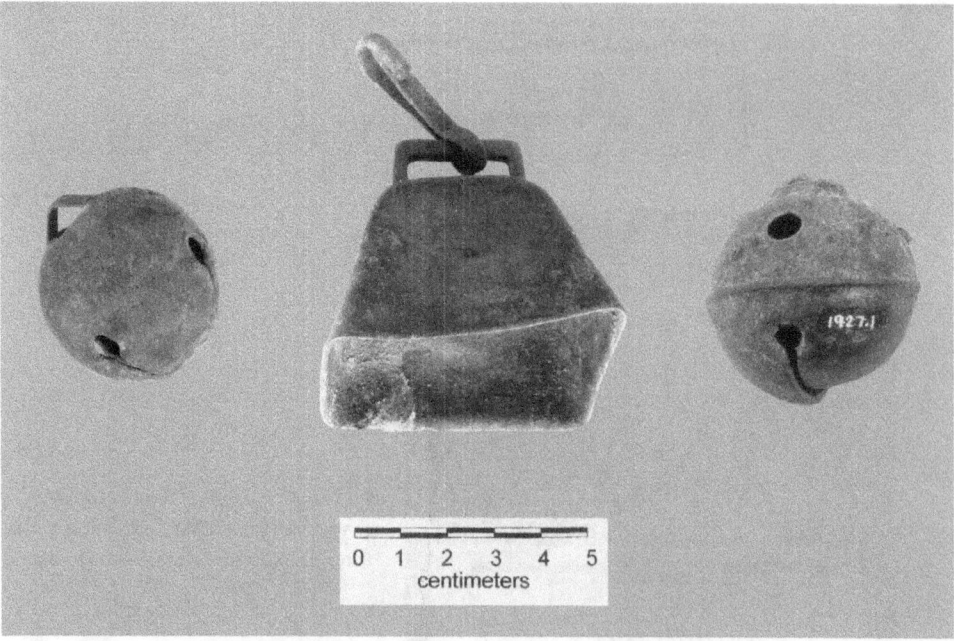

Figure 6.4. Three brass bells. *Left to right:* flushloop bell from 8DA11, open cast brass bell from 8DA11, brass rumbler bell from 8DA34. Collection of the Archaeological and Historical Conservancy.

in South Florida include two wooden statuettes found in the mangrove forest of Elliott Key by Virginia Tannehill in the 1970s. One is a Spanish corsair (fig. 6.5) and the other is Virgin Mary (fig. 6.6).

Left: Figure 6.5. Wooden statuette of a corsair found at Elliott Key. Collection of Everglades National Park.
Right: Figure 6.6. Wooden statuette of the Virgin Mary found at Elliott Key. Collection of Everglades National Park.

Acculturation

The response of the Tequesta, who were basically living in a shell and bone culture, to the metal culture of the Europeans was like dipping a hand into honey through a swarm of bees. Native Floridians probably viewed European metals, pots, cloth, and bottles as wonderful objects and their arrival as the most fortuitous of events. There can be little doubt that the numerous shipwrecks off the Florida coast were largely responsible for the natives' sudden wealth. Many ships en route to Spain after picking up cargo in Central America, Mexico, and Cuba sailed close to the South Florida coast and fell prey to the storms that dragged the ships across the treacherous reefs and sank them in shallow water.

Whereas one might imagine that the Indian sites of southern Florida are filled with the gold and silver of the Indies, the truth is that surprisingly little has been found in the way of precious metals. Instead, the Spanish wealth is represented by iron nails and spikes, sherds of Spanish pots and jars, and even ship ballast stones. To Florida's natives during the early sixteenth century, these utilitarian items were equal in value if not more valuable than gold and silver. What gold and silver that was salvaged by the Indians became the target of numerous Spanish trading expeditions, who worked hard at recovering their lost wealth. There is one account of how Florida natives were persuaded to trade their golden ornaments for a large iron spike.

A typical assemblage of Spanish artifacts recovered in Miami-Dade County was provided by the archaeological work at the Grenada site and DuPont Plaza, 8DA11, along the north bank of the Miami River. This was the site where two known Spanish missions were constructed. The location of the mission site is now common knowledge as a result of the translation of Spanish archival documents. But earlier ideas on the location of these sites were far off the mark. The Federal Writers Project in 1934 had located the missions in present-day El Portal. Other theories making the rounds among popular writers in 1930s–1940s were that the missions were located in Coconut Grove; one version had it that the missions were on San Ignacio Street in Coral Gables. As recently as the 1950s archaeologist John Goggin believed that the Tequesta mission was located on the Little River near NE Seventy-ninth Street, but he altered his opinion when he became aware of the relevant Spanish documents.

In recent years, a large assemblage of European artifacts has been uncovered at 8DA11, confirming the historical record. These artifacts reflect the typical Spanish cultural materials used in the Americas from the sixteenth through eighteenth centuries. The most common Spanish artifacts are ceramic sherds, which include olive jars, earthenware, and majolica. Majolica was a type of pottery commonly used in Spain and the American colonies. The majolica was shaped on a potter's wheel into a variety of dishes, cups, platters, and bowls. Colorful designs were often painted below the lustrous tin glaze. When the Spanish began their colonization of the New World, they quickly adapted their Old World majolica techniques to the ancient Indian pottery centers of the Caribbean and Mexico and began a variety of majolica traditions that continue to this day. Archaeologist John Goggin, who wrote a paper on majolica in the New World,[28] classified it into specific styles and dates of use, thus providing other archaeologists with a tool to date sites of Spanish contact. His work was greatly expanded by the studies done by Kathleen Deagan in both St. Augustine and the Caribbean.[29]

Although no complete majolica vessels have been found in Miami-Dade County, the numerous sherds found reveal a variety of types. Not surprisingly, 90 percent of the sherds in the Historical Museum of Southern Florida collection are from the Granada site. The remaining specimens were collected from six different sites, four of them located in the east Everglades and the other two at coastal sites. Most of the specimens date from the seventeenth century. About 20 percent are Puebla Blue on White (fig. 6.7A) and 40 percent are San Luis Blue on White (fig. 6.7B, 6.7C). One specimen of Aucilla Polychrome (fig. 6.7D) and Ichtucknee Blue on Blue are also represented, as well as three specimens of Columbia Plain, a type dating from prior to about 1650. These majolica sherds suggest that between about 1650 and 1700 the influx of Spanish materials in southeast Florida was at its peak. The sudden decline of majolica after 1700 probably reflects the decline of the Tequesta population rather than diminishing Spanish influence.

The most common Spanish ceramic type found in South Florida is the olive jar. Like majolica, the ceramic "olive jar," or tinaja, is commonly associated with Indian sites affected by Spanish contact. The rounded-bottom containers have their roots in Greek and Roman amphora. The olive jar was like the contemporary tin can. It provided a sturdy storage container that was used for storing and transporting food and spirits. An important secondary use for the vessels was as a container for water storage, and it is probable that the Florida Indians were reusing the jars for various types of storage.

John Goggin divides the chronological evolution of olive jars into three

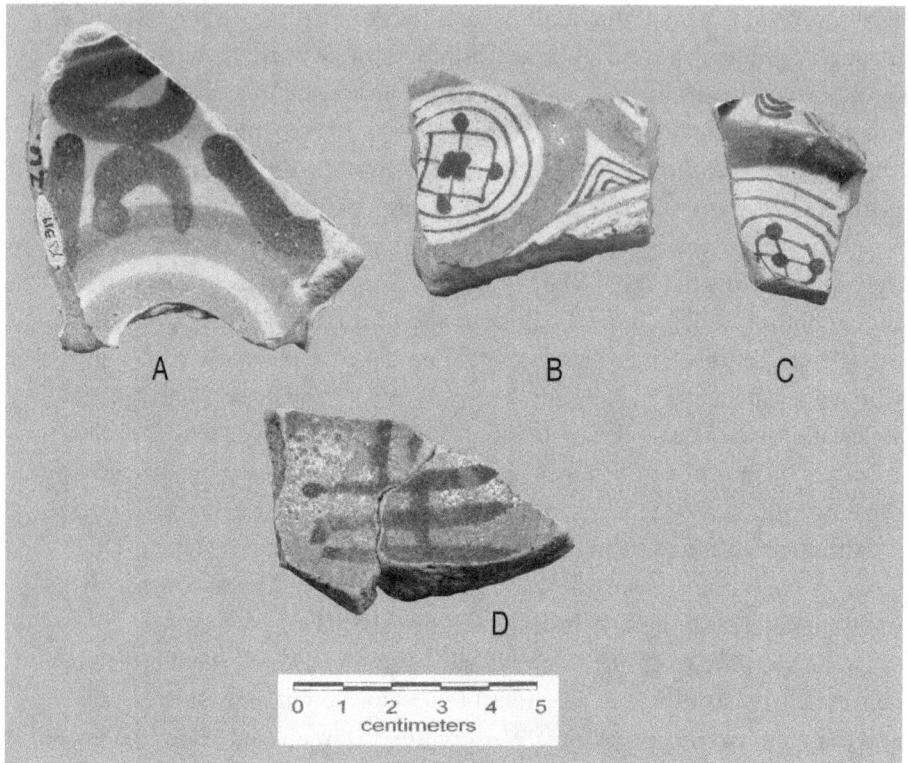

Figure 6.7. Majolica sherds: Puebla Blue on White (A), San Luis Blue on White (B and C), Aucilla Polychrome (D). Collection of the Historical Museum of Southern Florida.

styles.[30] He describes the early styles as a "medium-sized globular vessel with a small flaring, or collared, mouth, having a loop handle on each side." Goggin dates this early style as being manufactured between 1500 and 1575. No recognizable early-style specimens have been found at the Granada site, which is surprising since it is likely that the Granada site is very close to the Menéndez mission and fort.

Goggin divides the middle style into three different types, all varying in size and/or form but all basically egg-shaped with a ring or collared mouth. These types range in age from about 1580 to 1780. Most of the olive jar sherds found in southeast Florida are of the middle style. A number of specimens have green glazes, varying from olive to emerald green. Most of these sherds have been found at the Granada site, suggesting increasing Spanish-Indian contact during the seventeenth and eighteenth centuries. The recovery of complete vessels is fairly rare in Florida (aside from shipwrecks), but during the course of Miami-Dade's Historic Preservation Division's archaeological survey, a nearly complete middle-style jar was found in the eastern Everglades (fig. 6.8).

Late-style vessels have a large number of variations that include the previous types of the Middle period with the addition of a top-shaped vessel. They date from roughly 1780 to 1860. Several early-nineteenth-century American and Bahamian sites along Biscayne Bay have produced late-style olive jars sherds, indicating trade with Cuba. A specimen dating from circa

Figure 6.8. An olive jar found in the eastern Everglades. Collection of the Historical Museum of Southern Florida.

1858–60, now partially restored, was uncovered from the Arch Creek mill race during excavations there in 1981. Excavations of the Polly Lewis house site dating from about 1810–35 also yielded olive jar sherds. The presence of late-style olive jar sherds in early- to mid-nineteenth-century Bahamian and American pioneer homesteads suggest the importance of Cuban trade, and that olive jars were part of the household inventory of Florida's first pioneers.

In 1981 sherds from a yellow-clay water bottle, known as a hidroceramo, was uncovered in a solution hole beneath a parking lot on SE First Street. The jar is made of pale yellow clay and has a narrow mouth and two handles. A similar hidroceramo sherd was found at Arch Creek (8DA23). In 2006 a hidroceramo (grayware) sherd, circa 1780–1820, was recovered by the Archaeological Society of Southern Florida from salvaged sediments at the Dupont Hotel component of 8DA11.

There is little discernible effect from the influx of Spanish ceramics into the Tequesta community. Certainly the well-made olive jars and colorful majolica offered an attractive alternative, but traditional ceramics were not abandoned. Glades Tooled Rim and St. Johns Check Stamped were prevalent, and in one interesting occurrence, a St. Johns Check Stamped bowl was modified with an iron wire to create a handle. A sherd from this modified bowl was found at the Granada site, 8DA11. Another interesting modified ceramic was the use of a sherd of Spanish majolica to create a pendant.

The importance of the Florida Indian trade for the Spanish is reflected in a document uncovered by historian Eugene Lyons while doing research in Cuba.[31] The document is a claim put forth to the Cuban governor for an unpaid bill for *medelatas* of copper and brass made to sell or trade to the Florida Indians. These medals may refer to the metal tablets that have been found throughout southwest Florida and the Lake Okeechobee–Kissimmee area and now familiar to many scholars because of its use as a logo by the Florida Anthropological Society. These medals are usually engraved with a complex design featuring a sun above and a face-like design on the lower half. Sometimes crescents or moons are incised on the reverse. Although these metal tablets have been reported from other parts of Florida, none are known from southeast Florida or from any Tequesta site.[32]

Some of the most common trade items encountered in Indian sites are glass trade beads. Glass beads arrived in the New World with Columbus on his first voyage to San Salvador when he presented the Lucayans "with strings of glass beads to wear upon the neck."[33] Beads were destined to become part of the archaeological record of the New World in sites from as far north as Hudson Bay to as far south as Argentina. Bead manufacturing centers arose in Holland and in at least two locations in Spain. Apparently, no glass bead manufacturing ever occurred in North America.

A classification system for beads has challenged scholars for years, and several systems have been offered that classify beads according to manufacturing techniques (i.e., Kidd, Beck) and by descriptive types that are often confusing and misleading, such as "Hudson Bay," "Russian blues," and "Carnelian d'Aleppo," which refer to places where beads were found. Studies have determined these geographic associations are not necessarily correct; for example, the "Russian blues," found at native sites in Alaska and the Pacific Northwest, were actually manufactured in Belgium. Archaeologist John Goggin, prior to his death in 1964, attempted to culminate his years of experience with Spanish contact artifacts by writing a paper that described these artifacts.[34] His work is among the first to classify the beads of Florida.[35] It was his objective to provide useful chronological markers for the archaeologist studying contact period sites. More recently, a major study of early-sixteenth-century beads in Spanish sites was done by Marvin Smith.[36]

The glass beads uncovered on Tequesta sites in South Florida represent a great variety of types. The earliest types reported are chevrons and other wire wound varieties—mostly dating from the seventeenth century. No glass beads from the sixteenth century have yet been reported in Miami-Dade County, although they undoubtedly occur. A chevron bead was discovered by the Archaeological Society of Southern Florida at the Cheetum site, 8DA1058, and another likely chevron was found at the Granada site. One of the most interesting glass ornaments found at the Granada site is a Punta Rassa pendant. A small (1 centimeter long) blue specimen (fig. 6.9) was discovered during monitoring for the swimming pool at the Hyatt Center at 8DA11. The specimen dates from about A.D. 1650 to 1700.[37] Overall, the seventeenth- and eighteenth-century dates of the glass beads reported from the Granada site are consistent with the age of the other European artifacts from the site.

In addition to glass beads, Goggin discusses cut crystal beads, a signature artifact from early Spanish contact sites. Cut Florida crystals are probably European in origin and according to Goggin are typically sixteenth century. A crystal cut bead, possibly from a rosary, was uncovered at the Granada site. Cut and polished rock beads reported for the area include two specimens made from carnelian (fig. 6.9) and one of turquoise found at

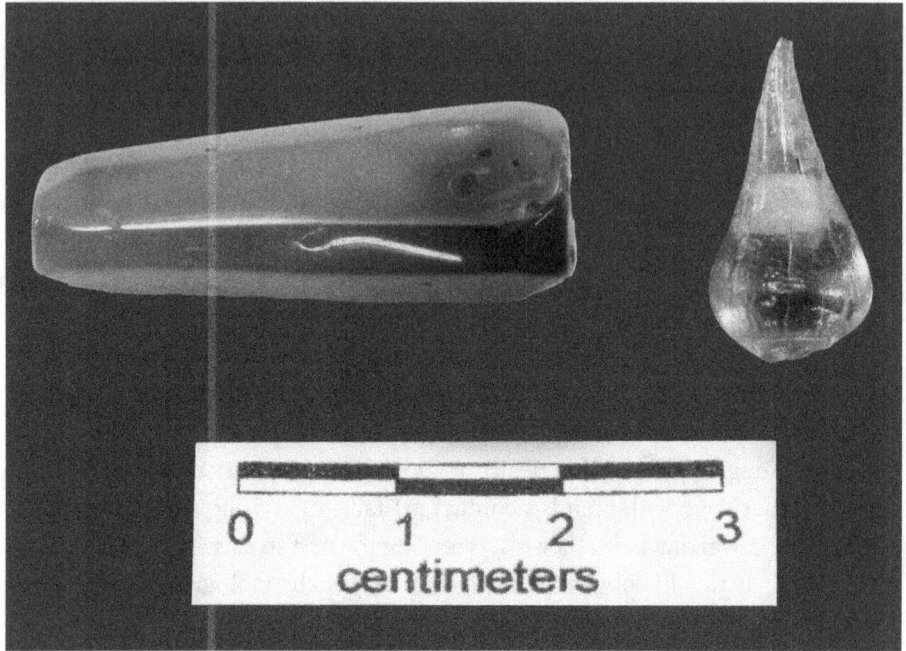

Figure 6.9. Carnelian bead from 8DA1058 and Punta Rassa pendant from 8DA11. Collection of the Historical Museum of Southern Florida.

Arch Creek. One of the carnelian beads was uncovered from an east Everglades site, 8DA1058, and the other from the Charles Deering Estate.[38] The turquoise bead may be evidence of Central American artifacts that were salvaged from shipwrecks or simply traded by the Spanish. Other Central American and Meso-American ceramic artifacts and copper artifacts have been found in southern Florida.

Perhaps the most common European artifacts are iron objects such as nails, spikes, scissors, and other miscellaneous utilitarian objects. Because they are subject to severe oxidation and are not easily identified, they often go unidentified. Many large iron spikes, most likely salvaged from shipwrecks, have been reported from contact period sites, including many in the Everglades. Other obvious shipwreck objects include ballast stones discovered at the now destroyed Trail site, 8DA34.

Spanish period glass bottles are particularly rare in Tequesta sites, although one broken "onion" bottle, 1710–15, was found at 8DA34. The distribution of European objects at Everglades sites reveals the movement of people from the coast to the interior and suggests the importance of Everglades sites as base camps—and not just as temporary camps.

7

The English and Bahamian Legacy

Twenty years of English rule over Florida, from 1763 to 1783, did not result in the ruins of a single fort, monument, or town in southern Florida. English colonial efforts focused mostly on northern Florida, while South Florida remained a wilderness. English rule, however, resulted in some of the most superb maps ever produced of the area. Gerard De Brahm's six-year survey of the Florida east coast resulted in the most detailed and accurate maps that had been done up to that time and include the first detailed map of the Biscayne Bay area published in 1770. Subsequently, surveyor Bernard Romans visited Florida and published a map of South Florida in 1774. These mapping efforts included the first surveys to traverse the county's coastal pinelands.

Archaeological evidence of English activities in Miami-Dade County is understandably scarce, but at least four sites associated with English and Bahamian activities have been discovered. One site produced evidence of a previously unknown English visit to the shores of Biscayne Bay. The site was discovered prior to construction work for the Villa Regina condominiums on Brickell Avenue in 1981. A small copper military cuff button inscribed from the British Fifteenth Regiment was found during a metal-detecting survey of the property by avocational archaeologist Bruce Eistadt while assisting the Dade County archaeologist before the site was destroyed. The button was associated with a few pieces of "black" bottle glass, suggesting that the site was probably a camp for a small group, possibly having arrived by boat for the purposes of securing provisions. Although no records have been uncovered that document such a specific event, McGregor's *Uniforms of the American Revolution* indicates that the Fifteenth Regiment served in Florida during the American Revolution and had an extensive battle record, including action in Charleston, Long Island, and Connecticut. Under the command of Lt. Col. Hugh Powell, they were finally deployed to East Florida in November 1778 and remained there until July 1779, when they were transferred to the island of St. Kitts in the West Indies.[1]

While the English may have left little more than footprints on the shores of Biscayne Bay, their intentions were certainly ambitious and included a proposal for a major settlement of the Biscayne Bay area complete with plantations and an initial colony of 20 families under the contract of the Cape Florida Society. If the Cape Florida Society had been successful, Miami's first English-speaking settlement would have been in the vicinity of Cutler. It was De Brahms's intention to build a town near the bay shore east of the 6,000-acre settlement. Article 19 of the society's charter stipulated: "Each member will be at full liberty to build houses at his own expense on the land which the said Lord Dartmouth shall Designate for the placement of a City."[2]

Although there is some vagueness about the proposed town's exact location, it seems most likely that the intended location was in what is now the Charles Deering Estate Park. But Lord Dartmouth's town was never built, nor did any of the prospective Protestant settlers arrive in South Florida. The plan fizzled because of conflicts among the charter members, particularly because of difficulties caused by De Brahm's abrasive personality. At least two other Miami settlements were proposed in 1770. De Brahm prepared a map for Samuel Touchett for 20,000 acres south of the Miami River.[3] By 1772, three claims had been mapped. A claim for John Augustus Ernst encompassed an area from the north bank of the Miami River northward to Arch Creek. Ernst, who was from Geneva, Switzerland, attempted to settle Swiss and German Protestants on the parcel granted to him on May 13, 1767. His first group of colonists was detained in England and his efforts stopped by the outbreak of the Revolutionary War. His colony would likely have focused on what is now downtown Miami. Touchett's finances fell on hard times and he committed suicide.

Although formal English plans for South Florida's settlements went unfulfilled, the area had already been a focus of activity for Bahamians, and their scattered homesteads appeared along the shores of Biscayne Bay. Not surprisingly, the arrival of Bahamian squatters in South Florida after the end of English rule in defiance of government land grants was received with great irritation by the Spanish governor of East Florida, and it is ironic that it was only after the Spanish regained control of Florida in 1785 that English/Bahamian influence gained a foothold in South Florida, an influence that would continue through the American acquisition of Florida in 1819. In 1817, it was reported that "two or three settlements of little consequence are about Cape Florida. All of these settlements are from Providence, Bahamas."[4] As late as 1854, U.S. Army officer J. M. Robertson noted:

From the mouth of the Miami south as far as the Punch Bowl the land is very high hammock with the exception of about one eighth mile of pine barren. All this land was under cultivation while in possession of the English before it came under Spanish rule the remains of the old stone fences still mark the fields.[5]

The Polly Lewis Home Site

Of the several Bahamian families that settled in South Florida, the Lewises and the Pents were among the earliest and the most prominent. Charles and Frankie Lewis settled on the banks of the New River in present-day Ft. Lauderdale in the 1790s (and possibly earlier). Their two sons began new homesteads along Biscayne Bay. One son, William, and his wife Mary (Polly) built a home on the bluffs overlooking the bay. For reasons unknown, only his wife was named as grantee by the king of Spain in 1805 for their 40-acre homestead. Possibly, by this time, her husband had already died. In 1813, the second Lewis brother, Jonathan, received a similar grant for land along Biscayne Bay south of Polly's.

In August 1982, archaeologists with the Dade County Historic Preservation Division discovered the William and Polly Lewis homesite (8DA2132) during clearing of a property on Brickell Avenue for what would eventually become the Santa Maria condominium. Pressed by the rapid construction schedule, volunteers and University of Miami students working under the direction of the Dade County archaeologist conducted salvage excavations before the site's destruction. A total of four test units and one test trench was excavated before construction work commenced. In addition, a metal-detecting survey was conducted of the area, which resulted in the uncovering of a large number of early-nineteenth-century artifacts. The artifacts are almost all utilitarian, most of them being fragments of ceramics that were typical of the period, including sherds of earthenware pots and jugs—obviously important for food and liquid storage. Some copper buttons, iron nails, a ballast stone, tobacco pipe fragments, and a bone game peg rounded out the artifact categories. Although the sample area was small, all of the materials excavated represented adult activities. No clay marbles or other items commonly associated with children were uncovered.

The most interesting feature of the site are steps cut into the rock that ascended the limestone bluff to the house. Some of the steps were altered with concrete in the twentieth century to modernize access for a more recent home that was built there. Evidence of the Lewis house architectural artifacts included brick and mortar fragments, as well as a portion of a cut limestone block. The remnants of a masonry wall foundation were observed in one of the test trenches.

Despite the recent clearing and pre-construction excavations at the Santa Maria site, it was not totally destroyed because the proposed new building was never constructed. Another opportunity to investigate the site occurred in 1994, when the Archaeological and Historical Conservancy conducted a more thorough examination of a small part of the site still preserved near the edge of the bluff.[6]

The investigations were based on a grid system that was established across the site. A total of 41 units were dug, representing a total excavation area of 147 square meters. It was discovered that the Lewis house had been built on top of a prehistoric midden, which lay beneath a thin horizon of historic artifacts varying from 15 to 25 centimeters in depth. Recovered historic artifacts include musket balls, ceramic sherds, olive jar sherds, pipe stems and bowls (fig. 7.1), bottle glass, iron spikes, nails, buttons, mortar, brick, and slate. Of particular interest was the discovery of 56 post holes

Figure 7.1. Terracotta tobacco pipe bowl from 8DA2132. Collection of the Historical Museum of Southern Florida.

cut into the bedrock later to be overshadowed by the discovery of cut holes at the Miami Circle at Brickell Point in 1998. However, the Santa Maria cut holes appear to be historic and linked to the Lewis structures. Reinforcing that conclusion is the fact that many of the holes contained historic refuse. Two of the cut holes were rectangular and measured approximately 20.5 by 26.5 centimeters across. No complete building footprint was discernible from the holes since much of the site had been previously destroyed by the adjacent construction of a high-rise building.

An important clue to the site's identity was revealed by the following account of an unidentified woman living alone on the Biscayne Bluffs in 1827:

> The point of land to which we steered our course was steep and perpendicular, consisting of a wall of limestone rock, twelve of fifteen feet above the level of the water. At one of these we landed, and ascending a rude flight of steps, I found myself at the door of a new palmetto hut which was seated on the brow of the hill. It was a quite romantic situation. The cottage was shaded on its western aspect by several large West Indian fruit trees, whilst on its eastern side we found a grove of luxuriant limes, which were bowing to the earth under the weight of their golden fruit. This was the residence of the old lady to whom I had been recommend and who was bordering on 80 years of age. I entered the house and made my devoirs. She received me graciously and placed before me some Palmetto and Icaca plums and after refreshing, politely conducted me herself over her grounds and showed me a field of potatoes and corn which she had cultivated. She generally employed several Indians for this purpose, who for their labor received a portion of the products.[7]

The above description is among the most compelling clues to the identity of the Santa Maria site as being the homesite of Polly Lewis. Her identity is plausible considering the woman's age. Polly Lewis had moved south after leaving her New River homestead at present-day Ft. Lauderdale to join her children. A second clue to her homestead is that the Tanner map of 1823 identifies the nearest point of land adjacent to the site as Lewis Point.

The Polly Lewis Biscayne Bay homestead was inhabited from as early as 1805 and was later sold by Polly in 1832. The median year of occupation based on the available historic documents is 1818.5. The average date of the site based on the historic ceramic types found is 1815.

Other likely Bahamian homesteads were discovered along Biscayne Bay, including that of Jonathan Lewis at the historic punch bowl, 8DA412, near Viscaya, and a previously undocumented site found during monitoring of the Bristol Condominium.[8]

Black Caesar: Fact or Fiction?

Those readers who have waited patiently for a true and full account of piracy on the South Florida coast to unfurl its black flag and crossbones might be gratified to read the following section. But if those expectations are for accounts of naval battles and buried doubloons, then be prepared for disappointment.

South Florida's most famous pirate, Black Caesar, has towered in local pirate lore because of a host of fanciful accounts by twentieth-century writers. Caesar has even been given dubious distinction by being listed in the *Pirates' Who's Who*.[9] Writers have trumpeted his exploits, complete with details of his alleged birth place (claims are made for both Haiti and Africa), his pirate colony on Caesar's Rock near Elliott Key with its harem of women, and the 30 tons of silver these writers claim he buried (incidentally, 60,000 pounds of silver would have been a respectable amount of material for anyone short of the king of Spain or a commodities broker).

A favorite explanation for many writers attempting to explain Caesar's 100-year reign of terror is that there was not one but two Black Caesars: one who lived in the eighteenth century and then a later character who was awarded the nineteenth-century franchise for the area and thus assumed the same name. In fact, there was a black pirate or slave who sailed with Blackbeard named Caesar, but there is no documentation to indicate that they were ever in South Florida. Blackbeard's Caesar was hanged off the coast of North Carolina in 1718. Unfortunately, there is not the smallest parchment of truth to substantiate any of these claims that Blackbeard's Caesar is the source of the local pirate lore, or that Black Caesar the pirate of Biscayne Bay was any more than fictional pulp.

A search of the historic records reveals that the earliest known reference to Florida's Black Caesar is the 1774 Bernard Romans map of the area. In that map, the channel between Elliott Key and what is now Caesar's Rock is depicted as "Black Caesar's Creek," a name that survives today. However, another map uses the term "Black Sarah's Creek," which opens the possibility of a Caesar of another gender.

One of the most important sources of the Black Caesar myth is Boe Pent, a South Florida resident of Bahamian descent (also known as Conchs) who shared his alleged firsthand knowledge with Charles Frow, an early pioneer of Coconut Grove. Frow then passed on this information to writers hired for the Federal Writers Project in the 1930s.[10] Boe was 105 years old when he died in Key West in 1925. He claimed that as a boy he had seen Black Caesar—obviously the nineteenth-century version. This account and others like it became the fodder that launched a legend that I'm sure even the most authoritative historic account will never fully put to rest.

There are numerous accounts indicating that Caesar's treasures had become well entrenched within the lore of nineteenth-century South Florida. In 1875, Henry E. Perrine, son of the famous botanist, confessed that his haste in excavating the prehistoric burial mound at the Charles Deering Estate was, in part, driven by his desire to find treasure. After uncovering human remains at the center of the mound, he reported:

> The arrangement of the skulls was such that it suggested to my mind some central object of great interest, and thoughts of "Caesar's Treasure" caused us to use our working tools with redoubled energy, as we slowly dug our way down through the central portion of the mound. Nothing of greater value than a plentiful crop of teeth rewarded our search, and we concluded to leave further exploration for some future antiquarian who may perchance pass this way.[11]

The longevity of Black Caesar was assured by local lore and in the 1940s given considerable credibility when a local restaurant named Black Caesar's Forge opened near Cutler (fig. 7.2). The restaurant claimed to harbor Caesar's hand-dug tunnels allowing his escape to Biscayne Bay. Fortunately, none of these were discovered by patrons wishing to avoid paying for the check. However, perhaps in an effort to enhance the tip, Black Caesar Forge's menu offers this encouraging information:

> A princely fortune in gold and treasure trove, including Black Caesar's favorite coins and jewels is believed to have been buried in the area centered by Black Caesar's Forge. . . . As you dine in the pleasantly cool, coral-walled cellar of the forge, who is to know how near, or far, the golden loot of countless ships lies hidden, awaiting but the lucky hand.[12]

No good legend is worth its salt if there isn't some physical evidence to bolster it. In the case of the Black Caesar legend, the most commonly offered evidence is the submerged iron ring that was once pinned into Cae-

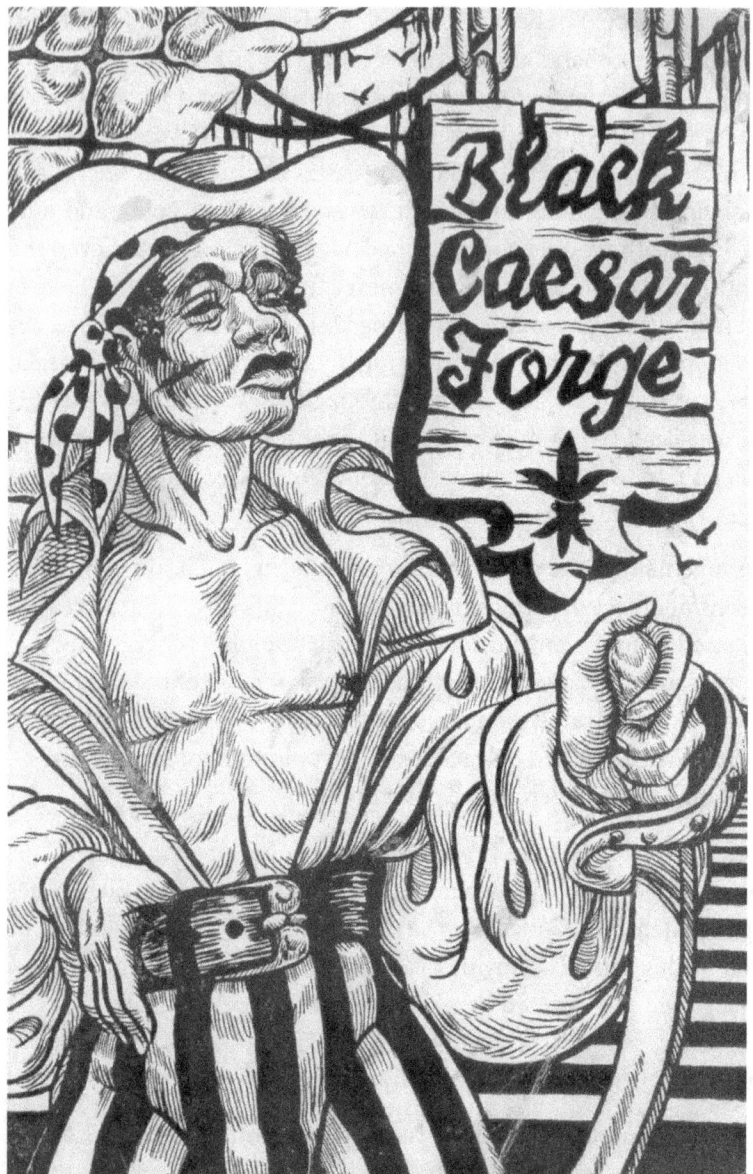

Figure 7.2. Menu cover for Black Caesar's Forge. Collection of Robert S. Carr.

sar's Rock. It was alleged that Black Caesar used the ring to keel his vessel on its side so that its masts would not be spotted by passing ships. The ring was commonly cited by many writers as the ultimate Black Caesar artifact (short of his hordes of silver). Thus it is not unusual that people began to worry about preserving the ring. There was a justifiable fear that either the dredging of Caesar's Creek or a souvenir hunter would end the artifact's place of prominence.

In 1943, a *Miami News* reporter, Edward Hughes, visited the site and described the ring. However, several years later he said the ring disappeared after the creek was dredged by the U.S. Corps of Engineers. In an interview I had with Charlie Brookfield, the one-time owner and operator of the Ledbury Lodge on Elliott Key, Brookfield reported that the ring had been removed by Claude Hill in the 1930s and sent to the Smithsonian Institution in Washington, D.C. Contradicting all of the above is the 1925 article by *Miami News* reporter Prunella Wood that stated that the ring already was missing by that date. Another version of what happened to the ring is offered by the late avocational archaeologist Wesley Coleman who told me that his father removed the ring in the late 1940s. Coleman stated the ring is somewhere in his back yard overgrown with weeds in Sweetwater, where he placed it in the 1960s.

What is certain to historians is that based on the Romans map, there was somebody, previous to 1775, named Black Caesar or Black Sarah who may have lived in the vicinity of Elliott's Key. As to whether this person was involved in piracy is not known, but considering the political realities of eighteenth-century South Florida, anybody seriously engaged in piracy would have become well known to his victims and some mention of his exploits would have appeared in the newspapers and official records of the time. Also, anybody (including pirates) living in southern Florida prior to the British rule of 1763 would have had to come to terms with the indigenous Tequesta population. Although their population had been seriously depleted by the eighteenth century, they still would have been a force to be reckoned with, particularly since the Tequesta were close allies with the Spanish at this time. A pirate victimizing Spanish ships would not have lasted long using southeast Florida as a home base, although a pirate preying on non-Spanish ships would have had a better chance of maintaining his operation.

A true account of known piracy in South Florida waters would, at best, fill several note cards. The account of piracy attributed to Levi James in 1816 in Biscayne Bay uncovered by historian Arva Parks is, thus far, the earliest documented tale of "piracy" in present-day Miami-Dade County.

However, one man's pirate is another's privateer. A contemporary account of one incident indicates that Levi James was a privateer who attacked the Lewis homestead because he believed Lewis was a loyal subject of Spain (which was true). He beat Lewis and robbed him. Undoubtedly, similar cases of "piracy" were occurring during the second Spanish period (1783–1819) because Spanish rule had grown weak and the local Indians had disappeared. However, it is doubtful that any pirate was successfully using the South Florida area as a home base, loading up on treasure and then conveniently dying or getting amnesia so that modern treasure hunters could find their loot.

Contributing to South Florida's paucity of pirates was Commodore David Porter's arrival in Key West in 1822 to rid Florida waters of "the alarming and widespread evil along the Florida and Gulf coasts." Much of this piracy was the work of simple thugs and thieves who took advantage of wrecked vessels and their crews. Porter's war on pirates was largely fought in Cuba and the West Indies, and ended when he invaded a Puerto Rican village, then under Spanish rule, to get his man. This incident led to his court-martial and subsequent resignation. Ironically, Dade County's second known account of piracy was reported in 1843. In the spirit of Black Caesar, and as one possible inspiration to Boe Pent's fertile imagination, the following account was reported in the *New York Daily Tribune*:

> Negro Pirates—The St. Augustine Herald of the 7th inst, contains some further account of the five runway Negroes who recently escaped from St, Augustine. It appears they penetrated as far South as Cape Florida, and there attempted to rob the settlers of the Miami River, but were driven off. They then crossed over to Key Biscayne where they concealed themselves from pursuit. Slaying out from here they plundered the house of a settler Geireen while he was away fishing. Returning and learning the fact, he went in pursuit of the robbers and was murdered. Two children of Geireen, who were left alone without food, were found a few days after by one of the workers who visited Key Biscayne, and taken to Indian Key. The affair has created great alarm among the settlers on the coast.[13]

Local settlers and the military were understandably concerned about the attack and mounted a naval force to intercept and capture them dead or alive. Concerned about the pirates aborted attempt to seize a small schooner *Vigilant* and possibly flee to the Bahamas, the revenue cutter *Flirt* arrived at Key Biscayne on September 5 and found that the pirates had fled the island.

On October 7, Lt. C. Hetzel of the U.S. Army, 18 privates, and two non-commissioned officers carrying 20 days of provisions and 600 rounds of ammunition landed at Key Biscayne on the transport schooner *Walter M.*

After scouring the key with negative results, he proceeded to what may have been Lewis Point on Biscayne Bay and went northward to the Miami River, visiting old Fort Dallas and a small settlement at the forks of the river. Hetzel reported:

> I ascertained from the settlers that the negroes had been seen going up that river and returning to its mouth a week or more previous in large whale-boat; but they being well armed and the persons seeing them not sufficiently strong to attack them, they were permitted to pass.[14]

After searching all of Biscayne Bay and its creeks, and then the "Hunting grounds," no trace of the marauders were found. Hetzel concluded that they had crossed the gulf stream and escaped to the Bahamas.

Southeast Florida's thin brush with piracy as attested to by archival records has not dissuaded modern-day treasure hunters from searching for any forgotten hordes. A favorite search area is Brickell Point.

In 1913, the Rickmers, who had acquired property from the Brickells on the present-day Brickell Presbyterian Church property, entered into an agreement with Capt. W. H. McIntyre to search for hidden treasure on their property. The agreement provided the good captain with the opportunity to search for wealth for exactly 11 days, with the agreement terminating at noon of August 31, 1913. The Rickmers wisely included in the agreement that "all property found, unearthed, or otherwise discovered, other than bullion, shall be divided before leaving the property."[15] The clause was never exercised as no treasure was found.

In the 1940s property owner Maude Brickell entered into an agreement with treasure hunters to harvest a large quantity of loot they were convinced existed there. Using a mechanical excavator, they dug a deep, large hole but found only water.

The facts, as revealed by historic research and archaeological investigations, are that pirates are often thieves and thugs and their alleged treasures are scarcer than dinosaur eggs in South Florida. Any serious, objective researcher will soon find that the myth of piracy in South Florida, conjured up by images of swashbucklers and ships laden with Spanish gold, is a dry hole and an empty chest.

Part III
Seminole Legacy

Hermann Trappman, *Construction of Fort Henry,* 1983. Pencil on paper, 8 × 10. Collection of the Archaeological and Historical Conservancy. By permission of the artist.

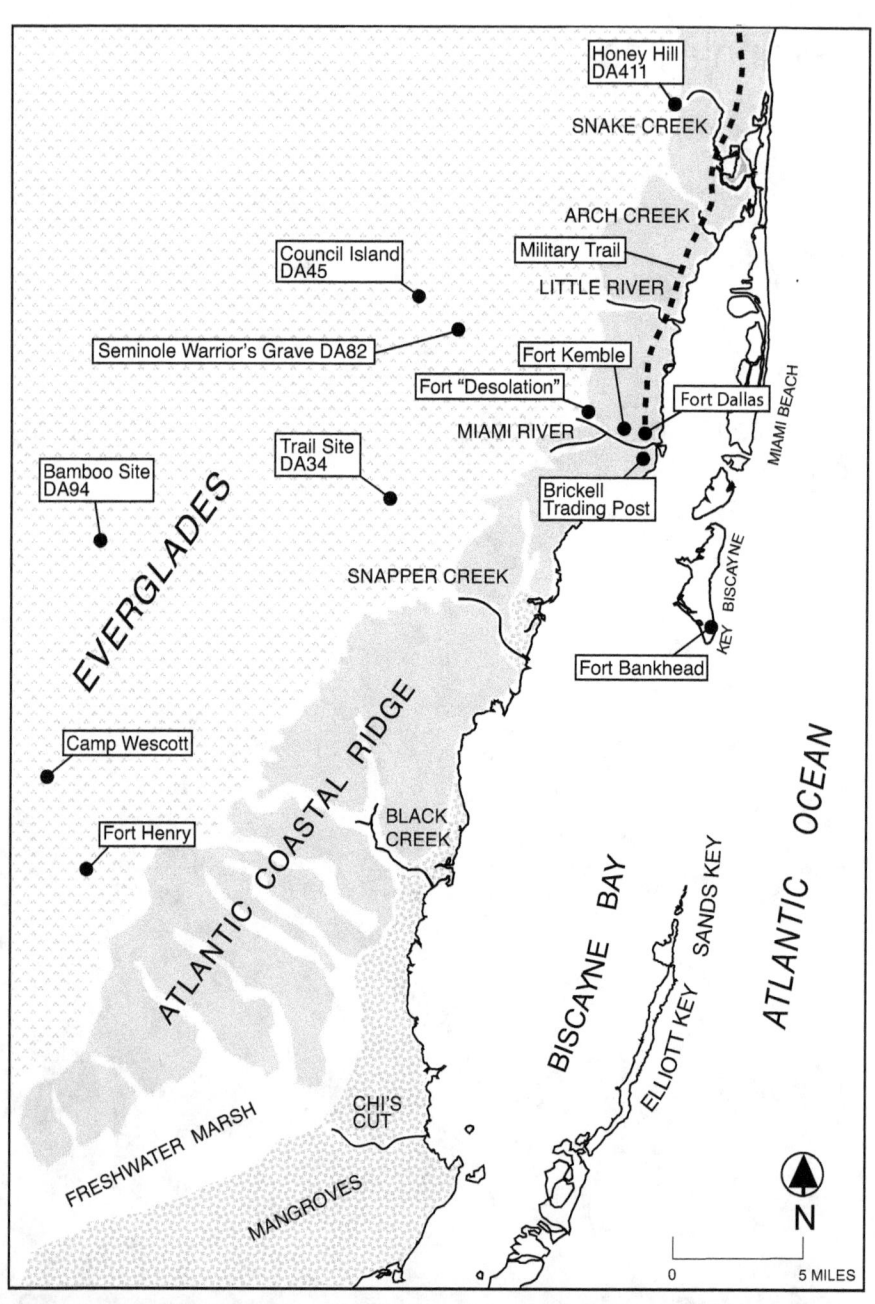

Seminole and Seminole War sites of Miami-Dade County. Map created by John G. Beriault. Courtesy of the Archaeological and Historical Conservancy.

8

Seminole Archaeology

There is debate among scholars as to the origin of the word "Seminole." Some say it is a corruption of the Creek words *ishti semoli*, meaning "separatist," according to Seminole Tribe historian Willard Steele, referring generally to people who have left their town, are living by themselves, or are runaways. However, other authorities believe that the word Seminole is a corruption of the Spanish word *cimarron*, which means "wild," "untamed," "unruly." In 1771, the Spanish used the term to refer to Indians from Alachua who were visiting in Havana. The corruption of *cimarrones* to Seminoles is suggested in a notation made by the English surveyor William De Brahm in 1765 on one of his Florida maps, where he refers to hunting parties of "Semiolilies." In a later report, in 1770, De Brahm uses the term "Seminolskees" to refer to "Indians which have separated themselves from the Creek nation, living by small tribes in towns lately built to the west and south of St. Augustine."[1]

In all probability, De Brahm was getting his information from Indian informants who were not part of these "separated" towns; thus it is doubtful that the Indians in question were referring to themselves as "Seminolskees." It is interesting that Joshua Giddings, who wrote *The Exiles of Florida* in 1858, stated that the word Seminoles was used by the Creeks to refer to the escaped Negroes (which may have been a term borrowed from the Spanish), while the pioneer white settlers were quick to make constant use of the word in referring to Indians. Obviously, the meaning and use of the word varied according to who used it and changed in context through time, particularly in its use by whites, until the word was firmly entrenched in the American vocabulary as being synonymous with all nineteenth-century Florida Indian tribes despite their differences in language or origin. Historian Patsy West believes that non-natives should use the native's own word of self-identity, *i:laponathli*, to describe the Miccosukee,[2] but the word Seminole is now deeply embedded into the English language and has been fully embraced by the Seminole Tribe, having become during the last century the official tribal name. In fact, the name Seminole became such a powerful and positive symbol of the noble virtues of the Native American that it was used as a brand name on hundreds of products in the late nineteenth century and early twentieth century across the United States to promote the sales of medicine, milk, and other products. In 1940 the U.S. Navy named one of its ships the USS *Seminole*, and in 1947 Florida State University named its football team the Seminoles.

Archaeologist Charles Fairbanks concluded in his important study of the Seminoles that 1813 was the approximate date in which the Seminoles finally coalesced as a separate unit.[3] Historian James Covington divides early Seminole activity in Florida into three distinct periods. The first period was 1702–50, when the native Florida Indians were the target of numerous Creek raids, often at the instigation of the English.[4] During this period of warfare there were no Seminole settlements attempted on the peninsula. In the second period, 1750–1812, some settlements were started in northern Florida, and hunting reconnaissance trips continued into the rest of the peninsula. During the third period, between 1812 and 1820, warfare and pressures from American settlers in Georgia and Alabama forced the Upper and Lower Creeks to move into Florida in a major exodus of several thousand people, swelling Florida's native populations by adding to numerous native Florida tribes, such as the Alachua and Yuchee.

The Creek migrations into Florida represented a complicated cross-cultural stream of people attempting to adjust to the dramatic political and demographic changes that affected Florida during the eighteenth and early nineteenth centuries. In many respects, Florida became an Indian melting pot where the dominant Georgia and Alabama Creeks splintered and regrouped into a variety of Indian bands that absorbed the remnants of native Florida tribes, runaway slaves, and the Spanish Indians. Despite the ease of assigning the simple label of "Seminole" to this diversity of Native American cultures and languages, in truth, the diversity has been retained. Even today, Florida's native populations are divided by language and tribal affinity. The Indians of the lower peninsula are divided into two political and tribal groups. First, the Miccosukee Tribe, Incorporated, who speak Mikasuki. Their tribal lands are located west of Miami along the Tamiami Trail and separate parcels in the Big Cypress near Alligator Alley. Second, the Seminole Tribe, Incorporated, speaking Muscogee, are divided among four principal reservations located in Hollywood, the Big Cypress, Immokalee, and Brighton, just west of Lake Okeechobee. Despite such distinctions, tribal lines are blurred by affiliations through marriage and clan.

The earliest reported contact between South Florida's native Indians and Indians from the north is alluded to by the English captain Thomas Nairne in 1709, who earlier had led a party of 33 Yamasee Indians on raids in search of Timicua Indians. Nairne stated that his raids in northern Florida had been so successful that England's Indian allies were "obliged to go down as far as the point of Florida as the firm land will permit, they have drove the Floridians to the Islands of the Cape, have brought in and sold many hundreds of them and daily now continue that trade."[5]

In 1743, Father Monaco attempted to operate the second Spanish mission on the Miami River and reported that the Tequesta Indians had been victims of continued "Yuchi" attacks. In 1775, Adair reported that the "Muskhoge carried their cypress bark canoes from the head of the St. John's black river, only about a half a mile when they launched them into a deep river which led to a multitude of islands to the N.W. of Cape Florida."[6]

This description of a "multitude of islands" probably refers to the numerous tree islands of the east Everglades, many of them being northwest of Cape Florida at the headwaters of the Miami River.

The north Florida Indians' increasing familiarity with the country of South Florida is suggested in De Brahm's advice to the prospective settlers of the Cape Florida Society when he advised them to acquire the services of the Indian "Juaniko" in St. Augustine,

> who is a relick of the ancient Jamarce Indians he speaks both English, Spanish, and Indian, has deserted from a Spanish Man of War, he has been in my service and proved himself an exceedingly good Sailer, fisherman and Hunter well acquainted with all the seas, Rivers, and woods in East Florida.[7]

The Creeks, and later the Seminoles, were very friendly to the English, largely because the English knew how to win their hearts and allegiance. The Indians evaluated their European neighbors according to their generosity. The Spaniards were lowly regarded because of the paucity of gifts they offered to the Indians. In contrast, the British established Indian dependence on a trade economy through licensed traders such as Panton, Leslie and Company. Government-sanctioned traders supplied the Indians with guns, metal kettles, glass beads, and liquor. This British trade system so excelled anything the Spanish had ever offered that it was necessary for the British to convince the Creeks to stop regarding the Spaniards with hostility when the Spanish regained control of Florida in 1783.

The importance of trade as an avenue for peaceful coexistence is demonstrated in the instructions of De Brahm to prospective settlers of the Cape Florida Society settlement (see chapter 7). He specifically described potential contact with the Indians with the following advice:

> As to Indians, you will find them in your first seeting out rather friendly and useful, if any in their way of hunting (being unlimited:) Should come near you, they will endeavor to gain your acquaintance and friendship by Supplying you with Venison, of which they will make practice, provided you present them with a little Corn, Rice, or salt (:by no means let them know you have stronger liquor than water:) they will readily Traffic with you and exchange Skins, furrs, bears oil, wax and honey for the following articuls. Belts leather with buckles Earbobs Silver slight Linsey woolsey Salt Blanket very small Flints Looking glasses small Bracelets, silver and Garters Needle coarse Shirts (Scizzaws) brass for arms & hands Guns very Slight Pots tin Strouts Bulletts Hatched Powder Gun Thimbles, Thread Calicoes Kettles brass Razors Vermillion Combs Knives Ribbon silks Wire brass & iron.[8]

After the British departure, the Spanish maintained good relations with the Creeks, but Indian anger was soon vented toward the United States, which had conducted a series of raids and brutal military operations in what was then Spanish Florida. In 1813, a force of Tennessee and Georgia militia burnt 386 Indian homes and captured hundreds of cattle and horses on an attack of Chief Payne's village near current-day Gainesville. After the raid, 20 of the tribal members and three blacks migrated southward to near Cape Florida, where they lived for several years. The Cape Florida area may have been familiar to the Alachua Indians as early as 1793, when hostilities between Georgian settlers and the Lower Creeks had broken out. Chief Payne stated that he would "remove the whole of his people down to Cape Florida, which is their hunting ground, and there remain, until the present troubles are over."[9] Although the exact site of Chief Payne's village is unknown—the Biscayne Bay area offered numerous settlement opportunities along its creeks and the Miami River—even though some Bahamian families had already located on some of the most desirable tracts, it is possible that these Alachua Indians were living on one of the numerous tree islands in the eastern Everglades.

It is noteworthy that Key Biscayne was a major point of departure for many of the Black Seminoles who fled Florida to evade southern slave catchers. Many of these Black Seminoles emigrated to Andros Island in the

Bahamas. It is possible that the Alachua Indians joined these other Seminoles for a new and safer life. Archaeologist John Goggin visited Andros in 1937 and attempted to discover links between the present inhabitants and those of the original Seminole migrations, but he found few, except for the use of the Seminole name Bowlegs.[10]

This era of turbulent change of native populations offers little that can be clearly isolated in the archaeological record in southeastern Florida. Several San Marcos–style pottery sherds uncovered on an Everglades island at Margate-Blount (8BD41) in Broward County hint at the arrival of Yamassee Indians from the St. Augustine area.[11] Items of European manufacture were also found there, but it is difficult to distinguish such items from the artifacts owned by local Indians. The San Marcos pottery probably dates from about A.D. 1700, when large numbers of coastal Indians from Georgia were driven southward, causing many to settle in the St. Augustine area. These groups conducted numerous raids on the remnant Tequesta (see chapter 6). A perforated copper English coin (fig. 8.1) depicting Queen Anne and King William discovered in the 1970s by avocational archaeologist Bill Lyons on a bulldozed tree island near the south campus of Florida International University may also be associated with a Yamassee or Uchi raid.

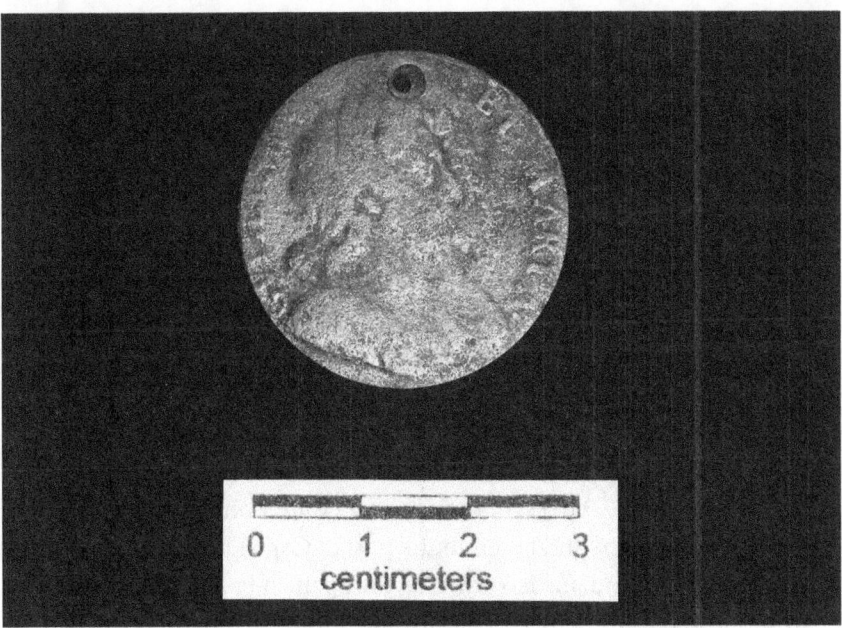

Figure 8.1. Perforated half-penny of William and Mary, Great Britain, c. 1689–94, found near Coral Way and SW 107th Avenue. Collection of the Historical Museum of Southern Florida.

The Spanish Indians

The Seminole and Creek bands that moved into southern Florida during the late eighteenth century did not move into a population vacuum. The last vestiges of the Calusa and Tequesta had been decimated by exposure to European diseases and were forced southward into the Florida Keys, from where they later emigrated to Havana when the British took over Florida in 1763. However, there is tantalizing evidence that some of these people may have returned to Florida and became known as the "Spanish Indians" by the British and Americans during the late eighteenth and early nineteenth centuries.

The Spanish Indians played a principal role in the Second Seminole War, first when their leader Chakaika led his forces in a successful raid on Colonel Harney's forces at the Caloosahatchee River on July 23, 1839. A year later, Chakaika's Spanish Indians delivered a fatal blow to the wrecking town of Indian Key and murdered Dr. Henry Perrine. Harney's personal vendetta against Chakaika was fulfilled when Harney led his dragoons deep into the Everglades and conducted a surprise attack on Chakaika's Island on December 10, 1840. Chakaika was killed, and his body was hung from a tree. Nine prisoners were hanged. Most of the other Spanish Indians were captured and forced to emigrate to the western reservations. Chkaika's Island, or the "hanging island" as it is known by the Miccosukees, is located in Everglades National Park. The event is described in the following newspaper account:

> With a force of about ninety men he entered the Everglades in canoes, guided by John, a negro who was captured by the Indians in 1835, from his master, Dr. Crows, and who escaped. The negro conducted the Colonel through the Everglades to the Indian town, and he surrounded it and fired upon them, killing one or two Indians, and taking thirty-eight prisoners. In the assault the chief of the band, Chai-ki-ka, escaped, but was pursued several miles by one of the dragoons, and overtaken and shot. Among the prisoners taken were ten warriors, nine of whom were hung; the life of the tenth being saved for a future guide. The rest of the prisoners were women and children, and were all spared and taken to the post at Cape Florida.
>
> This band of Indians is known as the Spanish band, and the same who murdered Mr. Cooley's family and several others at Cape Florida.[12]

The prisoners captured by Harney were taken to Key Biscayne and then shipped to Tampa and finally to Arkansas. Their eventful fate is indicated by several families of Oklahoma Seminoles who claimed to have "Spanish ancestry." One group of emigrating Indians appeared to have so much Spanish blood that an army lieutenant freed them in New Orleans en route to the reservation.[13]

While the major military activities of the Spanish Indians are well documented, their origins and history previous to the war are unclear. The late William C. Sturtevant, an anthropologist with the Smithsonian Institution, made a remarkable attempt to discover the origins of the Spanish Indians. His field work in South Florida in 1953 was partly funded by Yale University as part of their Caribbean Anthropological Program. He is among the first to use Seminole oral traditions to learn about certain historical events involving the Spanish Indians as viewed by the contemporary Indians. Sturtevant documented the earliest recorded use of the term "Spanish Indian": when Bernard Romans, the naturalist, used it to describe the guide he employed at the mouth of the St. Lucie River in 1769. In 1774, William Bartram recorded his conversations with an old "Creek," who indicated that an Indian town existed at Charlotte Harbor on the southwest coast that contained "Calosulgees" and "remnants of other different Nations atients [ancient] of the utmost [isthmus] called 'Painted People' and 'Bat Necks.'" Between 1814 through 1820, various Indian parties and their chiefs from the "coast of Tampa" arrived in Havana to visit and trade. Sturtevant believes from his linguistic analysis of the names of the chiefs and towns involved that these groups could have been a combination of Creek and Calusa Indians.

By 1824, American visitors documented at least four small settlements in the Charlotte Harbor area that were involved in exporting fish to Cuba. The people lived in palmetto-thatched houses and conducted some cultivation. In 1831, this population was estimated to be about 65 Spanish men, 65 Indian men, 30 Indian women, and 50 to 100 children. In 1837, John Lee Williams described in detail some of the Spanish-Indian fishing settlements. He indicated the separate character of these fishermen from that of the Seminole and how the former people were drawn into the war:

> The inhabitants of several large settlements around the Caximba Inlet, the heads of the Hujelos, St. Mary's, and other southern streams, never appeared at the agency, to draw annuities, but lived by cultivating their fields, hunting, trading at the Spanish ranchos, bartering

skins, mocking birds and pet squirrels, for guns, ammunition, and clothing, and sometimes assisting in the fisheries. This race of Indians would have remained peaceful to this day, had not an order been issued for the agency requiring them all to be removed. . . . Their knowledge of the passes of the country, and their long connection with the Spanish traders and fishermen afforded perfect facilities for supplying the Seminoles with arms and munitions of war.[14]

Eventually, the Spanish fisheries at Charlotte Harbor became a target for Seminole attacks, and Spaniards at the fishery aided Lieutenant Powell when he explored the Myakka River looking for the hostile Indians who had killed the Charlotte Harbor customs collector. The hostility of the Seminoles toward the Spanish and Indian fisherman at the fishing ranches suggests little kinship or alliance between these groups at that time.

However, historian James Covington favors the idea that the origin of the Spanish-Indian was a result of Seminole-Cuban intermarriage rather than descent from more ancient tribes.[15] Further, Sturtevant's informants insisted that Chakaika and his band were not Calusa but Miccousuki. One old man thought Chakaika and his band were members of the wind clan, because members of that clan had tried to claim Chakaika's possessions after his death. Interestingly, Sturtevant points out that his collection of oral interviews indicates that the Miccosukee tradition refers to the Calusa as a Spanish people. Specifically, their word for the Calusa, *Kalas: L:*, is sometimes a synonym for *ispa:na:L*, or "Spaniards."[16] It is likely, based on historical evidence, that the earliest attacks in Dade County, specifically at the Cape Florida Lighthouse and Indian Key, were conducted by "Spanish Indians" and not Seminoles as popularly believed.

Miccosukee spokesperson Fred Dayoff, while learning their language, told me that in his early years in the Glades in the 1950s he did not understand the dialect of the Tigertail group of Miccosukees, who were residing only a short distance from the "hanging island," where Chakaika was killed. When he asked other Miccosukees about the Tigertails' distinct vocabulary, they said they didn't understand it either. "The Tigertails not only spoke with a different dialect they were physically different," he reported. "They were bigger." An anonymous diary confirms the large size of the Tigertails: "H. G." reported on a trip to the Miami River in 1877 that "Big Tigertail" was reportedly seven feet tall.[17]

While the evidence is inconclusive, there is sufficient reason to believe that at least some of the Spanish Indians were the mixed-blood descendants of the Tequesta and the Calusa with the Spanish. The descendants of the Spanish Indians are now spread from Cuba to Oklahoma, with those few who survived in the Florida Everglades.

Seminole Settlement Patterns

The earliest documented Seminole settlement in South Florida may have been Payne's relocated Alachua village dating to the early nineteenth century, although its exact location is unknown. In 1829, John Lee Williams describes the Creek village of Snake Warrior, Chitto Tustenugee, which was later the target of a U.S. Army raid in 1841 during the Second Seminole War. Williams described the village in a report to Buckingham Smith: Chitto-tus-te-nug-gee, or Snake Warrior, . . . took possession of an island about 20 miles west of Little River; had procured to be cleared about 20 acres of first rate land; built upon it two small towns, and drew to it, from Sam Jones men, nearly 60 inhabitants.[18]

Archaeologists discovered what is believed to be Snake Warrior's Island in 1991 within the Perry Farm adjacent to the Dade-Broward County line in Miramar.[19] This site is located on an 11-acre island on the edge of the Everglades at the headwaters of Snake Creek, the present-day Oleta River, which at one time was the principal canoe access connecting the Everglades with Biscayne Bay. Its discovery led to the site's preservation within a 53-acre park created by the state of Florida and the Broward County Parks Department.

During the earliest period of the Seminole exodus into South Florida as a result of the Second Seminole War (1835–42), Seminole villages were hidden in the interior away from the coast, often in the Everglades and the Big Cypress. These reclusive settlement patterns continue through the Third Seminole War. Sites dating from the 1835 to 1858 period spanning the last two Seminole Wars are very rare, and only a few early Seminole occupations have been documented across South Florida. One of those is the Trail site (8DA34), a large tree island hammock destroyed for a suburban housing development in the early 1970s. This site revealed a long span of Seminole occupation, including one of southern Florida's only known specimens of possible Seminole pottery, a technology largely ignored by the Seminoles after their rapid move southward from central Florida during the war years, particularly since brass kettles and iron pots were so much easier to obtain and transport.

Other Everglades sites such as Maddens Hammock, 8DA45, have early-nineteenth-century Seminole components. This site, depicted as Council Island on numerous military maps from the period, was occupied during the Second and Third Seminole Wars. Abner Doubleday describes the island with its large hill and Everglades vista as the stronghold of Billy Bowlegs and his warriors. Doubleday attacked the island with 60 soldiers, but the Indians fled before the soldiers reached the village.[20]

After the end of the Third Seminole War and the subsequent American Civil War, the Seminoles began to cautiously breach the sanctity of coastal white pioneer settlements and establish relationships with individuals and families who were friendly, particularly those who were interested in trading or buying game and skins. Individual transactions soon led to more ambitious trading as white hunters and traders responded to these economic opportunities with gusto. Trading on the Miami River began as early as the 1870s. John Ewan traded from the old Fort Dallas barracks on the north side of the Miami River. His transactions spanned at least 15 years and he was one of the first whites to gain the trust of the Miami Seminoles, who likely were primarily at the Snake Creek settlements.

The anthropologist MacCauley noted during his visit in 1880 to the Miami River that a very interesting system of credit had evolved between Ewan and the Seminoles:

> At Miami a trader keeps his accounts with the Indians in single marks or pencil strokes. For example, an Indian brings to him buck skins, for which the trader allows twelve "chalks." The Indian, not wishing then to purchase anything, receives a piece of paper marked this way:
> "//// //// ////"
> J.W.E. owes Little Tiger $3."
> At his next visit the Indian may buy five "marks" worth of goods. The trader then takes the paper and returns it to Little Tiger changed as follows:
> "//// ///"
> J.W.E. owes Little Tiger $1.75."
> Thus the account is kept until all the marks are crossed off, when the trader takes the paper into his own possession. The value of the purchases made at Miami by the Indians, I was informed, is annually about $2,000. This is, however, an amount larger that would be aver-

age for the rest of the tribe, for the Miami Indians do a considerable business in the barter and sale of ornamental plumage.

This credit system based upon 25 cents was called by the Seminoles *Kan-cat-ka-hum-him*, apparently a Muskogee phrase for "one mark on the ground."[21]

Among the most successful of the Miami traders was William Brickell, who had brought his family from Cleveland, Ohio, purchasing 3,000 acres from the south bank of the Miami River extending several miles southward along Biscayne Bay. He built his house and a general store in 1871 on the south bank of the river, later known as Brickell Point. Seminoles began to converge on his store, bringing deer skins, alligator hides, and bird plumes. In return, the Seminole men, their wives having carefully instructed them since the women never spoke to the white traders, would purchase canned goods, sugar, flour, cloth, and beads, as well as ammunition, axes, and guns. The Brickell Trading Post and general store thrived from the 1880s to about 1900.

The Brickell Trading Post and store was originally located near the river bank, where a dock allowed Seminoles and other visitors to come ashore. When the building was demolished in 1909, much of the store's inventory, particularly the trade beads, were moved to the cellar of the new main house located on top of the bluff. Wooden crates and barrels filled with beads were stored there, and when Maude Brickell died in 1960, the empty Brickell house and property was left to the American Legion with the stipulation that the house would be preserved. Vandals searching for treasure, however, converged on the house, damaging it so badly that it was demolished in 1963. Prior to its demolition, I found hundreds of beads beneath and around the house, providing the first study collection of Brickell trade beads, which could now be compared to beads found in Seminole sites across South Florida.[22] The bead assemblage reflected approximately 30 years of trade from roughly 1871 to 1900. Interestingly, the glass beads had their origins in Europe, where many of them had been stockpiled for decades, thus the types include some dating from the early nineteenth century, particularly wire-wound beads, but the most common were faceted tubular blue and white beads. This bead assemblage, when compared to the beads of the Stranahan Store, which operated in Ft. Lauderdale between 1896 and 1907, showed some overlap of types between the two.[23] This is not a real surprise, however, since William Brickell had sold the land on the New River used for the trading post to Frank Stranahan, and undoubtedly had also sold him part of his bead stock after the decline of the Brickell Trading Post. The bead types associated with the Brickell-Stranahan stores have been uncovered at Seminole sites across the Everglades, including sites at Long Key and Snake Warriors Island.

After the demise of the Brickell Trading Post, the Girtman Brothers store in downtown Miami became the principal trade center in the Miami area. Operating from 1896 to 1915, the store was assessable by Seminoles canoeing to the Miami River landing. They then walked eastward on present-day SW First Street to the store at Avenue D (present-day Miami Avenue).

During this period of increasing trade and Seminole prosperity, from the 1870s to about 1900, the principal Miami area Seminole settlements were located at the eastern rim of the Everglades along the banks and islands of Snake Creek, which is present-day Oleta River, and on the tree islands of the Everglades. In addition, large villages and agricultural fields were located on the Pine Island group west of Ft. Lauderdale. There is no evidence that any permanent Seminole village occurred anywhere on the Miami River—the river would be occupied by Seminoles later during the rise of tourist attractions in the teens and 1920s. However, traditional sites such as Madden's Hammock continued as an important Seminole settlement. That site was also used for the green corn dance. Madden's Hammock, the largest of the eastern Everglades sites in Miami-Dade County, is located less than a mile west of the Palmetto Expressway in Miami Lakes.

Boom was soon replaced by bust when the government's Everglades drainage program began in 1906. Large steam-driven dredges began to dig their way between Lake Okeechobee to Ft. Lauderdale, Miami, and other coastal towns. When the rocky rapids on the north fork of the Miami River were breached by dynamite, Everglades water shot into the Miami Canal and into Biscayne Bay like a huge, muddy brown plume. The "sweet water" was no more. The Everglades began to shrink and dry out, and birds began to die by the thousands. Pete Tiger provided this view based on the passing of the greater Everglades:

> In the old times we could paddle our canoes for many days and hunt the deer and the alligator. Now the white man has drained the Glades with his canals to make fields for his tomatoes and sugarcane. Our canoes cannot run on the sand and it is forbidden to cross the white man's fences. And the deer and the alligator each day go farther away.[24]

Even before drainage, as the Everglades became more accessible to pioneer farmers, the Snake Creek settlements were displaced by whites making claims on the land. The typical white pioneer's attitude toward Seminole property rights was depicted in the following fictional dialogue written by Coconut Grove resident Kirk Munroe, a longtime friend of the Seminoles, who described the clash between pioneer homesteaders and the Seminoles in his book *Big Cypress*, in which a ruthless plume trader offers riverside land occupied by a Seminole to a white homesteader:

> Don't you see, ma'am, that he's an Injun, and don't you know that Injuns can't take up land? he may claim it all he wants to, but he hasn't got a deed for it, and he can't get one; only a citizen of the United States can obtain that. Oh, no, his claim don't amount to nothing, and the land is yours if you only say the word. These Seminoles haint got no rights that white folks is bound to respect.[25]

From the 1890s to 1920 white farmers forced the Seminoles out of their Pine Island and Snake Creek settlements. This loss of these larger islands with their pine and hardwood hammocks, which had been the perfect setting for supporting both villages and farming, led to a radical change in Seminole settlement and land use in southeastern Florida. For the first time since the Seminole Wars, the smaller Everglades tree islands would have to support almost all aspects of Seminole subsistence and habitation. This meant smaller groups living over greater distances from one another.

By 1915, scarce game, new laws protecting birds, and changing fashions ended the profitable plume trade. Fortunately, the booming tourist trade in Miami created an instant demand for winter tourists to see the unconquered Seminoles. Historian Patsy West reports how white entrepreneur Henry Coppinger had recognized the opportunity created by visitors' curiosity to see the Seminoles by opening his tropical gardens on the Miami River to Jack Tigertail and his family to camp there.[26] Thus began the era of Indian tourist camps along the Miami River. No camp, however, surpassed the commercial success of Musa Isle, located on the south bank of the Miami River east of present-day Twenty-seventh Avenue. This village was the brainchild of Seminole Willie Willie, who used the camp not only to attract tourists but also as a native trading post for hides, eliminating the white middle man and thus beginning one of the first successful ventures into Western-style capitalism by a Seminole.[27]

One of the advantages of the reassertion and opportunism offered by the tourist villages on the Miami River was not only access to cash and goods but also proximity to the coastal pinelands, where coontie was more plentiful. Tree island camps still thrived, and the infusion of manufactured goods was particularly evident at the camps of William McKinnley Osceola at present-day Chakika Park and Bamboo Mound (8DA94), later destroyed by clearing for a dynamite storage area by the Portland Cement Company in the 1950s.

The construction of the Tamiami Trail in 1926 connecting Miami to Naples across the Everglades was perhaps the final arrow into the heart of traditional Seminole settlement and transportation patterns. The road obstructed the sheet water flowing southward toward Florida Bay and blocked centuries-old canoe trails. Some Seminoles shifted their canoe trips to Miami by using the Tamiami Canal, which had been created from the construction fill to create the road. Because of their dependence on the canoe, and since few Seminoles at that time could afford automobiles, the road forced some Seminole families to select camp sites along the highway because of the convenient fill provided by the canal dredging and because they could no longer access certain islands, a pattern reflected today in the location of homes of the Miccosukee Indian Reservation.

The second blow to traditional Seminole access to the Everglades occurred in 1947 with the formation of Everglades National Park. All of the glades south of the Tamiami Trail became off limits to native habitation, hunting, fishing, and other traditional activities. Only the Everglades area north of the Tamiami Trail and the Big Cypress remained accessible.

Today, the Seminoles' use of tree islands is maintained for weekend camps, where a traditional chickee or other shelter might be erected. Some cultivation and plantings are done and sometimes the island is used as a focal point of Miccosukee airboat tours. One of the larger islands is still used for the traditional green corn dance.

Modern Seminole culture has come far from its impoverished nineteenth-century roots of survival and subsistence. Casino capitalism in the twentieth century has created a Seminole/Miccosukee society that has moved from open chickees to concrete homes, from canoes to pickup trucks, and with the economic clout to expand tribal land by simply buying it.

Seminole Artifacts

The Seminole archaeological record reflects the increasing impact of Euro-American material culture through time. When the first Creek/Seminole settlements began in southern Florida in the early nineteenth century, artifacts may have included some ceramic bowls, but by and large, machine-made trade items had replaced many of the traditional crafts except for basketry. Iron axes and adzes replaced those of stone. Brass kettles replaced ceramic cooking bowls. Conical metal arrowheads made lithic ones obsolete, and glass beads quickly surpassed shell beads in popularity. When the Seminole Wars began, opportunities to trade for manufactured goods virtually disappeared. Except for illicit trade with Cuban smugglers and booty captured from Indian raids, such as at Indian Key, which may have had as much an economic objective as a military one, materials acquired by the Seminoles may have been reduced to survival essentials such as guns, bullet molds, knives, and axes.

The Trail site, 8DA34, has produced evidence of the earliest known Seminole occupation in the area. It is the only known South Florida site with Creek brushed pottery as reported to me by Wesley Coleman.[28] Generally, the Seminoles had abandoned pottery by the time they migrated southward from northern Florida. An isolated crushed brass kettle perforated with "kill holes" from a square nail was found at this same site in the sawgrass in 1963.

Few other artifacts have been uncovered from this early period of Seminole culture. They include glass beads, miscellaneous trade items, and metal projectile points (known as Kaskaskia points by archaeologists) made from thin sheets of metal and rolled into a cone. Beyond a fairly narrow range of artifacts, there are few items that can be distinguished from those of the mid- and late nineteenth century. Even glass beads from different time periods, which can be classified according to manufacture and color, are not necessarily fail-proof indexes of a site's age. Beads were sometimes kept for long periods of time by both traders and Indians. It was probably not uncommon for an Indian woman to be wearing beads manufactured 50 to 100 years before she was born, and considering that beads were worn for a lifetime, one must be cautious about dating a site using glass beads alone.

The first reported Seminole mortuary site uncovered in Miami-Dade County was found by avocational archaeologist Dan Laxson in 1954, when he investigated a small tree island in Hialeah.[29] On the fourth and final day of his excavation, his daughter noticed an iron pipe protruding from beneath a ficus tree. The pipe turned out to be a .35-caliber gun barrel. Subsequent excavations there revealed a group of artifacts around the tree, including a mirror, a musket-ball mold made from steatite, brass military buttons, brass gun accouterments, and clay pipe fragments. The age of the material appears to be from the Second Seminole War, or about the 1840s. Laxson's recovery of these grave goods and associated human bones should be understood within the context of the times when there were no preservation laws to protect such burial sites. Six months after Laxson's dig, the site was bulldozed and a church was built on top of the site. Laxson donated all of the material to the Museum of Natural History in Gainesville, and from there the artifacts eventually were repatriated to the Miccosukee Tribe.

After the end of the Third Seminole War in 1858, the Seminoles maintained a cautious distance from white settlers, but by 1870–80 new trade patterns had begun to emerge based on the Seminole sales of animal skins, alligator hides, and bird plumes to white traders. Large quantities of manufactured goods, including axes, knives, bottles, and rifles, began to stream into Seminole villages along the edge of the Everglades and onto tree island camps in the Everglades heartland. This influx of goods probably reached its zenith between 1910 and the 1930s, when the growth of Seminole tourist villages reinforced a reliance on a cash economy that replaced trade.

The Seminole artifact assemblage can be divided into two general categories. The first includes those Euro-American items purchased or traded by Seminoles and then assimilated into Seminole daily life without any significant alterations, such as kettles, rifles, and bullet molds. Other unmodified artifacts encountered in Seminole sites include glass bottles, tin cans, watch fobs, iron harpoons, sewing machines, and even coffee grinders. Unaltered ornaments include such items as a beautiful Persian brass snuff box lid (fig. 8.2) found at Honey Hill, 8DA411, which was part of the Snake Creek settlement.

Another important unaltered diagnostic artifact type associated with Seminole sites is glass beads (fig. 8.3). Most were manufactured in Europe specifically for the purpose of trade and were used by the Seminoles for necklaces for women, but some were used to create beadwork for necklaces and as part of complex beadwork sashes, leggings, and other composite sewn pieces. Beads are the most common artifact type discovered at Seminole sites.

Perhaps no artifact that was found in Miami-Dade County is more intriguing than the brass U.S. lighthouse service cap insignia found at 8DA45 by James Schaffer in the 1960s (fig. 8.4). Research indicates that the insignia had been manufactured in 1883, suggesting that the cap was likely a gift or a trade item since relations with lightkeepers—such as with lightkeeper James Armour at the Jupiter lighthouse—were very important.

The second category of Seminole artifacts are those created from altering imported materials, such as lead and copper used to construct metal coontie graters, copper canoe patches, lead bullet molds, and metal ornaments.

Figure 8.2. Bronze Persian snuff box lid from 8DA411. Collection of the Historical Museum of Southern Florida.

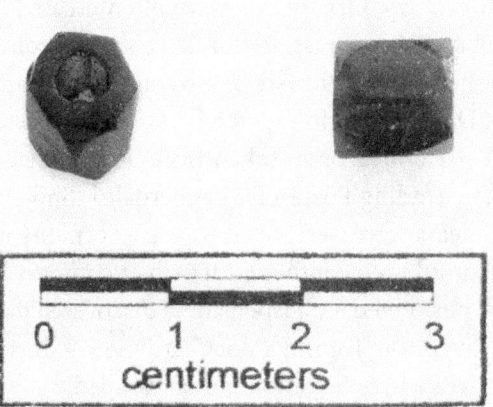

Figure 8.3. Faceted glass trade beads from the Brickell Trading Post. Collection of the Historical Museum of Southern Florida.

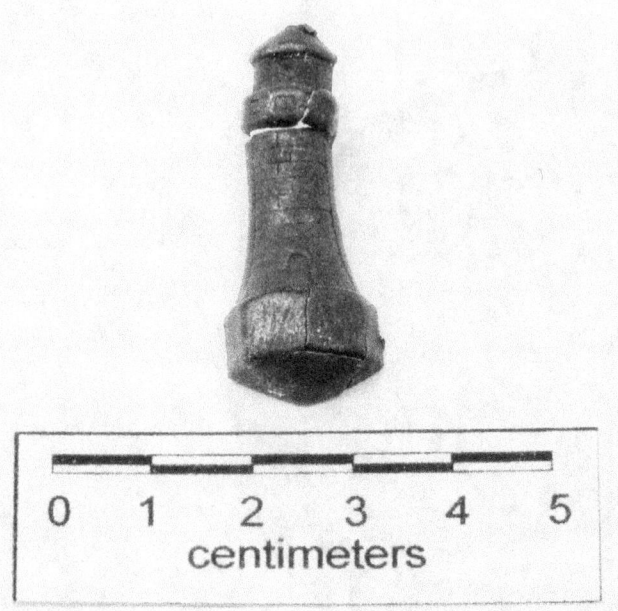

Figure 8.4. Copper insignia from a U.S. lightkeeper's cap found at 8DA45. Collection of the Historical Museum of Southern Florida.

It is this assemblage of altered artifacts that allows archaeologists to identify a site as Seminole, since unaltered manufactured goods might be associated with a white hunter's camp or other non-native historic activity. Seminole manufacturing techniques were varied. Copper was often snipped and cut, lead was melted and cast, and silver cut and hammered into ornaments.

Seminole artistry in the archaeological record is perhaps best represented by ornamental metalwork. John Goggin wrote about Seminole brooches in the 1950s.[30] These beautiful ornaments were cut from silver coins are often depicted in nineteenth-century engravings and photographs through the first half of the twentieth century. Ornaments were often created by perforating coins and pieces of copper or brass. Perforated coins are sometimes found at Seminole War sites, such as the two drilled half dimes dated 1839 and 1856 discovered at 8DA411. Also found at 8DA411 were two cut "star" ornaments (fig. 8.5). A perforated brass token from an Ohio store was uncovered at the Stranahan Trading Post in Ft. Lauderdale.[31] Shotgun shells and even pocket watch gears were perforated to use as ornaments. An unusual ornament is a beautiful nineteenth-century silver compact lid engraved with the name "Mae" perforated for suspension. I discovered it on the south bank of the Miami River near Tommy's Boat Yard in 1974 during bulldozing of the parcel in an area where Seminoles often camped.

The scarcity of Seminole ornaments is based, in part, on the fact that

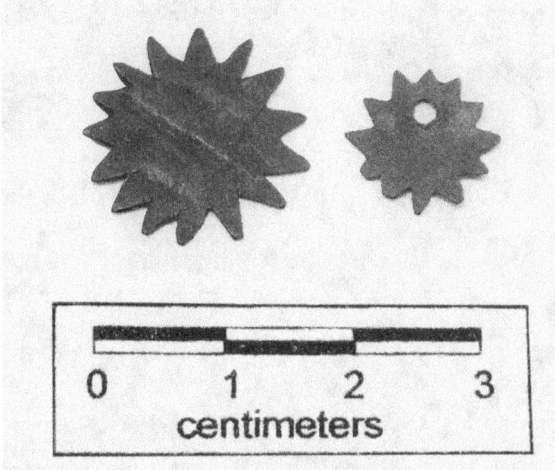

Figure 8.5. Cut copper ornaments from 8DA411. Collection of the Historical Museum of Southern Florida.

such items were not intentionally discarded but were either lost or placed with personal possessions in a Seminole grave. Grave sites should be dealt with the utmost respect and preserved whenever possible, and collecting artifacts from a preserved gravesite is strictly avoided by professional archaeologists.

Other important alterations to imported materials are those associated with mortuary behavior. Grave goods accompanying Seminole interments were often broken or defaced. For example, gun barrels were bent and holes were added to pots and kettles to "kill" them and release their spirits.

Other types of Seminole metalwork uncovered by archaeologists in southeast Florida since the 1980s represent typical examples of utilitarian artifacts created by the Seminoles. During excavations of the Honey Hill site (8DA411) and Snake Warrior's Island (8BD1867) several artifacts made of copper and lead were found. A ladle found at 8DA411 was made from a copper sheet (fig. 8.6). This carefully hammered artifact was made to be attached to a wooden handle. Cooper sheeting was also an important base material for other artifacts, such as canoe patches and graters for scraping coontie. A grater was found by avocational archaeologist Wesley Coleman at a site in present-day Kendall during construction of an elementary school. The grater had been manufactured from a rectangular sheet of copper that had been perforated with numerous nail holes. The jagged edge of the nail holes created the grating effect.

Other Seminole manufactured artifacts found at Snake Warrior's Island include replacement gun parts such as a shotgun or rifle butt plate

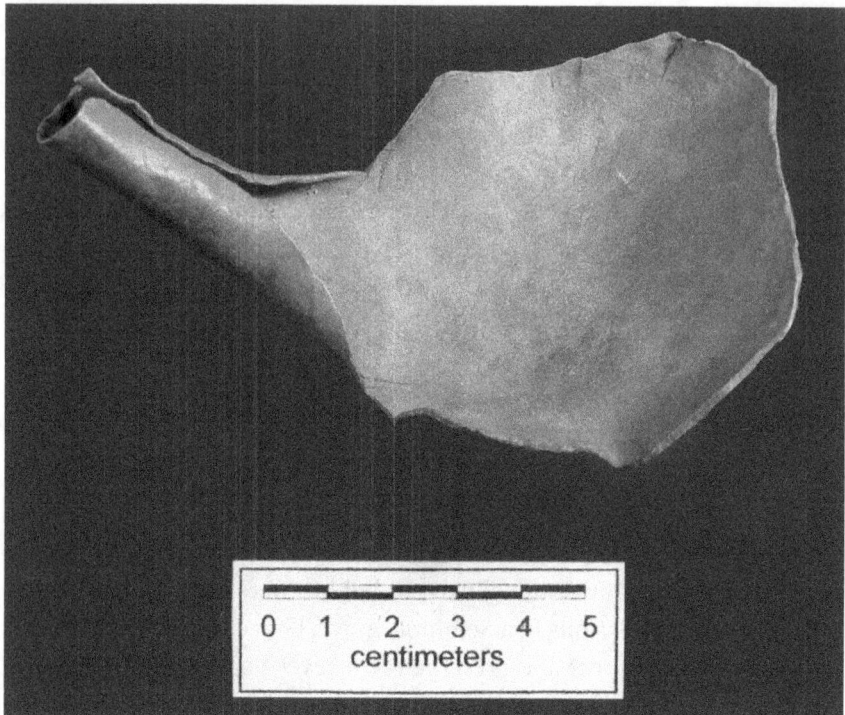

Figure 8.6. Ladle manufactured from copper sheet from 8DA411. Collection of the Historical Museum of Southern Florida.

made from lead. These artifacts demonstrate that simple repairs were part of Seminole gun maintenance and that working with lead had become a common skill. The Seminoles' versatility with lead was apparent when a musket-ball mold constructed from lead was discovered at Abiaka's camp, 8BD12, at Long Key in Broward County (fig. 8.7).

One of the most distinctive Seminole metal artifact types is the Kaskaskia projectile point (fig. 8.8). This arrowhead was manufactured by cutting a small, triangular strip of copper, brass, or iron and rolling it into a conical tube, creating a point on one end and an open socket at the other that fitted onto a wooden shaft. Recovered specimens in southeast Florida range from as small as 3.5 centimeters in length to one example 10 centimeters long found at the Loxahatchee Battlefield near Jupiter. Kaskaskia points have been found at camps along Snake Creek such as at Honey Hill, 8DA411, and Snake Warrior's Island. Even though the Seminoles were armed with muskets throughout their earliest occupation in South Florida, and used shotguns and rifles throughout the last half of the nineteenth century, bows

Figure 8.7. Lead musket-ball mold found at Everglades Island. Collection of the Archaeological and Historical Conservancy.

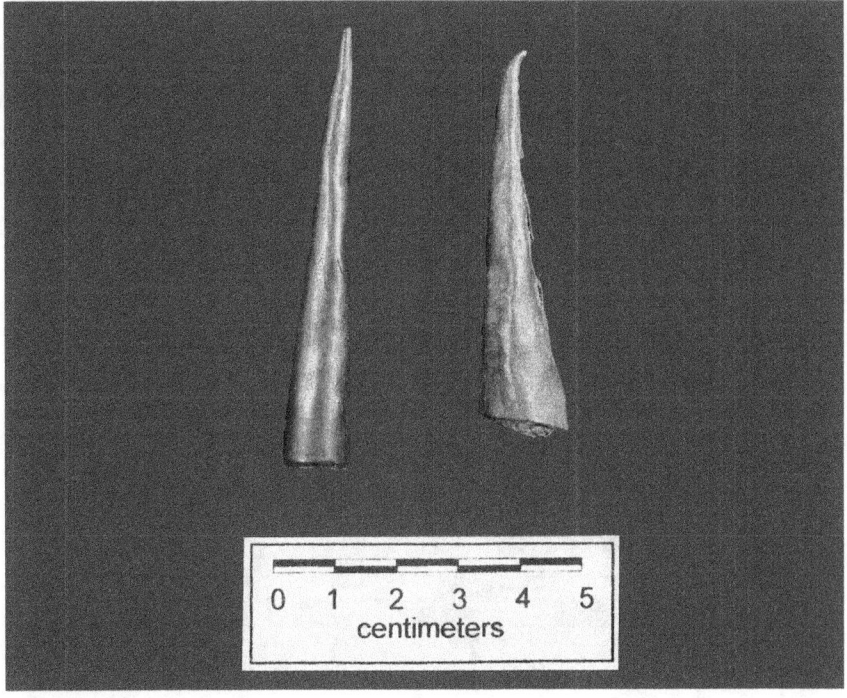

Figure 8.8. Kaskaskia projectile point cut from copper sheet from 8DA411. Collection of the Historical Museum of Southern Florida.

178   Part III. Seminole Legacy

and arrows continued in use until the 1930s, used by children for fishing and play.

Among the most innovative of Seminole artifacts were the scrapers and cutting tools created from glass bottles or other pieces of glass. Using the same techniques of percussion flaking that had been applied to flint and chert, glass was flaked into both thumbnail-sized and larger scrapers. One possible glass scraper was found on Pine Island in Broward County, but the best example is a large rectangular knife recovered from the Bamboo Mound, 8DA94, originally known to be William McKinley Osceola's camp, dating from a 1890–1930 context (fig. 8.9).

Undoubtedly, the stylistic development of Seminole clothing after the mid-nineteenth century is among the most powerful statements of the

Figure 8.9. Glass knife from the Bamboo site, 8DA94. Courtesy of the Archaeological and Historical Conservancy.

Seminoles maintaining cultural integrity despite dependence on imported cloth and sewing machines. Unfortunately, organic fabric and cloths are rarely preserved within the archaeological record.

This infusion of Euro-American manufactured goods into the Seminole material assemblage had a surprisingly minimal impact on tribal and cultural integrity. Basic religious and social traits remained largely unaltered. True acculturation of Seminole life ways into the tempo of Western culture only emerged in the twentieth century with the advent of missions and churches working to convert Seminoles to Christianity and the creation of government reservations. These new social and religious forces coupled with emerging economic patterns of cattle ranching and tourist camps shifted Seminole culture away from the Everglades subsistence to a life today in which traditional crafts of patchwork clothing and basketry are mostly produced for tourist consumption. Traditional wooden canoes were manufactured for utilitarian use and probably disappeared by the 1960s.

Despite setbacks, Seminole and Miccosukee communities now prosper. The Ah-Tah-Thi-Ki Museum established on the Big Cypress Reservation preserves and documents Seminole material culture, maintaining an extensive collection of crafts and artifacts as well as conserving original paper documents dating back to the Seminole Wars. Perhaps the most telling object of Seminole emergence into the position of cultural victor was the tribe's acquisition of General Zachery Taylor's report on the aftermath of the Battle of Okeechobee. Written in his camp on the only piece of paper he could find, it reported on his "victory." Bought for $80,000 at auction, it is the modern equivalent of counting coup—the ultimate Seminole battle souvenir.

9

Stockades and Musket Balls

> We should devote ourselves to [the preservation of the Ft. Dallas barracks] with the zeal that will cause our children and our children's children to look upon these old treasures and be inspired.
>
> Williams Jennings Bryan, 1925

The preservation of the Fort Dallas stone barracks in Lummus Park provides a good example of the public's desire to hold on to some vestige or monument of the dramatic conflict that engulfed South Florida during the Second and Third Seminole Wars. The Fort Dallas barracks building was situated on Julia Tuttle's property on the north bank of the Miami River, and when threatened with demolition in 1925 by the construction of the Robert Clay Hotel, Miami's first preservation movement was ignited under the guidance of the Daughters of the American Revolution and the Miami Women's Club. The one-story, 17-by-95-foot quarried limestone building was dismantled and reassembled at Lummus Park. It became obvious that the reconstruction was less than perfect when, after reassembling the building, there were a large number of bricks and blocks that had not found their proper place. Ironically, the building's most significant history had little to do with its limited role with the fort, but the message was clear. Miamians didn't want to lose their history, particularly those monuments associated with the Seminole Indian Wars.

When laborers demolished the Indian burial mound during the construction of the Royal Palm Hotel, the grave of Capt. Samuel Russell also was destroyed. Russell had been killed on the Miami River in 1839 during a Seminole ambush and buried in the mound. Ironically, when archaeologist Andrew Douglass in search of burial mounds along Miami River in 1883 was led to the large Tequesta mound at the river's mouth by resident E. W. Ewan, Douglass refused to dig there when he discovered that it contained the graves of soldiers.[1]

In an early newspaper account detailing the history of Fort Dallas, author Agnew Welsh described a soldier's missing headstone on the Royal Palm Hotel grounds as being painted white and marked with his name (Granger), his regiment and company, and a masonic emblem. He then made an appeal to the public: "If this old headboard has been preserved by anyone it should be presented to the local masonic bodies."[2]

The graves of dozens of soldiers and Indians are scattered across South Florida as a result of the wars. Indian graves were above ground and were quickly disturbed by the elements. Soldiers were placed in wooden coffins and marked with wooden headboards. Most graves were placed near the various forts and settlements. Today, the exact location of these graves is unknown. Many have been lost to development; others are unlocated because their wooden markers were lost or have decomposed. The only soldier's grave discovered by archaeologists was excavated at the Granada site on the north bank of the Miami River,[3] but other graves may still survive beneath the concrete of downtown Miami or in the sands of Key Biscayne. Only one Seminole warrior's grave has been documented, when avocational archaeologist Dan Laxson excavated the skeletal remains of a Seminole or Miccousuki warrior from a site in Hialeah before it was bulldozed (see chapter 8).

The two decades of the Seminole Wars represent a barely 2-inch stratum of sediment and artifacts in Florida sites. Yet in my experience, this period of time can conjure up more emotion than any other historical era for many Floridians. Perhaps it is the drama of those events or because land that has been bought or lost by blood is dear.

South Florida's 22 years of military conflict are a dark shadow on the area's human history. Those years caused tremendous hardships and losses to both Indians and non-Indians. Assistant Surgeon Ames wrote in 1836 from Fort Brooke in present-day Tampa that "there is neither honor nor glory in the Indian Wars."[4] Although honor and glory may have been in short supply, there was no shortage of disease and death. At Fort Dallas, the largest fort in Miami-Dade County, two died from battle and four from disease during the Second Seminole War.[5] Two subsequent occupations of the fort resulted in seven additional deaths.[6] At Fort Bankhead on Key Biscayne 17 deaths were reported.

Miami-Dade County was an area of strategic importance during the Seminole Indian Wars. Seminole War military sites include the locations of skirmishes, encampments, forts, and the graves of Indians and non-Indians who died during the conflict. The locations of battles or skirmishes are the most difficult to identify based on artifacts, since material evidence is usually limited to spent bullets and a few lost items. A skirmish moving quickly over a wide area of swamp holds little promise of leaving much for an archaeologist to find. An exception to this is the site of the lightkeeper's house on Key Biscayne. Attacked in 1836, the structure was burnt and looted by an estimated 50–60 Spanish Indians.

Archaeologists have made important contributions to our knowledge of this era because of several archaeological projects directed at the sites of Fort Bankhead and Fort Dallas, the former that led to the surprising discovery of a structure believed to be the lightkeeper's house on Key Biscayne burnt by the Seminoles in 1836. The historian has benefited because archaeologists have contributed new information about this period that is not available in the written record. The community has benefited from these discoveries by learning the exact locations where these sites occur, and by being able to see the artifacts associated with these sites, many of which are now in the Historical Museum of Southern Florida.

One of Florida's most significant sites of Indian attack is Indian Key, once the most populated settlement in Dade County. Shifting political tides moved the county boundary northward, leaving Indian Key in the newly formed Monroe County in 1838. The now vacant 16.48-acre island became a state park in 1970 and was the focus of an archaeological excavation directed by the Florida Division of Archives, History and Records Management.[7] More intensive excavations were recently conducted under the direction of Brent Weisman of the University of South Florida.[8] These excavations documented numerous foundations of structures and cisterns and thousands of artifacts, providing a wealth of information on nineteenth-century maritime culture in southern Florida.

In contrast to fortified coastal communities, military sites in the interior are more elusive. Troops encamping in the Everglades traveled lightly and brought few disposable supplies. Military buttons found in the Everglades were likely lost by soldiers or Indians (for example, buttons from a military jacket may have been a trophy taken from a dead soldier). Only three sites in the Everglades of Miami-Dade County have produced evidence of military activities. Madden's Hammock (DA45), located in Miami Lakes, reflects a century-long period of Miccosukee/Seminole occupation beginning in the early nineteenth century and lasting to the end of the nineteenth century, when it was a large village and the location of the green corn dance. It is likely the same location depicted as Council Island on Seminole War maps. The island was attacked by Abner Doubleday and army forces in 1856.[9]

A cuff button depicting a schooner possibly from the uniform of a U.S. Revenue Marine was found near the Snake Creek Canal at a site later destroyed for low-income housing. The Revenue Marines maintained a naval blockade around southern Florida during the Second Seminole War and launched occasional expeditions into the Everglades.

Honey Hill (8DA411) is among the most significant military sites in the eastern Everglades. There a camp dating from the Seminole Wars and the Indian scare of 1849–50 was discovered during clearing for the Dolphin Stadium parking lot. The military had dug a slit trench for use as a privy, and it yielded copper percussion caps, bullets, and the broken shards of a pictorial glass flask. The flask was embossed with a portrait of Zachery Taylor, president of the United States in 1849–50, and was likely created for his election campaign (fig. 9.1). This same site yielded two army artillery buttons, a naval button (fig. 9.2), brass epaulets, musket balls, and a minie ball (fig. 9.3) from the Third Seminole War (1855–58)—all testimony to the numerous military

Figure 9.1. Glass flask sherd depicting Zachary Taylor, 1849–50, from 8DA411. Collection of the Historical Museum of Southern Florida.

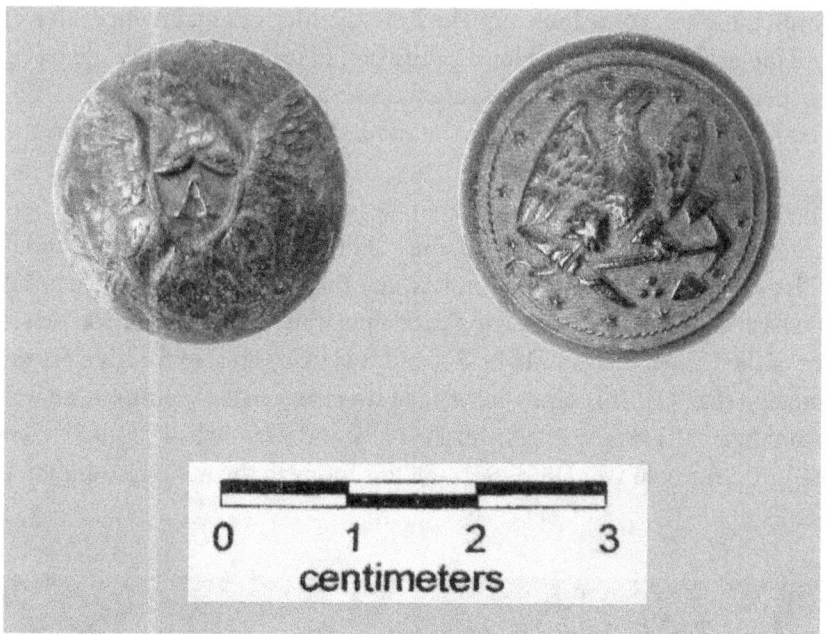

Figure 9.2. Military buttons from 8DA411: army button on the left, navy button on the right. Collection of the Historical Museum of Southern Florida.

Figure 9.3. Musket ball and minie ball from 8DA411. Collection of the Historical Museum of Southern Florida.

expeditions at this prominent site that commanded a view of the headwaters of Snake Creek.

Cape Florida Lighthouse

One of the most dramatic events of the Seminole Wars was the attack on the Cape Florida Lighthouse on July 23, 1836. The attackers were most likely the so-called Spanish Indians (see chapter 8), who had successfully attacked settlers across southern Florida, causing many to abandon their homes. Included in the exodus was lighthouse keeper John DuBose, who fled the Cape Florida Lighthouse with his family, leaving behind the assistant keeper, John W. B. Thompson, and his African American helper, Aaron Carter. Only minutes before the attack, Carter alerted Thompson that he had spotted Indians hiding behind the coconut trees. An estimated 50 to 60 Indians had landed by canoes on the lee side of Key Biscayne and had quietly crept toward the lighthouse. Carter and Thompson raced from their houses with the Indians in hot pursuit. They arrived at the light tower just in time and shut the wooden door behind them. Thompson had already been wounded—musket balls having passed through his clothes and hat. When Carter and Thompson raced up the steps, they shut an iron trap door at the top of the stairs but found themselves exposed to musket fire from the ground. Meanwhile, Indians set fire to the tower door. A tank filled with oil was ruptured by musket balls, soaking Thompson and Carter and the bottom of the lighthouse. Fire quickly spread to the wooden stairs at the center of the 90-foot tall tower.[10] Five musket balls killed Carter, whose body was eventually pushed off the tower by Thompson, who was wounded and severely burned. Believing that the two men were dead, the Indians burned down all of the houses, slaughtering the keeper's animals, and fled with their plunder. The towering inferno was spotted by the crew of the U.S. revenue cutter *Washington*. They rescued Thompson by shooting an iron ramrod attached to twine to the top of the tower, allowing seamen to reach the top and bring him down.[11]

The official assessment of the attack revealed not only the extent of damage but also Miami's first case of building corruption. The assessment revealed that the thick brick walls of the light tower were hollow. The contractor had neglected to place the interior bricks into the walls to cut costs. In 1856, the lighthouse was rebuilt, only to be disabled again during the Civil War by southern sympathizers who destroyed the lens.

In 1971 the lighthouse and the 400 surrounding acres became Bill Baggs State Park. In 1986, proposed improvements to stabilize the light tower and recreate the lightkeeper's house required prior archaeological testing. Park Ranger Don Mattucci, assigned to assist the archaeological team, played a key role in discovering the foundations of the original lightkeeper's house. The structure measured 32 by 16 feet and was constructed with tabby walls and brick foundations placed around the posts of the structure. During part of the attack, the keeper was trapped on top of the blazing light tower while he fired at the Indians looting his dwelling below. During archaeological excavations of the structure, numerous balls of lead shot, many obviously misshapen from striking the walls, were found, along with a variety of domestic artifacts that spanned the decade that the house was used by various lightkeepers and their families. Evidence of the Indian attack was confirmed when the sandy soils around the foundations were carefully sifted to reveal numerous artifacts, including melted glass and spent musket balls—likely fired by the attacking Indians.

Forts

Forts and military camps provide the best opportunity for archaeological research of military culture and subsistence in the South Florida frontier. At least six military posts within the present boundaries of Miami-Dade County earned the distinction of being called a fort. When one hears the term "fort," one usually pictures a substantial fortification surrounded by a stockade. In the Florida wars, however, a fort was often hastily constructed and used for only weeks or months rather than years.

Florida forts were of four major types. The most substantial were stockade forts with picket logs enclosing the position and buildings. Fort Lauderdale on the New River Inlet was of the stockade type. Another type used a stockade of horizontal logs creating a breast work. A faced fort used an earthen wall of soil as at part of the defensive work. Fort Dallas was an open fort without walls, although during its first incarnation as a naval fort in 1838 it may have had a stockade. Fort Bankhead on Key Biscayne was also open. Fort Henry may have been a star-shaped fort and was probably constructed as a breastwork. Fort Kemble was constructed with a breastwork, and Fort Miami on the Miami River is an unknown type—but logic suggests that its proximity to hostile Indian country necessitated at least a breastwork. Camp Wescott, located within Everglades National Park, may have had an earthen breastwork. A temporary fort established at the Ferguson Mill on the north bank of the Miami River may have been simply an open encampment using the mill building as the fortification.

Fort Dallas

Located at the mouth of the Miami River, this fort was the largest and most important in Miami-Dade County. Fort Dallas was constructed on February 13, 1838, however, local historians have debated as to whether the first fort was built on the river's south or north bank. The mystery was caused by several early maps that depict Fort Dallas on the south bank while others show it on the north bank. Reinforcing these contradictory map locations is a statement written to Capt. Martin Burke, who was ordered to occupy the fort in October 1839—the fort's third occupancy. Captain Burke was told to take the post on the "left bank of the Miami, near old Ft. Dallas."[12] Approaching from the bay the left bank would be the south bank at Brickell Point.

If Fort Dallas was initially located on the south bank, it was there for only a short time because, despite extensive archaeological excavations at Brickell Point, not a single military button or any convincing evidence of a military encampment has been found. Only a 4-inch ball of iron shot, typical of what might have been used by a small naval cannon, was uncovered in 1961 by the author. Of course, the absence of artifacts does not conclusively argue against the first Fort Dallas being on the south bank of the river, but when compared to the vast quantity of military artifacts found on the north bank, the importance of the north bank Fort Dallas site is obvious.

Fort Dallas was an open fort without any stockade. The 1849 Gerdes map shows the fort buildings spread across a wide area (fig. 9.4). During the Third Seminole War an army report indicates that new buildings added to the fort included a stable for seven mules, storage house, blacksmith, carpenters shop, two kitchens, a hospital kitchen, and a bake house. They were modest wood structures, many measuring only 15 by 20 feet. Some of the wood was hauled from the pine forest 2 miles distant. Other boards and shingles were purchased in Key West, Jacksonville, and Savannah.[13]

Most of the military artifacts excavated at the Granada site, 8DA11 (at present-day Knight Center) date from the Third Seminole War. In 1978, under the direction of State Archaeologist Carl D. McMurray, archaeologists uncovered several important architectural features associated with the two stone buildings built by William English (one being the "barracks" moved in 1925 to Lummus Park) and subsequently used by the military between 1855 and 1858. McMurray did not provide an inventory or description of any of

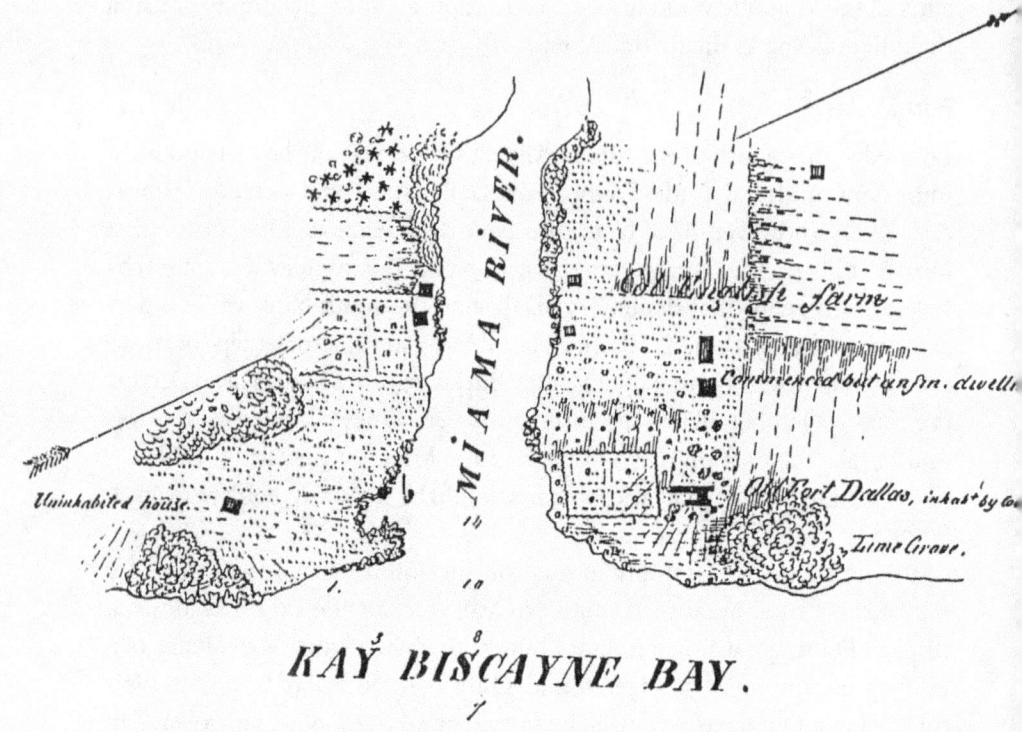

Figure 9.4. Gerdes map of Fort Dallas, 1849. Courtesy of the Historical Museum of Southern Florida.

the uncovered artifacts associated with the fort, stating that although such artifacts were found, they were never in a "closed historic provenience."[14] A grave of a male individual was discovered in the vicinity of what was then the William English home and slave quarters and later used as the officers' quarters and barracks respectively. Since the grave was unmarked and the only associated artifacts were bone buttons, his identity and the exact date of his death remain a mystery.

After the state assessment, the Miami-Dade County Historic Preservation Division conducted three different investigations at the Fort Dallas site. Monitoring of construction projects resulted in the discovery of several features associated with the fort. During construction of the Hyatt Center's swimming-pool deck, evidence of an outhouse was found. It had extended from the river bank over the water. The feature and the adjacent area yielded 10 general service pewter buttons, two brass army uniform buttons, five copper percussion caps, and numerous lead buck and balls.

A second fort feature was discovered in 1981 during the construction of the People Mover near the Hyatt Convention Center when a trash pit dating from the Third Seminole War was uncovered. This pit revealed food remains, several complete bottles, and an extraordinary effigy pipe bowl with the likeness of President Millard Fillmore. This pipe was likely manufactured for Fillmore's unsuccessful presidential campaign of 1856, although his pipes were manufactured from 1850 to 1855.[15] The food refuse found in this trash pit revealed a heavy dependence on domestic animals as opposed to the hunting of wild game and fishing. Although hardly a representative sample, the trash pit suggests that camp life at Fort Dallas relied on using available rations rather than exploiting local natural resources. It is likely that military personnel were limited in their mobility outside the fort area to conduct hunting and foraging expeditions.

The ceramics in this refuse pit were minimal, represented by only a few pieces of plain ironstone. This is not surprising considering that fine china is not normally part of a military inventory, being more likely associated with officers. It also reinforces the possibility that much of the colorful, decorated, nineteenth-century ceramics uncovered at other parts of the Granada site were from settlers rather than military personnel.

More recently, in 2005–7, more of the Fort Dallas site was uncovered by archaeologists at the site of the Royal Palm Hotel and its surrounding landscaped grounds and gardens. In 2005, the Archaeological and Historical Conservancy directed excavations on three vacant parking lots. It was anticipated that evidence of the fort's many out buildings might be found, but it soon was discovered that most of the soils below the parking lots had been disturbed and little structural evidence of the fort's buildings were found. Still, hundreds of artifacts and several trash features associated with the fort were located. The refuse features yielded bottles, kaolin pipes (fig. 9.5), musket balls, faunal bone, and buttons. Most of these artifacts date from the Third Seminole War, revealing that the enlisted men were camping at least a thousand feet from the river and the bay, which suggests that residence on the bay shore and river bank were reserved for the officers.

Fort Bankhead

Fort Bankhead was established on Key Biscayne on April 5, 1838, by Capt. L. B. Webster after Fort Dallas was temporarily abandoned. The fort was named after Lt. Col. James Bankhead, but after the death of Capt. Samuel Russell on the Miami River in 1839, the fort was renamed Fort Russell. The fort was used by both the army and the navy and constructed to protect the lighthouse, partly in response to the deadly Indian attack there in 1836.

The best description of the post survives through the eyes of Captain

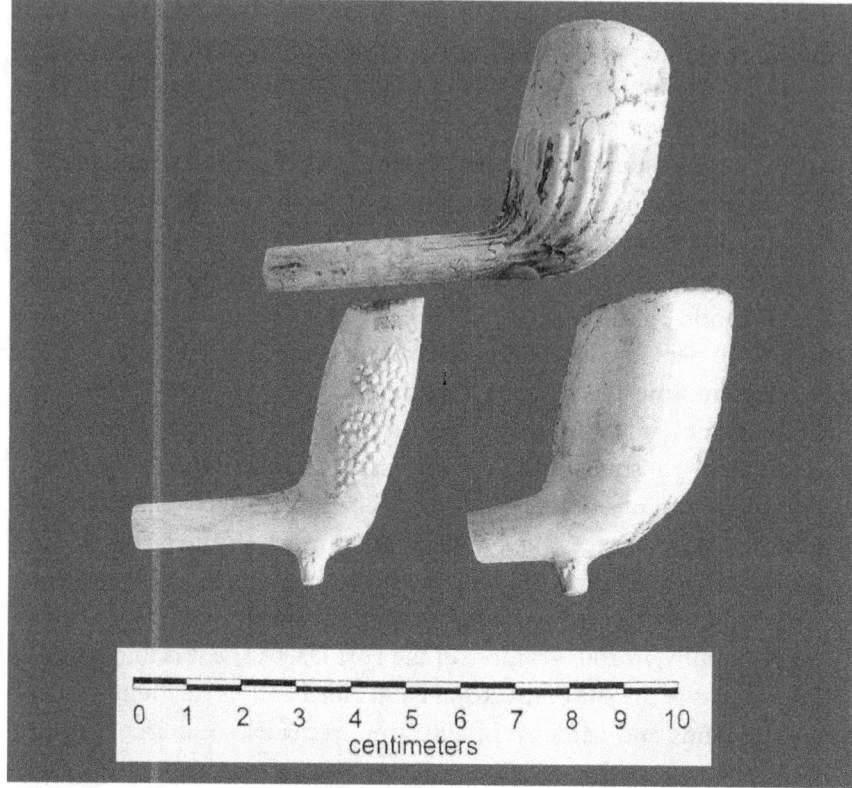

Figure 9.5. Kaolin pipe bowls from Fort Dallas. Collection of the Archaeological and Historical Conservancy.

Vinton, who sketched it in 1839 (fig. 9.6). His sketch shows a leisurely post with the officer's quarters and kitchen and two separate rows of tents near the lighthouse. Much of the fort site has since washed out to sea as a result of the extreme shore erosion that has occurred during the last 150 years. A survey map of 1897 shows that several hundred feet of shoreline had eroded since an earlier survey in 1837. The erosion continued until the 1960s, when the area around the lighthouse was bulk headed and refilled with beach sand.

After Hurricane Betsy in 1965, the sand at the base of the light tower eroded away, exposing pewter military buttons and gunflints (which I collected). The most significant artifact recovered was a hand-sized fragment of the lighthouse lenses, likely broken by the fire set during the 1836 Indian attack or from the confederate raid on the lighthouse during the Civil War. All of those artifacts are now in the Historical Museum of South Florida.

Archaeological testing conducted there in 1983–85[16] and monitoring after

Figure 9.6. View of Fort Russell by Capt. John Rogers Vinton, 1838–40. Courtesy of the Historical Museum of Southern Florida.

Hurricane Andrew in 1992 revealed undisturbed cultural deposits beneath the fill in the vicinity of the lighthouse, but no identifiable features directly associated with the fort have yet been discovered.

Seventeen soldiers were buried at this post.[17] Ten of these men were buried near the fort. A wooden coffin reportedly washed into the sea may have been a soldier's grave.[18] The other graves are still unaccounted for, and some may still be in the vicinity of the lighthouse, although it is more likely that most have been destroyed, victims of the rising sea level and storms.

Fort Kemble

This small temporary outpost was built on the Miami River on October 13, 1839, by naval forces from the steamer *Poinsett* by Commander Isaac Mayo. He reported that the fort was built a short distance from Fort Dallas under the command of Melaneton Smith with 45 men and two officers. Smith built the fort to protect his wood cutters and mounted guns, including a gun from the West Point Kemble Foundry, the namesake of the fort.[19] The location of the fort is unknown, but it was likely in the pinewoods abutting the river bank.

Fort Henry

Fort Henry was depicted on the Ives map of 1856 deep in the Everglades. The history and the exact location of the fort was a total mystery. No historian seemed to know when the fort was built or by whom, or what role it played in the wars. Numerous individuals, using early maps as a reference, searched for the fort site. The Peninsula Archaeological Society claimed to have found it in 1967.[20] They proudly displayed "cannonballs" to reporters and said that they had uncovered them from the fort site in the eastern Everglades. The truth is somewhat less spectacular. The "cannonballs" were, in fact, ball bearings from machinery from the Portland Cement Company. Their Fort Henry was actually the bulldozed remnants of a black-earth midden and Seminole camp (8DA94), located on a tree island adjacent to a rock quarry near Krome Avenue.

The mystery of Fort Henry was not solved until military historian and former Seminole tribal preservation officer Willard Steele tackled the task using the Ives map and additional documents secured from the National Archives. In 1981 Steele located a letter that revealed the origin of the fort. The letter, written on February 25, 1842, by Lt. John B. Marchand, the naval officer who built Fort Henry and was the commander of the steamer *Van Buren* during the Seminole Wars, stated:

> After our encampment yesterday I built Fort Henry about 15 miles from here and at early daylight left there after seeing Rodgers off, reaching this place at two o'clock pm without detection a moment in the way. in [sic] order to give Rodgers as many men as possible I came here with but four men and Joe our guide, leaving at Fort Henry Mid Lieutenant Westcot and fifteen men.
>
> ... and will on my return to Fort Henry which will be tomorrow carry a number of shoes for the men as some of them are nearly barefooted.[21]

Another description of Fort Henry is provided by the famous "father" of baseball, Abner Doubleday, while he was an army captain during the Third Seminole War:

Both going and returning I scouted an immense number of islands with one uniform result. Only two of them presented any Indian sign. One of these probably the island which is called Fort Henry has an immense rubber tree in the center. It is so lofty as to overlook the Everglades in all directions. I made a kind of ladder by which the trunk could be ascended. I found a path about a year old cut through this island, and a square plot of ground dug or turned up. On digging into this I found nothing.[22]

When Steele used the latitude and longitude on the maps depicting Fort Henry, he found only open Everglades prairie at the recorded coordinates. I obtained aerial photographs of the search area and, after several hours of interpretative review, pinpointed a general area where the fort may have been located. I reasoned that nineteenth-century latitudes could not be trusted in terms of accuracy but that the longitude was more likely to be accurate. I followed a mosaic of aerial photographs southward along the longitude bearing. Suddenly the perfect image of a fort in the shape of a four-pointed star was visible on a small island. The aerial camera from a height of 1 mile had captured the signature of the fort's foundation, scarred into the Everglades limestone bedrock still discernible over a hundred years after the navy had left the island.

Unfortunately, both Steele and I arrived at the site years too late. Cultivated rows of beans grew where the fort had once been. The 200-foot-diameter tree island had been rock-plowed. The soil, rock, and presumed artifacts had been chewed into little pieces and spread across the field. Hopefully, the fort will be interpreted some day with an appropriate historic marker. Fort Henry, a naval fort, was the last fort built in Florida during the Second Seminole War.

Fort Desolation

During the 1849 conflict, the Ferguson Mill at the Miami River Rapids was briefly used as a military outpost. The officer in charge, Anson Cooke, humorously referred to the place as "Fort Desolation." The following is an excerpt from his letter of November 1, 1849, to his wife:

You will see my own Dearest by the heading of this that I am some where so I will at once tell you that I am at the headwaters of the Miami with a detachment of six men guarding one man, (who is making coontie or Arrow root), from the Indians who are said to be in the vicinity. I am in supreme command here and five miles from Fort

Dallas and I live in the open loft of a mill, (built for a saw mill) so that if I talk too loud for you when I return you must charge the whole circumstance for one has to speak very loud here to be heard above the din of the waters and the grinding.

The mill shakes me so that I can scarcely write at all, and it is now quite dark, I could not write for before my men have been busy all day putting sides and ends to my room which was before entirely open to the weather and last night I slept very cold, which would not however have been the case if I could have had you my love in my arms. I cannot write with a light the mosquitoes are so thick and even now I have to keep one hand busy all the time to keep them off and even then I succeed very poorly. I must quit for I can no longer see what I am doing.[23]

The encampment associated with Fort Desolation was discovered during the construction of a parking lot near the Miami River. Prior to the construction, archaeological excavations had proved negative, however, during subsequent clearing historic artifacts were observed in the bulldozed soil. (It was later determined that the shovel testing had missed the site by 10 feet.)

A large quantity of historic artifacts were discovered, many with a distinctly military theme. The most common artifacts were ceramic sherds, which were scattered throughout the site. A total of 2,302 glazed ceramic sherds were recovered.

Most compelling of the ceramics was a thick, hard whiteware with a blue transfer print of a complex fortification (fig. 9.7). The plate's center depicts a fort separated by a field of grass, while the plate's rim is a motif of the fort's outer facies and redoubts. The plate is manufactured in Italy as indicated by the manufacturer's mark "Tuscan" with a bird motif/crest on the reverse on the plate's center. A total of 174 sherds, most of them burnt, representing different plates and trays from the service, were found.

The largest number of ceramic sherds are represented by fine, thin china characterized by a brown geometric design and a narrow band around the rim of the plates, cups, and bowls. It would appear that most of an entire service may be represented by the 707 sherds recovered of this ware. Most sherds are burnt. This ware has the distinctive manufacturer's mark of "Copeland & Garrett" within a wreath. This firm is identified as the Spode works in Staffordshire.[24] This particular mark's style is illustrated in Godden's *Encyclopedia of British Pottery and Porcelain Marks* as entry 1091 and was used

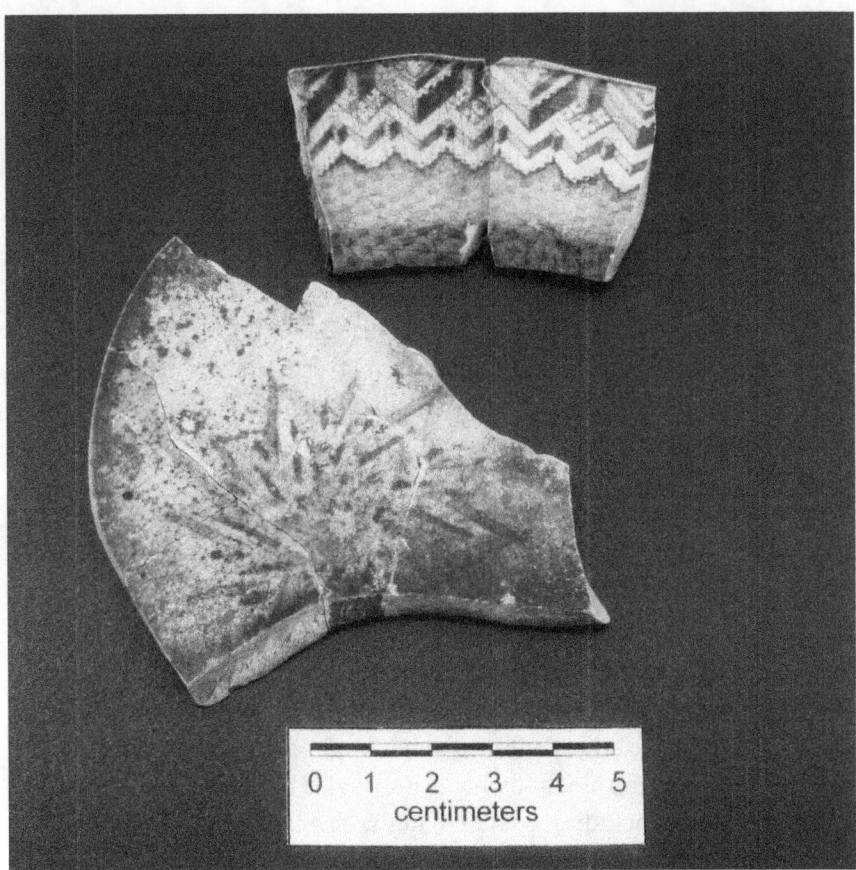

Figure 9.7. Whiteware with transfer print of fort motif from "Fort Desolation," c. 1840s. Collection of the Historical Museum of Southern Florida.

between 1833 and 1847, and, in fact, the registration mark adjacent to the manufacturer's imprint on the recovered plate bases indicates that this set was manufactured on March 5, 1845.[25]

Several large trays and dishes of a blue and yellow floral motif represented by 669 sherds, all burnt, were recovered. This whiteware was identified by the manufacturer's mark of an elaborate motif of flags with the manufacturer's name "Potts." Godden's *Encyclopedia of British Pottery and Porcelain Marks* indicates an identical design (3103) belonging to William Wainwright Potts, who produced "printed earthenwares" after the year 1830.

Other artifacts include hundreds of fused aqua and clear glass fragments—small bottles or vials that had melted. Only a single clear glass stopper was found intact. These fused bottle fragments suggest contents of either spice or medicine. Metal artifacts include a brass key, likely from a trunk and a melted brass compass.

Military-related artifacts include 25 military uniform buttons, most of them associated with a single concentration. The buttons have a standard design of a U.S. eagle with a shield on its chest. All have a soldered loop on the reverse. Most of the specimens are infantry as indicated by the letter "I" on the shield. One specimen has the letter "A," representing the army artillery on the shield. The buttons are of two sizes, 15 and 20 millimeters, representing cuff and breast buttons. Most of the buttons had been severely burnt. The manufacturer's mark on the reverse of the artillery button is stamped "Scovills/Waterbury."

Of particular interest is a cast-iron trivet decorated with an ornate floral design with an American eagle at the top. The eagle's style is typical of the U.S. military and U.S. coinage design of the 1840s–1850s. The artifact was found in five pieces, with a few smaller pieces missing. The artifact is well preserved because of a thick, red, lead-based paint covering the specimen.

These military artifacts are an intriguing inventory of objects that include army buttons and gunflints, which might be expected from any ordinary military campsite, but what is unusual is the large quantity of fine, expensive china, including a set of plates with a fort design—not exactly a mill worker's wife's first choice of tableware but, logically and more likely, the type of tableware associated with an army officer and/or his wife. Additional evidence of this career officer are the military buttons and the cast-iron trivet with a U.S. eagle design. It is probable that most of the artifacts represent material from a single episode of breakage or loss associated with the military occupation of the area during the 1849–50 Indian scare or "Phony War."

The broken plates and crockery represent the loss of an entire dining set and tableware that traveled with an officer or officer's wife assigned to the post. The risks of moving so much china into the interior near the edge of the Everglades are obvious. Since most of the artifacts are burnt, the shelter or structure likely caught fire and destroyed the contents, including much of the personal possessions. Another possible explanation is that the material was broken while being transported from the boat (the trunk holding the items could have been dropped, for example). Subsequently, these items and others were simply burnt in a trash fire. The least likely hypothesis is that this feature is a trash pit of broken and discarded items from everyday attrition. This seems unlikely because the number of ceramics uncovered is so high. There are at least 30 to 50 different bowls, plates, and cups present. The discovery of 25 military buttons (all burnt except for one) suggests the loss of an entire uniform. No matter how damaged a uniform might be, a soldier will always salvage the buttons since these had to be special ordered (and paid for) from the quartermaster. It is more likely that the buttons, the uniform, an expensive brass compass, as well as a table set of fine china were lost in a fire. The large quantity of iron fasteners found suggests that the objects were in a trunk possibly inside a structure. Undoubtedly, future historic research may uncover archival documentation of the Fort Desolation fire.

The Military Road

The most enduring achievement of the Indian Wars was the construction of Miami-Dade County's first road. Built under the command of Capt. Abner Doubleday in 1856–57, the 35-mile span connecting Fort Lauderdale with Fort Dallas was hacked through pinewoods and swamp, spanning creeks with wooden bridges. The incredible difficulty in building a road in the South Florida wilderness is indicated in this excerpt from a letter reporting on its construction:

> Having arrived at Little River, distance 5 miles, I commenced on the morning of the 16th the building of a bridge across that stream. The width of the river at this point is 70 feet and length of bridge 81 feet. Depth of river from 4 1/3 to 6 1/2 feet. On the north side of the river I found a prairie which is dry at this season, except near the river, where it is at present very boggy. It became necessary to corduroy the road from the bridge to a distance of 408 feet across the prairie—A ditch was dug, 4 feet wide and 3 deep, on either side, the earth being thrown in the center of the road & mixed in with sawgrass & branches from small bushes, making the road about 16 feet in width. Sleepers were lain in the road about 240 feet from the bridge, where the soil was found to be most yielding, between which earth was again thrown mixed with bushes. Logs were then laid across the bridge the sleepers & secured at the ends by about a foot of earth. This work was carried on while the bridge was being built.
> On the 27th, I sent to Fort Dallas 5 sick men, leaving me 39.[26]

After the war, the road evolved with the community and eventually became Dixie Highway, which followed much of the original route. Today only a few segments of the military trail survive. Although capped with asphalt and crushed limestone, a section near NE 160th Street and another segment that crosses the natural arch at Arch Creek and traverses the western edge of Carl Mertz County Park north of NE 135th Street still survive.

Part IV
Pioneer Miami

Hermann Trappman, *Operations at the Arch Creek Coontie Mill*, 1983. Pencil on paper, 8 × 10. Collection of the Archaeological and Historical Conservancy. By permission of the artist.

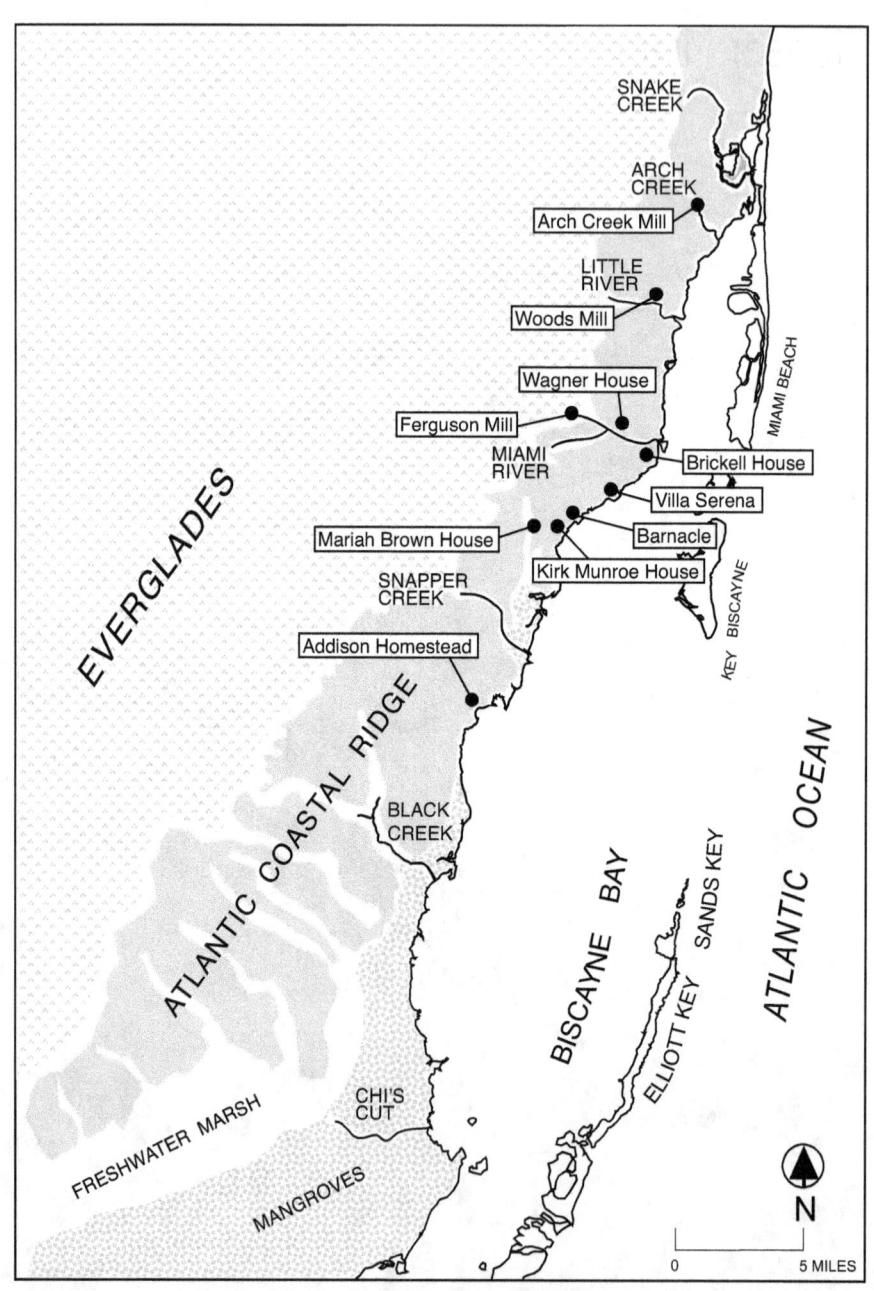

Pioneer sites of Miami-Dade County. Map created by John G. Beriault. Courtesy of the Archaeological and Historical Conservancy.

10

The Archaeology of Arrowroot

Miami's First Industry

After the United States purchased Florida from Spain in 1819, new settlers brought a new attitude toward the land and new economic strategies to survive in the South Florida frontier. Unlike earlier English settlers, who were maritime oriented, subsisting on an "island economy" that included catching sea turtles and wrecking, some American entrepreneurs began to shift their vision toward gaining wealth from intensive agriculture. As early as 1820, Peter Stephen Chazotte, a Frenchman who had formerly escaped a slave rebellion in Haiti, proposed developing coffee plantations on Key Largo and building a town south of the Miami River, to be named Jeffersonville, on the shores of Biscayne Bay.[1] Chazotte's coffee plantations never materialized, but other Americans learned that cultivating and harvesting tropical plants could earn them a livelihood. In 1836, Henry Perrine, a prominent New York botanist, petitioned the U.S. government to grant him land at present-day Cutler to introduce and cultivate a diverse assemblage of tropical plants, including sisal for making rope. Although the Perrine grant was eventually confirmed, Perrine's dreams ended when he was slain during the Indian attack at Indian Key in 1840.

Although much was made of introducing commercial plants into the South Florida environment, no one native plant captured the attention of pioneer settlers as did coontie. Growing profusely across the Atlantic Coastal Ridge, particularly in the pine flatwoods, it also thrived on many of the Everglades tree islands. Coontie (*Zamia pumila*), or comptie, as it was known by the pioneer settlers, is a cycad, an ancient, fernlike plant with thick, succulent tuber roots (fig. 10.1). This root is poisonous if eaten without appropriate processing, but when processed correctly, it yields a powdery white flour suitable for baking bread and cakes.

The pioneers may have learned from the Seminoles and other Native Americans that coontie was an important source of flour and starch. The

Figure 10.1. Photo of coontie (*Zamia pumila*). Courtesy of the Archaeological and Historical Conservancy.

natives likely shared their knowledge of this plant and how to remove its poisons with the settlers. In the nineteenth century the plant grew in Miami-Dade County in such abundance that the J. C. Ives map of 1856 shows a large area in present-day Cutler Ridge as the "Coontie Grounds" because this area was regularly visited by the Seminoles for harvesting. Coontie became the principal product for southeast Florida's economy during the mid-nineteenth century. It was so abundant in the pinewoods that a harvester could collect five or six barrels a day. Estimates vary considerably on how many barrels of root it took to make a 250-pound barrel of finished flour, but a contemporary of the early mills stated it took five barrels of root to make one barrel of flour.[2] Manual operations used perforated sheet metal, usually soft metals such as tin, zinc, or even lead, to grate the coontie. Larger operations used a grinder made "by driving rows of shoe peg nails into two short round logs and making one log turn against the other so that the nails chewed up the roots." The ground coontie was then placed in a sieve under which a container was placed for collecting the starch, which settled on the bottom of the tank, and the water containing the toxin was then drained off.

The remaining starch consisted of two layers, a white layer—the pure starch—covered by an impure yellow layer. Both layers were edible, but the white layer was more highly prized. Early manufacturers may have used both layers, but later producers did not. This may account for the discrepancy in estimates as to how many barrels of roots it took to make a barrel of flour. Gerdes gave the ratio at five to one, while Thelma Peters reported it at nine to one. The starch was then dried and placed into barrels. It was generally shipped by way of Key West to markets in New Orleans and Charleston.[3]

The finished product was similar to arrowroot, a close relative, which was produced in the Caribbean. The Caribbean arrowroot brought 75 cents a pound in the 1840s, whereas that made in Miami sold for 10 cents a pound, giving the Miami producers a clear advantage. The product apparently sold well, and any early settler who needed cash could grind a barrel and ship it to market.[4]

The pioneers used a variety of methods to process the starch. Horses or mules could be used to provide the power to turn the grinder—the device that would crush the plant into a pulp. In other instances, water power was used. Pioneer Charles W. Pierce, who arrived in South Florida in 1872, describes the construction of a grinding mill in his memoirs:

> At one time the making of starch from the coontie root was the main source of income for most of the settlers on the bay. Those who had a horse or mule rigged up power mills, but few were fortunate enough to have any power other than their hands and arms. When a man decided to make starch the first operation was to construct the grinding mill. A section of a large tree about eighteen inches long would be pressed to a perfect round, then shoe nails would be driven in diagonal rows about half an inch apart until the log was covered. About half the length of the nails were left above the surface. These nails were the teeth of the grinder. Then an axle was attached and on the end of it was the crank. The cylinder was then mounted on a box frame above which the hopper was attached. Close beside the grinder was a large tank that was filled by a hand pump. There was also close to the grinder a washing tank to wash the dirt from the coontie roots as they came from the woods. When the roots were washed clean they were dumped into the hopper. Then the grinder was cranked until the roots were ground to a pulp by the rows of shoe nails. Sliding down an inclined board into the water tank, the ground mass was thoroughly stirred, then drawn off into another tank and left to settle. When the white starch had precipitated to the bottom of the tank, the water, called "redwater" from its color that was caused by tannin in the root, would be run off, the

starch shoveled up and placed on cloth-covered frames to dry. When dry it was barreled and shipped to Key West for sale.[5]

The water mills were the most ambitious attempts to process the coontie. By the beginning of the Third Seminole War in 1855, every creek and river in Dade County had at least one coontie mill operating on its banks. Arch Creek, Little River, and Wagner Creek had one mill each, and the Miami River had no less than five operating mills.

Woods Mill

In 1843 Alva F. Woods, in fulfillment of the Armed Occupation Act, settled on 160 acres on the north bank of the Little River. There Woods constructed a water mill for coontie processing and a "wood frame and boarded structure."[6] This mill included a sluice extending several hundred feet north of the river. It was encountered by George McKay in 1845 when

Figure 10.2. Aerial photo depicting Woods's mill race, 1926. Courtesy of the Archaeological and Historical Conservancy.

surveying a section line. A 1926 aerial photograph reveals remnants of the mill race (fig. 10.2). The house was likely nearby. In 1980 I found ceramic sherds and stoneware dating from the 1840s in the area of the mill site, as well as steps cut into the bedrock descending into a root cellar structure also cut into solid limestone bedrock.

Arch Creek Mill

In 1979, the sluice run for the Arch Creek coontie mill was accidentally discovered by archaeologists from the Dade County Historic Preservation Division during archaeological investigations of the prehistoric Arch Creek midden (8DA23). Test excavations were being conducted on a portion of the midden north of NE 135th Street under the direction of Irving Eyster with students from Miami-Dade Community College. A strange feature had been observed cut in the limestone bluff on the west side of the creek next to the natural bridge. This feature was believed by some local historians to be the boat landing used by nineteenth-century settlers. As the volunteers dug into the rubble that covered the feature, no steps were found on the creek bank as had been expected. Eyster, a native of Indiana, quickly recognized it as a mill race. The rubble covered and filled the semicircular sluice that provided the water power for Arch Creek's coontie mill.

On April 13, 1981, the Miami-Dade Historic Preservation Division, with the help of students and members of the Archaeological Society of Southern Florida, began a 10-day excavation of the sluice. A backhoe was used to remove most of the rubble and fill from within the top 2 feet of the mill race, as well as the asphalt paving of Old Dixie Highway that covered the natural bridge and the sluice. The 80-foot-long sluice was divided into eight separate 10-foot sections and then excavated. Modern debris characterized most of the fill, but about a foot above the sluice bottom were large quantities of crockery, brown and white glazed stoneware, beer bottle fragments, and black bottle glass. Excavations revealed iron nails, cast-iron stove parts, and a clay pipe fragment, sherds of a late-style olive jar, and a curry comb (fig. 10.3).

The excavations revealed well-preserved details of the mill's operation. Large quantities of charcoal and wood were discovered in Section 3. Remains of the original wooden water wheel (Feature A) were found. Slots for the shaft of the water wheel were drilled into both sides of the sluice wall. Directly associated with this feature was the charred wooden axle, a portion of which was removed and placed in the research collection of the Historical

Figure 10.3. Curry comb from Arch Creek Mill, 8DA1655. Courtesy of the Historical Museum of South Florida.

Museum of Southern Florida. It was observed that a circular cut had been made 15 inches deep into the west wall of the sluice to allow for the wheel itself to be situated. The wheel base was only 4 inches above the floor of the sluice. Feature 3 represents two narrow niches that extend vertically on the sluice walls. It is believed that these niches allowed a wooden gate to slide up or down the sluice walls, enabling the water volume affecting the wheel to be partially controlled.

The extensive charcoal in the sluice indicates that the workings of the mill had been burnt. No conclusive historical documentation has been found indicating the date of the fire, but it is possible that the abandoned mill workings had been burnt by Union naval patrols during the Civil War, particularly since Union raids on other mills on the Miami River are recorded.[7] Most of the artifacts recovered from the sluice appear to date from the 1860s.

One of the surprises in the mill race were the numerous (over 40) cut limestone blocks, possibly foundation stones, that littered the bottom of the run. Each block was 2 feet square and weighed at least 40 pounds. The function of these cut stones is still a mystery. Did these stones once support the wooden mill or a nearby structure? After the excavation, the rocks were removed from the mill race and placed along an abandoned roadway inside the park. Unfortunately, two years later a park work crew cleaning debris hauled them to a dump and not one was saved. Although the sluice has since been refilled for liability concerns, hopefully the mill sluice and wheel will someday be reconstructed and interpreted as part of Arch Creek Park.

Ferguson Mill

The largest mill in Dade County was the Ferguson Mill, which was operated by two brothers on the north fork of the Miami River. The parents of the Fergusons were obviously patriots, naming two of their sons George Washington and Thomas Jefferson. Leaving New York, they were among the first to resettle Miami after the Second Seminole War. They arrived with their families at Key West about 1843 and moved to Miami in 1844.[8] There were at least two other Ferguson brothers, Daniel and Fernando. Daniel was with Thomas in California at the time of the 1850 census and does not appear on the 1844 Dade County jurors list. His success in the California gold fields suggests that his connection with the Miami operation was minimal. The fourth and youngest brother, Fernando, acted as a clerk for the Miami mill. Other Fergusons, Albert, Isaac, and William, appear on the 1844 Dade County jurors list, but their relationship to the family operation is unclear.[9]

Soon after arriving in Key West, the Fergusons came to Miami and established themselves at the head of the Miami River. Rose Richards, daughter of William Wagner, who arrived in Miami in 1858, stated in a 1903 *Miami News* article that the brothers built not only the coontie mill at the rapids but also a sawmill and homes for their families.[10] Contemporary maps of the area, correspondence between Thomas and his wife, and census records indicate that the families of the brothers lived in Key West, not Miami. Furthermore, the sawmill and coontie mill were one in the same. The Fergusons spent $5,000, their life savings, building the mill. Although built as a sawmill, it was converted to a coontie mill sometime before 1846. Adaptable functions are reflected by the fact that people who saw the mill in 1849, years after its conversion to a coontie mill, referred to its having been built as a sawmill.[11] There are no depictions of the mill other than the 1849 Gerdes map (fig. 10.4).

Since the Miami River was considered a navigable stream, George Ferguson petitioned Florida's legislative assembly and asked for permission to

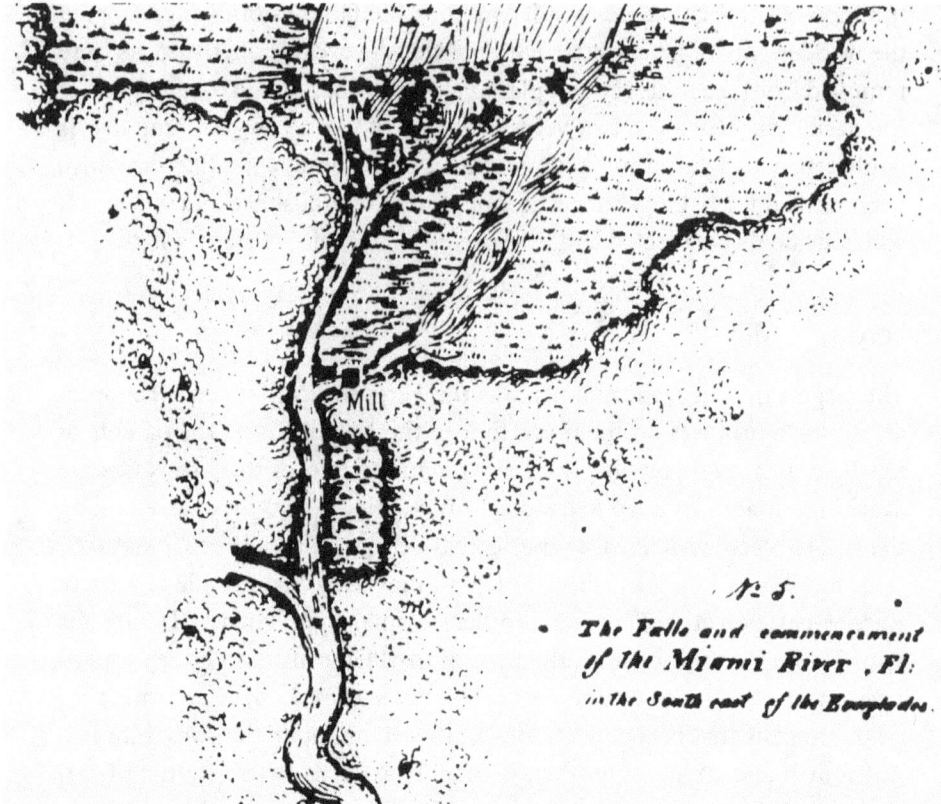

Figure 10.4. Gerdes map of Ferguson Mill, 1849. Courtesy of the Historical Museum of Southern Florida.

dam the Miami River aforesaid for the purpose of creating a water power at some numerous small tributary streams and within two miles of its headquarters wheresoever the land can be controlled for the purpose....

Believing the prosperity of Dade County to depend very much upon the petitioner hopes for a favorable response.[12]

Near where the mill was built the river divided into three branches. Each branch had rapids, but the middle or main branch, with the largest rapids, would become a tourist attraction in the late nineteenth century. Here the water from the Everglades fell 6 feet over a distance of 450 feet. The rapids were 45 to 60 feet wide and were apparently an impressive sight as the first survey of the state of Florida done in 1846 made note of it, referring to it as the "Falls."

The mill building was built directly over a northern prong of the north fork of the river. Early surveyors consistently show the mill but not the dam that powered it. This is probably because the mill, as at Arch Creek, was built over the dam. Surveyors' field notes indicate that the dam was 10 chains (660 feet) due west of the northeast corner of Section 33, Township 53 south, Range 41 east. This would be very near the location of the early-twentieth-century Miami Water Company and very close to the Miami Canal. The canal dredging may have destroyed it. This would fit with Ralph Munroe's comment that he did not see the remains of the mill after the construction of the canal.[13]

George Ferguson had a business arrangement with a Joseph Y. Porter of Key West to supply him with coontie flour in exchange for goods. Porter gave the Fergusons four cents a pound credit on the flour and then made arrangements to ship the flour from Key West to market in New Orleans. After deducting costs, Porter and the Fergusons would split the profits, which varied depending on the market. This agreement seems to have worked out amicably until Porter, believing he could get a better price for the flour in Charleston and being unable to arrange for the flour to be shipped to New Orleans, shipped 1,725 pounds of Ferguson's flour, valued at $140, by way of the small mail boat bound for Charleston. It might have been a good decision had not the mail boat sunk in a storm. Porter died soon after. George sued his heirs for the value of the shipment, claiming he had not authorized Porter to ship the flour to Charleston. The case went all the way to the Florida Supreme Court. In January 1851 the case was declared a mistrial.[14]

Undoubtedly, coontie flour sales by the Fergusons were among the highest in Dade County. The Fergusons also were the county's biggest employers. Historians Paul George and Joe Knetsch's report that "during one year in the late 1840's, the Ferguson Brothers employed twenty five laborers who produced 300,000 pounds of coontie starch, netting more than $24,000 from the sales; this figure represents about $650,000 in 1990."[15]

The particular prong of the river chosen by the Fergusons for their mill had several natural advantages. Unlike the main fork of the north fork, which is broad and shallow, the mill branch is narrow and deep with nearly vertical walls. The headwaters of the creek drained from the Everglades into the creek, which was characterized by a spring located in an open area of the headwaters that continued to provide water for the mill even during the driest times. The purity of this water probably assisted in the rinsing process as well. Later, when George Ferguson moved the operation several miles eastward on the river, the incursion of saltwater into his water supply due to a drought ruined a batch of his starch, the poor quality of which cost him considerable business.[16]

To make matters even more difficult for the Fergusons, a brief "war" broke out with the Seminoles. Only a footnote in the history books, the Indian scare of 1849–50, seemed at first to be the general outbreak that the settlers had predicted. It caused the abandonment of many settlements and the reopening of several forts in the area. Governor Thomas Brown received reports that "there remains but one single person south of New Smyrna on the Eastern shore." By this time Thomas Ferguson had joined his brother Daniel in Panama, from where they made their way to the California gold fields to seek their fortune. As Thomas put it in a letter to his wife Rosalinda, "Give me the digging of the root of all evil, not compty roots." George sought the safety of Key West for a short time but was soon back in Miami.

The brief conflict resulted in the placement of the U.S. Army at the mill (see chapter 9), but otherwise life was uneventful and George continued operating the mill during its last years with unusual success. At this time George had 25 people employed at the mill. The 1850 Dade County Census gives a partial listing of those working at the mill: George W. Ferguson, 38, of New York; George H. Parker, 32, of England; William I. Smith, 34, of Maryland; Andrew B. Pacety, 20, of Florida; George Mazlen, 21, of England; Peter Leith, 32, of Germany; James Davidson, 30, of Ireland; George Marshall, 50, of England; George Baker, 17, of Belgium; and Charles Lee, 22, of New York.[17]

The Search for Ferguson's Mill

One of the last accounts of anyone seeing the ruins or machinery of the mill operations was reported in 1903, when R. C. Richards wrote in a *Miami News* article that the grinding stones of the Ferguson mill were still visible near Miami River's north fork. In 1935, Commodore Ralph Munroe wrote that he last saw the mill ruins just prior to 1909, when the canal was being dredged, and never saw them after that event.[18]

It is difficult to believe that the Miami River Rapids was once a prime tourist attraction for the city's first visitors. From 1900 to 1909 it was the feature attraction of a daily boat trip from the mouth of the Miami River. This trip was often supplemented with a special train tram that ran through the tropical hammock, ending with the visitors disembarking and walking across wooden planks along the muddy river bank to a wooden observation tower built to allow visitors to view the vast Everglades stretching westward from the river's headwaters. Despite thousands of visitors and numerous postcards of the rapids, no historic marker pointed the way to this site and not one informant or document could be found to locate this site in relation to Miami's current streets and features. As difficult as it is to believe, in 70 years a major tourist landmark had disappeared without a trace. In 1980, I searched for the location of the rapids and the river's headwaters. At that time their location was unknown because of the tremendous alterations that had affected the Miami River: The river had been channelized, adjacent areas had been filled, and extensive development had occurred. The site's disappearance was augmented by the popular misconception that the rapids had been dynamited and destroyed when the Miami River was dredged in 1909. However, when archaeological investigations began in 1982, pieces of information began to surface to indicate that the popular notions about the rapids' demise were incorrect. Historian Arva Parks shared with me a number of maps, including the Gerdes survey of 1849, which identified the location of a coontie mill at the headwaters of the Miami River. Howard Kleinberg, former editor of the *Miami News* and author of many articles on Miami's history, joined the team to compare data and visit an area on the old north fork of the Miami River that I thought might be the site of the coontie mill. The location was adjacent to the Miami Canal in a large grassy lot with a concrete-block house structure converted for use for manufacturing storm shutters. Several subsurface tests dug on the property revealed compacted limestone rock fill across most of the parcel. On June 28, 1982, several backhoe test trenches were dug which penetrated the fill and uncovered a large sherd of blue transfer whiteware and a long wooden pine pole beneath the fill. The plate fragment was an important clue because it appeared to date from the mid-nineteenth century, exactly the time when the mill was in operation.

In 1986 the city of Miami designated the area as an archaeological site, the first site so designated by the city. The boundaries of the site included four lots, three of which included private parcels and the third a small city park then known as Paradise Point Park. As a result of the historic designation, the city park's name was changed to Miami River Rapids Park. The parcels on either side of the park were privately owned, one of them by a storm shutter company and the other by Bruce Sugar, who used several small CBS buildings on the property as part of a marine salvage business.

In 1989, Bruce Sugar advised me that he had acquired the LaRoca parcel and was attempting to conduct a land swap with the state of Florida that would provide him with property directly adjacent to the Miami Canal in exchange for the site parcel. The Miami-Dade Historic Preservation Division encouraged the transaction and in 1990, when the public acquisition was completed, the state transferred the property to the city of Miami.

Preservationists were shocked to learn that soon after Miami acquired the parcel it leased the property to Miami Bridge, a private not-for-profit corporation dedicated to working with children in need, to allow them to build a new facility with a 24-bed shelter home on the site. Tempering what appeared to be the imminent destruction of the site were assurances by the directors of Miami Bridge, Inc. and their architect, Raul Rodriguez, that they would construct a facility that would be designed to minimize adverse impacts to the site's archaeological remains and existing environmental features. Also, the existing park parcel would not be built upon, nor would the new building be constructed on the known site boundaries. In fact, the final building construction used a design which minimized subsurface construction, and no dirt below the building footprint was removed, except from the footers.

In March 1991 an archaeological plan was developed in conjunction with the state and the Miami-Dade Historic Preservation Division that included archaeological testing across the project parcel combined with monitoring of construction work by an archaeologist.

In the same month archaeological investigations were started on the parcel by the Archaeological and Historical Conservancy with volunteer assistance from the Archaeological Society of Southern Florida. Twenty-nine test units were excavated during the three-week study in the southwest corner of the property at the convergence of a small creek with the north fork of the Miami River, where I had conducted tests in 1982.[19]

Level 1 was limestone rock fill, likely dredged from the Miami Canal. Level 2 was a dark brown, silty sand averaging about 20 centimeters in thickness. The sediment was screened through a quarter-inch mesh. Cultural material was collected, bagged, and given field specimen numbers. Level 3, when present, consisted of a sterile white/tan mottled sand located directly above and on top of the bedrock.

A number of diagnostic historic artifacts were found, such as ceramic sherds and bottle glass, including fragments from a square case bitters bottle. Other artifacts are described below.

Coin

Only one coin was found during the investigations, a copper half cent manufactured in 1829 in Liege, Belgium. The coin's country of origin is of interest because the 1850 census records indicate at least one of Ferguson's workers, George Baker, was born in Belgium.

Wrought-Iron Wheel

A wrought-iron wheel measuring 66 centimeters in diameter was uncovered in unit 97N/65E. This wheel may be from a steam engine (possibly even mill related), but its function and age are unclear.

Copper Daguerreotype Plates

Two rectangular daguerreotype plates were uncovered. The first plate was uncovered during the 1982 excavations when trenches were dug. A second plate was discovered in 1991 in Unit 65N/53E. An examination of the copper three-inch plates revealed a makers stamp, the letter "A" embossed within a circle in the lower right-hand corner. A reference guide to early photographs indicates that this hallmark was used by Edward Anthony and Company in the 1850s, most likely after 1853.[20] Anthony's principal studio was in New York City. Whatever photographic image had existed on the plate had long since disappeared, a victim of organic soils and water.

Lead Musket Ball

One highly corroded 54-millimeter lead ball was uncovered from Unit 65N/50E.

Lead Baling Pin

A problematical lead pin with a plain circular head suggesting a baling seal was uncovered from Unit 99N/73E.

Percussion Cap

A fired copper percussion cap was found in Unit 97N/65E.

Copper Leather Boss

A fragmentary ornate copper boss, probably associated with a leather strap or saddle, was found in Unit 97N/65E.

•

Archival records indicate that the Ferguson Mill began operations in 1844 and continued through 1851 or 1852, when the mill operation was moved to another location on the Miami River after the Ferguson land claim was found invalid (the Fergusons apparently never filed their claim). By the 1890s arrowroot had lost its glitter. Miami's economic boom had been replaced by another: land sales and tourism. The mill site was located where a wooden observation tower would eventually be, allowing thousands of Miami's first tourists who were taken by boat up the Miami River to see the rapids and the pristine Everglades. Within 10 years that Everglades vista and the rapids were destroyed—a victim of the dredging of the Miami River Canal. Miami's growth spurt had begun.

11

Tropical Homesteads

Artifacts of Miami's Pioneers

There is a popular misconception that historic archaeologists are laboring to reach back to those hallmarks that define the beginning of the American experience, such as the settlement of St. Augustine or Jamestown. But archaeology is the study of material culture, and although many investigations focus on the distant past, some archaeological discoveries yield surprising revelations of a community's more recent past—the broad cultural patterns that shaped the social and economic growth of a community—and sometimes uncover artifacts associated with specific families or individuals that reach beyond the written record to provide a glimpse of a family's past or a long-lost secret.

Archaeological investigations have provided a tangible link to some of Miami's earliest pioneer families, including the Wagners, Addisons, Frows, Browns, and Brickells. These families arrived in the Miami area when southern Florida was still a frontier. South Florida had a loss of population during the Second Seminole War (1836–42), and after the war those who returned to their old homesteads did so slowly. With the final departure of U.S. troops at the end of the Third Seminole War in 1858, the Fort Dallas settlement at the mouth of the Miami River emerged as a rough-and-tumble frontier outpost. The Miami settlement was described at the end of the Civil War by John Wood, aide to General C. Breckridge, the former Confederate secretary of war, who was fleeing capture by Federal forces in June 1865:

> [There were] of all colors from Yankee to ebony Congo, all armed: a more motley and villainous crew never trod at Captain Kidd's ships. we saw all at once with whom we had to deal—deserters from the Army and the Navy of both sides, a mixture of Spaniards and Cubans, outlaws and renegades.[1]

Urban archaeology is in a unique position to examine and dissect its own urban and frontier history. Whether of white or black, rich or poor, patterns of land use, subsistence, and material consumption can be discerned by viewing cultural material assemblages at house sites. From the wealthy Brickells and presidential candidate William Jennings Bryan to African American hotel employee Mariah Brown, the archaeology of Miami's pioneers can reveal the patterns of daily life.

The Wagners

William Wagner was born in 1825, the son of German immigrants. He served in the U.S. military and was wounded in the Mexican-American War in 1847. At Fort Moultrie, South Carolina, he married a French Creole, Eveline Aimar, 15 years his senior. Wagner brought his wife to Fort Dallas in 1855, following his former army company, where he became partners with a Captain Sinclair to set up a sutlers' store to serve troops at the post during the Third Seminole War. Wagner stayed on past the war, the family having to survive the hardships of the Civil War, where imports of commodities and cash were scarce because of the U.S. naval blockade in place to suppress southern sympathizers, several of whom operated out of the Miami community.

Perhaps the Wagners appreciated their isolation 2 miles from Miami's principal settlement. Traveling from their homestead to the mouth of the river where most people lived meant either a boat trip from Wagner Creek to the Miami River or a long wagon ride or horse ride through the pinewoods. The Wagners brought some semblance of family values to the frontier, introducing Miami's first Catholic church since the Spanish mission of 1743—a wood-frame structure built near the banks of Wagner Creek in 1888.

The family prospered, growing crops, processing arrowroot flour, and raising livestock—enough to feed the family of five. Their daughter Rose wrote detailed accounts of their life for Miami's first newspaper, the *Miami News*, providing a rare insight into Miami's frontier life.[2]

Their story may have remained largely forgotten if not for the discovery of the original Wagner House in 1978 by historian Arva Parks, who discovered the house still standing at 1145 NW Eighth Avenue, covered by modern plaster. It was hard to believe: Miami's oldest house, outside of the Fort Dallas structure (which had been completely rebuilt in 1921) was still standing camouflaged beneath a plastered Mediterranean façade in a deteriorating low-income neighborhood. Research has revealed that this was not the house's original location. It had been moved in the early twentieth century from a location nearer the creek so that the house could straddle a lot that conformed to a newly platted neighborhood laid out in 1912. By that date, the Wagner church and other outbuildings had long disappeared.[3]

The archaeological chapter of Wagner story began in 1980, when Miami's new Metro-Rail corridor was announced. The Wagner's house was located uncomfortably close to the proposed Metro-Rail Culmer Station, which was to be located about 500 feet south of the house. As alarm bells sounded with local preservationists, the property owner pressured the county to remove the vacant structure and allow him to move forward with his plans to build a duplex on the property. Led by the Dade County Heritage Trust, the house's modern alterations were peeled away and the house moved to Lummus Park, where it would await restoration.

After the house was moved, I, while county archaeologist, with assistant archaeologist Irving Eyster and working with student volunteers, conducted archaeological excavations at the house site, digging where the porch once had been situated. Careful screening of the shallow, sandy soil uncovered dozens of artifacts, including numerous glass beads probably lost by the many Seminoles who had visited the family early in the twentieth century.

When Metro-Rail construction began, I monitored the area where the rail crossed Wagner Creek. A beautiful broken purple glass cross was discovered within the creek floodplain—perhaps an artifact from either the church or the Wagner family itself.

The Addisons of Cutler

After the Wagners settled on the outskirts of Miami's bustling Fort Dallas community, another family, the Addisons, arrived several years later in the wilds of Dade County's southern frontier. John and Mary Addison settled in the "Hunting Grounds," a lush tropical hammock that represents mainland Florida's last upland embrace of Biscayne Bay before the coastline disappears southward behind a mosaic of mangrove thickets and estuaries. John Addison was the son of one of Florida's first settlers. The Addisons arrived in Leon County from North Carolina about 1825. They then moved to Manatee County, where John was born in 1827. He and his three brothers served in their father's "Addison's Company of Florida Mounted Volunteers," mustered during the Third Seminole War. After the death of his father in 1858, John brought his wife, Mary Townsend Addison, to the Hunting Grounds.

This may have been in 1859 or 1860, when he was in his early thirties. Mary was 12 years his senior. Addison settled on the old Perrine Grant. His homestead was isolated and only easily accessible by boat.

By 1886 at least 36 settlers had moved into other vacant land in the Perrine Grant. Forming a squatters union, the group elected William Cutler as their leader, incorporating their community as the town of Cutler. By 1884, they had established their own post office and blazed a trail through the pinewoods connecting their communities to Coconut Grove by horse and buggy. In 1898, a satisfactory resolution was reached between the squatters union, the Perrine heirs, and the U.S. government, resulting in granting the Addisons 80 acres of land.

Henry Perrine Jr., son of the famous botanist, visited his family grant in 1876 and apparently was not alarmed by the presence of the Addisons squatting on his family's land. He described John Addison as being "a very good-hearted man, but illiterate" and his wife Mary as being "tall, thin, very pale and has long gray hair; has a kindly face and shows evidence of more culture than her husband."[4] He also described the Addison home as being "a very ordinary log kitchen about fifteen feet square, with a veranda on the north side of it; and a rough board building about the same size, containing one room, located about ten feet in front, between the kitchen and the Bay."[5]

The author Caroline Washburn Rockwood visited the Addisons with Commodore Ralph Munroe and described the bounty of the Addison's flower laden porch and yard, while Munroe photographed the house.[6]

John and Mary were childless, and to assure protection in his old age, John placed an ad in a newspaper offering to deed his property to anyone who would look after him and his wife during their old age. A man named A. T. Carter applied and was accepted as their caretaker. In 1906, Mary died at the age of 87 at Cutler and was buried at the Pinewood Cemetery in Coral Gables. John left Cutler in 1910 to visit relatives on the Gulf Coast, where, at the age of 81, he died in 1911 and was buried in Fort Myers.

The Addison House was at the intersection of the original Old Cutler Road and Addison Avenue. The wooden house was well constructed of board and batten, with an open porch. A photograph taken in the 1890s indicates that a stacked-rock feature was located in the front yard. It's possible that this was a baking oven, a common feature in pioneer South Florida. All of the rocks from the "oven" and the wall disappeared by 1922, apparently reused for the construction of Charles Deering's stone house. The house and all other structures associated with the town of Cutler were demolished when Deering purchased the settlement, lot by lot, to create his own estate and natural preserve. Deering used the Addisons vacant lot for his plant nursery and for the storage of equipment.

When the estate was acquired in 1985 by the state of Florida and Miami-Dade County, the vacant parcel's connection to the Addison homestead had been long forgotten and archaeologists were focused on the Cutler Burial Mound and midden as well as the newly discovered Cutler Fossil site. It was not until the county moved forward to develop plans for constructing an interpretive center for the new park that attention was paid to the grassy lot. It appeared that the location of the lot, ideally situated near the bay and commanding a key vantage point for visitors entering the park's lush hammock, would be perfect for a park interpretive center. On April 24, 1988, I expressed to Robert L. Line, the park's director, my concerns that the lot might have archaeological and historical significance. Test holes excavated across the parcel revealed numerous historic artifacts. Additional investigations at the homestead in 1991 uncovered the Addison trash dump: hundreds of broken bottles and china dropped into a natural solution hole near where their house was situated. The artifacts provide an exciting glimpse of decades of frontier subsistence and the everyday life in the town of Cutler. Also found at the Addison parcel were prehistoric artifacts that may have been redeposited from the Cutler midden site, 8DA9, by either the Addisons or the Deering caretaker to provide fertile soils for a garden or nursery.

Excavations of the trash pit uncovered sherds of ironstone plates, bottle glass, shell and porcelain buttons, a thermometer, two clay marbles, and a child's tea set, a curious find since the Addisons were childless. They may have used them to entertain the children of the Cutler community as the town began to grow up around them. Among the most interesting artifacts was a "Cuba Libre" pin that was fashionable in the months preceding and during the Spanish American War of 1898–99. This pin may have been given to the Addisons or a Cutler resident by a soldier stationed in Miami or a Cuban patriot, many of whom were based in Miami for operations during the Cuban campaign.

As a result of these discoveries, the interpretive center site was moved to a location outside the park, well away from any historic or archaeological sites.

The Brickells

William and Mary Brickell, wealthy merchants from Cleveland, Ohio, moved to the south bank of the Miami River in 1871. William Brickell was born in

Figure 11.1. Maude and Belle Brickell, daughters of William and Mary Brickell, c. 1900, Chamberlain Photo Studio. Courtesy of the Historical Museum of Southern Florida.

Ohio in 1825 and Mary Bulmer Brickell in 1836 in England. William had reportedly mined gold in the California and Australia, where he became a successful merchant.[7] With his wealth he acquired 640 acres of hammock and pinewoods, extending from the south bank of the Miami River southward along Biscayne Bay to Coconut Grove, for $3,000.[8] The Brickells' vast landholdings were a key to the development of Miami south off the Miami

River. Selling lots and creating plats in an orderly and thought-out manner, Mary Brickell also donated a 100-foot right-of-way to the city of Miami in 1913 that would become Brickell Avenue.[9] Mary championed attractive plat developments, new parks, and wide roads, in contrast to Henry Flagler, whose parsimonious platting of small lots and narrow roads helped guarantee higher returns on his land sales.

The Brickells built a house and store on the point at the mouth of the river facing the bay. In about 1896 they built a larger store with a dock. It was here that Miami's post office was located. By 1910 the store had been demolished, apparently damaged by the 1909 hurricane. Three multistory residential structures were built in 1906–7 from wood and rusticated block, including the principal residence. This grand Victorian mansion would survive until 1962, demolished after the last Brickell daughter, Maude, died there at the age of 89 in 1960. A long sidewalk extended from the front of the house on its east side to the prominent natural bluff on which the house sat—high enough to avoid the storm surges that occasionally pummeled the bay shore. In 2005, Archaeological and Historical Conservancy excavations uncovered the Brickell sidewalk prior to its final destruction beneath the Viceroy condominiums building.[10]

The Brickell presence brought a new landscape to Miami. Groves of coconut trees were planted between their house and the bay, creating a beautiful tropical vista. The bay shore and river bank were expanded by fill, an unintended benefit of Henry Flagler dumping dredged sediments from the mouth of the river upon the Brickell property. Today, the Brickell legacy is maintained by their namesake at Brickell Park and Brickell Avenue, Miami's principal commercial roadway in Miami.

Brickell Park survives as a 2-acre green space between the Viceroy and the Brickell Presbyterian Church. The park encompasses the Brickell family mausoleum constructed in 1921. Prior to its construction, the Brickells maintained a family plot in their garden on top the ridge on the southeast side of their house. The family plot and mausoleum were placed by the family, perhaps not without coincidence, on a Tequesta cemetery. When matriarch Mary Brickell died in 1922, she reportedly stated in her will, "I charge the beneficiaries and their descendants with the sacred duty of keeping (the family burial ground) in good repair and preservation." The city's park staff inherited those duties when the property was deeded to the city. Sometime in the 1970s, the mausoleum's art nouveau bronze doors disappeared, soon followed by the disappearance of the two large urns set on either side of the entrance.

During the Viceroy condo construction, the developer, the Related Group, placed wooden sheeting around the structure to protect it. It survived the construction of its towering neighbor without a scratch. Archaeologists from the Archaeological and Historical Conservancy conducted excavations around the mausoleum prior to and during the Viceroy development in 2005. No historic graves were found, confirming newspaper reports that the Brickell bodies had been moved to Woodlawn Cemetery. This conclusion is important because one treasure hunter told me that he had found a child's metal coffin in the Brickell garden in the 1950s, much to the horror of Maude Brickell, who apparently identified the body inside the coffin as being that of her sister Emma, who had died in 1874. The treasure hunter insisted that her grave was still there, but our archaeological investigations confirmed newspaper articles that Maude had moved her sister's remains to Woodlawn after the unwelcome discovery and permanently banned the treasure hunter from her property.

While we were students in 1961, Mark Greene and I carried out the earliest archaeological investigations documenting the historic component of the Brickell site. We collected hundreds of glass beads used for Seminole trade as well as numerous historic artifacts, including medicine bottles, brass thimbles, plugs of sealing wax, fancy kaolin pipes (fig. 11.2), and a small brass compass.[11]

Subsequent investigations at Brickell Point uncovered Brickell homestead artifacts, but the greatest number was found in 1981 during monitoring of the construction of the Holiday Inn. At that time excavations into the bay-shore fill in front of the house uncovered a privy that had once been on a dock over the bay. Scores of intact bottles were recovered, all predating 1900 (the date of the fill placement). Of particular interest was the discovery of numerous whisky and bitters bottles, unusual because of reports that William Brickell was a teetotaler and that the trading post did not sell liquor. The large number of bottles suggest that someone had enhanced their trips to the privy with occasional refreshment. Recent excavations at Icon-Brickell[12] uncovered the leg of a porcelain doll, probably lost by one of the Brickell daughters (fig. 11.3).

The remnants of the Brickell House foundations and its basement were destroyed during construction of the Viceroy, all monitored and documented by archaeologists. Part of the adjacent park was used as a construction staging area, but the park's archaeological deposits were protected with an environmental fabric and fill was placed across the site. The park, with

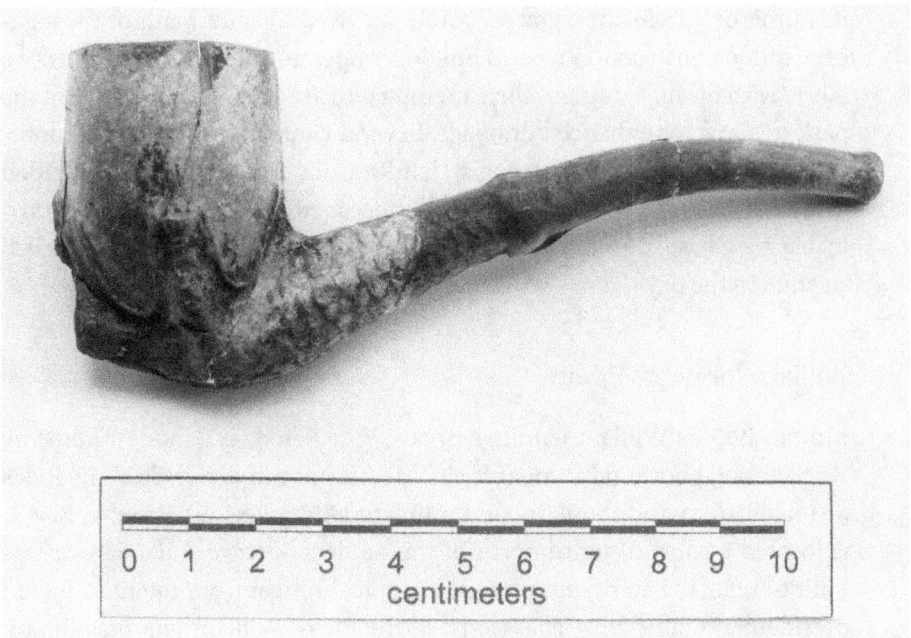

Figure 11.2. Kaolin pipe with effigy of eagle's claw. Collection of the Historical Museum of Southern Florida.

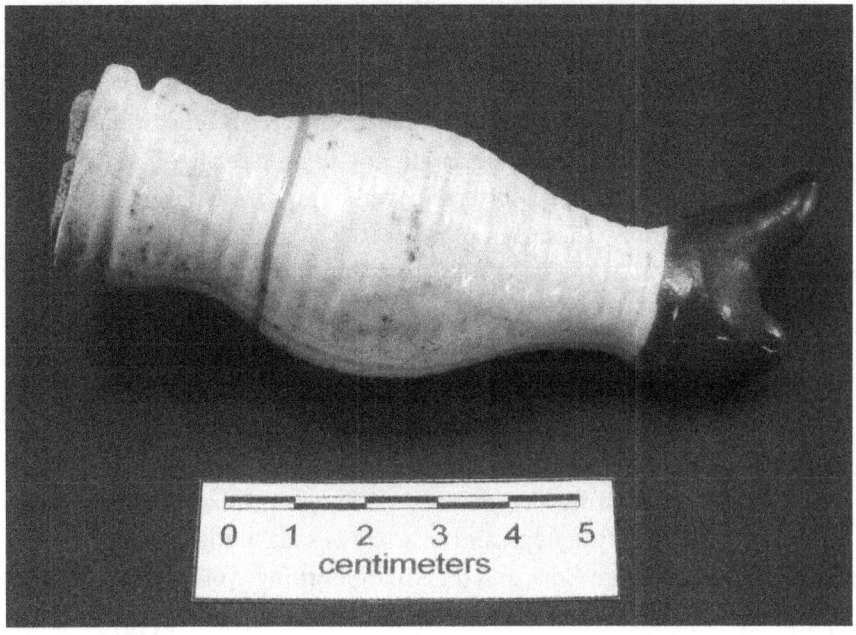

Figure 11.3. Brickell porcelain doll leg. Collection of the Historical Museum of Southern Florida.

its numerous prehistoric graves, barely survived the aftermath of the adjacent condo construction when a bulldozer operator removed the protective fabric with his machine and then attempted to grade the natural slope of the park to allow for enhanced drainage. Several vigilant archaeological monitors aided the county archaeologist, Jeff Ransom, to prevent an unintended disaster. Today the park is beautifully landscaped and the site is largely protected by a layer of fill, over which a walkway takes visitors from Brickell Avenue to the bay.

William Jennings Bryan

Built in 1913 by William Jennings Bryan, Villa Serena is a modest home by Brickell neighborhood standards. Its Mediterranean architecture includes a small atrium and fountain, and a breathtaking view of Biscayne Bay. It is located a short distance north of the opulent Viscaya. Villa Serena was built to relax the spirit and provide a tropical retreat from the hard-boiled presidential politics that characterized the life of William Jennings Bryan, who was a three-time unsuccessful presidential candidate (fig. 11.4). He was also the secretary of state under President Wilson, a great public speaker, and an expert witness for creationism at the Scopes "Monkey Trial" in 1923.

In 2007, Villa Serena was acquired by Adrienne Arsht, who subjected the parcel to an 18-month restoration and landscape project. Because of the parcel's location within an archaeological conservation area that included a known prehistoric Tequesta site, 8DA2009, the ground-disturbing activities required an archaeological assessment and monitoring. In addition to prehistoric artifacts, archaeologists uncovered three trash dumps associated with the Bryan family. These dumps reflect the common practice of disposal of household trash in the yard prior to the initiation of city trash pickup in 1921. The Bryan trash pits included not only family artifacts but also the ordinary utensils of the caretakers and servants. Not surprisingly, the Bryan trash includes refined objects of value and artistry, such as flow blue china and beautiful porcelain, including a delicate gold-braided tea cup, undoubtedly part of the family service. Recovered items include a bottle of veterinarian mange scrub—its contents preserved and ready for application, presumably for the Bryan dogs, and a variety of soda bottles, including from Coca-Cola, Royal Palm Cola, and the Miami Bottling Works. One bottle, labeled "Paul Westphal Auxiliator for the Hair," may suggest the understandable concerns of a person in the public eye. Also found were cast-iron pots and pans and copper window screens. Architectural artifacts include pieces

Figure 11.4. William Jennings Bryan at Villa Serena. Collection of Robert S. Carr.

of the original green barrel roof tile manufactured in Chicago and broken Cuban floor tiles still vivid with their brash colors.

The yard's largest dump included dozens of bottles used for condiments and medicine, including two from the Palm Pharmacy in downtown Miami and a milk bottle from the Biltmore Dairy. It is possible that this dump was associated with the laborers who built the estate, and/or the servants and caretakers who maintained Villa Serena. Bryan's powerful support for prohibition may be reflected by a general paucity of spirit bottles, although a few wine and beer bottles were found, including one wayward beer bottle from the West Side Brewery Company in Detroit, Michigan.

Pioneer Homesteads in Coconut Grove

Coconut Grove is one of Dade County's earliest pioneer settlements. Its proximity to Biscayne Bay and its relatively high ground adjacent to the bay made the area one of the most attractive to South Florida's visitors and settlers.

Among the earliest settlers was Simon Frow, who arrived in Coconut Grove in 1856.[13] His homestead was known as Twin Palms because of the landmark coconut trees located on his property. The land sloped from the high limestone ridge that parallels the bay down to a low, freshwater marsh that skirted the ridge. Fresh water flowed eastward through the oolitic limestone toward the bay, creating numerous freshwater springs at the foot of the bluff as well as in Biscayne Bay.

In 1881, Frow sold part of his land to Commodore Ralph Munroe, who would become the community's most famous resident, creating innovative boat designs for sailing in Biscayne Bay and building an extraordinary home, the Barnacle, on the bay. Fortunately, Munroe's legacy has been preserved through his numerous photographs and the preservation of his home as a state park.

The northern portion of Frow's homestead passed into the hands of Vincent Gilpin and eventually became the home of Joe Harrison. Harrison's home occupied only a small part of the 10-acre parcel, and eventually, as land values increased, he sold his property and moved his home by barge to Camp Biscayne, a quarter of a mile to the south.

Through much of the 1990s, the Harrison parcel became the focus of a tug-of-war between preservationists who wanted to purchase the property to add to the adjacent Barnacle State Park and developers who saw the parcel as an opportunity to create a townhouse development nestled against the bay in one of Coconut Grove's prime locations. In 1998, developer money trumped the city's anemic preservation efforts and the development of the 40-unit Cloisters began.

The Cloisters development triggered the city's historic preservation ordinance requiring that an intensive archaeological recovery program would need to be conducted. Excavations uncovered numerous nineteenth-century artifacts and an unexpected Spanish olive jar fragment dating from the eighteenth century. A box of square iron nails and Miami's first Pepsi bottle, circa 1910, were among the most interesting artifacts uncovered.

Kirk Munroe was a prominent author who lived south of the commodore's residence on Biscayne Bay. He had written numerous popular articles on South Florida and the Seminoles as well successful juvenile novels such as *Flamingo Feather* and *Canoemates*. He resided there from 1886 to 1920 in a beautiful house at what is now 3551 Main Highway. Nestled behind a fringe of mangroves, the swampy shore may have discouraged prehistoric habitation, but Munroe had a great appreciation of his property because of its native hardwood hammock. A freshwater spring was a highlight on his land, and he apparently made it prominent by building a limestone wall and drainage sluice around the well.

Kirk Munroe died in 1930 and the property was sold to the Semple family. They tore down many of the Munroe structures and built a large Mediterranean structure which is there today. Eventually, about 1940, the property was passed on to the anthropologist Henry Field, who lived there with his wife Julie. In 1993, archaeologist Richard Haiduven located several archaeological features on the property.[14] In 1994 Archaeological and Historical Conservancy archaeologists uncovered a historic trash dump in a large solution hole. Artifacts found there included a cast-lead soldier, a porcelain doll's head, and a gold-plated mechanical pencil—a fitting artifact for a celebrated author. One of the most unusual finds was a group of copper buttons depicting a family crest.[15]

In the shadow of the shoreline elegance of the homes of the Peacocks and Munroes was the Grove's African-Bahamian community, which was confined to the pine flatwoods that stood inland from the lush coastal hammock. Coconut Grove's black Bahamian community began on Charles Avenue, located several hundred feet west from the Frow homestead on a piece of land he sold to Mariah Brown and Charles Stirrup. Charles Avenue, then a dirt road, cut a line northward from Coconut Grove's Main Highway.

Mariah Brown was a black Bahamian born in Upper Bogue, Eleuthera, in 1851. She immigrated to Key West in 1880 and is listed in the 1885 census as living with three daughters on Emma Street in Key West and working as a washer woman. In 1890, Charles Peacock hired Mariah to come to Coconut Grove and work in the Peacock Inn. The fact that Mrs. Peacock also came from Eleuthera may have played a role in the job offer.

In about 1890, Mariah purchased a lot on 3298 Charles Avenue, then known as Evangelist Street. There she built a simple and small wood-frame vernacular home fig. 11.5). Little is known about Mariah and less about her husband, Ernest Brown. He married Mariah in 1892 and is listed in the 1900 census as a cook but was blind at the time. Mariah Brown died in January 10, 1910, at the age of 60. Perhaps what was most important about Mariah was simply that she was typical of many struggling, hard-working blacks trying to survive in Miami.

In March 1995, historians from Research Atlantica and archaeologists from the Archaeological and Historical Conservancy combined forces to investigate the Mariah Brown homestead, acquired in 1995 by the Coconut

Figure 11.5. African Bahamian settlement in Coconut Grove. Photograph by Ralph Munroe. Courtesy of the Historical Museum of Southern Florida.

Grove Cemetery Association. Thirty-seven test holes and three units were dug across the property. A trash dump was found on the west side of the house. Recovered artifacts include whiteware and porcelain sherds, bottle glass, marbles, buttons, a mechanical pencil, tin cans, and glass beads. Several circa 1920s soda bottles were found, including Lime-Cola, Cola-Nip, the Miami Bottling Company, Coca-Cola, and Chero Cola.[16]

Although the trash dump postdates the Mariah Brown occupancy, archaeology has provided a rare glimpse of everyday life in the black Grove through the mid-twentieth century, revealing the ordinary objects of daily life, including depression glass, soda bottles, medicine bottles, and one whiskey bottle. The presence of children is reflected by 19 marbles and a "Western Flyer, Western Auto Stores" bicycle plate.

Lemon City Cemetery

If life and survival for blacks in Miami was a daily challenge, death was no guarantee of peace thereafter. Miami's large population of blacks played a prominent role in the development of the city, providing labor for Flagler's railroad, building the Royal Palm Hotel, constructing roads and houses, and providing labor and staff for the growing number of hotels. Thousands of blacks poured into Miami from southern states and from the Bahamas. Hundreds died from the ordinary afflictions of daily life and scores from accidents. Some reports indicate that laborers who worked on railroad construction gangs and died during service were unceremoniously buried in solution holes along the railroad tracks. Whereas white pioneers had cemeteries such as the stately Miami Cemetery, with beautiful marble statutory and memorials for such families as the Burdines, as well as the more modest Pinewood Cemetery in present-day in Coral Gables, African Americans had the beautiful Coconut Grove Cemetery and the less elaborate Lemon City Cemetery in North Miami, located at NW Seventy-first Street near NW Third Avenue. Known at the time as the "Lemon City Colored Cemetery," it was the selected resting place for many of Miami's blacks, particularly those from Overtown.

The Lemon City Cemetery was lost and forgotten until April 2009, when the Carlisle Company uncovered human bones while constructing low-income housing. The cemetery, abandoned by the 1940s, somehow had disappeared from the community consciousness. No one seemed to notice or raise any protest when the YMCA constructed a building on the southern half of the cemetery in the 1970s. It is unlikely that the YMCA knew it was there. The neighborhood, now largely commercial with store fronts and auto shops and the Victory Gardens housing project a stone's throw away, had no apparent memory of the old cemetery. The cemetery wasn't on the city's radar when the YMCA permits were issued, and likewise, permits for the subsequent demolition of their structure and new construction of Village Carver were issued with little attention to the site. Even local African-American historians had no knowledge of the site. Only one citizen presented the city staff with a map of the cemetery, but the map never made its way to the historic preservation board for its review and the permits were issued without conditions.

Several months after the discovery of the human bones and coffin fragments during trenching, local historian Larry Wiggins conducted research which yielded death certificates for 523 blacks buried at the Lemon City

Cemetery. The death records indicate that the cemetery has over 60 percent juveniles, including stillborns. Almost 70 percent were Bahamian or of Bahamian descent. Although no conclusion could be reached as to how many individuals are still interred at the cemetery, archaeologists uncovered fragments representing about 20 individuals from the construction spoil piles and open trenches. It was obvious that previous construction had destroyed many graves, although records suggest that some families may have moved loved ones from the cemetery after it was apparently abandoned in the 1940s.

Once the cemetery location was confirmed with GPR (ground-penetrating radar) and archaeological investigations, the Carlisle Company redrew their plans and moved all new building construction to areas away from the cemetery. A memorial for the cemetery was completed in March 2011, while the displaced remains still await reinterment.

Part V

Urban Archaeology
A Past with a Future

Guy LaBree, *Tequesta Skyline*, 1984. Pencil on paper, 9 x 12. Collection of the Archaeological and Historical Conservancy. By permission of the artist.

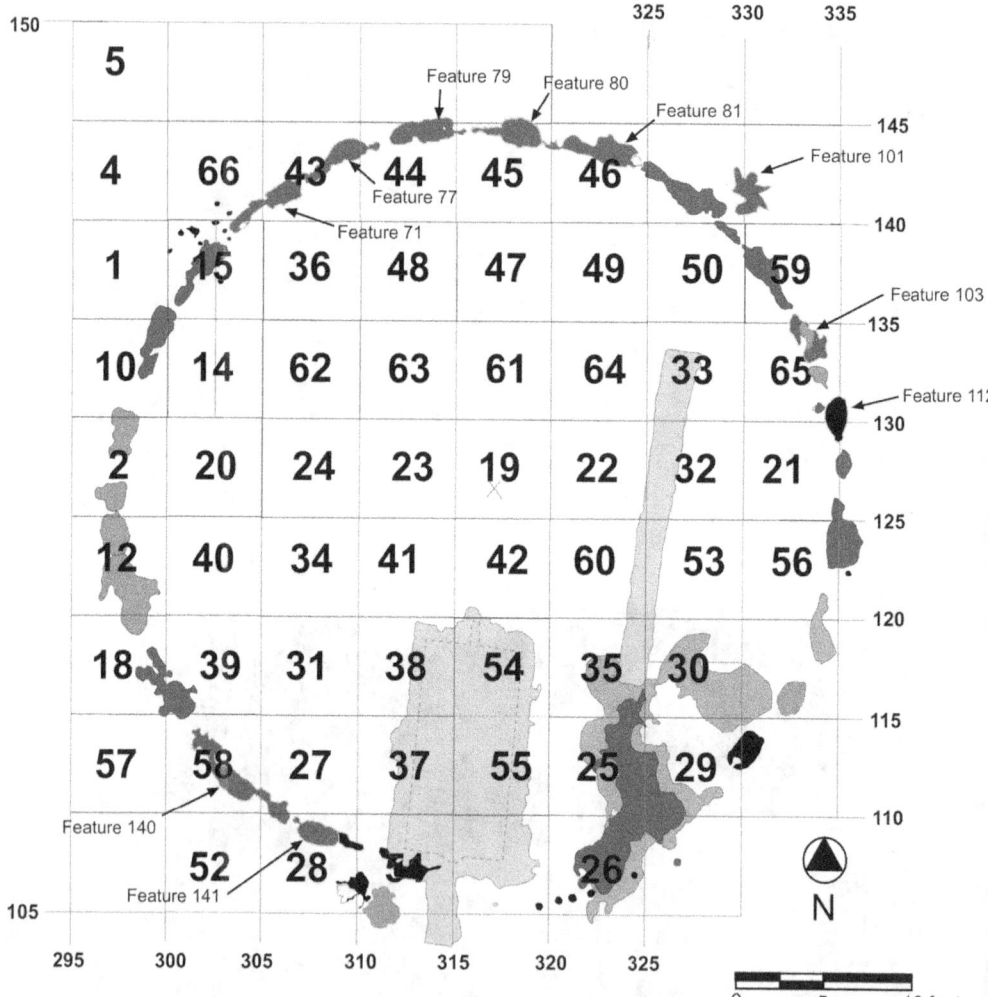

Map of the Miami Circle depicting test units and features selected for faunal analysis. Map created by John G. Beriault. Courtesy of the Archaeological and Historical Conservancy.

12

The Miami Circle and Beyond

In May 1998, urban archaeology and the community were put to the test when an important archaeological discovery collided with the Miami's historic preservation ordinance and private property rights. I was driving over the Brickell Bridge and saw a wrecking crane demolishing the vacant Brickell Apartments located on the south bank of the Miami River. The sense of alarm I felt was not over the loss of the 1950 multistory structures but the realization that no archaeologist had been notified to monitor the demolition. The parcel was located within the city's Miami River Archaeological Conservation Area, which meant there was a legal requirement for an archaeologist to be present. Surprisingly, the developer, Michael Baumman, had never been told by city staff that there was such a requirement, and no conditions for archaeology had been placed on his permits. Nonetheless, he was agreeable to hiring an archaeologist (Scott Lewis) to conduct monitoring during the demolition process.

As the concrete building foundations were being ripped from the ground, black-earth midden, shells, and artifacts became exposed across much of the 2-acre lot. The Miami-Dade county archaeologist, John Ricisak, with assistance from the Archaeological and Historical Conservancy, began excavating test units in one area once it had been fully cleared by the demolition crew. When archaeologists dug the second test hole, a peculiar feature was uncovered in the limestone bedrock 50 centimeters below the black-earth midden: a basin that appeared manmade and cut into the bedrock. The feature contained hundreds of prehistoric animal bones, shells, and pottery sherds. The absence of any historic or modern materials could only mean that the feature itself was prehistoric.

When additional archaeological testing revealed similar basins and numerous smaller circular holes cut in the bedrock, the project surveyor, T. L. Riggs, observed that the basin locations were not random but were aligned on an arc that he hypothesized was part of a circle. Based on his measurements, Riggs calculated the diameter and circumference of the circle and then spray-painted a circular footprint on top the ground. With only a week to go before construction was to begin, the archaeologists mechanically stripped the fill and part of the midden along the circumference of the painted circle. The backhoe bucket was never allowed to reach the bedrock. The remaining soils were dug by hand, revealing a perfect circle measuring 38 feet in diameter and composed of 24 basins. Nothing had ever been seen like this before in Florida—a circle of holes cut into solid rock (fig. 12.1).

The mystery of the circle, which became a media sensation, was pondered and debated by scholars. A campaign was waged by the public and preservation groups to save the circle, and in 1999, after considerable controversy and the expenditure of $26,700,000, the 2-acre site was acquired by the state of Florida and Miami-Dade County to be preserved as an archaeological park. Title for the parcel was held by the state of Florida, and in 2009 the park was placed under the management of the Historical Museum of

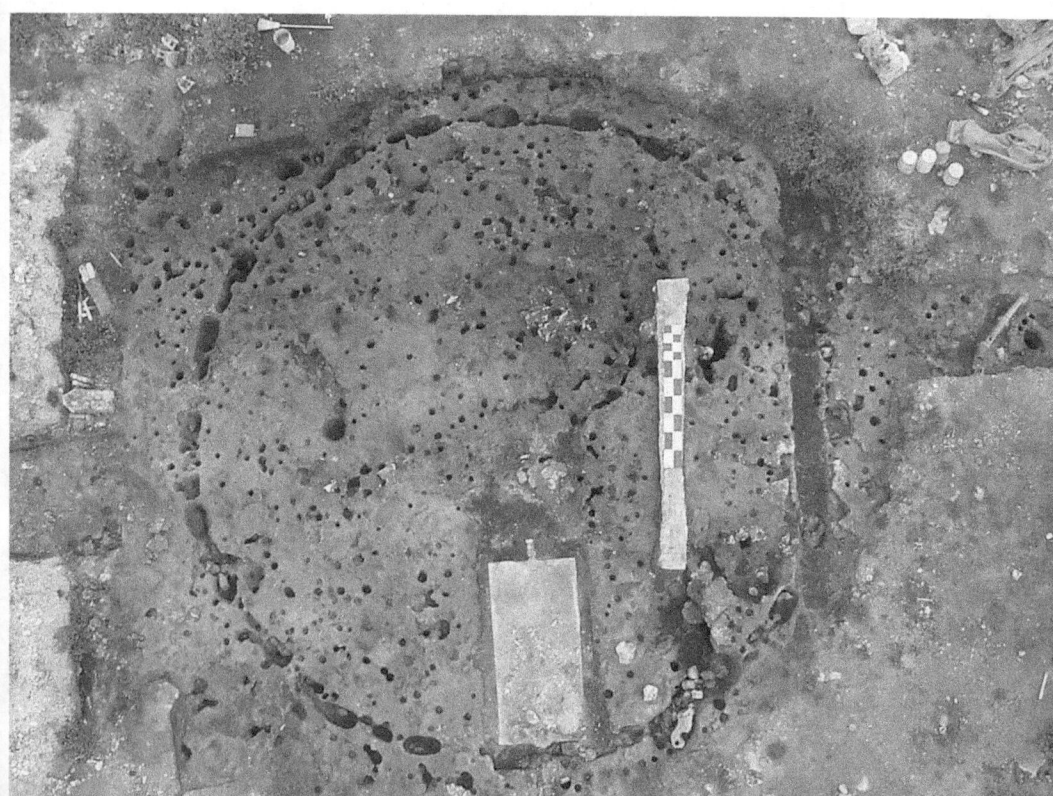

Figure 12.1. Aerial photo of the Miami Circle. Courtesy of the Miami-Dade County Historic Preservation Division.

Southern Florida but has since reverted back to the State. The parcel opened to the public in 2010, after repairs were completed to the crumbled seawall.

Part of the hoopla of the circle was the controversy over its origin and age, which ran a gambit of theories from the ridiculous—an alien landing pad—to the profane: a Stonehenge-like calendar, a council house, a chief's house, a fish weir, coconut tree planting holes dug by the Brickell family, and, the most deflating theory of them all, a drain field for the Brickell Apartment septic tanks. To determine the site's function and significance, a systematic survey was conducted across the parcel by Florida's Division of Historical Resources,[1] while intensive testing was conducted at other parts of the site.[2] Funds allocated by a Florida historic preservation grant were used to conduct scientific analyses of the site and its artifacts.[3]

The first line of analysis was the circle itself. A laser-scanned map and measurements of the circle's features indicated that each basin had been cut and shaped into the limestone bedrock. Grooves were observed on the walls of some of the basins, indicating that a narrow, chisel-like tool had been used. It was observed that shell columella chisels found at the site are a suitable match for the tool that may have been used to create the holes. As an experiment, John Ricisak was able to use a shell tool to create similar cut holes in about 10 minutes. The relative ease of using a shell tool to excavate through limestone bedrock is explained by the softness of the rock below the harder surface duricrust.

Most basins are loaf-shaped (fig. 12.2), varying in length from 56 centimeters to as long as 74 centimeters.[4] Their width varies from 36 to 47 centimeters. Each basin was dug to a depth of about 40 centimeters from the top of the bedrock, but it is unclear as to their actual depth from the surface because much of the original soils had been removed as a result of the construction of the apartment complex and it is not known how much soil had accumulated since prehistoric times. Each basin has slightly sloping sides and is characterized by circular post holes cut into the basin bottom. Clusters of rocks, many of them cemented by concretion, occur around the holes, suggesting that they were placed around wooden posts to provide support.

The challenge of determining the age of the Miami Circle was met by analyzing the geological and archaeological evidence. Geologists Thomas Scott and Guy Means from the Florida Geological Service examined the cut hole features with particular attention to the layer of duricrust that had formed on the surface of each hole. This duricrust is a thin layering of redeposited calcium carbonates created over time during periods of fluc-

Figure 12.2. Miami Circle foundation basins and post holes cut into the bedrock. Courtesy of the Archaeological and Historical Conservancy.

tuating water tables. The geologists compared the duricrust of the basins and post holes with modern trenches cut into the bedrock, including cuts made during the placement of a 1950 septic tank within the circle. They observed that no duricrust had formed on the bedrock cuts made during the construction of the apartment complex. In contrast, all of the circle features had measurable layers of duricrust. The geologists concluded that this duricrust would have taken hundreds and likely several thousand years to have formed, indicating that the circle is of considerable antiquity.[5]

The antiquity of the circle and overall site was bolstered when archaeologists analyzed the site's artifacts and conducted radiocarbon dating. I examined the pottery sherds uncovered at the circle, particularly those found within the basins. I hypothesized that the pottery sherds that were isolated and "trapped" within each basin were likely coeval with the construction of the structure associated with the circle's basins. I further hypothesized that the soil that entered the basins after the structure's construction and eventual demolition would represent a relatively short time span, and even if subsequent disturbances had introduced newer material into the basins, the overall ceramic assemblage would be similar in all of the basins and likely consistent or slightly newer than the structure's age.

A total of 26,281 ceramic sherds were recovered from the overall site. Of these, 23,281 are sand-tempered plain, 481 (about 2%) are of the St. Johns series, and 21 are nonlocal plainware and various decorated types.[6] A total of 189 pottery sherds were examined from 16 of the basins. Of these, 108 (55%) were sand-tempered plain and 83 (45%) were St. Johns wares, a nonlocal pottery. This ratio of St. Johns chalkyware to sand-tempered plain is significantly higher at the circle than from any other part of the site where sand-tempered ceramics are 90 percent of the ceramic assemblage. The frequency of St. Johns wares at most Miami sites during the Early to Middle Glades I period is less than 10 percent, and the wares virtually disappear during the Late Glades I and Glades II periods, not increasing in frequency until the Glades III period.

The quantity of St. Johns pottery in the circle suggests an emphasis on exotic materials in the feature. Seven of the St. Johns sherds were decorated by stamping: three simple stamped, three linear stamped, and one check stamped. The simple-stamped (fig. 12.3) and linear-stamped designs are in the tradition of Deptford pottery, a type that commonly occurred in northern Florida and always on sand-tempered ware. However, the stamped wares in the basins are St. Johns wares. I uncovered other examples of Deptford-like chalky stamped ware from several sites along Biscayne Bay and from the New River, 8BD202, in Fort Lauderdale—all sites dating from the Glades I period. John Goggin had reported similar St. Johns stamped wares in northeast Florida.[7] All of these St. Johns stamped wares from South Florida occur in a Glades I context. They represent a previously unclassified type, and after additional analysis they should be classified as St. Johns Simple Stamped and St. Johns Linear Stamped.

The ceramic evidence in the basins supports a Glades I period for the circle's construction. Reinforcing the interpretation of a Glades I age for the circle are two radiocarbon dates (Beta-128477, Beta-128478) collected from charcoal from one of the basins. These two samples yielded dates of 1950 ± 150 B.P. (cal. 365 B.C.–A.D. 415) and 1920 ± 70 B.P. (cal. 45 B.C.–A.D. 245). The two samples represent a mean calibrated age of about A.D. 50. Although it can be argued that the charcoal entered into the basins sometime after (or

Figure 12.3. Deptford Stamped pottery sherd uncovered at the Miami Circle. Courtesy of the Archaeological and Historical Conservancy.

possibility during) the construction of the structure, it reinforces an overall Glades I age for the circle.

Interpreting the circle's function has been daunting, in part because of popular misconceptions about the feature. All evidence to date suggests that the circle is the footprint of an architectural structure. The basins represent footers to support groups of wooden posts. Each post was firmly placed within a circular hole cut into the bedrock at the bottom of the basin. Other supporting posts occurred around the circle's circumference. Although the wooden posts have not survived, the indirect evidence of their existence is indicated by the cut post holes and the limestone rocks, now cemented, which are piled around the post holes.

The circle's location on the southern point of the mouth of the Miami River afforded a strategic view upriver and across the bay. Also, the circle foundations are better crafted and more substantial than other posted structures encountered in south Florida. All of these qualities suggest that it was an important structure, possibly a council house or the house of a cacique or some other high status individual.

There are several clues to the structure's special status. The cut basins are well constructed and vary in style by quadrant, suggesting that each group of basins was dug by different workers, each with their own stylistic touches for creating the basin's shape. The northwestern, northern, and part of the northeastern basins are relatively similar in their "tadpole" format, with a wide loaf-shaped basin followed by a more narrow connected tail, presenting a dot-dash appearance from a plane view (fig. 12.2). The southern basins (many of them indistinguishable because of associated solution holes and disturbances) are more irregular and tend to lack the extended "tails."

One cut hole located four degrees north of east is unique. It is elliptical, looking like an eye, and is 30 centimeters long (fig. 12.4). Its eye-like appear-

Figure 12.4. "Eye" basin cut into the eastern point of the bedrock at the eastern point of the Miami Circle. Courtesy of the Archaeological and Historical Conservancy.

ance is enhanced by the presence of a limestone rock wedged into the center of the hole. This appearance may be a coincidence caused by the rock being placed to shore up two small posts on either side, but only 50 centimeters away an intact polished basalt celt was uncovered within a post hole. The celt appears unused. An analysis of the artifact by geologist Jackie Dixon of the University of Miami determined its origin was the Appalachian Mountains of northern Georgia.[8] Archaeologist Randolph Widmer believes it is a dedication offering.

The special purpose of the Miami Circle structure is hard to deny. Some newspapers and scholars, including the late William Straight, have stated that the circle was a cemetery or a charnel house where bodies were prepared and stored for interment. Excavations at the circle, however, revealed only a few isolated human bones and teeth.[9] If it had been a charnel house, it is likely that numerous teeth and small bones would have been found during the excavations. Noteworthy and mysterious was the discovery of two human cervical vertebrae: a C-1 and a C-2, bones located below the cranium at the top of the spinal column. Interestingly, the two vertebrae are from two different individuals, although both were found within 6 feet of each other. Such a small sample can hardly be the basis for any conclusions, but isolated vertebrae rarely have been found at other Miami River sites on either side of the river. The occurrence of two vertebrae from two individuals within the circle suggests that it is likely nonrandom and may be related to the display or use of human skulls as a household totems or for sorcery, not unlike the zemi of the Caribbean Taino, where human skulls of family members were kept within the house. Escalante de Fontaneda, who was shipwrecked on the South Florida coast about 1543, provided a description of the Calusa in regard to severed heads: "Every year they kill a Christian captive to feed their idol with which they adore, and they say that it has to eat every year the eyes of a human man, and then they all dance around the dead man's head."[10]

No severed heads or buried craniums were found at the Miami Circle, but their absence is not critical evidence since if trophy heads had been mounted on posts, they would have not necessarily been subsequently buried at that location, and it is exactly the C-1 or C-2 vertebrae that might be lost from such displays. The point of this speculative discussion is that if trophy skulls were displayed at the Miami Circle, it may indicate that the structure was a council house, chief's house, or temple, where conversations with dead ancestors was part of maintaining the balance between natural and supernatural forces.

Reinforcing the ritual importance of the human head is the fact that isolated skull burials have been reported across southern Florida. A single skull burial was found during the construction of Jose Marti Park, located a mile up the river.[11] Skull burials also have been reported from the Surfside site, DA21.[12] Obviously, if cranial burials are a Tequesta mortuary trait, one would expect the occurrence of postcranial burials, those without skulls, and that is exactly the case when recent investigations were conducted at the nearby Icon-Brickell condominiums. Archaeological investigations uncovered a burial area about a thousand feet south from the circle. Fourteen concentrations of human remains were found, five of which had no crania.[13] Although there are other explanations for missing crania, it does suggest that cranial burials and interments without skulls were an important element of the Tequesta's mortuary behavior and belief system.

Rite and Ritual

Soon after its discovery, the Miami Circle was touted by Native Americans and much of the public as a sacred site, defined as a location tied to religious beliefs. In early 1999 the Five Indian Nations of Oklahoma, which includes the Seminole, Choctaw, Cherokee, Creek, and Chickasaw, passed a resolution that the Miami Circle was a sacred site, thus verifying to many the circle's sacredness. Its sacredness transcended archaeological evidence and became a fact simply by its pronouncement—not that the archaeological evidence offers a contrary view. The circle's various associated features, which include the "offering" of a beautiful unused basalt celt in the circle's eastern post hole, numerous exotic artifacts, and animal interments, all reinforce the idea of the Miami Circle as a sacred space where special rituals and offerings had occurred.

Among the most intriguing and problematic of the ritual features are the three animal interments documented within the circle.[14] A requiem shark measuring 5 feet in length (Feature 234) was discovered beneath a shallow footer wall that survived the Brickell Apartment demolition (fig. 12.5). The shark was 50 centimeters below the existing surface and was aligned on an east-west axis with its head facing west. Although the shark has no true bones and is composed largely of cartilage, its entire vertebrae—all articulated—had survived. Also present were the teeth and dermal scutes in the vicinity of where the head had decomposed. The presence of an articulated shark indicates it had not been used in the utilitarian sense and had been interred while still fleshed, likely as a ritual offering.

Figure 12.5. Shark skeleton at the Miami Circle. Courtesy of the Archaeological and Historical Conservancy.

Several meters north of the shark, a skull of a bottlenose dolphin (*Tursiops truncatus*) was uncovered (Feature 218). Although fragmentary, it too was aligned on an east-west axis. A short distance to the northwest of the shark and the bottlenose dolphin was the carapace of a loggerhead sea turtle (*Caretta caretta*). The carapace measured 65 centimeters in length and was placed in an east-west alignment. Particular to the turtle was a large quantity of rusted square iron nails uncovered within the carapace. The nails are historic, a sure indicator of a more recent date of the turtle relative to the age of the circle. In fact, radiocarbon dates calibrated at 2 sigma determined that the interments range from A.D. 1330 to 1680. The disparity of one thousand years between the animal interments and the age of the circle structure poses some interesting questions. If the Miami Circle structure existed or was rebuilt over a span of less than a hundred or even several hundred years, then the animals were interred independent of the structure. Was the site's sacredness maintained throughout time? It seems likely that this may be the case. Brickell Point, with its commanding position on the bay and river, with its eastward view of the ocean horizon and rising sun, was likely a powerful and important location in the Tequesta cultural consciousness.

Animal interments have been reported from other Tequesta sites—many directly associated with human burials. An alligator burial was reported at the Margate-Blount site, 8BD45,[15] and an alligator skull was found atop a human burial at the Trail site, 8DA34.[16] Recent excavations at Brickell Point, while the Icon Brickell condominiums were being constructed, uncovered five shark vertebrae interments, indicating the deliberate burial of shark spinal columns or shark "steaks."[17] Since the site is a black-earth midden with abundant refuse, it is not clear whether the shark "offerings" are linked to the human burials. Widmer recovered a similar group of shark vertebrae with no human remains in association, which he referred to as a "dedication cache."[18]

Another line of evidence of the importance of ritual behavior is the occurrence of exotic materials and artifacts in the archaeological record. The Miami Circle excavations uncovered a large assemblage of exotic materials with origins in central and northern Florida as well as more distant sources.

A total of five complete and fragmentary basaltic celts or axes were found at the circle.[19] Geologist Jean Dixon of the University of Miami compared two of the celt fragments with a database of 776 major and trace elements of basaltic rocks from across North America and the Caribbean.[20] She determined that the celt trace elements were consistent with basalt from the Piedmont region of Georgia in the vicinity of Atlanta and Macon.[21] Other exotica included galena from Missouri and copper, likely from Michigan or possibly Georgia.[22] More localized exotic materials include chert from central Florida and ceramic platform pipes similar to those at Fort Center at Lake Okeechobee. Also found were sherds of nonlocal ceramic vessels representing types manufactured on the Florida Gulf Coast and northern Florida.[23]

These rare objects suggest higher status individuals or special functions that may have been associated with the circle, but excavations at the Icon-Brickell portion of the site located 1,500 feet to the south yielded similar exotic objects, including a quartz pendant. A similar quartz pendant was found on the north bank of the river—both within a midden context, which indicates that although these "precious" objects are rare, they occur throughout the entire site. Their general distribution may reflect ritual offerings—a common thread of Native American culture, which gave thanks for fishing, hunting, or new house construction—or an effective redistribution system for elite residents, although some exotic materials such as copper beads, chert, and basalt celts may have been accessible to the general populace, perhaps because the town of Tequesta was a regional center of redistribution of goods. The redistribution of exotic and sacred commodities, as well as more common items, may have been an important task of the cacique and/or shamans.

Surprisingly, such exotica has not been found in any of the graves uncovered in recent archaeological investigations on both sides of the Miami River. Only one probable high-status individual has been found,[24] a scarcity that may indicate that elite graves are the victims of development, as happened with one burial mound, 8DA14, during construction of the Royal Palm Hotel.

Other burial mounds from southern Florida have revealed Hopewellian exotica, including mica and nonceramic vessels. Artifacts found at the Goodland Mound (8CR46) and the Oak Knoll Mound (8LL729) indicate that burial mound construction in South Florida began as early as A.D. 200–300. At the same time, earthwork construction was well established around Lake Okeechobee. The Ortona canals are the largest prehistoric canal system in North America, constructed in about A.D. 400.[25] These canals were dug to circumvent the falls of the Caloosahatchee River, providing an important leg in the trade and transportation corridor connecting Pineland on the Gulf Coast to Lake Okeechobee by way of the Caloosahatchee River. Trade corridors continued from Lake Okeechobee southward to the Miami River.

When these pulses of trade and associated exotica arrived in southern Florida about A.D. 200–400, it may have set into motion an effective break from egalitarian religious traditions. The control and redistribution of trade items may have led to the development of larger villages and organized labor for public construction, such as what would be needed for the Miami Circle.

Although ordinary secular life continued in the sense that the traditional economy, based on fishing, hunting, and gathering, was largely unaltered, some changes, such as how game and fish were distributed, may have occurred. No longer catch-as-catch-can by extended families and individuals, hunting and fishing may have been subject to tribute and redistribution organized by an elite leadership. "Ownership" of particular estuaries and tidal channels may have been enforced by tribal chiefs or clan leaders. Emphasis on the collection of certain shells, feathers, pumice, or shark teeth for long-distance trade may have become important.

By A.D. 700–800 the Glades ceramic tradition of incised and punctuated designs had become firmly established, with an apparent lessening of exotic ceramic imports. Decorative types, including Opa-Locka Incised,

Fort Drum Punctate, Dade Incised, and Key Largo Incised, appear to be distinctly local to southeast Florida and suggest a cultural continuity during this period. Exotica such as copper, galena, and basalt appear to dwindle.

By A.D. 1000–1200 a profound change had occurred at the mouth of the Miami River. The location of settlements had shifted from both the river's south and north banks to almost exclusively the north bank. This shift in population is reflected by the distribution of ceramic types and radiocarbon dates in the archaeological record. Ceramic types typical of the Late Glades II and Glades III periods, such as Glades Tooled Rim and Surfside Incised, are nearly absent on the south side of the river, while they frequently occur on the north bank. Sixteenth-century Spanish historical records refer to the Tequesta settlement and mission construction on the north side of the river.

What caused this shift in settlement from the south to the north bank? Archaeologists don't know, but it may be coincidental that at about the same time that this population shift occurred an important religious-social movement was sweeping through the Southeast. The Mississippian Culture had at its heart the development of social complexity and chiefdomship that were characterized by the construction of large, flat-topped mounds, religious ceremonialism that focused on the creation of symbolic icons associated with the elite class, and the trade of exotic commodities such as copper, galena, and ground-stone tools across the region. This exotica, some from as far away as present-day Michigan and Missouri, appeared in Florida just as it had during the earlier Hopewellian period. There is evidence that *Busycon* shells from the Gulf Coast traveled northward and were used for beautifully engraved gorgets and drinking cups such as those found at the Cahokia mounds in Illinois.

The central pulse of Mississippian Culture was the cultivation of maize, a plant that enabled a high level of food production that in turn stimulated the development of specialized skills because less time was needed for food gathering. It also was the impetus for social cooperation, as people organized to plant and harvest crops. The opportunity to intensely cultivate maize may have been available to South Florida's Native Americans, but it was not embraced, possibly because the area's plentiful marine resources provided ample subsistence. In fact, southern Florida and the Pacific Northwest were the only two regions of North America that developed complex chiefdoms based on marine resources rather than agriculture. The flux and effect of Mississippian traits in South Florida may have been marginal compared with other parts of the Southeast, however, there are changes that occurred during that time period.

There was a distinct shift in ceramic traditions in the area about A.D. 900–1000. Nonlocal ceramics such as St. Johns wares reappear in the area after at least a 500-year hiatus. Belle Glade pottery, a type typical of the Lake Okeechobee area, began to appear in small numbers in the ceramic assemblage by A.D. 1200. Typical Glades decorative types, such as Key Largo Incised, continued, but a new type, Surfside Incised, appeared about the same time. This type has deeply incised parallel lines below the rim. What makes Surfside Incised distinctive is that some bowl forms venture from the traditional hemispheric form in an entirely new direction characterized by shallow vessels with protruding lugs or extensions from the rim. These bowls are sometimes elongated or boat-shaped. The lugs are incised with multiple lines, creating a variety of geometric designs. Some lugs have zoomorphic designs suggesting a bird head on one end of the bowl and the tail on the opposite send. The sudden appearance of Surfside Incised is an enigma. It does not appear to have evolved from earlier local types. At approximately the same time period, A.D.1300–1400, another shallow bowl type, Glades Tooled Rim, was represented by a variety of incised or pressed lines or grooves placed upon an expanded, exaggerated rim, often giving the bowl a pie crust appearance.

The Glades Tooled bowl is innovative and not part of any style continuum. It is possible that this new type, with its shallow bowl, reflected a new food product—possibly a cassava-like bread that is fried within a bowl purposely designed with a thick, expanded, crenulated rim to facilitate peeling the bread out of the bowl. It may be a ceramic innovation linked to culinary innovations.

Possible influences on the emergence of Surfside pots may have come from one of two possible sources, one being the Fort Walton tradition of northwestern Florida, which was characterized by lug-rimmed bowls, a style identified as an earmark of Mississippian influence. A second possible influence is Cuba. Boat-shaped vessels from central Cuba that are surprisingly similar to South Florida examples have been reported.[26] Bowls with similar Glades Tooled rims and bowl shapes also occur in Cuba.[27]

The idea of circum-Caribbean and even Meso-American influences on South Florida Indians has teased scholars for the last century, and many in the public believe that South Florida's prehistoric people migrated northward from Cuba or Meso-America. The compelling draw of a Meso-American culture and its diffusion into North America has been offered as an explanation for the complex shellworks of Florida's Gulf Coast. The

Rock Mound in Key Largo has been offered as evidence of a Mayan connection.[28] In truth, little evidence has been uncovered that indicates such prehistoric migrations ever occurred. However, there is evidence that after initial Spanish contact in Cuba some Taino Indians may have canoed to Florida and resettled. Fontaneda describes how the father of the Calusa chief Carlos allowed Indians from Cuba to resettle in his domain, this establishing what may have been an Taino settlement somewhere in southern Florida—possibly in the Keys. Perhaps it is this influence that changed Tequesta pottery styles after A.D. 1300–1400 with the introduction of Glades Tooled Rim and Surfside Incised lugged bowls.

Among the most intriguing artifacts found in southeastern Florida that fall close to a Meso-American smoking gun is a cache of three metal objects found by Wesley Coleman in the eastern Everglades in the 1970s. Coleman recounted how he found three copper shell effigies resembling Tellin shells (*Tellina radiata*) within the concretion 1 meter below the surface. Their Meso-American origin is almost certain, as one of the effigies is manufactured from "tumbaga," a copper-gold alloy. However, it is possible that this cache found its way to the Tequesta during the period of Spanish contact.

During the pre-European contact era of the Glades III period (A.D.1200–1500), ceramic innovations were coupled with other developments. Artistic expression, particularly of geometric and naturalistic forms, reached their zenith during this period.[29] Animal carvings on bone pins are beautifully executed, using deer, birds, parakeets, vultures, and turtles as favorite subjects. The rise of animal depictions in art may reflect a fundamental belief in animal worship, or animal totems assigned to individuals, extended families, or clans. One of the most beautiful zoomorphic carvings discovered was a shell carved into a buzzard pendant found at the Coleman site, 8DA1058 (fig. 12.6).

It is during the Glades III period that mound building becomes the signature of Tequesta mortuary architecture. The construction of mounds and elaborate shellworks are firmly in place by this time throughout southern Florida and Lake Okeechobee. The rise of mound construction, the development of "cult" and totem art motifs, and new ceramic forms may reflect the farthest ripple of Mississippian influences from its northern epicenter. However, some influences may stem from refugees from the Spanish onslaught of Native Americans in Cuba. South Florida may have been the recipient of new ideas about religion—and with it, an influx of exotic commodities with

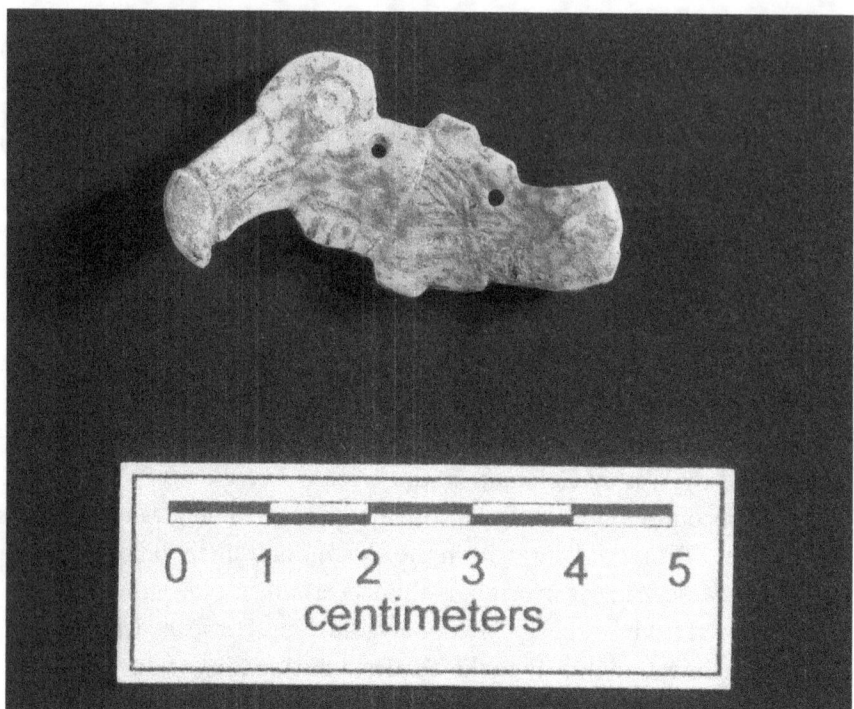

Figure 12.6. Shell buzzard ornament found at 8DA1058. Collection of the Historical Museum of Southern Florida.

local resources moving northward in exchange. *Busycon* shells, shark teeth, and bird plumes had considerable value a thousand miles to the north of Florida, and, indeed, *Busycon* shell masks and gorgets have been uncovered from numerous burial mounds in the Mississippi River Valley.

The rise of the Tequesta chiefdom denotes increasing social organization and a celestial-earthbound hegemony in which chiefs are linked to gods. Perhaps the plentiful fish provided by communal harvests of the tidal estuaries and creeks set the stage for organizing village clans and families for mound and canal construction and other public projects. It is unclear whether the Mississippian influences of A.D. 1200–1400 represent the movement of ideas and materials, people, or both. What is clear is that the prehistoric Miami of that time was a place of flux. Profound changes were underway that would culminate with the arrival of the Spanish in the sixteenth century and the eventual extinction of the Tequesta.

Epilogue

In modern life, the pace of change since the incorporation of the city of Miami has been staggering. The land and sea that had breathed easily from the light touch of several thousand Tequesta is now congested with roads and a million people. There is a constant buzz of human activity, and the sightings of panthers in Miami are now only a matter of historical record. Towering buildings bite into the sky and a million artificial lights dim the sea of stars that once hugged the earth's horizon. The city is larger now, yet somehow smaller and less mystical.

It is impossible to know what songs were heard millennia ago in a dark hole below the Cutler forest or the chants and prayers made inside the Miami Circle. Although we can piece together splintered bones and analyze artifacts to tell a story, the richness of the moment is gone. We are wiser because of this knowledge, these new connections made, and the sober realization that we are custodians of far more than what we bargained for by having to preserve and document a past that our direct ancestors did not create. Preserving the past is the small print of the implicit agreement that binds us to those who lived and died before us.

We preserve our past because it defines us as a civilization and a community. We connect to our history because it reveals a deeper part of who we are and who we should not be.

Acknowledgments

This book was an effort long in the making. My good fortune to become Miami-Dade County's first archaeologist was the beginning of a multitude of experiences that helped shape the contents of this book. I am profoundly indebted to Ivan Rodriquez, former director of the Miami-Dade County Historic Division, and historian Nancy Hoffmann, who hired me for that position.

My work was improved by the contributions of countless others, including scholars, volunteers, and students. Some of those who were particularly helpful in reviewing the prose and facts of this book include Dr. John Reiger, Christopher Eck, George Luer, and Jim Clupper, who brought his skill as a librarian to this book. I am also indebted to Betty Jo Brownfield, Kim Perry, and especially my wife Debbie, who helped prepare the final drafts of this book. I want to particularly thank Tim Harrington for his graphics excellence in preparing this volume and his extraordinary patience helping to complete it.

I am thankful that as a boy growing up in Miami I had the good fortune to meet Dan Laxson and attend his archaeological summer camp at the Museum of Science. Likewise, I was fortunate to meet my school chum Mark Greene, who was my first partner in archaeology. He and I documented some of the last vestiges of the Brickell Trading Post, which started me on a lifetime journey of curiosity and discovery about Miami's past.

Another boy searching Brickell Point was the late Stan Cooper. Although I didn't meet him until we were adults, his stories of his boyhood Miami explorations greatly aided in my knowledge of the archaeological sites in the area.

The earliest incarnations of this work bore the fruit of research conducted by historians Arva Parks and Margot Amnidown. Their research of Miami's earliest pioneers was particularly valuable.

The contributions of Willard Steele, historian and former officer of the Seminole Tribal Historic Preservation Office, have been significant. His fresh insights and exhaustive research about the Second Seminole War unraveled the location of many of Miami's most important historic sites. He played a principal role in those investigations and was the catalyst for the discovery of Fort Henry.

Contributions in the field by former park ranger Don Mattucci, particularly at Bill Baggs State Park, were important. Student contributions by David Allerton and Gina Demigone were invaluable. The field work and reports of Dr. Marilyn Masson, carried out at the Cutler Fossil site while she was still a student, were outstanding.

Irving Eyster was an assistant to the county archaeologist in the early 1980s. He directed field classes at Brickell Park and Arch Creek, and his efforts added to the pool of knowledge about these sites. Other archaeological assistants to the county program included Debra Sandler and Jo Southard, both dedicated and diligent in their work.

Volunteers Sue Goldman, Barbara Tansey, Jeannie McGuire, Beth Read, Lynda Green, and other members of the South Florida archaeology family provided tireless enthusiasm for advancing archaeological research in South Florida.

Recent work by archaeologists from the Archaeological and Historical Conservancy, such as Joseph Mankowski, Ryan Franklin, and Bill Schaffer, provided important field data and analyses that helped shape this volume. Current Miami-Dade County archaeologist Jeff Ransom has been a continual force in preserving the community archaeological record.

Other important contributors to the county's archaeological programs have been former county archaeologist John Ricisak and former director of the Historic Preservation Division Chris Eck.

A special thanks to surveyor Ted Riggs, who has always been available to provide professional surveys and maps for the numerous archaeological sites uncovered over the past thirty years. The late Dr. William Straight, an avocational historian, was a tireless researcher of the details of local archaeological discoveries and was generous with his time and knowledge.

The Historical Museum of Southern Florida—now known as History Miami!—has provided long-term commitment to preserve Miami's past. A tip of the hat to former director Randy Nimnicht of the Historical Museum, who helped develop the museum's outstanding material collection from South Florida sites. Patricia Barahona, Dawn Hughes, and Becky Smith have greatly supported research for this book by making HMSF's vast archives available. Thanks to Jorge Zamanillo of the Historical Museum of Southern Florida, who spent many years working with the Archaeological and Historical Conservancy aiding in the documentation of local archaeological sites and now plays a leadership role in interpreting the Miami Circle Park.

I am particularly thankful to my late friend Wesley Coleman, who played a pivotal role in inspiring my professional development as an archaeologist. Wes was always there and always ready to help. I also thank the late Jim Lord, who shared his knowledge about the prehistoric artifacts of South Florida. Other avocational archaeologists, such as Bill Carson, James Lee, Ed Barberio, and Bruce Eistadt, added to my knowledge of area sites.

I want to acknowledge the special contributions of my good friend John Beriault, who was a major co-investigator of projects across southern Florida and whose notes, photos, and drawings were invaluable in my research.

In recent years many archaeologists have left their mark in documenting Miami-Dade County archaeological resources, including Dr. John Gifford and, particularly, Richard Haiduven, who conducted extensive cultural resources management work across the county, and former county archaeologist Gary Beiter, who earnestly pursued excavating at the county's many local and state parks in his quest to prove that there is a high correlation between Tequesta sites and public parks. Investigations at the Miami Circle by Dr. Randolph Widmer are also an important influence on my recent work.

A tip of the hat to former State Archaeologist Ryan Wheeler, who was always available to provide insight into tough preservation questions and has been an effective force in interpreting and opening the Miami Circle Park. Likewise, former and present Florida Division of Historic Sites staff Laura Kammerer, Bob Taylor, Fred Gaske, Kevin Porter, Louis Tesar, and others contributed to preserving the archaeological sites of Miami-Dade and Florida.

Contributions by bioarchaeologists Amy Felmley, Cynthia Condon, and Keith Condon deserve special recognition, as does the work of Ryan Franklin and the work of William Schaeffer, who conducted the analysis of the MDM site's human remains with Ashley Gelman, with contributions by Rose Drew and a completed analysis by Cristina Echazabal. An acknowledgment to Allison Elgart, who with the others completed analysis of other prehistoric human remains in Miami-Dade County that greatly added to our knowledge of the region's bioarchaeology and mortuary patterns. Archaeologist Jim Pepe—owed a special nod for coining the term "South

Florida Archaic"—was a positive force during his South Florida work. Appreciation also goes to Dr. Jerry Milanich, whose quest for the truth inspired a rich tapestry of research at the Miami Circle.

A particular thanks to the Archaeological and Historical Conservancy for providing the time and resources needed to produce this work.

Finally, the support of my wife Debbie, and my two children, Christopher and Cathy, have been constant source of love that has allowed this book to finally come to fruition.

Notes

Chapter 1. Diggers, Scientists, and Antiquarians: History of Archaeological Research

1. True 1946.
2. Hann 1991.
3. Dickinson 1945.
4. Romans 1962.
5. Smith 1848.
6. Ibid.
7. Eck 2000: 286–93.
8. Ibid., 288.
9. Ibid., 289.
10. Perrine 1875.
11. Douglass 1884: 138.
12. Straight 2002: 188.
13. Douglass 1884: 141.
14. Ibid., 146.
15. Sewell 1926: 47.
16. Weatherly, n.d.
17. Eck 2002: 292.
18. Peters 1984: 21.
19. Writers' Program (Fla.) 1941: 21.
20. Weisman 2002.
21. Ibid., xiv.
22. Goggin 1948.
23. Coe 1935.
24. Hrdlička 1935: 11-12–35.
25. Lamme 1934a.
26. Lamme to Carr, personal communication, 1974.
27. Goggin and Sommer 1949.
28. Gilpin 1890: 73.

29. Luer 2006: 253–62.
30. Goggin 1947.
31. Laxson 1955.
32. Laxson 1957a: 1–16.
33. Laxson 1964: 215–20.
34. Laxson 1954: 111–18.
35. Luer 2006: 253–62.
36. Mallard 2009.
37. Carr 2002: 187–206.
38. Schwadron 2005.
39. Carr 1975.
40. Gagel 1976.
41. Daniel 1979.
42. Griffin et al. 1985.
43. Griffin 1982.

Chapter 2. The First People: The Cutler Fossil Site

1. Clausen 1979: 609–13.
2. Cockrell 1978: 1–13.
3. Dunbar, Webb, and Cring 1989: 473–97.
4. Gifford and Wentz 2007.
5. Weisman and Newman 1992.
6. Carr 1986b: 231.
7. Morgan 2002.
8. Ibid.
9. Morgan and Elmslie 1998.
10. Gifford 1986.
11. Morgan 2002: 24.
12. Austin 2008.
13. Ibid., 4.
14. Ibid.
15. Masson 1987.
16. Armelagos 1986.
17. Ibid.
18. Morees, Fanning, and Hunt 1963: 1490–1502.
19. Newsom 2007.
20. Edwards and Merrill 1977.
21. Dunbar 1992.
22. Scholl, Craighead, and Stuiver 1969.
23. Morgan 2002.
24. Mead and Meltzen 1984.
25. Kerr 2009: 26.

Chapter 3. The South Florida Archaic

1. Carbone 1983; Delcourt and Delcourt 1981.
2. Carr and Steele 1992.
3. Carr and Steele 1993.
4. Carr, Sandler, and Felmley 1992.
5. Newman 1986.
6. Masson, Carr, and Goldman 1988: 336–50.
7. Schwadron 2005.
8. Carr and Davis 1990, 1991.
9. Carr and Davis 1990.
10. Carr 2002.
11. Carr and Masson 1988.
12. Carr et al. 1979; Gifford 1991.
13. Gifford 1991.
14. Carr et al. 1979.
15. Cockrell 1971.
16. Carr 1981b.
17. Widmer 1988: 210, Table 10.
18. Quitmeyer and Blessing 2006.
19. Fradkin 1996.
20. Fradkin 2004.
21. Quitmeyer and Blessing 2006.
22. Condon, Condon, and Carr 2001.
23. Carr 1981c; Felmley 1991.
24. Carr, Iscan, and Johnson 1984: 172–88.
25. Ibid.
26. Ibid.
27. Carr 1981c.
28. Carr, Iscan, and Johnson 1984.
29. Carr et al. 2010 (revised 2012).
30. Carr 1990: 249–61; Felmley 1990: 262–74.
31. Felmley 1991.
32. Carr, Elgart-Berry, and Ransom 2009.
33. Condon, Condon, and Carr 2001.

Chapter 4. The Perfect Balance: Adapting to the Land and Sea

1. Goggin 1947.
2. Griffin 2002: 187.
3. Ibid., 232.
4. Ibid., 270.
5. Wing 1984.
6. Griffin et al. 1985.

7. Wing and Loucks 1985: 259–345.
8. Ibid., 269–74.
9. Ibid., 278, Table 59.
10. Scarry, Newsom, and Masson 1989.
11. Ibid.
12. Scarry 1985: 1–248.
13. Ibid.
14. Ibid.
15. True 1944: 27–28.
16. McNicoll 1941: 17.
17. Goggin and Sommer 1949.
18. Carr 2006: 142–48.
19. Carr 2006.
20. Ibid., 140.
21. Sears 1982: 32–36.
22. Gilliand 1989.
23. Goggin, n.d. [1949].
24. Carr et al. 2010.
25. Reiger 1990: 227–39.
26. Austin 2004: 90.
27. Kish 2006: 229–37.
28. Gilliland 1989.
29. Reiger 1990.
30. Stirling, 1934–36, dated 1936.
31. Reiger 1990: 230.
32. Gilliland 1989.
33. Ibid.
34. Solis de Merias 1964.
35. Griffin et al. 1985.
36. Hann 1991.
37. Carr et al. 2010.
38. Carr et al. 2006.
39. Coleman 1989: 257–62.

Chapter 5. Sacred Geography: The Prehistoric Settlement System

1. Goggin 1940: 7.
2. Iscan, Kessel, and Carr 1993.
3. Carr, Iscan, and Johnson 1984: 173.
4. Carr et al. 2010.
5. Carr, Shaffer, and Gelmer 2007.
6. Echazabal 2010.
7. Sears 1982.

8. Carr 1985: 288–301.
9. Griffin et al. 1985.
10. Carr and Greene 1961.
11. Laxson 1959: 57–62.
12. Carr 1981d.
13. Carr et al. 2001.
14. Carr and Ricisak 2000: 275.
15. Wheeler 2000b: 294–323.
16. Carr et al. 2006.
17. Ives 1856.
18. Goggin 1931.
19. Lamme 1934.
20. Iscan, Kessel, and Carr 1995: 7.
21. Coleman 1989: 257–62.
22. Ibid.
23. Ibid.
24. Ibid.
25. Shirley to Carr, June 2009.
26. Laxson 1957a: 1–16.
27. Gifford 1989.
28. Carr 2005.
29. Miller 1899.
30. Laxson 1957a: 1–16.
31. Carr 1975.
32. Lamme 1935.
33. Russo 1990.
34. Small 1929.
35. Lamme 1934.
36. Ibid.
37. Ibid.
38. Lamme 9-31-34.
39. Reichard 1936.
40. Carr, Ransom, and Elgart-Berry 2009.
41. Goggin 1940: 7.

Chapter 6. European Contact: The Transition to Extinction

1. Nuñez Cabeza de Vaca 1993.
2. True 1944.
3. Carr 1986a: 164.
4. Ibid., 167.
5. True 1944.
6. Ibid.

7. Lyon 1976: 187; Parks, n.d.
8. Parks, n.d.
9. Solís de Merás 1964.
10. Parks, n.d.; Solis de Merás 1964.
11. Rogel 1570 in Zubillaga 1941.
12. Villarreal to Father Francisco Borgia in Zubillaga 1941.
13. Parks, n.d.
14. Zubillaga 1941.
15. Manucy 1965.
16. Lyon 1995: 8.
17. Ibid., 9.
18. Rouse 1951.
19. Ibid.
20. Martínez 1765.
21. Parks, n.d.
22. Governor of Cuba to the king of Spain, July 26, 1743.
23. Alaña 1743.
24. Governor of Cuba to the king of Spain, September 28, 58-2-10/15, Archivo General de las Indias, Seville, Spain.
25. Ibid.
26. Romans 1775.
27. Smith 1987.
28. Goggin 1968.
29. Deagan 1987.
30. Goggin 1964.
31. Lyon to Carr, personal communication, 1986.
32. Allerton, Luer, and Carr 1984: 7.
33. Casas 1989.
34. Goggin 1968, 1960a.
35. Goggin 1960b.
36. Smith and Good 1982.
37. Deagan 1987.
38. Haiduven 2001.

Chapter 7. The English and Bahamian Legacy

1. McGregor 1985.
2. Chardon 1975: 7.
3. Frazier 1975: 77.
4. *Niles Register,* 1817.
5. Robertson 1854.
6. Heinz 1994.
7. Hammond 1961: 68–69.

8. Smith 1994.
9. Gosse 1924.
10. Federal Writer's Project 1939.
11. Perrine 1877: 3.
12. Caesar's Forge Menu, c. 1950s.
13. *New York Daily Tribune*, October 27, 1843.
14. Hetzel 1843.
15. Rickmer 1913.

Chapter 8. Seminole Archaeology

1. De Brahm 1770.
2. West 2002.
3. Fairbanks 1957.
4. Covington 1992.
5. Nairne 1988.
6. Adair 1775.
7. Chardon 1975: 33.
8. Ibid., 32.
9. Seagrave to Knox 1793.
10. Goggin 1946: 201–6.
11. Williams 1983: 146.
12. Marvin 1840.
13. Sturtevant 1953: 54.
14. Williams 1837.
15. Covington 1992.
16. Sturtevant 1953: 35–37.
17. Straight, n.d.
18. Smith 1848.
19. Carr and Steele 1991.
20. Chance 1998.
21. MacCauley 1883.
22. Carr 1981.
23. Ibid.
24. Burman 1956.
25. Munroe 1894.
26. West 1981.
27. Ibid.
28. Coleman 1989.
29. Laxson 1954.
30. Goggin 1940.
31. Carr 1989.

Chapter 9. Stockades and Musket Balls

1. Douglass 1885: 141.
2. Welsh 1925.
3. McMurray 1985.
4. Ames 1836.
5. Straight, n.d.
6. Ibid., 23.
7. Baker 1973.
8. Weisman, Collins, and Driscoll 2001.
9. Doubleday 1856.
10. Blank 1996.
11. Leib 1836.
12. Shappee 1961.
13. Morris 1855.
14. McMurray 1985.
15. Bell 2004.
16. Carr 1987.
17. Straight, n.d.
18. Woodman 1961: 18.
19. Mayo 1839.
20. Hudson 1974.
21. Marchand 1842.
22. Chance 1998: 188–89.
23. Cooke 1849:NP.
24. Godden 1964: 173.
25. Ibid., 527.
26. Branan 1857.

Chapter 10. The Archaeology of Arrowroot: Miami's First Industry

1. Kleinberg 1985: 126.
2. Ibid., 126.
3. Ibid., 125.
4. Pierce 1975: 155.
5. McKay 1845.
6. Eyster 1981.
7. U.S. War Department 1880–1901.
8. George and Knetsch 1990: 5.
9. Bonawit 1980: 12.
10. Richards 1903.
11. Cooke 1849: n.p.
12. George and Knetsch 1990.

13. Munroe 1974: 95.
14. Supreme Court of Florida 1850: 27–41; Supreme Court of Florida 1852: 102–11.
15. George and Knetsch 1990: 5.
16. Richards 1903: n.p.
17. National Archives 1850.
18. Munroe 1974: 95.
19. Carr et al. 1991.
20. Mace 1990: 193, Fig. A-3.

Chapter 11. Tropical Homesteads: Artifacts of Miami's Pioneers

1. Wood 1893: 318.
2. Richards 1903.
3. Parks 1978.
4. Perrine 1875.
5. Ibid.
6. Rockwood 1891.
7. McMahon and Wild 2007.
8. Bell 1960.
9. Brickell 2011.
10. Carr et al. 2006.
11. Carr and Greene 1961.
12. Carr, Mankowski, and Franklin 2008.
13. Parks 1978.
14. Haiduven 1994.
15. Heinz and Carr 1994.
16. Heinz 1995.

Chapter 12. The Miami Circle and Beyond

1. Wheeler 2000c.
2. Widmer 2004: 11–58.
3. Carr 2006; Wheeler 2002, 2006; Dixon et al. 1998; Kish 2006.
4. Carr and Ricisak 2000: 277.
5. Means and Scott 2000: 324–27.
6. Carr 2006: 133–60.
7. Goggin 1952: 99.
8. Dixon et al. 2000: 328–41.
9. Elgart and Carr 2006: 241–50.
10. Fonteneda 1569.
11. Carr 1981b.
12. Lamme 1934.

13. Carr, Mankowski, and Franklin 2008.
14. Elgart 2006: 179–90.
15. Williams 1983: 142–53.
16. Coleman 1989: 257–62.
17. Carr, Mankowski, and Franklin 2008.
18. Widmer 2004: 52–58.
19. Dixon et al. 1998: 326–39.
20. Ibid., 332.
21. Ibid., 336.
22. Ibid., 326–39.
23. Carr 2006: 133–60.
24. Carr et al. 2010 (revised 2012).
25. Carr, Zamanillo, and Pepe 2002.
26. Harrington 1909.
27. Ibid., Plate LXVII.
28. Gifford 1931.
29. Wheeler 1994: 47–60.

References Cited

Adair, James
1775   *The History of the American Indians; particularly Those Nations Adjoining to the Mississippi, East and West Florida, Georgia, South and North Carolina, and Virginia.* London: E. and C. Dilly.

Addison, Ferguson
1990   "Unveiling of [a] Portrait of Joel Addison Sheriff of Manatee County, 1861–1866. Speech. Bradenton, Fla.

Alaña, Joseph Xavier
1760   Report on the Indians of Southern Florida and Its Keys by Joseph Maria Monaco and Joseph Javier Alaña, Presented to Governor Juan Francisco de Guemes y Horcasitas, 1760. Translated by John H. Hann. In *Missions to the Calusa*. Gainesville: University Press of Florida.

Albert, Alphaeus H.
1976   *Record of American Uniform and Historical Buttons, Bicentennial Edition.* Boyertown, Pa.: Boyertown Publishing.

Allerton, David, George Luer, and Robert S. Carr
1984   Ceremonial Tablets and Related Objects from Florida. *Florida Anthropologist* 37 (1): 5–54.

Ames, Assistant Surgeon, U.S. Army
1836   Letter to Hon. Gideon Lee. Written from Fort Brooke, November 1, 1836. Copy on file, Archaeological and Historical Conservancy, Davie, Fla.

Ammidown, Margot
1982   The Wagner Family: Pioneer Life on the Miami River. *Tequesta: The Journal of the Historical Association of Southern Florida* 42:5–37.

Anonymous
1912   *Genealogy: A Weekly Journal of American Ancestry* 2, no. 4.

Armelagos, George
1986   Untitled manuscript. On file, Archaeological and Historical Conservancy, Davie, Fla.

Austin, Robert J.
2004   Chipped Stone Artifacts from the Miami Circle Excavations at Brickell Point, Florida. *Florida Anthropologist* 57 (1–2): 85–32.
2008   Lithic Artifacts from the Cutler Site, 8DA2001. Report on file, Archaeological and Historical Conservancy, Davie, Fla.

Baker, Henry
1973   *Archaeological Investigations at Indian Key, Florida.* Tallahassee: Florida Division of Archives, History and Records Management.

Bell, Jack
1960   "When I die," said Maude, "write me a story, Jack." *Miami Herald,* November 24, 1960.

Bell, Max
2004   Collecting American Face Pipes. *Bottles and Extras Magazine* (Raymore, Mo.), 52–54.

Berning, C. G.
1948   Brickell Point: Trade Post to Tourist Inn. *Miami Herald,* August 22.

Blank, Joan
1996   *Key Biscayne: A History of Miami's Tropical Island and the Cape Florida Lighthouse.* Sarasota, Fla.: Pineapple Press.

Bonawit, Oby J.
1980   *Miami Florida Early Families and Records.* Miami: Privately published.

Branan, J. M.
1857   Letter to 1st Lieutenant P. L. Wyman. January 10. M1084, NA.

Brickell, Beth
2011   *William and Mary Brickell: Founders of Miami and Fort Lauderdale.* Charleston, S.C.: History Press.

Brooks, Marvin J., Jr.
1956   Excavations at Grossman Hammock, Dade County, Florida. *Florida Anthropologist* 9 (2): 37–46.

Brown, Canter, Jr.
1991   The East Florida Coffee Land Expedition of 1821: Plantations or a Bonapartist Kingdom of the Indies? *Tequesta: The Journal of the Historical Association of Southern Florida* 51:7–28.

Brown, Robin C.
2008   *Florida's Fossils: Guide to Location, Identification and Enjoyment.* Sarasota, Fla.: Pineapple Press.

Bullen, Ripley P.
1975   *A Guide to the Identification of Florida Projectile Points.* Rev. ed. Gainesville, Fla.: Kendall Books.

Cabeza de Vaca, Alvar Núñez
1993   *The Account: Alvar Núñez Cabeza de Vaca's Relación: An annotated translation by Martin A. Fauata and José B. Fernádez.* Houston: Arte Público Press.

Carbone, Victor
1983   Late Quaternary Environments in Florida and the Southeast. *Florida Anthropologist* 36 (1–2): 3–17.

Carr, Robert S.
1975   Excavations at the Arch Creek Site (8DA23) Dade County, Florida. Unpublished typescript. On file, Florida Division of Archives, History and Records Management, Tallahassee.

1981a   The Brickell Store and Seminole Trade. *Florida Anthropologist* 34 (4): 180–99.
1981b   Dade County Historic Survey Final Report: The Archaeological Survey. Metropolitan Dade County Office of Community and Economic Development, Historic Preservation Division, Miami.
1981c   Salvage Excavations at Two Prehistoric Cemeteries in Dade County, Florida. Paper presented at the 45th annual meeting of the Florida Academy of Sciences, Winter Park, Fla., May 1.
1981d   Brickell Point Monitoring Field Notes. Manuscript on file, Archaeological and Historical Conservancy, Davie, Fla.
1985   Prehistoric Circular Earthworks in South Florida. *Florida Anthropologist* 38 (4): 288–301.
1986a   Historical Use Interpreted from a Conch Shell Feature in Southern Florida. *Florida Anthropologist* 39 (3, pt. 1): 164–70.
1986b   Preliminary Report on Excavations at the Cutler Fossil Site 8DA2001 in Southern Florida. *Florida Anthropologist* 39 (3, pt. 2): 231–32.
1987   An Archaeological Survey and Investigation at Bill Baggs State Park, Key Biscayne. Report on file, Miami-Dade County Historic Preservation Division, Miami.
1989   Archaeological Investigations at the Stranahan House (8BD259). *Florida Anthropologist* 42 (1): 7–33.
1990   Archaeological Investigations at Pine Island, Broward County. *Florida Anthropologist* 43 (4): 249–61.
1991   *Archaeological Monitoring of Trenching at Barnacle State Historic Site, Dade County, Florida.* AHC Technical Report 33. Archaeological and Historical Conservancy, Davie, Fla.
1994   *A Post-Hurricane Archaeological Survey and Assessment of Bill Baggs State Park, Key Biscayne, Dade County, Florida. Archaeological and Historical Conservancy.* AHC Technical Report 91. Archaeological and Historical Conservancy, Davie, Fla.
2002   The Archaeology of Everglades Tree Islands. In *The Tree Islands of the Everglades*, edited by Fred H. Sklar and Arnold van der Valk. Dordrecht: Kluwer Academic.
2006   Analysis of Ceramics from Brickell Point, 8DA12. *Florida Anthropologist* 59 (3–4): 133–60.

Carr, Robert S., and John Beriault
1992   *Archaeological Survey of the Sands Key Site 8DA4582 Biscayne National Park Miami-Dade County, Florida.* AHC Technical Report 895 (revised June 2009). Archaeological and Historical Conservancy, Davie, Fla.

Carr, Robert S., John Beriault, Irving Eyster, and Margot Ammidon
1979   An Archaeological and Historical Survey of the Site 14 Replacement Airport and Its Proposed Access Corridors, Dade County, Florida. Report on file, Archaeological and Historical Conservancy, Davie, Fla.

Carr, Robert S., Simon Daniels, Joe Davis, W. S. Steele, and Jorge Zamanillo
1996   *Archaeological and Historical Assessment of the Everglades Stormwater Treat-*

ment Areas, Palm Beach County, Florida. AHC Technical Report 145. Archaeological and Historical Conservancy, Davie, Fla.

Carr, Robert S., and Joseph Davis
1990 *An Archaeological Survey of the Southern Citrus Division Property, Hendry County, Florida.* AHC Technical Report 14. Archaeological and Historical Conservancy, Davie, Fla.
1991 *Archaeological Testing on U.S. Sugar Site #12 (8HN55), Hendry County, Florida.* AHC Technical Report 32. Archaeological and Historical Conservancy, Davie, Fla.

Carr, Robert S., Amy Felmley, Patsy West, Marilyn Masson, and Wesley Coleman
1991 Historical and Archaeological Investigations at the Honey Hill Site, Dade County, Florida. Report on file, Archaeological and Historical Conservancy, Davie, Fla.

Carr, Robert S., and Mark Greene
1961 Brickell Point Excavations Report. Unpublished report. Copy on file, Historical Museum of Southern Florida, Miami.

Carr, Robert S., M. Yasar Iscan, and Richard A. Johnson
1984 A Late Archaic Cemetery in South Florida. *Florida Anthropologist* 37 (4): 172–88.

Carr, Robert S., Shannon Iverson, William Shaffer, Ryan Franklin, Ashley Geleman, Brad Mueller, and William Rombola
2010 *Phase III Archaeological investigations of Parcel D, MDM, Miami, Florida.* AHC Technical Report 580. Revised 2012. Archaeological and Historical Conservancy, Davie, Fla.

Carr, Robert S., Joseph Mankowski, and John G. Beriault
2008b *A Phase II Cultural Resource Survey of the Bonnet House Parcel Landscaping Project, Broward County, Florida.* AHC Technical Report 876. Archaeological and Historical Conservancy, Davie, Fla.

Carr, Robert S., Joseph Mankowski, and Ryan Franklin
2008 *An Archaeological Assessment of 3031 and 3115 Brickell Avenue, Miami-Dade County, Florida.* AHC Technical Report 846. Archaeological and Historical Conservancy, Davie, Fla.

Carr, Robert S., and Marilyn Masson
1988 *An Archaeological Survey of the Silver Lakes Project, Broward County, Florida.* AHC Technical Report 12. Archaeological and Historical Conservancy, Davie, Fla.

Carr, Robert S., J. Ransom, and A. Elgart-Berry
2009 *Archaeological Investigations of the Long Lakes Parcel, Broward County, Florida.* AHC Technical Report 347. Archaeological and Historical Conservancy, Davie, Fla.

Carr, Robert S., Jeff Ransom, Mark Lance, and Alison Elgart-Berry
2001 *A Due Diligence Archaeological Assessment of Brickell Park, Miami, Florida.* AHC Technical Report 312. Archaeological and Historical Conservancy, Davie, Fla.

Carr, Robert S., and John Ricisak
2000   Preliminary Report on Salvage Archaeological Excavations of the Brickell Point Site (8DA12), Including the Miami Circle. *Florida Anthropologist* 53, no. 4 (December): 260–85.

Carr, Robert S., Debra Sandler, and Amy Felmley
1992   *An Archaeology Survey and Assessment of the Westridge Property, Broward County, Florida*. AHC Technical Report 48. Archaeological and Historical Conservancy, Davie, Fla.

Carr, Robert S., Debra Sandler, Jorge Zamanillo, and W. S. Steel
1994   *Archaeological and Historical Investigations of the Miami River Rapids Site, Dade County, Florida*. AHC Technical Report 36. Archaeological and Historical Conservancy, Davie, Fla.

Carr, Robert S., William Schaffer, Ashley Gelman
2008   *Archaeological Investigation of the Icon-Brickell Parcel, Miami, Florida*. AHC Technical Report 830. Archaeological and Historical Conservancy, Davie, Fla.

Carr, Robert S., and Willard Steele
1991   *Archival and Other Evidence on the Location of Snake Warrior's Island, Broward County, Florida*. AHC Technical Report 45. Archaeological and Historical Conservancy, Davie, Fla.
1992   *An Archaeological and Historical Assessment of the Weston Increment 3 Area, Broward County, Florida*. AHC Technical Report 46. Archaeological and Historical Conservancy, Davie, Fla.
1993   *A Phase II Archaeological Survey and Assessment of the Weston Pond Site, Broward County, Florida*. AHC Technical Report 72. Archaeological and Historical Conservancy, Davie, Fla.

Carr, Robert, Willard Steele, and Jorge Zamanillo
1994   *A Phase I Archaeological Survey and Assessment of the Santa Maria Parcel, Dade County, Florida*. AHC Technical Report #84. Archaeological and Historical Conservancy, Davie, Fla.

Carr, Robert S., Jorge Zamanillo, and Jim Pepe
2002   Archaeological Profiling and Radiocarbon Dating of the Ortona Canal (8GL4). *Florida Anthropologist* 55 (1): 3–24.

Casas, Bartolomé de las
1989   *The Diario of Christopher Columbus's First Voyage to America, 1492–1493*. Abstracted by Bartoloméde las Casas, translated into English by Oliver Dunn and James E. Kelley Jr. Norman: University of Oklahoma Press.

Chance, Joseph E.
1998   *My Life in the Army: the Reminiscences of Abner Doubleday from the Collections of the New-York Historical Society*. Fort Worth: Texas Christian University Press.

Chardon, Roland E.
1975   The Cape Florida Society of 1773. *Tequesta: The Journal of the Historical Association of Southern Florida* 35:1–36.

Clausen, C. J., A. D. Cohen, C. Emiliani, J. A. Holman, and J. J. Stipp
1979   Little Salt Spring, Florida: A Unique Underwater Site. *Science* 203:609–13.
Cockrell, Wilburn A.
1970   Glades I and Pre-Glades Settlement and Subsistence Patterns on Marco Island, Florida. Master's thesis, Florida State University, Tallahassee.
Cockrell, Wilburn A., and L. Murphy
1978   Pleistocene Man in Florida. *Archaeology of Eastern North America* 6:1–13.
Coleman, Wesley F.
1989   Salvage Excavations at the Trail Site, Dade County, Florida. *Florida Anthropologist* 42 (3): 257–62.
1997   Excavation of a Late Archaic Everglades Site, Da141, Dade County, Florida. *Florida Anthropologist* 50 (3): 133–35.
Condon, Cynthia, Keith Condon, and Robert S. Carr
2001   *Archaeological Assessment and Monitoring of the Monarch Lakes Sites, Broward County, Florida.* AHC Technical Report 294.
Connor, Jeannette Thurber
1930   *Colonial Records of Spanish Florida: Letters and Reports of Governors, Deliberations of the Council of the Indies, Royal Decrees, and Other Documents.* Vols. 1 and 2, 1570–80. Deland: Florida State Historical Society.
Cooke, Anson
1849   Letter to Mrs. Cooke, November 1. Copy on file, Historical Museum of Southern Florida, Miami.
Copeland, D. Graham
1947   Data Relative to Florida, Compiled by D. Graham Copeland, Everglades, Florida. Unpublished manuscript. Copy on file, Collier County Museum, Naples, Fla.
Covington, James W.
1992   *The Seminoles of Florida.* Gainesville: University Press of Florida.
Daniel, Randy
1979   Test Excavations at Chekika State Recreation Area, Dade County, Florida. Report on file, Florida Department of Historical Resources, Tallahassee.
Day, Jane S.
1995   Mariah Brown House. Report of the City of Miami Preservation Officer to the Historic and Environmental Preservation Board on the Potential Designation of the Mariah Brown House as a Historic Site. Report on file at Historic Preservation Division, Miami.
Deagan, Kathleen
1987   *Artifacts of the Spanish Colonies of Florida and the Caribbean 1500–1800.* Vol. 1, *Ceramics, Glassware, and Beads.* Washington, D.C.: Smithsonian Institution Press.
2002   *Artifacts of the Spanish Colonies of Florida and the Caribbean 1500–1800.* Vol. 2, *Portable Personal Possessions.* Washington, D.C.: Smithsonian Institution Press.

Dean, Love
1982   *Reef Lights: Seaswept Lighthouses of the Florida Keys.* Key West, Fla.: Key West Historic Preservation Board.

De Brahm, William Gerard
1771   Chart of the South End of East Florida and Martiers. Surveyed and drawn by Wm. Gerard de Brahm.

Delacourt, Hazel, Darrell C. West, and Paul A. Delacourt
1981   Forests of the Southeastern United States: Quantitative Maps for Aboveground Woody Biomass, Carbon, and Dominance of Major Tree Taxa. *Ecology* 62, no. 4.

Dickinson, Jonathan
1945   *Jonathan Dickinson's Journal, or, God's Protecting Providence: Being the narrative of a journey from Port Royal in Jamaica to Philadelphia between August 23, 1696 and April 1, 1697.* Edited by Evangeline Walker Andrews and Charles McLean Andrews. New Haven, Conn.: Yale University Press.

Dieterich, Emily Perry
1987   Arch Creek: Prehistory to Public. *Tequesta: The Journal of the Historical Association of Southern Florida* 47:49–67.

Dixon, Jacqueline Eaby, Kyla Simons, Loretta Leist, Christopher Eck, John Ricisak, John Gifford, and Jeff Ryan
1998   Provenance of Stone Celts from the Miami Circle Archaeological Site. *Florida Anthropologist* 53 (4): 328–41.

Doubleday, Abner
1857   Letter to Bvt. Colonel J. Dimick. September 26, 1857. M1084, Roll 7, frames 1203–7, NA.

Douglass, Andrew E.
1885a Earth and Shell Mounds on the Atlantic Coast of Florida. *American Antiquarian and Oriental Journal* 7, no. 3.
1885b Andrew E. Douglass Florida Diary—Letters. Unpublished manuscript. Copy on file, Historical Museum of Southern Florida, Miami.

Dunbar, James S.
1981   The Kaskaskia Projectile Point: A Seminole Indian Metal Arrow Point Type Recently Recognized in Florida. *Florida Anthropologist* 34 (4): 166–68.

Dunbar, James S., S. D. Webb, and D. Cring
1989   Culturally and Naturally Modified Bones from a Paleoindian Site in the Aucilla River, North Florida. In *Bone Modification*, edited by Rob Bonnichsen and M. Sorg, 473–97. Orono, Maine: Center for the Study of the First Americans.

Dunbar, James, S. David Webb, and Michael Faught
1992   Inundated Prehistoric Sites in Apalachee Bay, Florida, and the Search for the Clovis Shoreline. In *Paleoshores and Prehistory: An Investigation of Method*, edited by Lucille Lewis Johnson. Boca Raton, Fla.: CRC Press.

Echazabel, Christina
2010 Life in the Florida Everglades: Bioarchaeology of the Miami One Site. Master's thesis, University of South Florida, Tampa.

Eck, Christopher
2000 A Picturesque Settlement: The Diary of Dr. Jeffries Wyman's Visit to Miami and the First Archaeological Excavations in South Florida, 1969. *Florida Anthropologist* 53 (4): 286–93.

Edwards, R. L., and A. S. Merrill
1977 A Reconstruction of the Continental Shelf of Eastern North America for the Times 9,500 BP and 12,000 BP. *Archaeology of North America* 5:1–43.

Elgart, Alison A.
2006 The Animal Interments at the Miami Circle at Brickell Point Site (8DA12). *Florida Anthropologist* 59 (3–4): 279–90.

Elgart, Alison A., and Robert S. Carr
2006 An Analysis of the Prehistoric Human Remains found at the Miami Circle at Brickell Point Site (8DA12). *Florida Anthropologist* 59 (3–4): 241–50.

Emslie, S. D., and Gary S. Morgan
1995 Taphonomy of a Late Pleistocene Carnivore Den, Dade County, Florida. In *Late Quaternary Environments and Deep History: A Tribute to Paul S. Martin*, edited by D. W. Steadman and J. I. Meade. Hot Springs, S.D.: Mammoth Site of Hot Springs.

Erenhard, John E., Robert S. Carr, and Robert C. Taylor
1978 The Big Cypress National Preserve: Archaeological Survey Phase I. Southeast Archaeological Center, National Park Service, Tallahassee, Fla.
1979 The Big Cypress National Preserve: Archaeological Survey Season 2. Southeast Archaeological Center, National Park Service, Tallahassee, Fla.
1982 Everglades National Park Cultural Resources Inventory: Interim Report—Season 1. Southeast Archaeological Center, National Park Service, Tallahassee, Fla.

Escalante Fontaneda, Hernando de
1944 *Memoir of D d'Escalante Fontaneda Respecting Florida: Written in Spain, About the Year 1575. Translated from the Spanish with Notes by Buckingham Smith: Washington: 1854. Reprinted, with Revisions and Edited by David True.* University of Miami and the Historical Association of Southern Florida. Miscellaneous Publications 1.

Eyster, Irving
1981 Notes on Excavations of the Arch Creek Starch Mill Site, 8DA1657. Performed for the Dade County Historic Division of the office of Community and Economic Development, Miami.

Fairbanks, Charles H.
1957 *Ethnohistorical Report on the Florida Indians.* 3 vols. Tallahassee. New York: Garland.

Federal Writer's Project
1939 *Florida: A Guide to the Southern-most State.* New York: Oxford University Press.

Felmley, Amy
1990   Osteological Analysis of the Pine Island Site Human Remains. *Florida Anthropologist* 43 (4): 262–74.
1991   Prehistoric Mortuary Practices in the Everglades Cultural Area, Florida. Thesis submitted for a master's degree, Florida Atlantic University.

Forbes, James Grant
1821   *Sketches, Historical and Topographical of the Floridas; More Particularly of East Florida*. New York: C. S. Van Winkle.

Fradkin, Arlene
1996   Animal Resource Use Among Early Human Inhabitants of the "River of Grass": The Faunal Assemblages from the Everglades Archaeological Sites of McArthur #2 (8BD2591) and Sheridan Hammock (8BD191). Report on file, Archaeological and Historical Conservancy, Davie, Fla.
2004   Snake Consumption among Early Inhabitants of the River of Grass, South Florida, USA. *Archaeo Fauna* 13.
2007   The Role of Fish in Ancient Time. Proceedings of the 13th meeting of the ICAZ Fish Remains Working Group, Basel, October 4–9.

Frazier, James C.
1975   The Samuel Touchett Plantation, 1773. In *Tequesta: The Journal of the Historical Association of Southern Florida* 35:75–89.

Gagle, Katherine
1976   *Survey of DA139 (DA33)*. Tallahassee: Florida Division of Archives, History and Records Management.

George, Paul, and Joe Knetsch
1990   When Coontie was King. *South Florida History* 4 (Fall): 5–9.

Gerdes, F. H.
1849a   Everglades Touching the Upper Falls of the Miami River. Drawn by F. H. Gerdes.
1849b   Mouth of the Miami River, Fl. Kay Biscayne Bay, W of Cape Florida. Drawn by F. H. Gerdes.

Giddings, Joshua
1858   *The Exiles of Florida*. Columbus: Follett, Foster.

Gifford, John A.
1991   Archaeological Investigations at Black Island. Report on file, Miami-Dade Historic Preservation Division, Miami, Fla.

Gifford, John A., and Rachel Wentz
2007   Florida's Deep Past: The Bioarchaeology of Little Salt Spring (8SO18) and Its Place among Mortuary Ponds of the Archaic. *Southeastern Archaeology* 26, no. 2.

Gifford, John C.
1931   Letter to Matthew Sterling. National Anthropological Archives, Washington, D.C.

Gilliland, Marion S.
1989   *The Material Culture of Key Marco, Florida*. Port Salerno: Florida Classics Library.

Gilpin, H.
1890   Diary. Historical Museum of Southern Florida, Miami.

Godden, Geoffrey A.
1964   *Encyclopedia of British Pottery and Porcelain Marks.* New York: Crown.

Goggin, John M.
1931   Report on the Indian Mound in Flagami Hammock. Unpublished notes. John M. Goggin Papers. Special Collections, P. K. Yonge Library of Florida History, University of Florida, Gainesville.
1940a   Field notes. John M. Goggin Papers. Special Collections, P. K. Yonge Library of Florida History, University of Florida, Gainesville.
1940b   Silver Work of the Florida Seminole. *El Palacio: Journal of the Museum of New Mexico.*
1942   A Prehistoric Wooden Club from Southern Florida. *American Anthropology* 44.
1946   The Seminole Negroes of Andros Island, Bahamas. *Florida Historical Quarterly* 24 (3): 201–6.
1947   A preliminary Definition of Archaeological Areas and Periods in Florida. *American Antiquity* 13.
1951   The Snapper Creek Site. *Florida Anthropologist* 3:50–64.
1952   *Space and Time Perspective in Northern St. Johns Archaeology, Florida.* Yale University Publications in Anthropology 47.
1960a   *The Spanish Olive Jar, an Introductory Study.* Yale University Publications in Anthropology 62.
1960b   Spanish Trade Beads and Pendants. Manuscript on file, Florida Museum of Natural History, University of Florida, Gainesville.
1964   *Indian and Spanish Selected Writings.* Coral Gables, Fla.: University of Miami Press.
1968   *Spanish Majolica in the New World.* Yale University Publications in Anthropology 72.
n.d. [1949]   The Archaeology of the Glades Area, Southern Florida. Manuscript on file. John M. Goggin Papers. Special Collections, P. K. Yonge Library of Florida History, University of Florida, Gainesville.

Goggin, John M., and Frank H. Sommer
1949   *Excavations on Upper Matecumbe Key, Florida.* Yale University Publications in Anthropology 41.

Gosse, Philip
1924   *The Pirates' Who's Who: Giving particulars of the lives and deaths of the Pirates and Buccaneers.* London: Dulau.

Griffin, John W.
1946   Field Notes, 1946–47. Unpublished Papers of John W. Griffin, Box 4, National Anthropological Archives, Suitland, Md.
1987   The Bear Lake Site: A Report Prepared for the National Park Service Southeast Archaeological Center. Southeastern Frontiers, Tallahassee, August.

1988 *The Archaeology of Everglades National Park: A Synthesis*. Tallahassee: Southeastern Frontiers.
2002 *Archaeology of the Everglades*. Gainesville: University Press of Florida.

Griffin, John W., et al., eds.
1985 *Excavations at the Granada Site: Archaeology and History of the Granada Site.* Vol. 1. Tallahassee: Florida Division of Archives, History and Records Management.

Haiduven, Richard
1994 Phase I Archaeological Survey of the Gray Estate and Kirk Munroe Home Site (8DA5254). Report on file, Miami-Dade Historic Preservation Division, Miami.
2001 Archaeological Monitoring and Mitigation at Charles Deering Estate Park. Report on file, Archaeological and Historical Conservancy, Davie, Fla.

Hammond, E. A., ed.
1961 Dr. Strobel Reports on Southeast Florida, 1836. In *Tequesta: The Journal of the Historical Association of Southern Florida* 21:65–75.

Hann, John H.
1991 *Missions to the Calusa*. Gainesville: University Press of Florida.

Harrington, M. R.
1909 Archaeology of the Everglades Region, Florida. *American Anthropologist* 11:139–42.

Heinz, Kim
1995 A Phase I Archaeological Assessment at the Mariah Brown House, 3298 Charles Avenue, Coconut Grove, Florida. Report on file, Archaeological and Historical Conservancy, Davie, Fla.

Heinz, Kim, and Robert Carr
1994 *Archaeological Investigations of a Historic Dump at the Gray Estate Dade County, Florida*. AHC Technical Report 92. Archaeological and Historical Conservancy, Davie, Fla.

Hetzel, Lieutenant C.
1843 Letter from Lt. Hetzel to E. A. Ogden. October 16. General's Papers and Books, General Thomas Jesup Papers. RG 94, NA.

Hrdlička, Aleš
1918 *Recent Discoveries Attributed to Early Man in Florida*. Smithsonian Institution Bureau of American Ethnology Bulletin 66. Washington, D.C.
1935 Letter to Ernest F. Coe. November 12. From the unpublished papers of Aleš Hrdlička. Correspondence File, Everglades National Park Folder, National Anthropological Archives, Washington, D.C.

Hudson, Frank (Peninsular Archaeological Society)
1974 Personal communication with Robert S. Carr.

Hughes, Edward
1943 Black Caesar's Hideout Practically Hidden by Nature. *Miami News*, September 12.

Iscan, M. Yasar, Morton H. Kessel, and Robert S. Carr
1993   Human Remains from the Brickell Bluff Site. *Florida Anthropologist* 46 (4): 277–82.
1995   Human Skeletal Analysis of the Prehistoric Flagami South Site. *Florida Anthropologist* 48 (1): 54–60.

Ives, J. C.
1856   *Military Map of the Peninsula of Florida South of Tampa Bay. Compiled from the Latest and Most Reliable Authorities by Lieut. J. C. Ives, Topographical Engineers.* April. War Department.

Jones, B. C., and L. D. Tesar
2000   The Wakulla Springs Lodge Site (8Wa329): A Preliminary Report on a Stratified Paleoindian through Archaic Site, Wakulla County, Florida. *Florida Anthropologist* 53 (2–3): 98–116.

Kerr, Richard A.
2009   Did the Mammoth Slayer Leave a Diamond Calling Card? *Science Journal* 323, no. 5910.

Kidd, Kenneth E., and Martha A. Kidd
1970   *A Classification System for Glass Beads for the Use of Field Archaeologists.* Canadian Historic Sites: Occasional Papers in Archaeology and History No. 1. Ottawa.

Kish, Stephen H.
2006   Geochemical and Petrologic Characterization of Pumice Artifacts from the Miami Circle-Brickell Point Archaeological Site Plus Other Sites in Florida—Potential Provenance Locations. *Florida Anthropologist* 59 (3–4): 209–40.

Kleinberg, Howard
1985   Miami, the Way We Were. *Miami News.*

Lamme, Vernon
1934a   Field Notes. Unpublished manuscript, part of manuscript 4307, Field Notes, Maps and Photographs Relating to Archaeological Work in Florida, 1934–1937, U.S. Civil Works Administration. Copy on file, National Anthropological Archives, Washington, D.C.
1934b   Mound Near Indian Creek, Miami Beach, Florida. Unpublished manuscript, part of manuscript 4307, Field Notes, Maps and Photographs relating to Archaeological Work in Florida, 1934–1937, U.S. Civil Works Administration. Copy on file at National Anthropological Archives, Washington, D.C.

Laxson, Dan D.
1954   An Historic Seminole Burial in a Hialeah Midden. *Florida Anthropologist* 7:111–18.
1955   Letter to Pioneers Club of Miami, July 30.
1957a   The Madden Site. *Florida Anthropologist* 10 (1–2): 1–16.
1957b   The Arch Creek Site. *Florida Anthropologist* 10, nos. 3–4.
1959   Three Salvaged Tequesta Sites in Dade County, Florida. *Florida Anthropologist* 12 (3): 57–64.

1964 Strombus Lip Shell Tools of the Tequesta. *Florida Anthropologist* 17 (4): 215–20.

Leib, Lt. Thomas J.
1836 Letter to Alexander J. Dallas, Commander U.S. Naval Forces in the West Indies. August 17. Copy on file, Operational Archives, U.S. Naval Historical Center, Washington, D.C.

Le Moyne de Morgues, Jacques
1591 *Brevis narration eorum quae in Florida . . . acciderunt . . . Iacobo le Moyne.* Frankfurt: Theodore de Bry.

Lowery, Woodbury
1905 *The Spanish Settlements Within the Present Limits of the United States.* New York: G. P. Putnam's Sons; London: Knickerbocker Press.

Luer, George
2006 Obituary: Dan D. Laxson. *Florida Anthropologist* 59 (3–4): 253–59.

Lyon, Eugene
1976 *The Enterprise of Florida: Pedro Menéndez de Avilés and the Spanish Conquest of 1565–1568.* Gainesville: University Presses of Florida.
1995 The Fate of the Florida Indians, as Recorded in Spanish and Cuban Archives and as Particularly Related to the Florida Keys. Report on file, Key West Maritime Historical Society, Key West, Fla.

MacCauley, Clay
1887 The Seminole Indians of Florida. In *The Fifth Annual Report of the Bureau of Ethnology to the Secretary of the Smithsonian Institution, 1883–1884,* by J. W. Powell. Washington, D.C.

Mace, O. Henry
1990 *Collector's Guide to Early Photographs.* Radnor, Pa.: Wallace-Homestead.

Mahon, John K.
1967 *History of the Second Seminole War 1835–1842.* Gainesville: University of Florida Press.

Mallard, Paul
2009 Interview. Conducted by Bob Carr.

Manucy, Albert
1965 *Florida's Menéndez: Captain General of the Ocean Sea.* St. Augustine, Fla.: Saint Augustine Historical Society.

Marchand, John B.
1842 Letter to Lieutenant John G. McLaughlin, Commander of Florida Expedition. February 24. M148, Roll 143, frame 29. P. K. Yonge Library of Florida History, University of Florida, Gainesville.

Martinez, Fernan de
1765 Signed document. On file, chronological file folders, St. Augustine Historical Society, St. Augustine, Fla.

Marvin, Judge William
1840 Letter to *Tallahassee Democrat.* December 31.

Masson, Marilyn
1987   Chipped Limestone Artifacts from Dade County, Florida. Manuscript on file, Archaeological and Historical Conservancy, Davie, Fla.

Masson, Marilyn, Robert S. Carr, and Debra S. Goldman
1988   The Taylor's Head Site (8BD74): Sampling a Prehistoric Midden on an Everglades Tree Island. *Florida Anthropologist* 41 (3): 336–50.

Mayo, Commander Isaac, USN
1839   Letter to Secretary of the Navy reporting the establishment of Fort Kemble. October 13. Copy on file, Archaeological and Historical Conservancy, Davie, Fla.

McGregor, Malcom, and John Mollo
1985   *Uniforms of the American Revolution, 1775–1781*. Poole, UK: Blandford.

McKay, G.
1845   Copy of surveyor notes on file at the Archaeological and Historical Conservancy, Davie, Fla.

McMahon, Denise, and Christine Wild
2007   William Barnwell Brickell in Australia. *Tequesta: The Journal of the Historical Association of Southern Florida* 67:5–18.

McMurray, Carl D.
1985   Archaeological Remains of Fort Dallas. In *Excavations at the Granada Site: Archaeology and History of the Granada Site*, vol. 1, edited by John W. Griffin et al. Tallahassee: Florida Division of Archives, History and Records Management.

McNicoll, Robert E.
1941   The Caloosa Village Tequesta: A Miami of the Sixteenth Century. *Tequesta: The Journal of the Historical Association of Southern Florida* 1:11–20.

Mead, Jim I., and David J. Meltzen
1984   North American Late Quaternary Extinctions and the Radiocarbon Record. In *Quaternary Extinctions: A Prehistoric Revolution*, edited by P. S. Martin and R. G. Klein. Tucson: University of Arizona Press.

Means, Guy H., and Thomas Scott
2000   A Geological Assessment of the Miami Circle Site. *Florida Anthropologist* 53 (4): 324–27.

Miller, Florence
1899   My First Winter in Florida. Unpublished manuscript. Copy on file with Thelma Peters. Papers at the Historical Museum of Southern Florida.

Moorees, C. F., E. A. Fanning, and E. E Hunt
1963   Age Variation of Formation Stages for Ten Permanent Teeth. *Journal of Dental Research* 42:1490–1502.

Morgan, Gary S.
2002   Late Rancholabrean Mammals from Southernmost Florida, and the Neotropical Influence in Florida Pleistocene Faunas. In *Cenozoic Mammals of Land and Sea: Tributes to the Career of Clayton E. Ray*, edited by Robert J. Emry. Washington, D.C.: Smithsonian Institution Press.

Morris, Lt. Lewis
1855   Letter to Major General Thomas Jesup, Quartermaster General, Washington, D.C., written from Fort Dallas, July 1, 1855. General's Papers and Books, General Thomas Jesup Papers. RG 94, NA.

Munroe, Kirk
1894   *Big Cypress: The Story of an Everglade Homestead.* Boston: W. A Wilde.

Munroe, Ralph Middleton, and Vincent Gilpin
1974   *The Commodore's Story.* Narbeth, Pa.: Livingston.

Nairne, Thomas
1710   A Letter from South Carolina Giving an account of the soils, air, products, trade, government, laws, religion, people, military strength &c. of that province. Printed for A. Baldwin, London.
1988   *Nairne's Muskhogean Journals: The 1708 Expedition to the Mississippi River.* Jackson: University Press of Mississippi.

National Archives, Washington, D.C.
1850   Dade County Census. Microfilm Publication.
1870   Dade County Census. Microfilm Publication. John Addison is listed as being 41 years old.
n.d.   Historical Information Relating to Military Posts and Other Installations 1700–1900. Microfilm Publication 661. Records of the Adjutant General's office. Various microfilm reels, RG 94, NA.
n.d.   Papers Relating to Richard Fitzpatrick's Claim for Damages Caused by Indian Depredations During the Seminole War and for Losses Sustained Because of U.S. Troops Quartered on His Plantation in Southern Florida from 1838–42. M689, Roll 466, NA.
n.d.   Treasury Department. Annual Report File and Clipping File for Cape Florida Lighthouse. RG 26, NA.

Newman, Christine
1986   Archaeological Investigations Conducted at the Cheetum Site, Dade County, Florida. Report on file, Archaeological and Historical Conservancy, Davie, Fla.
1993   The Cheetum Site: An Archaic Burial Site in Dade County, Florida. *Florida Anthropologist* 46 (1): 37–42.

Newsom, Lee A.
2007   Untitled report. On file, Archaeological and Historical Conservancy, Davie, Fla.

Parks, Arva Moore
1973   Key Biscayne Base Marker. *Tequesta: The Journal of the Historical Association of Southern Florida* 33:3–16.
1977   *The Forgotten Frontier: Florida through the Lens of Ralph Middleton Munroe.* Miami: Banyan Books.
1978   Preliminary History of the Wagner Homestead. Unpublished report. Miami.
n.d.   *Where the River Found the Bay: Historical Study of the Granada Site.* Tallahassee: Florida Division of Archives, History and Records Management.

Perrine, Henry E.
1875   A *True Story of Some Eventful Years in Grandpa's Life*. Buffalo, N.Y.: Press of E. H. Hutchinson.
1876   *Biscayne Bay, Dade Co., Florida, Between the 25th and 26th Degrees of Latitude. A Complete Manual of Information Concerning the Climate, Soil, Products, etc., of the Lands Bordering on Biscayne Bay, in Florida*. Albany, N.Y.: Weed, Parsons.
1877   Burial Mounds in South Florida. *Semi-Tropical: A Monthly Journal Devoted to Southern Agriculture, Horticulture, and Immigration Literature, Science, Art, and Home Interests* 3 (7): 414–16.

Peters, Thelma
1976   *Lemon City: Pioneering on Biscayne Bay*. Miami: Banyan Books.
1984   *Miami 1909 with Excerpts from Fannie Clemons' Diary*. Miami: Banyan Books.

Pierce, Charles W.
1970   *Pioneer Life in Southeast Florida*. Edited by Donald Walter Curl. Coral Gables: University of Miami Press.

Pineda, Alonso Álveres de
1519   Map of the Gulf Coast. Copy at Archivo de las Indias, Seville, Spain.

Quitmeyer, Irving R., and Meggan Blessing
2006   The Stranahan House Archaeological Site (8BD259), Ft. Lauderdale, Florida: The Zooarchaeology of a Native American Shell Midden Hyde Park Parcel. Report on file, Archaeological and Historical Conservancy, Davie, Fla.

Quitmeyer, Irving R., and Erin E. Kennedy
2002   The Zooarchaeology of the Miami Circle, Brickell Point (8DA12) Florida. Environmental Archaeology Laboratory, Department of Natural History, Florida Museum of Natural History, Gainesville.

Reiger, John F.
1981   Analysis of Four Types of Shell Artifacts from South Florida. *Florida Anthropologist* 34 (1): 4–20.
1990   "Plummets"—An Analysis of a Mysterious Florida Artifact. *Florida Anthropologist* 43 (4): 227–39.
1999   Artistry, Status, and Power: How "Plummet"-Pendants Probably Functioned in Pre-Columbian Florida—and Beyond. *Florida Anthropologist* 52 (4): 227–40.

Richards, Rose C.
1903   "Reminiscences of the Early Days of Miami." *Miami News*.

Rickmer
1913   Written contract between Rickmer and W. H. McIntyre. Copy on file, Archaeological and Historical Conservancy, Davie, Fla.

Robertson, J. M.
1854   Letter from 1st Lieutenant J. M. Robertson to Mr. Haines. April 18. M1084, Roll 3, frames 1050–52, NA.

Rockwood, Caroline Washburn
1891   The Seminoles at Home. *Frank Leslie's Popular Monthly* 32 (July–December).

Romans, Bernard
1774   Bernard Romans' Map of Florida. Surveyed and drawn by Bernard Romans.
1962   A Concise Natural History of East and West Florida: A Facsimile Reproduction of the 1775 Edition. Gainesville: University of Florida Press.

Rouse, Irving
1951   *Survey of Indian River Archaeology.* New Haven, Conn.: Yale University Press.

Russo, Michael
1990   Report I on Archaeological Investigations by the Florida Museum of Natural History at Horr's Island, Collier County, Florida. Manuscript on file, Florida Museum of Natural History, Gainesville.

Scarry, C. Margaret
1985   Paleoethnobotany of the Granada Site. In *Excavations at the Granada Site: Archaeology and History of the Granada Site,* vol. 1, edited by John W. Griffin et al. Tallahassee: Florida Division of Archives, History and Records Management.

Scarry, C. Margaret, A. Newsom, and Marilyn Masson
1989   Calusa and Tequesta Plant Use: Evidence from Archaeobotanical Data. Paper presented at the 46th annual meeting of the Southeastern Archaeological Conference, Tampa, Fla.

Schmidt, Lewis G.
1989   *The Civil War in Florida.* Vol.e 1, *Florida's East Coast.* Allentown, Pa.: Self-published.

Scholl, D. W., F. C. Craighead, and M. Stuiver
1969   Florida Submergence Curve Revised: Its Relation to Coastal Sedimentation Rates. *Science* 163 (3867): 562–64.

Schwadron, Margot
2005   Archaeological Investigations of Eastern Everglades Tree Island Sites, Everglades National Park. Paper presented at the Florida Anthropological Society meeting, Gainesville, Fla., May 14.

Seagrave, James
1793   Letter to Henry Knox. May 24. Papers of the War Department. 3rd Cong., House, Sec War Confidential Rep. RG 233, NA.

Sears, William H.
1982   *Fort Center: An Archaeological Site in the Lake Okeechobee Basin.* Gainesville: University Press of Florida.

Sewell, John
1987   *Miami Memoirs.* New pictorial edition of John Sewell's own story by Arva Moore Parks. Tulsa, Okla.: Arva Parks.

Shappee, Nathan D.
1961   Fort Dallas and the Naval Depot on Key Biscayne. *Tequesta: The Journal of the Historical Association of Southern Florida* 21:13–40.

Shirley, Tom
2009   Personal communication with Robert S. Carr.

Siebert, W. H.
1929 *Loyalists in East Florida, 1774 to 1785; the Most Important Documents Pertaining Thereto.* Boston: Gregg Press.

Sklar, Fred H., and Arnold van der Valk, eds.
2002 *Tree Islands of the Everglades.* Boston: Kluwer Academic.

Small, John Kunkle
1924 *The Land Where Spring Meets Autumn.* New York: New York Botanical Garden.
1928 Botanical Fields, Historic and Prehistoric: A Record of Exploration in the Southeastern Coastal Plain in the Spring of 1923. *Journal of New York Botanical Garden* 29. New York.
1929 *From Eden to Sahara: Florida's Tragedy.* New York: New York Botanical Garden.

Smith, Buckingham
1848 Report on Reconnaissance of the Everglades Made to the Secretary of the Treasury, June 1848. *Senate Report Comm. No. 242,* 30th Cong., 1st sess., August 12, 1848. Washington, D.C.

Smith, Marvin T., and Mary Elizabeth Good
1982 *Early Sixteenth Century Glass Beads in the Spanish Colonial Trade.* Greenwood, Miss.: Cottonlandia Museum.
1987 *Archaeology of Aboriginal Culture Change in the Interior Southeast: Depopulation during the Early Historic Period.* Ripley P. Bullen monographs in anthropology and history. Gainesville: University Press of Florida.

Smith, Patrick
1994 Lewis Family, Early Land Grantees. In *Broward Legacy,* 17. Fort Lauderdale: Broward County Historical Commission.

Solis de Merá, Gonzalo
1964 *Pedro Menéndez de Avilés; Memorial.* Translated by Jeannett Thurber Connor. A facsimile of the 1923 edition. Gainesville: University of Press of Florida.

Stirling, Matthew W.
1934–36 The Unpublished Correspondence of Matthew Stirling. (Letters from D. L. Reichard, various dates, 1934–35.) Matthew Williams Correspondence File, National Anthropological Archives, Suitland, Md.

Straight, William M.
2001 Archaeological and Historical Events at Brickell Point. Unpublished manuscript. On file, Archaeological and Historical Conservancy, Davie, Fla.
2004 The A. E. Douglass Cup from the Brickell Mound. *Florida Anthropologist* 57 (1–2): 187–90.
n.d. Fort Dallas: A Most Salubrious Post. Manuscript on file, Archaeological and Historical Conservancy, Davie, Fla.

Sturtevant, William C.
1953 Chakaika and the Spanish Indians. *Tequesta: The Journal of the Historical Association of Southern Florida* 13:35–73.
1978 The Last of the South Florida Aborigines. In *Tacachale: Essays on the Indians*

of Florida and Southeastern Georgia during the Historic Period. Gainesville: University Press of Florida.

Supreme Court of Florida

1850   Reports of Cases Argued and Adjudged in the Supreme Court of Florida at January Term 1850.

1852   Reports of Cases Argued and Adjudged in the Supreme Court of Florida at Terms Held in 1851–52.

Swanton, John R.

1939   *Letter from the Chairman, United States De Soto Expedition Commission Transmitting the Final Report of the United States De Soto Expedition Commission*. Washington, D.C.: Government Printing Office.

Tanner, Henry S.

1825   Map of Florida by H. S. Tanner, Improved to 1825 [with] West Part of Florida. Published by H. S. Tanner, Philadelphia.

True, David O.

1944   The Freducci Map of 1514–1515. *Tequesta: The Journal of the Historical Association of Southern Florida* 4.

1946   Pirates and Treasure Trove of South Florida. *Tequesta: The Journal of the Historical Association of Southern Florida* 6.

U.S. War Department

1880–1901   *The War of the Rebellion: A Compilation of the Official Records of the Union and Confederate Armies*. 128 vols. Washington, D.C.

Weatherly, Capt. W. H.

n.d.   Manuscript memoir regarding the early history of the City of Miami. Probably written in the first half of the twentieth century by the anonymous daughter of Captain Weatherly. Copy on file, Miami-Dade County Office of Community and Economic Development, Historic Preservation Division, Miami.

Weisman, Brent

2002   *Pioneer in Space and Time: John Mann Goggin and the Development of Florida Archaeology*. Gainesville: University Press of Florida.

Weisman, Brent, Lori Collins, and Kelly Driscoll

2001   Historical Archaeology of Indian Key (8MO15), Monroe County, Florida. Report of the 2001 Investigations. Manuscript on file, Department of Anthropology, University of South Florida, Tampa.

Weisman, Brent R., and Christine L. Newman

1992   Archaeological Testing at Selected Wakulla Springs State Park Sites. Florida Bureau of Archaeological Research, C.A.R.L. Archaeological Survey, Tallahassee.

Welsh, Agnew

1925   Pioneer Days in Dade County: Article One—Old Fort Dallas. *Miami News*, April 20.

West, Patsy

1981   The Miami Tourist Attractions: A History and Analysis of a Transitional Mikasuki Seminole Environment. *Florida Anthropologist* 34 (4): 200–224.

2002 *The Seminole and Miccosukee Tribes of Southern Florida.* Charleston, S.C.: Images of America, Arcadia.

Wheeler, Ryan

1994 Early Florida Decorated Bone Arts: Style and Aesthetics from the Paleo-Indian Through Archaic. *Florida Anthropologist* 47 (1): 47–60.

2000a Treasure of the Calusa: The Johnson/Wilcox Collection from Mound Key, Florida. *Monographs in Florida Archaeology* 1. Tallahassee.

2000b The Archaeology of Brickell Point and the Miami Circle. *Florida Anthropologist* 53 (4): 294–323.

2000c *Cultural Resource Assessment of Brickell Point and the Miami Circle.* Florida Archaeological Reports 10. Bureau of Archaeological Research, Division of Historical Resources, Tallahassee.

2006 Pumice Artifacts from the Miami Circle at Brickell Point (8DA12). *Florida Anthropologist* 59 (3–4): 191–208.

Widmer, Randolph J.

1988 *The Evolution of the Calusa: A Nonagricultural Chiefdom on the Southwest Florida Coast.* Tuscaloosa: University of Alabama Press.

2004 Archaeological Investigations at the Brickell Point Site 8Da12 Operation Three. *Florida Anthropologist* 57 (1–2): 11–58.

Williams, John Lee

1837 *The Territory of Florida, or Sketches of the topography, civil and natural history, of the country, the climate, and the Indian tribes from the first discovery to the present time.* New York: A. T. Goodrich.

Williams, Wilma B.

1983 Bridge to the Past: Excavations at the Margate-Blount Site. *Florida Anthropologist* 36 (3–4): 142–53.

Wing, Elizabeth S.

1984 Faunal Remains from Seven Sites in the Big Cypress National Preserve. *CNRS Notes et Monographies Techniques* 16:169–81. Paris.

Wing, Elizabeth, and L. J. Loucks

1985 Granada Site Analysis. In *Excavations at the Granada Site: Archaeology and History of the Granada Site,* vol. 1, edited by J. W. Griffin et al. Tallahassee: Florida Division of Archives, History and Records Management.

Wood, John Taylor

1893 The Escape of General Breckenridge. In *Famous Adventures and Prison Escapes of the Civil War,* edited by G. W. Cable et al. New York: Century.

Woodman, Jim

1961 *The Book of Key Biscayne: Being the Romance of Cape Florida and Containing the Chronicle of the Island from Aboriginal Days to the Present.* Miami: Miami Post Publishing.

Writers' Program (Fla.)

1941 *Planning Your Vacation in Florida: Miami and Dade County, including Miami Beach and Coral Gables.* New York: Bacon, Percy & Dagget.

Zamanillo, Jorge
1996 *Archaeological Monitoring and Investigations at the Cape Florida Lighthouse Complex*. AHC Technical Report 165. Archaeological and Historical Conservancy, Davie, Fla.

Zubillaga, Félix
1941 *La Florida: La Misión Jesuítica (1566–1572) y La Colonización Española*. Bibliotheca Instituti Historici S.I. Rome.

Index

Abiaka, 176
Acculturation, 136, 179
Adair, James, 159
Addison family, 215, 217–19
Adze, 52, 74, 76–77, 79, 171
Agriculture, 63, 201
Aimar, Eveline, 216
Alaña, Father Joseph Xavier, 131–32
Allerton, David, 252
de los Almas, Alonso (Spanish governor of Florida), 130
Amphibians, 32–33, 54, 57
Amulet, 56, 84, 134
Anchor, 77, 80–81
Andros Island, Bahamas, 160–61
Anhinga, 50
Animal burials, 242–43
Antilles, 82
Archaic, 13, 46–57, 59, 61–63, 72, 78–79, 88, 90, 111, 113–14
Arch Creek Burial Mound, 8, 26
Arch Creek Coontie Mill 8DA1657, 24, 140, 199–200, 204–5, 207
Arch Creek Site 8DA23, 8, 18, 21, 26, 111–13, 144
Armadillo, 35–36
Armelagos, George, 39
Armor, 55
Arquebusiers, 126
Arrow, 121, 170, 193
Arrowroot. *See* Coontie
Arsht, Adrienne, 224
Artillery, 183, 196

Atlantis archaic cemetery 8DA1082, 58–59
Atlantis site 8DA1082, 23, 26, 52–54, 59, 73, 97
Atlatl, 79
Aucilla Polychrome, 137–38
Aucilla River, 29
Avifauna, 32
de Avilés, Pedro Menendez, 2, 121, 124–25
Azores, 82

Bahamas, 121, 130, 144, 152–53, 161, 229
Bahamians, 15, 144
Ballast stones, 136, 142, 145
Bamboo Mound 8DA94, 120, 170, 178
Barnacle State Park site 8DA10, 8, 100, 200, 226
Bartlett Estate site 8BD1102, 123
Bartram, William, 163
Basalt celt, 240
Basketry, 171, 179
Beads: carnelian, 141–42, 142f; chevron, 141; cut crystal, 141; bone, 84; general, 8, 40–41, 82, 130; glass, 10–11, 140–42, 159, 222, 228; rosary, 133, 133f; shell, 84; Seminole, 167–68, 171–73, 173f, 217, 222; stone, 37; turquoise, 142
Beadwork, 172
Beal Smith site 8DA1043, 49
Bear Cut, 116
Bear Lake site 8MO30, 21, 63–64, 166
Bears, 160
Beiter, Gary, 24
Belle Glade Plain, 73–74, 246
Bells, 134, 134f, 217

Beriault, John, 26, 30, 60, 87, 89, 116, 120, 156, 200
Bering Strait, 27
Bill Baggs State Park 8DA3, 116, 186
Biscayne National Park, 2, 21, 23, 117
Biscayne Plain. *See* Saint Johns Plain
Blackbeard, 148
Black Caesar, 148–52, 156
Black Caesar's Creek, 148
Black Caesar's Forge, 149, 150*f*
Black Sarah's Creek, 148
Blessing, Meggan, 54–55
Bobcat, 32, 35, 56
Boca Chita, 116, 131
Boca Raton (Indian tribe), 131
Bocas de Miguel Mora, 129
Bonath, Shaun, 21
Bone artifacts: awls, 79, 80*f*; bone socket handle, 79; general, 78–79, 80*f*; incised bone, 52, 52*f*; pins, 52; points, 52, 79, 80*f*
Botanical analysis, 41, 65
Bowlegs, Billy, 166
Bowlegs family name, 161
Breastwork (Seminole War), 186
Breckridge, General John C., 215
Brickell, Belle, 220
Brickell, Mary, 219–21
Brickell, Maude, 104, 153, 167, 220–21
Brickell, William, 6, 167, 219, 222
Brickell Bluff site. *See* Atlantis site 8DA1082
Brickell family, 103–4, 153, 215–16, 219–22, 220*f*, 233
Brickell house, 6–7, 103–5, 167, 221–22
Brickell Park, 74, 104–5, 221, 250
Brickell Point cemetery 8DA12, 97
Brickell site 8DA12, 6–7, 23, 54, 65, 74, 81–82, 90, 103–5, 147, 153, 187, 222
Brickell Trading Post, 17, 120, 167–68, 173
Brighton Seminole Reservation, 158
Brookfield, Charles M., 12, 17, 96, 117, 151
Brown, Mariah, 216, 227–28
Brown family, 215
Bryan, William Jennings, 180, 216, 224, 225*f*
Buckles, 160
Burdine family, 229
Burials, 6–7, 8–11, 14–15, 18, 26, 56–59, 61, 75, 88, 90–91, 96–97, 104, 106–10, 111–15, 117, 149, 172, 180, 219, 221; cremation, 41
Burnt bone, 34–36, 35*t*
Buschelman, Walter, 116
Buttons, 143, 145–46, 171, 182–84, 184*f*, 187–90, 196–97, 219, 227–28

Cabeza de Vaca, Alvar Núñez, 121
Cacique, 124, 126–29, 236, 238
Caesar's Rock, 148
Caloosahatchee River, 162, 244
Calosulgees, 163
Calusa Indians, 2–3, 14–15, 66, 68, 86, 118, 122, 124, 126–28, 130–32, 162–65, 240
Camel, 32, 42–43
Camp Biscayne, 226
Camp Wescott, 120, 186
Canal (prehistoric), 116, 168
Cane Patch Jab and Drag, 64*f*, 69
Cannibalism, 41
Cannonball, 17*f*, 192
Canoe, 51, 64, 74–75, 77, 80–86, 92, 94–95, 100–101, 105–6, 108–9, 111, 113, 115–18, 132, 159, 162, 165, 168, 170, 172, 175, 179, 185
Canoemates (Munroe), 226
Canoe trail, 100, 100*f*
Cape Canaveral, 122
Cape Florida, 130, 144, 152, 159–60, 162, 164
Cape Florida Society, 144, 160
Cape Sable, 118
Captive, 2, 66, 86, 124, 126–27, 129, 240
Caracara, 32
Card, Ron, 19
Carlos (Calusa cacique and village), 21, 124, 126–28, 131, 134
Carr, Robert S., 15, 21, 23–24, 99–100, 104–5, 107*f*, 150, 225
Castaways, 123. *See also* Shipwrecked
Catamaran, 86
Catfish, 54, 63
Cattle, 160, 179
Caximba, 163
Cayo Hueso, 118, 132
Cemeteries: Atlantis, 23, 59; Flagami, 23, 57, 106–8, 107*f*; Fort Bankhead, 191; Fort Dallas, 180–81; Historic, 181; Lemon City

Colored Cemetery, 229–30; Long Lake, 61; Madden's Hammock, 109–11, 110f; Miramar, 61; Miami Midden 1, 101–3; MDM, 89f; prehistoric, 23, 57–61, 88–91, 93, 103, 105, 108; Santa Maria, 23, 57–59, 60f; solution hole, 97; Trail Site, 108–9. *See also* Cheetum site 8DA1058
Ceremonial tablets, 140
Chakaika, 162, 164, 170
Charles Deering Estate Park, 6, 27, 29, 45, 142, 144, 149
Charnel house, 57, 132, 240
Chazotte, Peter Stephen, 201
Cheetum site 8DA1058, 19, 26, 48, 50–52, 57, 141
Chequesta, 122
Chert, 31, 36–37, 47–48, 50–51, 62, 81, 178
Chickees, 86, 170
Chitto Tustenugee, 165
Cimarrones, 157
Cisterns, 182
Clausen, Carl J., 29
Cloisters site at 8DA10, 226
Clovis, 29
Clupper, Jim, 19
Cockrell, Wilburn "Sonny," 29
Coins, 161, 161f, 174, 212
Coleman, Wesley, 18–19, 52, 102, 108, 134, 151, 171, 175
Collins Canal, 11
Columbia Plain, 137
Comptie, 201, 210. *See also* Coontie
Concha (Indians), 131
Concretion, 10, 13, 34, 44, 52, 114–15, 235, 247
Condor, 32
Cooley family, 162
Coontie, 24, 62, 66, 169, 172, 175, 193, 199, 201–5, 207, 209, 211; arrowroot, 203; grater, 172, 175; mill, 23–24, 140, 186–87, 193–94, 196, 199–200, 202f, 203–11, 213–14
Cooper, Stan, 249
Copper artifacts: canoe patch, 175; grater, 175; ladle, 176f; ornaments, 140, 173–74, 175f; Kaskaskia points, 176, 177f; general, 142; insignia, 172, 174f
Coppinger, Henry, 169

Coral Gables, 86, 136, 218, 229
Costas Indians, 130
Coyote, 32, 35
Creole, 216
Crystal, 133, 141
Cuba, 3, 121, 127, 130–32, 136, 139–40, 152, 163, 165, 219, 244–45
Cubans, 215
Cushing, Frank Hamilton, 77, 79, 84, 86
Cutler, William, 218
Cutler (town), 27, 29, 117–18, 144, 149, 201–2, 217–19, 249
Cutler Burial Mound 8DA8, 6, 26, 96–97, 117, 149, 219
Cutler Fossil Site 8DA2001, 23, 26–33, 28f, 30f, 35–46
Cutler Midden, 117

Dade Circle earthworks 8DA1642, 26, 98–99, 99f
Daguerreotype plate, 213
Danielson family, 30, 117
Dayoff, Fred, 21, 164
Deagan, Kathleen, 137
De Brahm, Gerard, 143–44, 157, 159–60
Deering, James, 11
Deering family, 117, 218
Deering Hammock, 29
Demigone, Gina, 252
Deptford Stamped, 73, 237–38, 238f
De Soto expedition, 4
Dickinson, Jonathan, 3, 86
Dire wolf, 32, 42–43, 45
Dog, 56, 224
Dolphin, 56, 65, 183
Doña Antonia, 127–28
Doubleday, Abner, 166, 182, 192, 197
Douglass, Andrew E., 6–8, 13, 180
Dragoons, 162
DuBose, John, 185
Duda, Mark, 58
Duggar, C. M., 19
Dugout canoe, 85–86
Dupont Plaza component of 8DA11, 133–34, 136, 140
Duricrust, 234–35

Earthenware, 3, 6–7, 137, 145, 195
Earthworks, 3–4, 98–99, 99f
Echazabal, Christina, 98
Eels, 49
Ehrenhard, John, 21
Eistadt, Bruce, 143
Eleuthera Island, Bahamas, 227
Elgart, Alison A., 61
Elliott Key, 135, 148, 151
Elmslie, Stephen, 31–32, 35–36, 41
El Portal burial mound DA20, 14, 96
Ernst, John Agustus, 144
Escalante Fontaneda, Hernando de, 2, 66, 124, 127, 238
Estero, 126
Everglades, 2–3, 8, 10–14, 16–17, 19, 21, 23, 42, 46, 48–50, 54–57, 59, 62–65, 69, 71, 77–78, 85, 90, 92–95, 98, 100–101, 105–6, 108–9, 135, 137, 139, 142, 159–62, 165–66, 168–70, 172, 177, 179, 182–83, 186, 192–93, 196, 201, 208–10, 214
Ewan, John W., 7, 166, 180
Extinction, 42–45
Eyster, Irving, 205, 217

Fairbanks, Charles, 158
Falcon, 32
Felmley, Amy, 61
Ferguson family, 209–10
Ferguson Mill site 8DA1655, 23, 186, 193, 200, 207–8, 210
Ferrer, Maurice, 57, 97
Fiber-tempered pottery, 53, 59, 67, 97
Fisheating Creek, 98
Flagami Island, 105–7, 106f
Flagami Mounds 8DA36, DA1053, DA1073, 11, 23, 26, 96, 106–7
Flagami site 8DA36, 57, 107–8, 107f
Flamingo Feather (Munroe), 226
Flint, 81, 160, 178
Flirt, 152
Florida lion, 32, 42–43
Florida panther, 32, 56, 64
Folsom, 29
Fort Center site 8GL13, 74, 98, 241
Fort Drum Incised, 72
Fort Drum Punctated, 64, 69

Forts: Fort Bankhead, 120, 181–82, 186, 189; Fort Brooke, 181; Fort Castillo de San Marcos, 131; Fort Center, 74, 98, 241; Fort Dallas, 4, 7–8, 120, 153, 166, 180, 182, 186–90, 197, 215–17; Fort Desolation, 120, 193–95, 197; Fort at "The Head of the Martyrs," 130; Fort Henry, 120, 155, 192–93; Fort Kemble, 120, 186, 191; Fort Lauderdale, 54, 186, 197, 237; Fort Miami, 186; Fort Moultrie, 216; Fort Myers, 218; Fort Russell, 189, 191, 191f
Fradkin, Arlene, 55–57
Frazier, J. S., 20
Frow, Charles, 149
Frow, Simon, 226–27
Frow family, 215

Galena, 241, 243
Geireen (settler on Key Biscayne), 152
Gerdes, F. H., 187–88, 203, 207–8, 211
Giddings, Joshua, 157
Gifford, John, 33, 111
Gilliland, Marion S., 82, 85
Girtman Brothers, 8, 168
Glades I period, 69
Glades II period, 69–70, 72–73, 79, 90, 98, 115
Glades IIC period, 68, 70
Glades III period, 68–69, 72–73, 79, 103, 115–16, 119
Glades IIIA period, 63, 72
Glades IIIB period, 65, 73
Glades IIIC period, 73
Glades Tooled Rim, 71f, 72, 116–17, 140, 245–47
Glass: bottles, 142, 146, 172, 205, 212, 219, 222, 228; cross, 217; flask, 183; melted, 186, 195–96; scraper, 178, 178f. *See also* Beads
Goggin, John M., 11–17, 12f, 63, 67–68, 71–72, 75–77, 82, 96, 101, 104, 106–9, 112, 116–17, 136–38, 141, 161, 174, 237
Goldman, Sue, 252
Goodland Site 8CR46, 242
Gorgets, 74, 82
Granada site component of 8DA11, 4–5, 21–23, 63–65, 78–79, 85–86, 101, 133, 137–38, 140–41, 181, 187, 189
Grayware, 140

Green, Lynda, 250
Greene, Mark, 19, 104, 222, 249
Griffin, John, 21, 48, 63, 68, 70, 101
Grossman Hammock site 8DA80, 16
Gunflints, 190, 196
Guns, 159–60, 164, 167, 171, 192

Haiduven, Richard, 59, 97, 227
Harney, Lieutenant Colonel William S., 162–63
Havana, 126, 130, 132, 157, 162–63
Hazelnuts, 40–41
Headstone, 180
Helisoma snails, 50
de Herrera y Tordesilla, Antonio, 122
Hetzel, Lieutenant C. U.S. Army, 152–53
Hialeah, 16, 67, 110, 171, 181
Hidroceramo ceramics, 140
Honey Hill site 8DA411, 14, 65, 120, 172, 175–76, 183
Hopewellian, 244–45
Host press, 134
Hrdlička, Aleš, 13
Huna, Ted, 18
Hunting Grounds, 153, 160, 217
Hurricanes, 75, 90, 116, 190–91, 221

Ibarra, Pedro de, 130
Ichtucknee Blue, 137
Immokalee Seminole Reservation, 158
Indian Key 8MO15, 6, 152, 162, 164, 171, 181–82, 201
Invertebrates, 36, 54
Iscan, Yasar M., 58–59, 108
Ives, J. C., 192, 202

Jaguar, 32, 33f, 42–43
James Deering Estate, 11
Jobe, 86, 131
Jupiter, Florida, 10, 86, 114, 122, 172, 176

Kaolin pipe, 189, 190f, 222, 223f
Karsification, 27
Karst, 46
Kaskaskia projectile points, 171, 176, 177f
Kennedy, William, 21
Kettle, 10, 159–60, 166, 171–72, 175

Key Biscayne, 20, 42, 92–93, 115–16, 122, 129–30, 152, 160, 163, 181–82, 185–86, 189
Key Biscayne Burial Mound 8DA4, 26, 115–16
Key Biscayne Lighthouse, 20, 164, 185–86, 189–91
Key Biscayne Midden 8DA5, 26, 115–16
Key Biscayne Survey Marker, 20, 20f
Key Largo, 201
Key Largo Incised, 67, 70–72, 71f, 115, 245–46
Key Largo Rock Mound 8MO27, 245
Key Marco site 8CR48, 8CR49, 53–54, 75, 77–79, 82, 84–86
Keys, 15, 43, 67, 69, 71, 76, 82, 92, 95, 116, 118, 124, 130–31, 162
Key Vaca, 121, 132
Kleinberg, Howard, 211
Knetsch, Joe, 209
Knowles, Joe, 116
Knowlton, A. L., 8

LaBree, Guy, 231f
Lamme, Vernon, 13–14, 106–7, 113–15
Laxson, Dan, 16–18, 17f, 104, 108, 110, 110f, 112, 171–72, 181
Ledbury Lodge, 151
Lemon City Colored Cemetery, 229–30
Lewis, Polly, 119, 145, 147, 156
Lewis, William, 145
Lightkeeper, 172, 174, 182, 186
Liguus, 36, 49
Limestone sea turtle carving from 8DA15, 15
Lithic artifacts: chert, 36–37; chert bifaces/projectile point, 36–37, 37f, 47, 50, 51f; flint, 190, 196; general, 79–80; limestone anchor, 80, 81f; limestone balls, 81; limestone biface, 50, 51f; limestone plummet/pendant, 80–81; limestone tools 36, 37, 38f, 50
Little River, 96, 120, 136, 156, 165, 197, 200, 204
Lord, Jim, 19, 253
Lorento, Santa Maria de, 120
Loucks, Jill, 65
Loxahatchee, 10, 176
Lucayan Indians, 121

Lummus Park, 180, 187, 217
Lyon, Eugene, 140
Lyons, Bill, 19, 161

MacArthur 2 site 8BD2591, 55
MacCauley, Clay, 166
Maddalino, Patrick, 111
Madden's Hammock site 8DA45, 16–17, 26, 109–11, 166, 168, 182
Maiyami (Indians), 131
Majolica, 11–12, 137, 138*f*, 140
Mammoth, 29, 32, 35–36, 42–43
Manatees, 56
Mankowski, Joseph, 59
Maracas (Indian tribe), 131
Marchand, Lieutenant John B., 192
Margate-Blount site 8BD41, 161, 241
Mariah Brown house, 200, 227
Martinez, Carlos, 21
de Martínez, Fernan, 130
Masson, Marilyn, 37, 252
Mastodon, 32
Matecumbe Incised, 71, 71*f*
Matecumbe Key, 118
Mattucci, Don, 186, 250
Mayami, Lake of, 124
Mayo, Commander Issac, 191
McGuire, Jeannie, 250
McIntyre, Captain W. H., 153
McKay, George, 3–4, 98, 204
McMurray, Carl D., 187
MDM site Component of 8DA11, 87, 89, 97–98, 251
Medelatas, 140
Megafauna, 34–35, 43–44
Menéndez de Avilés, Pedro, 2, 121, 124–29, 125*f*, 132, 138
Menéndez Marquez, Pedro, 126, 128
Mestizos, 132
Miami Canal, 10, 168, 209–12, 214
Miami Circle at Brickell Point 8DA12, 23, 55, 65, 73–74, 81–82, 88, 104–5, 147, 232–48
Miami News, 151, 207, 210–11, 216
Miami River earthwork, 4
Miami River rapids, 168, 193, 207–8, 210–11, 214

Miami Sand Mound #1 8DA14, 7–9, 26, 180, 242
Miami Sand Mound #2 8DA15, 7, 15, 26
Miami Sand Mound #4 8DA13, 104
Micco Island, 106
Miccosukee, 86, 132, 157–58, 162, 164, 170, 172, 179, 182; Miccousuki, 181
Militia, 160
Minie ball, 183, 184*f*
Mink, 56
Mission, 3, 128–29, 131–34, 136, 138, 159, 179, 216
Mississippian, 244–48
Moorees, C. F., 40
Morrell, Ross, 21
Mound, 4–11, 13–15, 18, 26, 63, 75, 91, 94–96, 104, 106–7, 109–10, 112–17, 126, 132, 134, 149, 170, 178, 180, 219
Mound Key, 126, 134
Mulattos, 132
Mules, 187, 203
Munroe, Ralph, 8, 96, 209–10, 218, 226, 228
Munroe, Kirk, 8, 17, 200, 226–27
Musa Isle Seminole village, 169
Musepa (Indians), 131
Musket, 123, 146, 171, 176–77, 180–81, 183–87, 189, 191, 193, 195, 197, 213
Musket balls, 123, 146, 171, 176–77, 180, 183–86, 189, 213
Muskhoge (Indians), 159
Muskrat, 56
Mutineers, 126–28

Nairne, Thomas, 159
Navy, 158, 184, 189, 193, 215
Negroes, 8–9, 152–53, 157, 162
Nerita peloranta, 36
Nets, 85
Netting, 209
Newsom, Lee, 41
Nuestra Señora de las Maravillas, 130

Oak Knoll mound 8LL729, 244
Ocher, 39, 69
Oleta Burial Mound 8DA25, 18

Index 293

Oleta River, 18, 95, 165, 168. *See also* Snake Creek
Olive jar, 12, 137–40, 139f, 146, 205, 226
Onion bottle, 142
Opa-Locka, Florida, 14, 15f, 18
Opa-Locka 1 site 8DA48, 15
Opa-Locka Incised, 64, 68–70, 242
Opossum, 35, 55–56
Orchid Jungle site, 75
Ortona Canals 8GL4, 244
Otter, 55–57

Paleolama, 32, 36, 42
Panton, Leslie and Company, 159
Peabody Museum at Harvard University, 4–5, 17
Peacock, Charles, 227
Peacock Inn, 227
Peccary, 32, 43
Pendants, 74, 78, 80–82, 83f, 84, 140–42
Pent, Boe, 148, 152
Pent family, 145
Peregrine, 32
Perrine, Doctor Henry, 162, 201
Perrine, Henry E., 6, 96, 117, 149, 218
Perrine land grant, 201, 218
Peters, Thelma, 203
Pineda Map, 122
Pipe (prehistoric), 73–74
Piracy, 11, 148, 151–53
Plainware, 68–69, 73, 235
Plantation Pinched, 70
Plantations, 130, 144, 201
Polly Lewis Homesite 8DA1655, 119, 145, 147, 156
Poppenhager, Donald, 12
Porcelain, 194–95, 219, 222–24, 227–28
Porpoise, 56
Postholes, 86–87, 94, 103–5, 115, 146, 235–36, 238, 240–41
Posts (wood), 88, 186, 233, 236, 238
Primary burials, 45, 57, 59, 61, 88, 90–91, 97–98, 108, 114
Privateer, 151
Puebla Blue on White, 137–38, 138f
Puma, 32

Pumice, 37, 39, 51, 81–83
Punta Rassa pendant, 141–42

Quarry, 37, 62, 81, 192
Quartz, 68, 73, 109; pendant, 243
Quitmyer, Irving R., 54–55

Rabbit, 35, 55–57
Raccoon, 35, 56–57
Radiocarbon dates, 11, 21, 29, 41, 43, 46–50, 59, 61, 67, 88, 107, 123, 236–37
Rancholabrean, 31
Ransom, Jeff, 24, 224, 252
Rattlesnakes, 55
Read, Beth, 251
Reichard, D. L., 14, 84, 115
Reiger, John, 19–20, 77, 80, 84
Reinterment, 96–97, 110–11, 230
Reptiles, 32, 36, 54–56, 63
Richards, R. C., 210
Richards, Rose, 207
Ricisak, John, 20, 24, 105, 231, 235
Rickmers family, 153
Riggs, Ted, 19–20, 105, 233
Rio Seco (Indians), 131
Rockwood, Caroline Washburn, 218
Rodriguez, Ivan, 23
Rodriguez, Raul, 212
Rogel, Father Juan, 127–28
Romans, Bernard, 3, 132, 143, 148, 151, 163
Roome House, 10, 57
Rosary, 133, 141
Rose, Captain C. J., 10
Royal Palm Circle at 8DA11, 87–88, 87f
Royal Palm Hammock, 50
Royal Palm Hotel, 7–9, 87–89, 97, 102–3, 180, 189, 229, 242
Russell, Captain Samuel, 180

Saber-toothed tiger, 32, 42
Saint Johns Check Stamped, 71f, 73, 115–17, 140, 235
Saint Johns Plain, 72
Saint Lucie River, 163
Salt, 29, 64, 149, 160
Sands Key site 8DA2, 8DA4582, 116

Sanibel Incised, 67
San Luis Blue on White, 137–38, 138f
San Marcos, 161
Santa Luzes (Indians), 131
Santa Maria archaic cemetery 8DA2183, 23, 26, 54, 57–58, 92
Santa Maria de Loreto, 131, 134, 156
Santa Maria site 8DA1658, 54, 57, 146–47
Santa Maria West archaic cemetery 8DA11246, 26, 59, 60f, 97
Santa Marta (Key Biscayne), 122
Scarry, C. Margaret, 65
Schaffer, James, 172
Scholtz, David, 13
Schwadron, Margot, 21
Sears, William H., 74, 98
Secondary burials, 57, 59, 61, 88, 90–91, 98, 108, 114
Sedeno, Father Antonio, 129
Semiflexed burials, 61, 109
Seminoles, 86, 100, 111, 132, 157–61, 163–72, 174–76, 179, 182, 201–2, 210, 217, 226
Seminolskees, 157
Semiolilies, 157
Semoli, 157
Semple family, 227
Seville, Spain, 127
Sewell, John, 8
Shafer, James, 19, 111–12
Shaman, 127
Sharks, 4, 54–55, 63, 65
Shark teeth, 13, 40, 52–53, 78–79, 114–15, 239, 242, 246
Shell artifacts: anchor, 77; awl, 52, 62, 77–78; axe, 51–52, 63; beads, 84; celt, 74–75, 75f, 105–7, 107f; columella hammer, 77; cups, 75; dippers, 75; gorgets, 80; ladle, 75–76, 76f; *Busycon*, 52, 82; *Busycon* adze, 76–77, 79; *Busycon* scraper, 36; necklace, 112; pendant, 82–83, 83f; radiocarbon dated, 49; shell buzzard, 248f
Sherwood Forest Subdivision, 96
Shipwrecked, 2–3, 86, 121, 123–24, 126–27, 129–30, 238
Shipwrecks, 130, 136, 138, 142

Simons, Jim and Wonda, 29
Sinclair, Captain, 216
Skeletons, 8–10, 14, 58, 112
Skull burials, 58, 108, 114, 241
Slaves, 121, 130, 148, 158, 160, 188, 201
Smithsonian Institution, 7, 13–14, 115, 151, 163
Snake Creek Canal, 182
Snake Creek, 26, 120, 156, 165–66, 168–69, 172, 176, 185, 200. *See also* Oleta River
Snake Warrior. *See* Chitto Tustenugee
Snake Warrior's Island site 8BD1867, 165, 168–69, 172, 175–76
Snapper Creek site 8DA9, 12, 26
Solis de Merá, Gonzalo, 2
Solution hole cemeteries, 97
Sommer, Frank, 14
South American spectacled bear, 32
Spanish Fort at Tequesta, 3, 127–28, 138
Spanish Indians, 132, 158, 162–65, 182, 185
Sparke, John, 84
Squires, Karl, 13–14, 106, 112–14
Steatite, 171
Steele, Willard, 157, 192–93, 249
Steward, Julian, 13
Stirling, Gene, 13
Stirling, Matthew W., 13–14, 115
Stockades, 180–81, 183, 185–87, 189, 191, 193, 195, 197
Stoneware, 205
Stranahan House and Trading Post 8BD259, 167–68, 174
Sturtevant, William C., 163–64
Surfside Burial Mound 8DA22, 11, 14, 26, 113–14
Surfside Incised, 71–72, 85, 117, 245–47
Surfside sites 8DA21, 8DA22, 11–14, 26, 71–72, 84–85, 113–15, 117

Taino Indians, 238
Tamiami Canal, 170
Tamiami Trail, 158, 170
Tampa, 37, 121, 163, 181
Tannehill, Virginia, 116, 135
Tansey, Barbara, 110

Tapir, 42
Taylor, General Zachary, 179, 183
Tegesta, 124
Tekesta, 14
Tequesta, 2–3, 15, 18, 21, 25, 62, 67–68, 73, 85–86, 92–95, 97, 100–103, 105–6, 109, 111, 113, 115–18, 122–24, 126–32, 136–37, 140–42, 151, 159, 161–62, 165, 180, 221, 224
Terracotta pipe, 145, 146*f*
Thimbles, 160, 222
Thompson, John W. B., 185
Tigertail (Seminole), 164, 169
Timucua Indians, 3, 84, 159
Touchett, Samuel, 144
Trade, 50, 62, 66, 68, 129, 134, 136, 139–40, 159, 163, 167–73, 222
Trail site 8DA34, 17, 26, 79, 108–9, 120, 134, 142, 165, 171, 241
Trappman, Hermann, 25*f*, 119*f*, 155*f*, 199*f*
Triton, 76
Trivet, 196
Tuttle, Julia, 11, 180

U.S. Revenue Service, 152, 182–83, 185
Uchises Indians, 132, 161
Upper Bogue, Eleuthera, Bahamas, 227
Upper Matecumbe Key site 8MO17, 14, 77

Valdéz, Bishop Gerónimo, 130
Veracruz, Mexico, 121
Vero Canal fossil site, 29
Villareal, Brother Francisco, 3, 127–29
Villa Regina site 8DA1656, 143
Villa Serena, 65, 200, 224–25
Viscaya, 148, 224

Vizcayanos Indians, 130
Vole, 32

Wagner, William, 207, 216
Wagner church, 217
Wagner Creek, 204, 216–17
Wagner family, 215–17
Wagner House, 200, 216–17
Weatherly, Captain W. H., 9
Weir, 98, 233
Weisman, Brent R., 11, 182
Welsh, Agnew, 180
West Indian Monk Seal, 56, 65
West Indies, 129, 136
Weston Pond, 46, 47*f*
Whale, 56, 65, 153
Whiteware, 194–95, 211, 228
Widmer, Randolph, 54, 238
Wiggins, Larry, 229
Willey, Gordon R., 84
Willie Willie, 169
Withlacoochee quarry, 37
Wooden artifacts: club, 11; pestle, 85, 85*f*; statuette, 135, 135*f*
Woodworking, 49, 76
Wreckers, 156
Wrecking, 162, 201, 231
Wyman, Jeffries, 4–5, 5*f*

Yale University, 14, 163
Yamassee Indians, 130, 159, 161
Yuchi Indians, 158–59

Zemi, 240
Zoomorphic, 82, 84

Robert S. Carr is executive director of the Archaeological and Historical Conservancy. He was Miami-Dade County's first archaeologist and became the county's historical preservation director in 1999. He is the former editor of the *Florida Anthropologist* and former president of the Florida Archaeological Council.

www.ingramcontent.com/pod-product-compliance
Lightning Source LLC
Chambersburg PA
CBHW061933220426
43662CB00012B/1895